K

Ronald Hayman worked in the theatre, acting and directing, before he became a full-time writer, starting with a series of critical books about such playwrights as Beckett, Pinter and Stoppard. He has written biographies of Nietzsche, Brecht, Sartre, Proust, Sylvia Plath, Thomas Mann and Jung. His other books include *How to Read a Play* (which is published in a new edition in 2001), *Secrets: Boyhood in a Jewish Hotel* and *Hitler and Geli*. His play *Playing the Wife*, was staged in 1995 at the Chichester Festival with Sir Derek Jacobi as Strindberg. He has just finished a play called *Becoming Noël Coward*, and he is working on a musical called *Doll*.

Also by Ronald Hayman

De Sade: A Critical Biography

Artaud and After

Theatre and Anti-Theatre: New Movements since Beckett

British Theatre Since 1955: a Reassessment

How to Read a Play (new edition)

Techniques of Acting

The Set-Up: an Anatomy of English Theatre Today

John Gielgud

Nietzsche: a Critical Life

Brecht: a Biography

Writing Against: a Biography of Sartre

Proust: a Biography

The Death and Life of Sylvia Plath

Thomas Mann: a Biography

Hitler and Geli

Nietzsche's Voices

A Life of Jung

Contemporary Playwrights Series:

Samuel Beckett

Harold Pinter

John Osborne

John Arden

Tom Stoppard

John Whiting

Arthur Miller

Edward Albee

Eugène Ionesco

Leavis

Tolstoy

The Novel Today 1967–75

K
A Biography of Kafka

Ronald Hayman

PHOENIX
PRESS

5 UPPER SAINT MARTIN'S LANE
LONDON
WC2H 9EA

A PHOENIX PRESS PAPERBACK

First published in Great Britain
by Weidenfeld & Nicolson in 1981
Phoenix edition first published in 1996
This paperback edition published in 2001
by Phoenix Press,
a division of The Orion Publishing Group Ltd,
Orion House, 5 Upper St Martin's Lane,
London WC2H 9EA

A CIP catalogue record for this book
is available from the British Library.

Printed and bound in Great Britain by
Butler & Tanner Ltd, Frome and London

ISBN 1 84212 415 3

For My Mother

Contents

Illustrations

Acknowledgments

I am aware of having accumulated more debts of gratitude than I ever have before on a single book. I am genuinely grateful to all the people who have helped me. Not all of them will be mentioned in what follows.

First I must thank the Arts Council of Great Britain, the Phoenix Trust and the Crompton Bequest for awarding me grants during the years 1978–80 when I was working on the book. Without the generosity of these bodies it would not have been easy for me either to spend so much time on the work or to make research trips to Berlin, Vienna, Prague and Tel Aviv.

I am grateful to Kafka's niece, Marianna Steiner, and her husband, George Steiner, to Catharine Carver and to Aaron and Mary Esterson for reading the book in draft and making useful comments. I am also grateful to Marianna Steiner and to another of Kafka's nieces, Věra Saudková, for their reminiscences. Věra Saudková was also hospitable and helpful when I was in Prague: I am deeply indebted both to her and to Frau Ilse Esther Hoffe, Max Brod's former assistant, who not only gave me access to unpublished papers when I was in Tel Aviv but devoted a good deal of time to helping me decipher difficult handwriting. George Steiner was also kind enough to go through the typescript and to give me Czech equivalents of all the German place-names (see the Glossary at the end of this book).

For help in contacting the right people and in locating unpublished material in archives and manuscript collections, I must thank Dr Jürgen Born, Professor Eduard Goldstücker, Mendel Kohansky, Murray Mindlin, Stephen Trombley, Klaus Wagenbach and W. L. Webb.

I am grateful to Dr Anne Oppenheimer for lending me her unpublished doctoral thesis on *Franz Kafka's Relation to Judaism*, to Meyer Levin for sending me his *Classic Hassidic Tales*, to Calvin Hall for sending me *Dreams, Life and Literature: a Study of Franz Kafka*, and to Philip Roth for showing me his manuscript of the speech Kafka made when Robert Marschner was promoted.

I must thank Dr Norbert Winkler for taking me to the house in Klosterneuberg where Kafka died, and for providing photographs.

Of the many conversations about Kafka which have stimulated me and contributed to this book, the ones I must mention were with František Kautmann, Jeffrey Meyers and Jiří Stromsič. I would also like to thank Eva Bornemann, Angel Flores, Dr Herta Haas, Calvin Hall, Leo Hamalian, Valer Mocak and Anthony Rudolf for their letters.

I am grateful to Dr Robert Baldock and Ms Paula Iley at Weidenfeld for help and encouragement, while, as usual, my secretary, Mrs Juliet Salaman, has done very much more than merely type the book out.

The translations from the German are my own, and I am glad to acknowledge help from Della Couling.

Chronological Table

Chronological Table

1 The Turning Point: 1912

At ten o'clock in the evening of 22 September 1912 the twenty-nine-year-old Franz Kafka sat down to begin his story 'Das Urteil' ('The Judgment'). When he finished it at six in the morning, his legs so stiff he could hardly pull them from under the desk,[1] he knew he had used his talent as never before. He had discovered 'how everything can be said, how for everything, for the strangest fancies, a great fire is ready. They're consumed and resurrected.'[2] The equation of destruction with creation is characteristic. He frequently destroyed his own writings, as if the less successful ones were weeds that could choke worthwhile work before it emerged.

During the night of writing 'Das Urteil', in spite of pains around his heart, tiredness vanished as the narrative gathered momentum. 'It's only like this that it's possible to write, only with this much continuity, this complete an opening of body and soul.'[3] He was not in the habit of reading his work to other people, but he read this story to his three sisters almost as soon as it was finished,[4] read it the next day to several friends[5] and, two weeks later, to Max Brod, after offering it to him for publication in his year-book *Arkadia*.[6] Two months later Kafka gave a public reading of it at a hotel, during an 'evening of Prague authors'.[7]

In February, when the story was in proof, he wrote that it had 'come out of me like a birth, covered with filth and slime, and my hands are the only ones able or eager to reach the body'.[8] While writing it he had thought of Freud,[9] and without Freud he might never have come to take so much interest in his own dreams: 'Nothing but Kafka's dreams seem to interest him any more,' Brod had written in a 1911 diary. The story has an anti-Oedipal ending in which the father condemns the son to death by drowning, and the son lovingly carries out the sentence. But it was not the influence of Freud that was new in Kafka's work, it was the method of opening the throttle fully to the autobiographical impulse. Obliquely and subtly, but more fully, more openly and more boldly than before, he was using fiction to confront his fear of his father, the big, burly, bull-necked, bullying, self-confident, successful businessman whose unpredictable outbursts of rage still frightened him. The long letter to his father that Kafka wrote when he was thirty-six is full of accusations, though no less full of self-accusations. 'I'm not going to say I'm what I am because of you, but I'm inclined to this exaggeration.' This is a typical sentence which

1

almost cancels itself out as it begins, and ends with a partial recantation. The main source of his misery was the guilt feelings cultivated by this domineering and insensitive man, who used to reproach his children in public. They had the feeling of being on trial, and, meeting in the bathroom, they would discuss the case for the defence. 'It's not in order to plot something against you that we sit together but in order to discuss, as energetically as we can, jokingly and seriously, lovingly, defiantly, angrily, with revulsion, submissively, with guilty consciences, with all our mental and emotional strength – to discuss this fearful trial . . . in which you still go on claiming to be judge.'[10] Kafka's failure to win his father's love never ceased to depress him, and he never came to recognize how unintelligent his father was, how ill-equipped to judge him.

As a child, Kafka's eldest sister Elli was no less timid and guilt-ridden than he was. 'I could scarcely bear to look at her . . . so strongly did she remind me of myself.' But she broke free by marrying young. In Kafka's life, as in his work, the failure to marry bulks large. 'Marrying, starting a family, accepting all the children that come, supporting them in this uncertain world, while still guiding them a little – this is, I'm convinced, the most extreme form of success available to a human being.'[11] Some of the sequences in 'Das Urteil' make little sense outside the biographical context, and in one of these Georg is told by Frieda, his fiancée, that he had no right to become engaged if his friends are like the unnamed bachelor who is living in Russia. She seems to think there are two categories of men – confirmed solitaries and those capable of marrying. The friend is a confirmed solitary, and Georg is nervous that if he came to the wedding, he would afterwards find solitude intolerable. Re-reading the story in proof five months after writing it, Kafka commented on the way that the father 'sets himself up as Georg's antagonist', using the friend and

other, smaller common factors namely the love and dependence of the mother, loyal memories of her and the clientele which the father originally built up for the business. Georg has nothing. The fiancée is easily driven away by the father, having no life in the story except in relation to the friend – to what father and son have in common – and since there has been no marriage yet she cannot enter the blood relationship that encircles father and son. What they have in common is all stacked up around the father; Georg feels it only as something that has grown independent and foreign, something he has never sufficiently protected.[12]

The more aggressive a father is, the less likely the son is to be objective about paternal power, and suppressed patricidal impulses can produce a need to exaggerate the damage that the father has been inflicting. The real damage inflicted by Hermann Kafka was undoubtedly substantial, but to his son the idea of living without him was more frightening than exciting – more frightening even than the idea of extinction. Kafka's death-wish, which was abnormally strong, was certainly intensified (if not induced) by his father.[13] Georg dies protesting that he still loves his parents. The ambiguity of the final sentence is untranslatable: 'In diesem Augenblick ging über die Brücke ein geradezu unendlicher Verkehr.' A stream of traffic is going over the bridge but the German words introduce the idea of intercourse. The implication is that the sadism of the old man can excite his son more than the yieldingness of the young woman. There is nothing in the action of the story about the girl's being driven away by the father: she simply fades out of Georg's consciousness as the old man takes over.

In his early story 'Kinder auf der Landstrasse' ('Children on the Country Road', 1904–5) the children, when pushed, fall willingly into a grassy roadside ditch. (The German word for it, *Graben*, can mean graves.)

If you turned on your right side with your hand under your ear, you'd have wanted to fall asleep there. Except that you wanted to clamber up again, chin raised, only to fall into a deeper ditch. Then you wanted to throw yourself out into the air again, your arm held across you, your legs dragging askew, and again fall certainly into a still deeper ditch. . . . How you could, at the extreme point, stretch yourself out properly for sleep in the last ditch – especially on your knees, scarcely occurred to you yet, and you lay on your back, disposed to weeping, as if you were ill.[14]

He could play – verbally at least – with his suicidal inclinations. 'I suppose one must earn one's grave,' he wrote in 1908, when the Cech Bridge was being built. 'Last week I really belonged in this street where I live and which I call "Suicide Approach". For this broad street leads to the river, where a bridge is being built.' There was a Belvedere on the other side but for the moment, with the bridge still incomplete, the street seemed to lead only to the river. But 'it will always be pleasanter to go across the bridge to the Belvedere than through the river to heaven'.[15] So one of the ideas basic to Georg's death had been in Kafka's mind for several years.

Literature looked like an alternative to suicide, but it was also the alternative to living:

Everything I possess is directed against me; what's directed against me I no longer possess. . . . If my stomach hurts it's . . . effectively indistinguishable from a stranger who starts wanting to assault me. But that is true of everything. I consist of nothing but spikes that go into me, if I try to resist and use force, it only pushes them further in. . . . From today onwards I shall believe firmly, constantly and uncontradictably that a bullet would be best. I'll simply shoot myself away from the place where I'm not.[16]

Believing he was not really there, he needed, above all, to find out where he was. In the early story 'Gespräch mit dem Beter' ('Conversation with the Suppliant', 1904–5) the tormented young man confesses: 'At no time have I ever been convinced from within myself that I was alive. You see, I've only such a fleeting awareness of things around me that I always feel they were real once and are now melting away. My constant longing, dear sir, is to catch a glimpse of things as they might have been before they showed themselves to me.'[17] So objects all round him become infected. For the writer the compulsion is to track down images of them in their uncontaminated state. Any price may be paid. No stratagem is too humiliating or too painful: unable to depend on the normal functioning of his body to remind him that he was alive, he jerked himself into awareness of it by doing mental violence to it. 'The regular diet of my imagination is fantasies like this one: I'm lying outstretched on the floor, sliced up like roast meat, and with my hand I am slowly pushing a slice towards a dog in the corner.'[18] But at the same time he believed that by inflicting pain on himself he could rise to a higher level of existence: he wrote to Felice Bauer about 'a desire and commandment to torment myself for a higher purpose'.[19] It was only the lower self that was animal: 'Just give the horse a good whipping. Dig the spurs into him slowly, then pull them out with a jerk, but now press them into the flesh with all your strength.'[20]

Not that the word *masochism* can explain the 'systematic destruction of myself' which Kafka achieved. For him writing was not so much an alternative to living as a terminal cure for it. Novalis had called self-destruction (*Selbsttötung*) 'the true philosophical act, the real beginning of all philosophy', and certainly it is right to emphasize what is positive in Kafka's negativism. He refused to shut his eyes either to death, which he acknowledged to be 'only an ingredient in the sweetness of life',[21] or to sadistic impulses. His story 'In der Strafkolonie' ('In the Penal Colony') may look forward, with an apparent refusal to be horrified, at the death camps of a war he did not survive to see, though his sisters survived to die in them. But the story contains its own judgment on the torture machine, on the Commandant who devised it and on the officer who operates it. The central conceit is characteristic of Kafka's work: the device which inscribes on the victim's body the law he has ignorantly broken. The assumption in the penal colony is that the guilt of the accused is never to be doubted. While on sentry duty the condemned man should have bowed every hour towards the door of his superior; he is now to have his body engraved with an injunction to honour his superiors. But when the officer understands that there is no hope of saving the old penal system from being discredited and abandoned, he releases the prisoner, programmes the machine to write: 'Be just', and puts his own body under the needles. He succeeds in killing himself but fails to have the sentence inscribed on him, because the machine goes wrong and starts to disintegrate.

In 'The Death of Ivan Ilyich', which was one of Kafka's favourite Tolstoy stories,[22] death and enlightenment are simultaneous. The dying man is conscious only of joy and love; pain disappears as soon as he stops trying to clutch at life. As for Prince Andrei in *War and Peace*, death is an awakening. In Kafka's story the officer's reverence for the machine is based partly on faith in its ability to bring the dying man enlightenment: 'It starts in the eyes. Then it spreads. A sight that could seduce one into lying down with him under the harrow. Nothing else happens, the man just begins to decipher the script, he purses his lips. You've seen, it's not easy to decipher the script with your eyes, but our man deciphers it with his wounds.'[23] *Schrift* (script) is also the German word for scripture, and the officer had treated the old Commandant's plans like a holy book when he showed them to the traveller. (Edwin and Willa Muir mistranslate *Reisender* as 'explorer'.) All he could see was a labyrinth of lines, but from this the officer could read – or believed he could – the sentences to be inscribed on the guilty bodies. He is like the priest of a vengeful god, and when the machine is finally put to the test on his body, it does not measure up to his claims: 'there was no sign of the promised redemption ... the lips were pressed firmly together, the eyes were open, had the same expression as in life, the gaze calm and convinced, through the forehead went the point of the great iron spike.'[24] His beloved machine has let him down, but as an anti-Tolstoyan machine Kafka's story functions efficiently.

2 After the Ghetto

Kavka is the Czech for jackdaw, and as a Bohemian Jewish surname Kafka had existed in the seventeenth century, but it was probably in 1788 that one of Franz Kafka's ancestors adopted it, following the decree from the Austrian Emperor Joseph II that Jewish fathers must pick new names. For centuries all but the most privileged of Bohemian Jews had been virtually anonymous, known only by their Hebrew names – Chaim ben Jakob, for instance, Higham the son of Jacob – or by their town of origin; now, suddenly, they were compelled to assert a new identity, choosing from a limited range of available names. Ruling out the more dignified sur-names, Christian hostility coloured the identity that the Jews had to choose, and with the choice of the name Kafka the first step had already been taken towards Franz Kafka's imaginative identification with insect, ape, dog, rodent – species whose names are borrowed as terms of abuse. Deprecation encourages self-deprecation, and one of Kafka's defensive strategies was to outbid his father and everyone else who appeared to be setting a low value on him, whether as an individual or as a Jew. He never used the word 'Jew' in his fiction, never made any of his characters Jewish. This would have been like putting on a Jewish mask; animal masks served him better.

Since the middle of the eleventh century, pogroms in Eastern Europe and Russia had kept Jews on the move. With the closing of the North Italian trade route to the Orient and the opening of the Russian route, Prague became one of the main centres of Jewish trade between London and Persia, despite the rampant xenophobia. In the pogroms of 1389, mobs lynched about 3,000 Jews in Prague. But in the first half of the nineteenth century victimization did not prevent the Jews from playing a leading role in the economic revolution that was to make Bohemia into the industrial centre of the Austrian Empire. On the contrary, since it was illegal for Jews to own land they could farm, or to work as craftsmen, they were forced into trading and money-lending. The great majority of the 70,000 Jews in Bohemia were pedlars. Some became money-lenders, and generally the Jews succeeded in developing a virtual monopoly over the wholesale trade in industrial and agricultural products, while the pedlars – Pinkeljuden they were called – necessarily proficient in both German and Czech, formed a complex network linking production of raw material to manufacture.[1]

The motive behind imperial tolerance was largely economic. If Western Europe was more advanced, economically and industrially, it was partly because the Jews were more emancipated. Austria was about forty years behind Germany in giving them civic rights, and in Germany confinement to ghettos had ended sooner and more suddenly. Joseph II's *Toleranzpatent* of 1782 made it possible not for all Jews but at least for founders of manufacturing enterprises to settle outside the ghettos, while it became illegal to speak Hebrew or Yiddish in commercial transactions. This increased the Jews' dependence on the German language, the language of the laws that were beginning to give them their freedom, but it did not automatically increase their loyalty to the Empire. As fellow-victims of imperial oppression, Czechs and Jews had something in common, and, until 1844, it seemed possible that Czech nationalism would rally support from the Jews who would be given the prospect of full civic rights. But the first strike of Czech labourers (1844) was directed against German-speaking employers, mainly Jewish – especially factory-owners. The Czechs regarded the Germans as a minority of intruders, invaders, robbers. Even in the fourteenth century, when Latin was the *lingua franca*, it had already been a grievance that German settlers did not trouble to learn the Czech language. To the Germans the Czechs were a minority because Bohemia was German territory, and Prague was one of the greatest cities in the Holy Roman Empire of the German nation.

Joseph II's tolerance gave way to a period of oppression. During the first half of the nineteenth century the vast majority of the Jews in Bohemia were still excluded from the community by strict legal control over what jobs they could do, what they could own, whether they could marry and where they must live. Despite the extortionate taxes levied on them, there was no limit to how much they could earn: the persecution that precluded the possibility of happiness made wealth the most desirable alternative.

In the aftermath of the 1848 revolution, when the Jewish population of Prague was 10,000, Jews were given full civil rights, and in 1852 ghettos throughout the Empire were formally abolished, but not immediately pulled down. The Prague ghetto was renamed the Josefstadt. In 1870, half the Prague Jews were still living in it; at the turn of the century, less than a quarter.

The transition from ghetto living to full citizenship could not possibly have been made smoothly. Doors were smeared with blood, windows were smashed, property-owners about to clinch deals with Jewish buyers were threatened. The unpopularity of the Jews had been apparent during the revolution, when, according to a book Kafka was later to read, the ghettos had been vandalized almost every night:

7

A wild rabble, bellowing, is bottlenecked into the narrow alleys, mostly boys and drunken louts but unfortunately a few women too. The mob has broken into two houses, the windows are thrown open, furniture and possessions flung down into the street and the crowd yowls. . . . Now a million feathers are floating through the air, like a snowstorm.

One of the vandals is using his knife on pillows and bedding.[2] It was not surprising that Jews should cheer when the Austrian army crushed the revolt.

Jakob Kafka, the Yiddish-speaking grandfather, was born in 1814. He was a butcher who probably, in the village community, also had the role of *schochet* or ritual slaughterer. (Meat cannot be *kosher* unless the animals' throats have been cut by the authorized butcher in the rabbinically approved way.) Jakob Kafka, a man strong enough to lift a sack of flour with his teeth,[3] did not succeed in obtaining a licence to marry until the liberalization that ensued on the revolution. In 1849 he was thirty-five and his bride thirty-eight. They lived in a low, thatched cottage with three rooms in the south Bohemian village of Wossek, which had only about a hundred inhabitants. They then had six children. The first was a girl, and Hermann, the eldest of his four sons, was born in 1852. They all slept in the same room. The other sons were given German names (Philipp, Ludwig, Heinrich) and sent to the Jewish school in the village, where they learned German. By the age of ten Hermann had proved his powers of physical endurance, getting up early in the morning to help his father, pushing a small cart through the villages, wearing the same scanty clothes summer and winter, putting up with open sores on his legs.[4] The rhythms and the itinerary of this peddling life were dictated by the Jewish sabbath: the pedlars would be on the road for six days, returning home to the *shtetl* for the seventh. In the ghetto community, culture was inseparable from religion, which, together with persecution, held the community together. Life was laborious and uncomfortable, but the Jews all enjoyed a luxury later denied to Franz Kafka – the sense of belonging to a clearly defined group. The word 'we', which he almost never used, would have come easily to his grandparents.

At the age of fourteen Hermann Kafka was sent away from home and had to take care of himself. He worked for a shop in Pisek.[5] His sister Julie was sent out to work as a cook from the age of ten. He learned to survive as a new member of a generation which had both to confront social problems that were not entirely new and to make decisions which were. There were still outbreaks of violence and there was still the gentile assumption – not always tacit – that Jews were racially different and congenitally inferior. If, like Sigmund Freud's father, you had your hat knocked off by a group of anti-Semitic louts who forced you off the

8

pavement, your only choice was between picking your hat up peacefully and fighting them. (Freud never quite forgave his father for accepting humiliation.) The area in which initiative could be taken – had to be taken – was over the degree of assimilation you tried for. And over the degree of dissimulation. The more ambitious you were, the greater the temptation to escape stigma by implicitly or explicitly denying your Jewish identity. You could give up your religion: 'The certificate of baptism', said Heine, 'is an entrance ticket to European culture'; or, without becoming a Christian, you could give up the religious practices of your parents, as Hermann Kafka did, and involve yourself in one or other of the surrounding institutions or organizations. During three years of army service which began when he was nineteen, Hermann Kafka rose to the non-commissioned rank of *Zugführer*, and, even in old age, went on talking about his army experiences and went on singing patriotic military songs.[6] Max Brod's parents sent their son to a Catholic elementary school, where he was instructed in German literature by Czech priests.[7] Certainly Hermann Kafka's chronic need for security was characteristic of his generation. His underlying anxiety was of losing the material advantages he had won by thrusting determination and relentless hard work in building up his fancy-goods business. He could never forgive his son for his sins of omission, and one of the most offensive, I suspect, was disinclination to co-operate in building financial bulwarks against the danger – it was not a real one – that Hermann Kafka and his children would be victimized as Hermann Kafka and his parents had been. Fundamentally it was fear of victimization that made the fancy-goods dealer victimize his sensitive son.

Between Hermann Kafka's birth in 1852 and his son's in 1883 it was not easy for Jews to take advantage of the mobility that Austrian law had finally given them. In 1859 there were anti-Semitic demonstrations by workers in south Bohemia. In 1864 poison pen letters were written: the people will 'destroy the Jews and the usurers . . . soon Prague will look quite different'.[8] In 1861 there were three days of anti-Jewish rioting in Strakonitz, six miles from Wossek, and the first anti-Jewish riot in Prague, bad enough for the army to be called in. In the spring and summer of 1866 there were anti-Semitic demonstrations, incited by labourers, throughout Bohemia. In 1867, after the *Ausgleich* which united Hungary with Austria in a dual monarchy, the Jews benefited from the liberalism of the regime.

Hermann Kafka came to Prague in 1882, and before the end of the year he was married – to a twenty-six-year-old woman from Podiebrad, Julie Löwy, the daughter of a fairly prosperous brewer. Her maternal grandfather had neglected his large shop in order to study the Talmud; her paternal grandfather was a cloth-merchant, sufficiently assimilationist to call one of his sons Siegfried, while one of Julie's great-uncles had been baptised – an example one of her brothers was to follow. Her mother was only twenty-eight when she was killed by a typhus epidemic. Brought up from the age of three by a stepmother, Julie had to work in the house, helping to look after her three younger brothers, though her father's income was sufficient for him to retire early and move from Podiebrad to Prague.[9] Marriages were normally arranged, and he cannot have set a high value on a daughter he married off to a man who had been a pedlar.

Hermann Kafka was living cheaply in the Josefstadt. His decision to settle in Prague belongs to a general drift: in spite of Austrian liberalism, Czech nationalism was eroding the small Jewish communities in the country. To the Czechs the Jewish German language schools seemed like boils that had to be lanced, and many of his married contemporaries moved to Prague simply because they would not have been able to get their children educated in the country.

Hermann Kafka had been dealing in buttons, threads and shoe-laces; in 1882, shortly before his marriage, he went into partnership with a man called Schmolka to open a fancy-goods shop in Zeltnergasse, not far from the Altstädter Ring in the centre of the old city. They sold hardware, haberdashery, novelties, gloves, slippers, umbrellas and parasols. In contrast to Julie's studious grandfather and her placid father, Hermann Kafka was dynamic, ambitious, extrovert. Considerably shorter than he was, she admired his physique and his business prowess. Her enormous capacity for devotion was to be oriented to him, and she made herself indispensable, fitting the daily routine of her life closely around his needs. Throughout their married life she would busy herself in the shop during the day, staying up to play cards in the evening as long as he wanted to.

The infant Franz saw little of his mother. Soon after his birth on 3 July 1883 she went back to work in the shop, leaving him in the care of a nurse, who stayed only till he was in his first or second year, when she was replaced by another. His early childhood was highly unsettled. They were living in the old city in a small flat in Maiselgasse, and Franz was not yet two when they moved to another small flat in Wenzelsplatz. His mother was then five months into her second pregnancy. Franz must have been happy to see more of her as she needed more time to rest at home, and must have felt betrayed on discovering that not only was it not on his account that she was coming home, but, worse still, he was to have a rival. Georg, the baby, was the only one of her three sons that Julie describes in her memoir as 'beautiful'. He survived for less than two years, but this was long enough to make Franz feel displaced. Though he became accustomed to seeing so little of her, he never became reconciled to it. One of the pleasures in childhood illnesses was that although, even then, she was not given leave of absence from the shop, she was able, when she came home, to cheer him up so much that it felt as if the day were beginning all over again.[10] In his impotent infantile bitterness at losing his mother to the masculine world of his father and to the beloved baby brothers, he must have felt intensely aggressive towards them and may have felt irrationally responsible for causing their deaths. Certainly he was thrown back more than most children on the comforts and discomforts to be found from inside his own train of thoughts. When he started going to school he was identifiable as a boy accustomed to solitude.[11]

They stayed in the Wenzelsplatz flat only seven months before moving again, this time to Geistgasse, which was near the original flat in Maiselgasse, and in the year of Georg's death they moved again, to Niklasstrasse, a pleasant street even closer to the original flat. Julie was about three months pregnant when Georg died. Heinrich was born at the end of September 1887, but lived only for six months. Measles caused Georg's death; an infection of the inner ear killed Heinrich. Kafka was later to blame both deaths on the inefficiency of the doctors;[12] Julie was left with the feeling that both lives could have been saved if only her husband had let her stay at home with the boys.[13] He was as compulsive about having her with him as he was about building up the business.

Even if there had been no major domestic upheavals, Franz would have had too little parental attention. As it was, in the first six years of his life he also had to withstand the birth and death of both brothers, the change of nurse and a total of five moves. The next occurred in 1888, when they rented a flat at No 2 Zeltnergasse, but though Hermann Kafka's shop was at No 12, they moved again in June 1889, this time into their first large flat. It was in a house that separates the Grosser Ring from the Kleiner Ring, which leads into the Maiselgasse. All these flats were in the old city, which was a less fashionable area than the Stadtparkviertel where Rilke, Werfel and Max Brod grew up.

At least there was less discontinuity in Franz's life from the moment that his parents engaged a Jewish Fräulein, Marie Werner, who settled down with the family. She was a kindly, simple woman, who came from a Czech village and who had no German. In Hermann Kafka's presence she hardly dared to express an opinion: 'I don't say that this is so. I only *think* it is....'[14] She was kind to the children, but the sensitive Franz reacted strongly to any hint of punishment. Told that he would not be taken to see the ducks in the park, he would dissolve into tears and hide in the dark space between the sideboard and the linen cupboard in the dining-room.[15] But at least she

11

provided stability. Nurses and cooks would leave and be replaced but she would stay on.

Until he went to school, then, Franz spoke more Czech than German. His parents, who mostly spoke German to him, wanted him to master the Czech language, and later employed a Czech girl to teach him.[16] They sometimes spoke Czech at home, but found it exhausting to sustain long conversations in the language.[17]

Franz had little contact with either of his parents except at meal-times. He remembered peremptory encouragement from his father to eat faster ('Eat first, talk afterwards.' 'You see, my plate's been empty for ages.').[18] Hermann Kafka was determined to teach his young son good table manners, but set a bad example. He would call the food 'pigswill' and accuse 'that cow' the cook of ruining it, but no one else was allowed to criticize the cooking. Franz must not crunch bones or lap up vinegar or let scraps of food fall to the floor, though his father did all these things. 'The main point was that bread must be sliced straight, but it was all right if you did it with gravy on the knife. . . . Nothing must be done at table except eating, but you cleaned your nails and cut them, sharpened pencils, used a toothpick to clean your ears.'[19] Hermann Kafka had learned his table manners in the *shtetl*, where customs were different from those of bourgeois Prague. His impatient decisions to move from flat to flat were symptomatic of his greed for prestige and respectability. His son must learn the appropriate eating habits, while his own betrayed the insecurity of the upstart. The only mouthful you can be sure of enjoying is the one rapidly on its way to your mouth.

Isolated by the death of his brothers, Franz found himself living alone in a world subject to parental orders, which were neither binding on the authority that issued them nor issued to other adults.[20] He was not even allowed to start talking about something he wanted to talk about: so far as he could remember, his father never entered calmly into discussion of a subject he had not introduced himself. His 'frightful hoarse undertone of rage and total condemnation'[21] would terrify the child, who felt deprived of the faculty of speech by 'your threat: "Not a word of contradiction" and the raised hand that accompanied it.'[22]

It can be inferred from Hermann Kafka's later reactions to the birth of nephews and grandchildren that he must have taken enormous pleasure and pride in the birth of his first son, but, conditioned by memories of his own childhood, he did badly, from the beginning, in evolving a relationship with the child. So far as Kafka could remember his father never read to him,[23] but taught him how to march, how to salute and how to sing military songs,[24] let him drink beer, tried to encourage him with shouting, hand-clapping, mimicry and laughter, which no doubt seemed more unsympathetic than it was, and all these efforts to give the boy more confidence had the opposite effect. [25] It became increasingly obvious that he was failing to please his big father, and the failure became increasingly frightening. Of course there must also have been moments of cuddling and shared laughter between father and infant son, but, significantly, it was not these that Kafka was to remember.

Julie Kafka lived lovingly in her husband's shadow, laughing at his sarcasm, listening to his complaints, sometimes arguing, invariably submitting. She alternated between brightness and melancholy without ever asking for sympathy and without apparent self-consciousness. Her voice was high and clear, 'too loud for ordinary conversation'. [26] (In her old age she was soft-spoken.) [27] She would sometimes try to defend her son against his father, pleading for the boy to be exonerated, and compensating by being extra nice to him when his father was not there, but she would never defend him forcefully and, though he was hardly ever beaten, Franz continued to live in terror of being shouted at, of his father's reddening face, of the braces hastily undone and laid threateningly over the back of the chair. [28]

Early on, therefore, Franz's attitude to the business changed. At first it was a pleasure to be in the shop, especially in the evening when the lights were on, to help occasionally, to look admiringly while his big father sold things, made jokes, wrapped parcels, opened crates, gave orders. But before long Franz was constantly ill at ease, and especially upset to see how his father would shout, rage and swear at the Czech staff – 'paid enemies' he called them – who could not understand when he spoke to his wife in German. [29] Why be nasty to people who were nice? At home, when his father raged at him, he always thought himself in the wrong, but in the shop it was obvious that his father was often unjust. The staff, unable to answer back, must be 'in a terrible state of indignation', [30] which made the child nervous and anxious to placate them. What he felt was an extreme form of what most Prague Jews felt, knowing themselves to be aliens among the Czechs both as Jews and Germans, and to be better off, financially, socially and culturally.

The most traumatic experience of his childhood seems to have occurred when he was about four. This is the earliest episode that survived intact in his memory. In bed one night, unable to sleep, he went on whimpering for water, ignoring his father's threatening attempts to silence him, until the man picked him out of bed, carried him out to the balcony and left him there alone in his nightshirt. 'Years later I still suffered from the tormenting fantasy that the gigantic man, my father, the supreme authority, could come at night, almost without any grounds, and carry me from my bed to the balcony and that I was therefore, for him, such a non-entity.' [31]

In *Der Prozess* Josef K. is in bed when two men come to tell him he is under arrest. In *Das Schloss* K. is in bed when he is woken up and told he has no right to be in the village.

When he was six, Franz started going to the German school in the meat market, and on 22 September, six days after the beginning of term, Julie Kafka gave birth to a daughter, Elli (Gabrielle), so the boy must once again have felt that he had lost what little claim he had had on his mother's attention. For the first year it was the cook, Frau Anna, who walked him to school, taking advantage of the opportunity to revenge herself on the timid child of her tyrannous master. She was 'small, dry, lean, with a sharp nose and hollow cheeks, yellowish but firm, energetic and superior'. When they left home – Kafka writes as though events followed the same pattern every day – she threatened to tell the teacher he had been naughty at home. He was always uncertain of whether she would dare to speak to someone so formidable, but as they got nearer to the school – the walk seemed longer than it was – he would grow increasingly nervous, and the more he pleaded, the more she enjoyed her power. The virtual loss of his mother and the hostility of his father had made him an easy prey to intimidation.

I stood still and begged for forgiveness. She dragged me along. I threatened to get my own back through my parents. She laughed. She was omnipotent *there*. I held on to corners and the doors of shops, I didn't want to go any further till she'd forgiven me, I tore at her skirt – it wasn't easy for her, either – but she dragged me on, promising that this, too, would be reported to the teacher. It was getting late. The Jakobskirche clock struck eight. The school bell rang. Other children started running. I was always terrified of being late. We had to run, too, and always with the thought: 'She'll tell, she won't tell.' Well, she never did tell, but she always had the opportunity.[32]

Above the entrance of the neighbouring Czech school was the inscription: 'A Czech child belongs in a Czech school.'[33] Between boys of the rival schools fighting was frequent and vicious: one seven-year-old boy, victimized either as a German or as a Jew, was hit over the eyes so hard with a pencil box that the retina came away from both, blinding him for life.[34]

Franz Kafka had been born into an environment that strongly rebuffed the assimilationist inclinations of Jews, who were reminded of their Jewish identity more painfully than in the more liberal period 1867–81. The economic crises in Austria and anarchistic subversion were inflaming anti-Semitism, and in Vienna leaflets were being circulated urging people to boycott Jewish shops.[35] In November 1882 a professor of theology at Prague University published an article maintaining that the Jews were committed by their religion to working for the destruction of all Christians and all their property.[36] The slander was repeated in Professor August Rohling's book *Der Talmudjude*, and in a spate of rabidly anti-Semitic leaflets, which coincided with the first in a series of damaging allegations that Jews were perpetrating ritual murder. In 1883 there was a trial in Tisz-Eszlar, a Hungarian village, where Jews were accused of slaughtering a Christian girl. From the beginning of 1883 Prague was inundated with anti-Semitic leaflets in Czech and German, thanks mainly to the activities of the printer Skrejsovsky, who had played a leading role in the emergence of the Young Czech Party, which was radicalizing the petty bourgeoisie and the proletariat, while the Old Czech Party drew its support from the upper classes, the big farmers, clergy, industrialists and officials. The propaganda drew Jewish voters into supporting the Old Czechs in the elections of 1883, and this exacerbated the hostility of the Young Czechs, but the loyalty of the Jews to the Austrian Empire and to the German language was being seriously eroded. In the census of 1880 only one Bohemian Jew in three gave Czech as his everyday language; in 1900 over 50 per cent did. In 1890 74 per cent of the Jews in Prague gave German as their everyday language; in 1900 only 45 per cent,[37] though most Jews still sent their children to German schools.

Hermann Kafka was involved during the eighties in the Czech–Jewish movement at least to the extent of being on the board of the Heinrich Synagogue, the first reformed community in which services were held in Czech. He was also a member (together with the fathers of Franz Werfel and Max Brod) of the *Centralverein zur Pflege judischer Angelegenheiten* (Central Organization for Promotion of Jewish Affairs) which was founded in 1885 to combat anti-Semitism. It was almost like a political party, and when the Young Czechs won an overwhelming victory in the elections of 1891, there was a rush of new members. But little could be done against the appearance in west Bohemia of facsimile Austrian railway tickets offering Jews free one-way transport to Palestine in cattle-trucks.[38] Against this background, Hermann Kafka's attitude to his 'paid enemies' is understandable. But it wasn't understandable to his son.

The major misfortune of the Bohemian Jews was that emancipation and the ensuing attempts at assimilation coincided with the upsurge of a nationalism fomented by demagoguery. Demagogues invariably need scapegoats, while amongst the shopkeepers, artisans, students and even amongst the old Catholic aristocracy there were inchoate feelings that could easily be drummed up against the Jews. In Prague the Jews had virtually a monopoly of wholesale merchandising and of fashionable goods – furniture, fabrics, millinery, lingerie. So many bankers, so many newspaper proprietors and editors, and so many department store owners were Jewish that it was possible to denounce 'Semitic rule' over these key areas of commercial activity. Meanwhile pogroms in South Russia were producing an unwelcome influx of Jewish immigrants. It was easy to inflame the jealous aggressiveness that was given an outlet in organized demonstrations and vandalism. In Bohemia the German-speaking Jews were vulnerable to both Austrian anti-Semitism and Czech anti-Germanism, and, as in the crusades and the Inquisition, self-righteousness served as a mask for sadism in which violence provided an outlet for secret guilt-feelings. Pan-Slav paramilitary sporting and gymnastic organizations were modelled on the German student fraternities, and their rallies played an important role in raising Czech national consciousness, while the loose imperial hold on outlying districts would sometimes be tightened out of all proportion to the need. In 1891, for instance, when a superior court was established with German as its official language at Trutnov, a town in north-east Bohemia with a mixed German and Czech population, it provoked the Czechs in Prague into violent demonstrations and anti-Habsburg riots. The imperial government responded repressively. Both Czech organizations and magazines were suppressed, while there were a great many arrests. Referring to the incident thirty years later, Kafka said: 'It took only a triviality to make the throne in Vienna begin to sway.'[39] In May 1893 a hangman's noose was found around the neck of a statue of the Emperor Franz I. On 17 August, the eve of the reigning emperor's birthday, military music was disrupted and subversive leaflets distributed. Using evidence faked by an informer, the police staged a trial, and sixty-eight members of the *Omladina*, a radical youth organization, were imprisoned for terms varying between seven months and eight years.

Whenever the cook was late in collecting him from school, Kafka became involved in street fighting. He'd go with the roughest boys in the class to the Ziegengasse, where he tried to prove that he was neither a Jewish weakling nor a spoiled mother's boy. Usually he came home in tears with bruises, buttons missing and clothes torn. 'You're a real *ravachol*,' the cook would tell him. When he asked his father what the word meant, he was told 'a criminal, a murderer', and, seriously believing she had recognized a murderer in him, he fretted so much that he became ill with an inflammation of the throat, bad enough to keep him away from school. After that he never joined in the street fights.[40] Ravachol was the name adopted by a French anarchist, Königstein, who, disliking his father's name, assumed his mother's. The press took so much interest in him that in Prague slang the name became synonymous with ruffian or bully.[41]

What Franz suffered at the hands of the cook may have been partly provoked by anti-German or anti-Jewish feeling, and partly by his father's treatment of the 'paid enemies', while the child's uneasiness about this must have made him more awkward in dealing with her hostility. In many ways, emotionally, Franz seems to have sided with the Czechs. Later on he would feel sufficiently at one with them to refer to Prague, in their way, as 'little mother', and, as he later told his friend Milena Jesenská, he felt the Czech language was 'warmer' (*herzlicher*) than German. From the beginning, the German language seems to have highlighted the barrier in his relationship with his mother.

We call a Jewish woman a German mother, but forget the contradiction, which sinks all the more heavily into the feelings. . . . So the Jewish woman who's called 'Mutter' becomes not only funny but strange. Mama would be a better name, if only 'Mutter' didn't have to be imagined behind it. I believe it's only memories of the ghetto that are preserving the Jewish family, for the word *Vater* too is a long way from meaning the Jewish father.[42]

Not that Franz, as a child, had any positive sense of Jewishness. He did not learn Hebrew, and the odd words of Yiddish that survived in his father's vocabulary were mostly expletive. The only ritual observed at home was the *Seder* service on the first evening of Passover; and the few times – four days a year – his father went to synagogue, he did not seem to take the proceedings seriously, while the child, given no explanations, felt very bored. At the opening of the 'ark' which contained the scrolls of the law, he was reminded of the shooting-stands at which a cupboard door would open when one scored a bull's eye, but nothing interesting came out: 'here it was always the same old dolls without heads'.[43] Later he would describe the hours of boredom in synagogues as 'preliminary studies, arranged by hell to prepare me for life in an office'.[44] He desperately needed a sense of his own identity as a Czech or a German or a Jew, but his father would talk with equal scorn about Czechs, Germans and Jews, condemning them all 'in every respect until it seemed no one was left except you'.[45] Kafka's story 'Zur Frage der Gesetze' ('On the Problem of the Laws') starts with the sentence: 'Our laws are not generally known, they are the secret of the few noblemen who rule us.' This feeling has its roots in his childhood: desperate though he was to win favour, to deserve love, he did not know what code of rules to obey. How could he prove himself to be meritorious when his father was consistent neither about religion nor about manners? His personal situation *vis-à-vis* his father was running parodically parallel to the situation of the Czechs *vis-à-vis* the Empire. The superb castle, the Hradčany, which sits high on the west side of the Moldau, visually dominating so much of the city, was an impressive symbol of imperial power, but the emperor, who disliked the Czechs, never came to Prague, so the castle was permanently empty.

Pictures of the emperor were to be seen, but without radio or televison his presence could be felt only through military uniforms and bureaucratic officials.

None of this would have mattered so much if Franz had been made to feel that he was loved or at least that he was good-looking. As a small child he was well dressed; as a boy he totally lost faith in his appearance. His parents bought clothes for him from customers at their shop, and he learned to be extraordinarily aware of how people were dressed – clothes would figure prominently in his dreams – but not to take any pleasure in his own appearance. 'I was convinced it was only on me that clothes assumed this board-like stiffness and later this crumpled droopiness. New clothes I didn't want at all. . . . So I let the shabby clothes affect even my posture, walked around with hunched back, drooping shoulders, unrelaxed arms and hands. I was afraid of looking-glasses because they reflected an ugliness which seemed inescapable.'[46] He knew that posture was partly a matter of choice, but keeping his back straight made him feel tired, and he failed or refused to see what harm a crooked back could do him in the future.

His lifeline to the future was abnormally frail:[47] he did not feel entitled to the self-indulgence of looking beyond the miserable present. He believed his appearance to be contemptibly childish and to be disqualifying him from striding forward into the manly future. It felt as though each step forward involved a fraudulence which would sooner or later be detected.[48] In bed at night he would cheer himself up with fantasies of becoming rich, driving in a coach and four into the Jewish quarter, rescuing a beautiful girl from the man who was beating her, driving off with her.[49] But, given the opportunity to join a dancing-class, he baulked.

Inadequate in his father's eyes, he was inadequate in his own, ashamed of his frail physique and vicariously proud of his father's bulk, though simultaneously depressed by it.

We often undressed together in the same bathing hut – I skinny, frail, slight, you strong, big, broad. Already, inside the hut I thought myself pathetic – not only to you but to the whole world, since for me you were the measure of all things. But then, when we stepped out of the cabin in front of the people, I holding your hand, a small skeleton, uncertain, barefoot on the planks, afraid of the water, unable to copy your swimming movements, which you, well-meaningly but profoundly humiliatingly, kept on demonstrating, I was desperate, and at moments like this, all my bad experiences of all kinds came egregiously together.[50]

Afterwards they would sit together at the buffet, both holding a sausage and a glass of beer. To save money his father would usually bring sausages with him instead of buying them at the buffet.[51]

18

Kafka loved swimming and took pleasure – probably not unmixed with pain – in the sight of other people's half-naked bodies. The love of swimming-pools was to persist through his life, and once he would stay at a nudist colony. But the pleasure was in seeing, not in being seen. One summer, holidaying on the Elbe, he longed to go bathing in the river but dreaded the crowded bathing establishment. 'I roamed about alone like a lost dog on the narrowest paths on the hills alongside the river, watching the little bathing establishment for hours in the hope it would suddenly empty and be accessible for me.'[52] Mostly he bathed in the evenings when the desire to swim had almost left him.

Outings provided relief from the claustrophobic grimness of school life. Hugo Bergmann, who had also started at the school in the Fleischmarkt in September 1889, testifies: 'This higher-grade elementary school, enclosed by narrow alleys with shops and meat-stalls, made a totally prosaic and unromantic impression on us.'[53] It was a fairly new, bleak, four-storeyed building with no playground. During break the boys had to stay either in the classrooms or in the corridors, which were bedecked with such sayings as 'Speech is silver, silence is golden'.[54] To Hermann Kafka it may have seemed that once his son became a schoolboy he was always studying.[55] To Franz it seemed more as if he studied little and learned nothing.[56] In fact his achievement at the school was above average, handicapped though he was by lack of self-confidence. He thought he was never going to survive the first year of school, but he ended up with a prize.

Though the continuity of his existence was no longer disrupted by moves from one flat to another, he had the feeling of losing his mother again and again. Almost exactly a year after Elli's birth and a few days after Franz had started his second year at school, his mother gave birth to another daughter. Valli (Valerie) was born on 25 September 1890. A nursemaid was employed to look after the children. The third daughter, Ottla (Ottilie) was born after a gap of slightly more than two years, on 29 October 1892, when Franz was nine. She was to become his favourite sister.

At school the clothes, deportment and self-importance of the teachers must have encouraged the tendency he would have had anyway to regard them as belonging to the realm of paternal authority, while the hierarchical structure of educational institutions encouraged them to regard themselves as superior by virtue of their seniority. But at least he could enjoy their accessibility. 'Even the greatest parental love is, as an educational factor, more selfish than the slightest love of the paid educator.'[57] 'Whereas parental love is animal, mindless and incapable of distinguishing between the child and the self, the teacher has concern for the child, and educationally that is incomparably more, even when no love is involved.'[58]

At the Volksschule the form master did nearly all the teaching, and, for both his third and his fourth years at the school, Franz was in the hands of the same teacher, the sympathetic Matthias Beck, who advised the Kafkas to let their son stay on for a fifth year at the school, on account of his frailty. 'Too much harassment will take its toll later.'[59] But in the summer, when Franz sat the Gymnasium examination in divinity, German and arithmetic, expecting to fail, he passed.

3 Gymnasium

On 20 September 1893 the ten-year-old boy started at the Altstädter Deutsches Gymnasium on the first floor of the eighteenth-century Kinsky Palace on the Altstädter Ring. Said to be the strictest school in Prague, it was more hierarchical than the Volksschule. Only the teachers could go up the steps to the main entrance; the boys had to use the servants' doors. Kafka's subjects included Hebrew and natural history. When Kafka started, the eighty-four new boys were divided into two parallel classes, but year by year the less scholarly boys were weeded out, only twenty-four surviving to take the *Abitur* (school-leaving certificate) at the end of the eighth year.

To his classmates Kafka seemed withdrawn, unapproachable:

> There was nothing striking about him. He was always clean and tidy, unobtrusive and solid, but never elegantly dressed. For him school was always something that failed to reach through to the innermost self. . . . We could never become really intimate with him. Something like a glass wall constantly surrounded him. With his quiet, kindly smile he opened the world up for himself, but he locked himself up in front of it. He never joined in our conversations. He only once came with us to a pub that was out of bounds. There, too, he was just the same as usual – a guest who looked with interest at the unfamiliar surroundings, smiled at them whilst keeping himself at a distance.[1]

Of the thirty-nine boys in Class Ia, thirty were Jewish (the others, except for one Protestant, all being Catholic), so Franz's isolation had nothing to do with his Jewishness. According to him he had so much anxiety

> over asserting my spiritual existence that everything else was a matter of indifference. Jewish secondary schoolboys in our country are often slightly remarkable – the most improbable things are to be found among them, but since then I have never found anything comparable to my cold, scarcely disguised, indestructible, childishly helpless, almost ridiculous, brutally self-satisfied indifference – that of a self-sufficient but coldly whimsical child. Here it was the only protection against the nervous disturbance that came from anxiety and guilt feelings.[2]

Looking back in 1922 on his schooldays he remembered: 'in my class there were probably only two Jews who had courage, and they both shot themselves while still at school or shortly afterwards'.[3] What saved Kafka

21

from suicide or breakdown was probably the same kind of balancing that saved him when he was nearly forty:

A weakness, a failing, easy to discern but hard to describe: a mixture of shyness, reserve, garrulity, half-heartedness. I mean to designate something specific, a group of weaknesses which under a certain aspect constitute a single clearly characterised weakness. . . . This weakness holds me back from madness but also from making any headway. . . . From fear of going *mad* I give up hope of going forward.[4]

According to one of his classmates, he was never a spoil-sport and never told tales; he joined in everything when invited, but never took the initiative.[5] There were only two months of holidays during the school year: the first term lasted from mid-September to February, and then, after a few days' break, the second continued from mid-February till early July. Four days a week there was school in the afternoons. Nor were there more than occasional outings to interrupt the strenuous routine. The four junior classes were taught in the rear building of the palace. At mid-morning break the boys joined the senior school for ten minutes when they could buy a piece of dry bread for one kreuzer or a sandwich for two, but they were still under supervision, having to bow whenever one of the masters passed, and the only diversion was the geographical and historical pictures on the wall.[6]

Instead of changing form-masters from year to year, Kafka was under the same teacher, Emil Gschwind, throughout his eight years at the school. Gschwind, an ordained priest who lived in a monastery, was a short, thickset man who liked to grip the boys by the chin.[7] A good classical scholar and a stern disciplinarian, he was not content with the eight weekly hours of Latin afforded by the timetable during the first two years. He demanded extensive private reading, while the better Latinists, including Kafka and his friend Hugo Bergmann, had to write out passages of Latin in exercise books, with the translation in parallel, and to visit Gschwind in the monastery, where he would look over their extra homework. 'We learned one language,' writes Bergmann, 'right down to the finest details, and that was of lifelong value.'[8] Though Kafka failed to remember his enthusiasm for Latin, he did work extremely hard at it. In his fifth year he was among the three boys doing the most reading in their own time.[9]

Gschwind believed in arousing the interest of his pupils by relating lessons to contemporary reality,[10] and involving pupils in active recording of their own observations,[11] while his own interests were wide enough for him to be interested in psychology: he reviewed books on the subject in an educational periodical.[12] He taught Latin syntax by making the boys copy out model sentences and memorize them. It must have been an ordeal for Kafka to translate or recite with a teacher and thirty-eight boys as his audience. He seems to have retained no favourable memories of Gschwind, who was probably in his mind when, in *Der Verschollene (Amerika)* he made Karl Rossmann remember the hated Latin teacher, Dr Krumpal, who used to prop himself up with his elbows, pressing his fists into his temples.

Though Kafka was to disparage his achievements at school, he did – even without wholehearted commitment – distinguish himself. In the register the boys who were graded as 'excellent' on their overall achievements were marked down as 'excellent pupils' (*Vorzugschüler*), and Kafka had this distinction each of his first three years at the school, sharing it with about eight of his classmates. In everything but maths he was well above average.

Another teacher whose influence on him, like Gschwind's, he seems to have underrated, was Ferdinand Deml, who taught him German litera-ture during his first three years at the school. Deml aimed at helping his pupils to achieve 'simplicity, clarity, accuracy and specificity' in the use of language.[13] Aware of the way that overuse devalued pictorial figures of speech, he gave the boys practice in analysing model sentences and composing sentences of their own. Especially during the first year he made copious use of fairy stories, including those of the Grimm brothers, and in the second half of the year introduced written exercises in style.[14] About a third of the time was spent on grammar. In the second half of the second year he gave the boys practice in description, moving on, in the first half of the third year, to syntax. Teaching the technique of narrative, he encouraged the boys to model their sentences on Goethe's. Almost certainly Kafka was learning more than he realized.

At the beginning of each year the school rules were read out – to Bergmann it felt as though the school community was being required to take an oath of allegiance.[15] At the end of the year, when the reports were given out, the teachers, all imperial officials, appeared in uniform, wear-ing their ceremonial swords. 'But their get-up', writes Bergmann, 'made the impression of an operetta. . . . The idea of a multi-national Austrian state would have been the acceptable solution if there had been any inner strength in it.'[16] Looking back on his education, another ex-pupil found it odd that so little was done to inculcate Austrian patriotism.[17]

Czech was obligatory in the first two years for boys who could not already speak it – Kafka took Czech lessons in spite of being able to – but no other modern languages were taught.[18] Music, art and physical train-ing were optional and only perfunctorily taught. Franz took violin and piano lessons, but made little headway, never even coming to derive

23

much pleasure from listening to music. In the third year, with only thirty-three of the original thirty-nine boys left in the class – there had been thirty-six in the second year – they started on Greek with Gschwind; from now on half the total time available was divided between Greek and Latin. Only three hours a week – later two – were devoted to maths.

Religious instruction centred on Hebrew lessons and the study in German of extracts from the Bible and the Talmud. Some of the boys in the class came from orthodox families, and Bergmann, the youngest, Kafka's junior by five months, was in real danger of losing his faith under pressure from Kafka's cogent atheism. They talked incessantly about school affairs, religion, philosophy and politics, but never, in the twelve years of their friendship, about sex. [19]

In the spring of 1896 the Kafka family moved yet again – this time to the Zeltnergasse, only a few doors away from the shop. It was an old building with narrow angular rooms and a pleasant atmosphere. [20] Franz was now given a room of his own. The flat was so close to the Teyn Church that it was almost like living inside it: prayers, hymns and organ music were loudly audible, especially in the room which must once have belonged to a priest and had a window looking into the church. If he had pulled the curtain aside during a service Kafka could have been seen to the right of the picture above the altar. But he was involved, during the first few months after moving into the flat, in preparing for a different kind of religious ceremony, his Barmitzvah. He was accustomed to memorizing passages of German, Greek and Latin verse and prose, so it was not especially taxing to memorize the passage of Hebrew he would have to chant in the Zigeuner synagogue, reading from the Torah, which contains only the consonants (vowels in Hebrew appearing underneath the letters). He had not been looking forward to coming of age as a Jew and being 'called up' for the first time to read from the Torah. The boredom of synagogue attendance was interrupted only by a 'ridiculous piece of learning by rote, and led only to something like passing an examination'. [21] For Hermann Kafka, to be called up to read from the Torah was an opportunity to acquit himself well – 'to my way of feeling an exclusively social event'. [22] So, apparently, was his son's Barmitzvah. Like many of his assimilationist contemporaries in Vienna and Prague, he used the Christian word 'confirmation' on the invitations to the reception. But Franz Kafka felt confirmed only in his lack of faith.

Elli was now nearly seven, Valli nearly six, and Ottla nearly four. He did not play with them much, and his life might have become slightly pleasanter if one of them had been a boy, so that he would no longer have been the one frail male sailing along in his hefty father's wake. The presence in the home of three small girls and a nursemaid was a negative advantage: at least there was more semblance of family life, a smoke-screen which made it less noticeable when he tried to escape conformist pressures:

> To a boy in the middle of reading an exciting story in the evening, it will never be intelligible why a command directed solely at him should make him stop reading and go to bed. . . . That was my individuality. It was suppressed by turning down the gas and leaving me without light. The explanation was: 'Everyone's going to sleep, so you must.'. . . I went sadly to sleep and a hatred began which conditioned my life.[23]

He did not revenge himself consciously, but if he later refused to play cards with his parents, he was preserving something of his right to be himself. And instead of seizing the first opportunity to move out of the parental home, he would stay on, snail-like, in the shell he had grown to protect himself from the family.

It was soon after his Barmitzvah that he became enthusiastic about theatre. The Neue Deutsche Theater had opened at Prague in 1888 under the artistic direction of Angelo Neumann, presenting operas by Wagner and Verdi side by side with plays by Ibsen, Hauptmann and Sudermann. There were schoolboy arguments about symbolism and naturalism, and boys would read out their own attempts at playwriting. Kafka only listened, never reading his own work,[24] but at home he would scare his sisters by making abrupt appearances in outrageous, improvised costumes,[25] and he would write plays for performance by them at his parents' birthday parties. None of the texts survives, but some of the titles do: *Der Gaukler* (*The Juggler*), *Photographien reden* (*Photographs Talk*) and *Georg von Podiebrad*. Georg of Podiebrad was a Hussite leader who in 1458 was elected as King of Bohemia in the Old Town Hall, which Kafka passed every day. Like the British in India, most Prague German Jews lived in ignorant indifference towards native culture and native history, and it cannot have been merely the association with his mother's birthplace that attracted Kafka to the subject.

It may have been his incipient interest in theatre that made him take more pleasure in reading aloud at school. According to his classmate Hugo Hecht, he excelled as Mark Antony when *Julius Caesar* was read out in a German translation, and did well during the fourth year, in readings from Homer and from Ovid's *Metamorphoses*,[26] which may have begun to prepare him for his own stories about transformation.

At school the teacher who probably exerted the most direct personal influence on him was Adolf Gottwald, who taught him natural history, physics, botany, zoology, mineralogy and astronomy during his first six years (except the fourth) at the school. Gottwald 'was very impressive, buoyed up with human warmth and enthusiasm for his subject. The last period in each week was devoted to philosophical discussion, in which he showed an optimism based on natural history.'[27] According to Hecht, Gottwald 'had the knack of using simple words to bring the wonders of nature closer to his pupils'.[28] He would make interesting digressions into geology or paleontology and discuss the benefits that might be expected from new discoveries in physics and chemistry. 'It was up to us, the younger generation, he told us, to elevate humanity to a higher cultural level.'[29] Gottwald was a disciple of Ernst Mach, a philosopher and physicist who believed in the primacy of the descriptive mode. He held that it was only sensory impressions which connected the individual to the external world, that a new synthesis of the natural sciences could be achieved through philosophy, and that the Darwinian principle of natural selection applied to mental processes. Mach lived in Prague and influenced both Robert Musil, who made him the subject of a doctoral thesis, and, indirectly, in his early writing, Kafka, who gave primacy to the descriptive, and whose Darwinism derived from Gottwald's. According to Hugo Bergmann, Kafka was sixteen when he started to read Darwin and became highly enthusiastic.[30]

It can only have been insecurity that made Kafka retain less specific memories of teachers and events at the Gymnasium than his classmates did. In 1910, the year he started keeping a diary, he made several reproachful attempts at summarizing the effects of his education, redrafting the statement again and again. The second version starts:

When I consider it, I must say that my education was in many ways very harmful. This criticism takes in a lot of people – my parents, some relations, individual visitors to our house, various authors, one particular cook who took me to school for a year, a crowd of teachers (whom I must press tightly together in my memory, otherwise, here and there one would elude me. But since I've pushed them all so close together, the whole thing's crumbling away in certain areas.).[31]

In each redraft there is considerable emphasis on education but very little on teaching: the focus is on damage and failure. 'My education tried to make me into a different person from the one I became.'[32] A part of him has been spoiled: 'a good, beautiful part – in dreams it often appears to me as a dead bride does to others'.[33] None of the teachers is mentioned individually as harming him, but none is mentioned as helping.

The photographs of him as a child are revealing. At about five he was appealingly fearful, appallingly vulnerable, cowed, tense, unhopeful. A few years later his face shows that some kind of defence system has been erected. The set of the features indicates more stubbornness than strength, but he is less vulnerable if only by virtue of being more with-

drawn. The withdrawal resulted less from schooling than from his private
attempts to deal with pressures he had to sustain: 'Those of us whose
education, fundamentally, was completed in a boy's bed, lonely, too cold
or too hot, say "I am cursed." It's not quite true but one comes to feel like
saying it.'[34]

The cryptic remark about the suicide of the only two brave Jews in the
class is the only pointer to his feelings about anti-Semitism. It is not
mentioned in his analysis of what damaged him, and even in the letters
and diary entries that look back on his childhood there is no mention of
the mobs that attacked Jews in the street and broke the windows of their
homes and businesses or of the ritual murder trials – there were no fewer
than twelve of them in the Empire between 1867 and 1914.[35] In April 1893
at Kolín in Central Bohemia, the town where Hermann Kafka's brother
Philipp had set up as a businessman, the body of a servant-girl was found
in the Elbe, and rumour had it that her Jewish master and his friends had
murdered her in order to use her blood in the unleavened bread for
Passover.[36] The anti-Jewish rioting that ensued may have been instigated
by the Young Czechs: in the recent local elections the Jews had mostly
supported Old Czechs.[37] Other Jews, reacting against Czech nationalism,
joined pro-German political organizations where the word Jew was never
mentioned, though the membership was entirely Jewish.[38]

But in Prague, as in Vienna, Jews were never allowed to forget their
Jewishness. Like Freud, who joined the Jewish organization B'nai B'rith
in 1897, when he was forty-one, Theodor Herzl would have preferred not
to think of himself as a Jew. At the age of twenty he joined one of the
nationalistic duelling fraternities, only to resign, three years later, in 1883,
when Wagner's death occasioned an anti-Semitic demonstration. After
the condemnation of Dreyfus in December 1894, Herzl committed himself
– as his precursor, Moses Hess, had in *Rom und Jerusalem* (1862) – to
Zionism and secessionism. As a schoolboy Kafka was to become almost
fanatically opposed to both Zionism and Judaism, and later still to become
deeply interested in both.

Religion was taught at school by Nathan Grün, librarian of the Prague
Jewish community, a small inoffensive man with a white beard, a soft
voice and a much imitated habit of interrupting his flow of words to clear
his throat of phlegm as unobtrusively as he could.[39] Kafka, in any case,
was less inclined to listen sympathetically to Grün than to the course in
formal logic and empirical psychology Gschwind was conducting in a cell
at the monastery, using books by Gustav Adolph Lindner, who took the
behaviour of the wolf and the tiger as proof of 'predatory nature's
cruelty'.[40] Apart from Latin, this was the only subject Gschwind was now
teaching the class. A formidably strict teacher, Gustav Effenberger, was

taking physics and mathematics, which meant that Kafka began to need –
and to accept – a good deal of help from Bergmann. Kafka still argued with
him about religion, talking in

a talmudic style which I had either evolved from inside myself or copied from
him. At that time I enjoyed grappling with a comparison I had found in a Christian
magazine – *Die christliche Welt*, I believe – between a clock and the world, and
between the clockmaker and God: the existence of the clockmaker was supposed
to prove that of God. . . . Against Bergmann I could refute that very well. . . . Once
I refuted it while we were walking around the tower of the town hall. [41]

The tower of the old town hall, which Kafka would have passed every day
– and seen every day from his window when he lived in the Altstädter
Ring – has an astronomical clock in it. At every hour death, holding a
sand-glass in one hand and striking at a chime of bells with the other,
presides over a procession of apostles who march out of one little doorway to disappear into another. The whole of this small area of old Prague
– and Kafka was hardly ever to escape from it – is overshadowed with
church towers and *mementi mori*. One of Kafka's earliest verses, written in
Bergmann's album on 20 November 1897, was

> Es gibt ein Kommen und ein Gehn
> Ein Scheiden und oft – kein Wiedersehen.
> (We come and go, part and often – never meet again.)

At the end of November Czech and German students began to clash
ferociously in the streets. On the 28th the Prime Minister, Count Badeni,
resigned, having failed to make peace between the factions in the
Reichsrat. To celebrate his downfall members of patriotic German student
fraternities sang the *Wacht am Rhein* in the streets. Czech students
attacked them. The police intervened brutally. Czech mobs attacked
German and Jewish shops, houses and cafés. Thousands of windows
were broken, including those of the Brod family. Hermann Kafka's shop
was spared: 'Leave Kafka alone. He's a Czech.' [42] Stones were thrown at
synagogues, and on the third day of the terror, martial law was pro-
claimed. Suspecting that Young Czech agitators had stirred up the
unrest, the government ordered an official enquiry.

The Altstädter Ring was a focal point for political demonstrations, and
Kafka cannot have failed to remember what he saw, but, apart from a
reference in 'Der Kaufmann' ('The Tradesman') to police on galloping
horses dispersing mobs, [43] he seems to have repressed these memories.
Inevitably there must have been interconnections between the self-
dislike that had accumulated from deprivation of parental love, the
self-dislike that rubbed off from anti-Semitism, and the death-wish he
never lost.

28

At school it affected him most strongly when he was doing badly. He disliked gymnastics and competitive sports; he did badly at maths. Terror at his inadequacy led straight to daydreams of escape. What if he could get up invisibly from the school bench, slip like a ghost past the teacher, through the door and out into the undemanding air? One incident he never forgot was being called to the front of the class and asked to solve a problem for which he needed a book of logarithms. Thinking the teacher would lend him one, he said, untruthfully, that he had left it in his desk. He was sent back to the desk, and, with an alarm that did not have to be faked, said it was not there. 'You crocodile,' said the teacher, giving him a bad mark, which was convenient, because it absolved him from the problem. 'Under favourable circumstances one could "disappear" even in the room, and the possibilities were infinite and one could "die" even in life.'[44] Literature was to provide a permanent escape route to a temporary death.

For Kafka, school books offered a refuge from paternal bullying, and, sensing this, Hermann Kafka felt personally rejected by his son's absorption in them, just as later he felt rejected by his son's writing. What evolved in Kafka was an almost complete dichotomy between two areas: he could feel at home only in literature. Marriage, family life and business were all situated in enemy territory. Julie Kafka, though less unsympathetic, was nervous of irritating her husband by supporting her son, while the age-gap precluded serious conversation with the three sisters. The only way these elements could all be brought together was through the plays Kafka wrote or produced for family entertainment. When he was about sixteen one of the textbooks used at school contained selections of Hans Sachs's work, and he directed his sisters in some of the playlets.[45] The family tradition of performing a play on his mother's birthday persisted at least until he was in his twentieth year. He was described as a strict director by Anna Pouzarová, who was housekeeping for the Kafkas and acted with the three sisters in the 1903 production, wearing a large pair of spectacles with no glass in them. They had to learn his text by heart and rehearse it. The dining-room was the acting area. The audience, consisting of Herr and Frau Kafka, her brother, Richard Löwy, and his family, sat in the drawing-room with the folding wooden partition as curtain.[46]

As a schoolboy Kafka was 'innocently uninterested' in sexual matters, and 'would long have remained so if I had not forcibly been thrust up against them.... Only trivialities – and even these only after precise indoctrination – made an impact on me. For example, that it was the most attractive and most attractively dressed women in the street who were supposed to be evil.'[47] The precise indoctrination came from two classmates: one of them was later a syphilitic, the other a sexologist. The most tangible result of what they said was that Kafka, who was not to lose his virginity until he was twenty, picked a quarrel with his parents for failing to educate him sexually. One evening, while the three of them were out walking, 'I began to talk about those interesting things in a manner that was stupidly boastful, superior, proud, cool (disingenuously) cold (genuinely) and stammering, just as so often when I spoke to you.' He reproached them for leaving him to be instructed by schoolboys, and he complained that he had been

in great danger (here I was lying unashamedly in my usual way, to show myself in a bold light, for, in consequence of my timidity I had no exact knowledge of the 'great dangers'). . . . You took it characteristically very simply. You only said more or less that you could give me advice about how these things could be done quite safely. Perhaps it was just such an answer I'd wanted to coax out of you, for it matched the prurience of the child over-fed with meat and all good things, physically inactive, constantly occupied with itself. Nevertheless my outward sense of shame was so hurt by this – or at least I believed it must be – that . . . with arrogant impudence I broke off the conversation. . . . What you were advising me to do was in your own opinion and, what's more, in my opinion at that time, the filthiest thing there was. It was incidental that you should make sure I'd bring none of the filth home with me: you were protecting yourself, your house. . . . And it was you who were pushing me, with a few frank words, down into the filth as if it were my destiny.[48]

In his last two years at the school his friendship with Bergmann was cooling, partly because Kafka was inclining more towards socialism – his Czech classmate, Rudolf Illowý, probably exerted an influence on this – while Bergmann was a passionate Zionist. On 24 April 1899, when the Prague Zionists held their first meeting, it was broken up by Jewish socialists.[49] After Illowý left the school in 1889, Kafka was the only socialist in the class sufficiently committed to wear the traditional red carnation, and in 1900 when the Boer War broke out, he sympathized with the Boers, roundly condemning the English. At a meeting of the Altstädter Kollegentag, the student fraternity which had recruited members from the school, Kafka and Bergmann remained sitting when the 'Wacht am Rhein' was sung – with the result that they were both ejected.

One element in Kafka's radicalism may have been reaction against his father's despotism – in the family, in the household, in the shop. It was at this point that Kafka, together with some of his classmates, joined the anti-clerical society 'Freie Schule', and that he was becoming more friendly with Ewald Felix Příbram, who was held in awe by his classmates for having broken decisively with the Jewish faith and the community.[50]

By putting more pressure on the Jews, the anti-Semitism fomented by the Young Czechs was sharpening the rift between Zionists and socialists. One of the most damaging allegations of ritual murder was made in 1899 when an unemployed Jew, Leopold Hilsner, was indicted for killing Anežka Hrůzová at Polná, in north-eastern Bohemia. The idea that her blood had been used in Passover matzos was encouraged in pamphlets, newspaper articles and speeches, and the situation was exacerbated by post-mortem reports that the body had lost large quantities of blood. After being sentenced to death, Hilsner confessed, but afterwards retracted the confession as having been made under duress. In October mobs rampaged through the old city in Prague, overturning stalls and attacking shops, while similar incidents occurred in many Moravian towns. Tomáš Masaryk, eight years before he became the leader of the Czech Realists, published a pamphlet ridiculing the legal proceedings against Hilsner, and, by doing so, he alienated the Young Czechs, the National Socialists and all the radical nationalists.

As the grandson of a ritual slaughterer (*schochet*) Kafka must have been particularly sensitive to the anti-Jewish hysteria whipped up by the allegation; seventeen years later when he read Arnold Zweig's *Ritualmord in Ungarn* (*Ritual Murder in Hungary*) he was reduced to tears.[51] In the play, which is based loosely on the Hilsner scandal, a boy falsely denounces his father and co-religionists. Finally he stabs himself in a synagogue. Kafka's vegetarianism may have had one root in revulsion at the idea of his father's father's daily activity – ritually slitting the throats of animals, hacking up their bodies, feeding his family with money earned from butchering. The butcher's knife will be recurrent in Kafka's nightmares, fantasies and fictions; the animal identifications may have seemed, at one level, like a means of making amends to the animals, or, at least, siding with them against slaughterous humanity. He even started to write a story himself about ritual murder in Odessa, but he destroyed the manuscript (see below, p. 296).

If German Jews were now having to choose, as Martin Buber said, between being German and being Jewish, the choice apparently open to Kafka's Jewish classmates was between Zionism and assimilationist socialism. Though a substantially smaller proportion of Prague Jews gave German as their primary language in the census of 1900 than in 1890,[52] Hermann Kafka on both occasions declared his family to be Czech-speaking. But records do not necessarily reflect facts, and the prospect of assimilation could be no more than a mirage when there was so little social contact between Christians and Jews. Now, as later, nearly all Kafka's friends were Jewish.

When the boys, in their final year, had to deliver a miniature lecture,

Kafka was the only one to choose Goethe as his subject. He also became interested in Kleist, whose writing had emerged out of a hopeless lifelong battle to contain the residue of guilt left by parental and family disapproval, and whose life prefigured Kafka's both in abortive marriage plans and in resentment against a dreary office job. But from fear of the impending *Abitur*[53] he spent much of his evenings and weekends on Greek and Latin. At school five periods a week were now being devoted to each; three to history and geography, and to physics; two to religious instruction, to mathematics and to 'Philosophical Propaedeutics'.

At the beginning of the summer holidays in 1900 Kafka went to stay with his favourite uncle, Siegfried Löwy, a doctor who later became the model for his story 'Ein Landarzt' ('A Country Doctor'). He lived in Triesch, a small village in western Moravia, about eighty miles from Prague, to the south-east. Kafka called him 'the twitterer' because 'there's such an inhumanly thin, old-maidish, birdlike wit that comes piping out of his constricted throat'.[54] Staying at Triesch with him Kafka could go swimming, lie naked in the grass by the pool, help with the hay harvest, wander in the park, make friends with the local girls, join in ring games, take cows and goats to pasture, go for long walks, and in the evening play billiards with his uncle.[55]

The rest of the summer holidays he spent living with his parents at Roztok, seven and a half miles north of Prague, on the left bank of the Moldau, living on the first floor of the house of the chief postmaster, Kohn. Kafka spent a great deal of time in the forest with the postmaster's daughter, Selma. Sitting under an old oak tree he read Nietzsche to her.

> We fell for each other. . . . I was pretty and he was very clever and both of us were so divinely young. . . . And our garden opened out into a high mountain. There was a bench at the end, and in the evenings we often went to this bench, Franz with a burning candle in his hand . . . he tried to persuade me to make up my mind to study. But it was no use. My father wouldn't allow me to – in those days we obeyed our fathers – and so we parted.[56]

On 4 September 1900 he wrote in her album: 'But there's a living thoughtfulness that has passed gently over everything memorable, as if with a caressing hand. And when from these ashes the flame shoots up, glowing and hot, powerful and strong and you gaze into it, as though spellbound by magic, then—'[57] But memories of this kind do not survive in Kafka's consciousness. Later he was to admit to having a poor memory, but wrote of his boyhood as if there had been no intervals of happiness in it.

His best friend at that time was Oskar Pollak, a serious-looking boy, one of the maturest in the class, 'temperamental and exuberant in his speech. He was more interested than the rest of us in art history, natural science and Indian philosophy.'[58] Though he could not yet confide in him sufficiently to show him his writing, their friendship developed during their last two years at school. They both chose Cicero's speeches for their private reading in Latin, and Pollak introduced Kafka to the periodical *Der Kunstwart*, edited by Ferdinand Avenarius. Some of his contributors had been recommended to him by Nietzsche. It was in *Der Kunstwart* that Kafka started reading Hofmannsthal, and he was strongly influenced by the verse it published. He also became interested in Nietzsche, taking *Also sprach Zarathustra* with him in 1900, when he went on holiday to Roztok. The school authorities were nervous of the atheistic tendencies in the top form, and when Pollak chose Darwinism as the subject for his practice lecture, it was vetoed.[59]

Though the Empire made no attempt to keep an ideological grip on education in the subject territories, political questions were often raised in school work. In the 1901 *Abitur* examination one of the essay topics was: 'What benefits accrue to Austria from its situation in the world and from the quality of the soil?' Only two of the twenty-four boys left in the class failed the exam; of the twenty-two who passed, three (including Bergmann and Utitz) were given a distinction; Kafka passed, but without distinction. Five of the boys were in their ninth year at the school, and five had already passed their twentieth birthday. This was the point at which decisions had to be made about university courses and therefore about future careers. Jews were hardly ever admitted to the army or civil service unless they became Christians, as many did. The 'free' professions open to them were medicine and law. Declaring their choice of university course, six of the twenty-two, including Kafka and Utitz, put down philosophy, four including Bergmann put law, and two including Pollak put chemistry. Jews were accepted in the local chemical industry.

In August, after leaving school, Kafka went outside his native Bohemia for the first time, travelling alone to the North Sea islands, Norderney and Heligoland.[60]

4 University

After eight years of intermittently intensive work within a fairly tight disciplinary system, Kafka had gained freedom, but the loss seemed greater than the gain. Being so insecure, he had needed at each instant 'a new confirmation of my existence'.[1] It was a relief that the dreaded examination no longer lay ahead, but he had no sense of achievement, feeling that he had escaped failure only by cheating.[2] The main deception had been to conceal the fact that study had never really involved him: 'I was interested in the teaching – and not only the teaching but everything around me at that formative age – about as much as a thievish bank clerk, still in his job and terrified of being found out, is interested in the trivial everyday business of the bank.'[3] Now unemployed, Kafka was free from that particular tension, but, 'If already, despite the pressures of the Gymnasium, I'd been concerned only with myself, how much worse it was now that I was free.'[4] His valuation of himself still depended on his father, and at home he still felt 'despised, condemned, beaten down'.[5] He could not escape this by going on a fortnight's holiday from it, and it would take ten years to achieve the degree of inner freedom that is revealed in his diaries.

Registering at the Deutsche Universität in November 1901, Kafka put his name down for the chemistry course that Bergmann and Pollak were going to take. Professor Goldschmied, who directed it, was himself a converted Jew, and, after an interview with him, Kafka was accepted. But, like Bergmann, he was surprised that so much work had to be done in the laboratory. 'Our hands weren't deft enough', wrote Bergmann, 'to carry out experiments.'[6] He persevered for a year, but after two uncertain weeks, Kafka switched to law, which pleased his father better. A degree in law might lead to a job in a bank or the post office, in industry or in local government. For Kafka – retrospectively, at least – the choice of career was, 'compared to the main issue, as much a matter of indifference as all the teaching at the Gymnasium: it was a problem of finding the career that would best indulge this indifference without hurting my vanity too much'.[7] For the first four terms he had to spend twenty hours a week listening to lectures on Roman law, ecclesiastical law and German law.

His friendship with Pollak was still developing, but not sufficiently for them to communicate freely. As later with women, Kafka could better

34

overcome his nervous reserve when writing a letter than when looking into another human face. 'When we talk the words are hard, we step over them like an uneven pavement. The subtlest things acquire clumsy feet, and there's nothing we can do about it. We're almost in each other's way. I bump into you, and you – I don't dare, and you—.'[8] One obstacle to intimacy was the difficulty of talking about Pollak's girlfriend. 'You go about with her here or there or at Roztok, and I sit at my desk at home. You talk to her and in the middle of a sentence someone pops up and bows. That's me with my rough-edged words and quadrangular countenance.'[9] At least he was now enlisting his literary talent to serve a personal relationship. He ended the letter: 'Are we enemies? I am very fond of you.' And the friendship continued.

Since 1882 the university buildings had been used by what were, in effect, two separate universities, one Czech, the other German. Students had to register with either one or the other, but they could safely ignore the rule that forbade them to attend lectures in the other language, while lecturers could ignore the veto on working in both languages. The buildings were all divided internally into Czech and German sections: the Carolinum, where Kafka went for law lectures, had two entrances, one in the Eisengasse, used by the German-speaking students, and one in the Obstmarkt. The archives, the library and the Aula, where degrees were conferred, were used on alternate days by the two universities, but in examinations students of both universities could choose between German and a combination of German and Czech. Only in legal history could they opt for only Czech.[10]

The course of lectures Kafka attended on art history did not provide sufficient diversion from the law, and in the spring of 1902 he seized gladly on his chance of switching to a course in German literature and art history. Law students at Prague were obliged to devote one term to the humanities. Kafka attended three courses of literary lectures by the heavyweight reactionary August Sauer, who since October 1901 had been editing the nationalistic monthly *Deutsche Arbeit*, which tended to denigrate Czech achievements while eulogizing the primacy of German culture. Fifteen years later Kafka would dream about girls attending a lecture mainly because Professor Sauer was going to be in the audience,[11] but Kafka found him highly unattractive.[12]

He also attended the philosophy lectures of Anton Marty, a pupil of Franz Brentano, who had noticed that antinomies and insoluble problems arose from a separation – which was in any case unnecessary – between consciousness and its objects. The assumption that all consciousness must be consciousness of something is the simple basis for Brentano's doctrine of intentionality as defining the essence of consciousness. It was

Brentano who introduced into modern philosophy the term 'intentionality', which had been used in the Middle Ages. He divided psychic phenomena into three categories: ideas, judgments and mood-changes. Strongly influenced by the English utilitarians, he regarded only the faculty for judgment as trustworthy.

Kafka exposed himself regularly, if indirectly, to the influence of Brentano. 'Every day from twelve to one,' writes Utitz, 'Marty read his lecture, speaking slowly and softly with pedagogic mastery, renouncing all rhetorical affectation. In discussion he let no observation pass without careful critical scrutiny. Participants gradually learned to weigh their words: the clear cool atmosphere of scientific precision ennobled each unforgettable period. . . . He was shy and nervous.'[13] It may have been through Marty that Kafka was given an entrée in the summer to the exclusive Brentano circle which met once a fortnight at the Café Louvre in Ferdinandstrasse. 'We found ourselves', says Utitz, 'among a large circle of fellow-campaigners who gathered in numbers for evenings of endless discussion. Franz Brentano was naturally not present, but his mighty shadow fell across all the dialogue.'[14]

They studied Brentano's books, as well as those of Gustav Fechner, a more traditional psychologist, whose ideas had been expounded by Gschwind. Kafka failed the oral examination which Marty held in his flat at the end of the lecture course,[15] but he went on attending the meetings in the café until the autumn of 1905.[16]

In August 1902, Kafka was invited to join Oskar Pollak, who was visiting places important in classical German literature, including Weimar and Ilmenau, a town nearby, with mines that had interested Goethe. But the invitation arrived too late,[17] and he spent the month at Liboch, a village on the Elbe, twenty-five miles north of Prague, staying with some people called Windischbauer. But he interrupted the holiday when his Uncle Alfred, his mother's eldest brother, arrived from Madrid, where he was director general of the Spanish railways.

> Shortly before his arrival I had the quaint (very quaint, unfortunately) notion of begging him, no not begging, asking, whether he couldn't help me out of this mess, couldn't take me somewhere or other where I could make a fresh start. Well, I started cautiously. . . . He began to talk smoothly, though he's normally good-hearted. He comforted me. Fine. Let it pass. Reluctantly I stopped talking, and the whole two days I've been in Prague because of him, I haven't mentioned it again, though I've been with him all the time.[18]

After his uncle left on the evening of 24 August, Kafka went back for another week in Liboch, where he did very little. 'I needed a strange time like this, a time of lying for hours on a vineyard wall, staring into the rainclouds, which refuse to go away.'[19] He played hide-and-seek with the children, told them stories, built sandcastles for them, went for walks by himself, watching the long shadows cast by the late afternoon sun on the furrows. 'Have you noticed how late summer shadows dance on dark, tilled soil, how they dance physically?'[20] He had a great deal to ponder: he was on the point of making his first attempt to leave home. From Liboch, he would go on to stay with his Uncle Siegfried for a week at Triesch, and later on, in October, he would visit Munich, where he was hoping to join his former classmate Paul Kisch in studying at the university.[21] But the plan fell through, presumably because of his father's resistance. Kafka had now had his one obligatory term of humanities and in any case he did not want to study literature in a faculty controlled by Professor Sauer; to study it at Munich would have been quite different. But, submissively, he returned to the legal fold at Prague. 'Prague doesn't let go,' he wrote to Oskar Pollak. 'This little mother has claws.... One has to give in or else—.'[22] But the sense of being landlocked was common among Prague authors: Gustav Meyrink, for instance, felt incarcerated by the city's demonic magic.

Kafka's letter develops into what was possibly his first attempt to distil abjection into allegory. He tells the story of Shamefaced Lanky (*schamhafter Lange*) who has crept away to an old village where the rooms are so low that when he stands up, his big angular skull goes through the ceiling. One day before Christmas Lanky is sitting with his legs dangling outside the window, knitting woollen socks with his clumsy, skinny, spidery fingers, and almost skewering his grey eyes on the needles, for it is dark. When a well-dressed visitor arrives, Untrue-in-Heart (*Unredlicher in seinem Herzen*, who represents Emil Utitz), Lanky feels ashamed of his height and his room and his woollen socks. The visitor's waistcoat buttons and his stories of the city make the room seem airless, and while he speaks he jabs Lanky in the stomach with his walking stick. Finally left alone again, Lanky weeps. 'With the socks he wiped the big tears away. His heart hurt, and he could tell nobody. But sick questions crawled up his legs to his soul.... Am I weeping from pity for him or for me?... He picked up the socks again. He almost dug himself in the eyes with the knitting needles, for it was even darker.'[23] Had this not been part of a letter it would subsequently have been destroyed by Kafka; surviving it serves to exemplify his immature technique of using self-hatred as a trampoline for unambitious fictional exercise.

Most of the law lecturers were Jewish; all of them were tedious. The rector of the university, Josef Ulbrich, permanently dishevelled and unshaven, lectured on political law, speaking flatly with lowered head, although there was no script on the table.[24] Professor Heinrich Singer, a baptized Jew, lectured on canon law. Brod, who was also studying law, describes him as a character from E. T. A. Hoffmann, 'creeping on to the rostrum, senile and shaking, a frail and crotchety little man'.[25] In Kafka's room at this period, on the desk beside the permanently open door were two volumes of Roman law.[26]

His friendship with Brod began on 23 October 1902. His junior by a year, Brod was small, and had been hump-backed since the fourth or fifth year of his life.

Kafka struck him at first as an untalkative, unassuming student, cheerful and amusing. There was nothing in his behaviour to indicate the cast of mind revealed in his letter to his father.[27] They met at the German Students' Union Reading and Lecture Hall, in the Lese- und Redehalle, in Ferdinandstrasse. Except for the nationalistic anti-Semites and the orthodox, anti-assimilationist Jews, every student who passed *Abitur* at a Prague school joined the Union, and wore the black, red and gold ribbon of the 1848 revolution. The committee of the Union was at loggerheads with the members, but the committee always won votes because the socially privileged student fraternities that wore colours – though they belonged only loosely to the Union – turned up in larger numbers to the general meetings, where their votes were decisive. The most influential member of the committee was Bruno Kafka, Franz's cousin, who became President in the summer term of 1903; the most independent section of the Union was the 'Section for Literature and Art', which held regular debates and lectures. On 23 October Brod, who was in his first year at the university, read a paper on Schopenhauer,[28] eulogizing him, while denouncing Nietzsche as a 'swindler'. Kafka, who regularly attended the section's meetings, was sufficiently upset to overcome his shyness and walk home with Brod, arguing. The conversation spread to other literary disagreements. Brod, who admired Meyrink, quoted by heart a passage comparing butterflies to great open books of magic.[29] Kafka was unimpressed. 'As a counter-example of what he liked himself', says Brod,

Kafka quoted a passage of Hofmannsthal: 'The smell of damp stone in a hall.' And he fell silent for a long time, adding nothing, as if this esoteric, unornamented phrase must speak for itself. That made such a deep impression on me that I still remember the street and the house in front of which the conversation took place.[30]

In fact his memory was deceiving him. The Hofmannsthal phrase, which Brod misquotes, substituting 'wet' for 'damp', occurs in 'Das Gespräch über Gedichte' which was not published till 1904. Either Kafka must have quoted another Hofmannsthal phrase or the memory belongs to a later period of the friendship. Brod was also a gifted musician, and Kafka attended student concerts featuring him as composer and pianist.

In November Kafka resumed his legal studies, from which there would now be no reprieve until he graduated in 1906, and during the first year of settling down to the law he wrote 'almost nothing'.[31]

He had to attend at least twenty hours of lectures each week, preparing for his first state examination on 18 July 1903, 'and in the few months before the examination, taking a heavy toll on my nerves, I was feeding myself mentally on sawdust, which had – what's more – already been chewed in the mouths of a thousand other people'.[32] It was in July – after his twentieth birthday on the third, and before the examination on the eighteenth – that he had his first sexual experience. Retrospectively he would associate it more with anxiety than with desire.[33] A shopgirl used to stand in the doorway of the dress-shop opposite the Kafkas' house in Zeltnergasse, and while he was pacing up and down his room, memorizing legal facts that did not interest him, their eyes met. This is how he remembered the incident seventeen years later:

It was summertime, very hot, quite unbearable, and I stopped at the window each time, rebarbative Roman legal history between my teeth. Finally we came to an agreement by signs. I was to pick her up at eight o'clock, but in the evening when I came down there was another man there, well that didn't make much difference, everybody made me feel afraid, so this man did too; if he had not been there I'd have been afraid of him in any case. But the girl, though she took his arm, made signs to me that I should follow them. So we went to Schützen Island, drank beer there, I at the neighbouring table, then went, I following, slowly back to the girl's room, somewhere near the meat market, and there the man said goodnight, the girl ran into the house, I waited a little while until she came out again to me, and then we went to a hotel in the Kleinseite [on the west side of the river]. It was all, before the hotel, charming, exciting and vile; in the hotel it was no different. And when, towards morning, we went home over the Karlsbrücke, it was still hot and beautiful, and I was certainly happy, but this happiness consisted only in my finally having peace from the constant whining of the body, but above all the happiness consisted in the whole thing's not being still more vile, still more filthy. Then I was with the girl once again, I think, two nights later, but since I then went away on my summer holidays, and played around a bit out there with a girl, I couldn't look at the shopgirl in Prague any more, and I never talked to her again, she was (from my point of view) my bitter enemy, though she was a good-hearted, friendly girl, always afterwards pursuing me with her uncomprehending eyes. I won't say it was the only reason for my hostility (certainly it wasn't) that in the hotel the girl did something slightly vile (not worth mentioning) and said something slightly filthy (not worth mentioning) but the memory remained, I knew immediately I'd never forget it, and at the same time knew or believed I knew that this vileness and filthiness, apparently quite unnecessary, were necessarily connected inwardly with the whole thing and that it was precisely this

39

vileness and filthiness (the only small signs of them being her small gesture and words) that had drawn me with such frantic force into this hotel which I would otherwise have used all my strength to avoid.[34]

The summer holiday Kafka took was with his parents at Zálezly, near Aussig, where the local girl played tennis with him, went for cycle rides with him and flirted with him. One of his reasons for looking forward to the summer reprieve from legal studies was that he wanted to write: 'what I believe I have inside me – I don't always believe it – (I wanted) to bring out at one stroke'.[35] This was over-optimistic, and he wrote little during the holiday, but by the end of the summer the weight of what he had written previously was pressing down on him hard enough for him to need someone else's reaction to it.

Something is tearing my lips apart . . . and someone standing behind a tree is saying softly: 'You'll do nothing without others.' But now I'm writing meaningfully and in elegant syntax: 'Isolation is repulsive, eggs should be laid honestly in the open, the sun will hatch them, it's better to bite into life than into one's own tongue.'[36]

What he wanted to do was to send Pollak a bundle containing everything he had written except the things from his childhood – 'You see, the misfortune has been sitting on my hunched back from early on'[37] – and except what he no longer had or considered 'valueless in this context', and the plans for the future and 'the things I can't show even to you, for one shudders to stand there quite naked and be fingered by someone else, even when one's begged on one's knees for that very thing'.[38] He was not asking Pollak 'whether it would be pleasant to wait for a while or whether to set a match lightheartedly to the whole bonfire'.[39] All he wanted was that another pair of eyes see the material. 'My maximum of warmth and hardness is only cool, in spite of the sun, and I know that the eyes of an outsider will make everything warmer and livelier.'[40] His vehemence about the repulsiveness of the solitary life belonged mainly to an argument he was having with himself, but this is the unmistakable desperation of the man who knows he has no chance of convincing himself. He went on to send Pollak poems, fragments of a novel to be called *Das Kind und die Stadt* (*The Child and the City*) and other pieces of prose.

By November, when the new academic year started, with its taxing routine of legal lectures, he had still done no writing:

God does not want me to write, but I must. So it is a constant up-and-down, finally, though, God's the stronger, and there's more unhappiness in it than you can imagine. So many forces inside me are tied to a stake, which might possibly grow into a green tree, while they could be useful, once released, both to me and the state.[41]

He was writing to Oskar Pollak, who had left Prague to start working as a tutor at Castle Ober-Studenec, south of Pilsen. Kafka felt not only bereaved of his closest friend but debilitated, as if he had lost an instrument of vision, a periscope.

> Really, of all the young people, I have spoken only with you, and if I spoke to others it was only incidentally or on your account or through you or in relation to you. You were, among many other things, something like a window through which I could look out at the street. Alone I couldn't do that, for in spite of my height I don't yet reach up to the windowsill. [42]

But he was already aware of how little anyone could ever know of another person's feelings:

> We're abandoned like lost children in the woods. When you stand before me and look at me, what do you know of the pain within me, and what do I know of yours? And if I threw myself to the ground in front of you, and wept, and explained, what more would you know of me than you do of hell, when someone tells you it's hot and frightful? For that reason alone we human beings ought to confront one another as reverently, as thoughtfully and as lovingly as we'd confront the entrance to hell. [43]

The only consolation for Pollak's departure was that it would be reassuring to have someone reading his work, and aware, at a distance, of his existence. 'I'm perhaps glad you've left, as glad as people would have to be if someone climbed up on the moon to watch them from there.' [44]

It was probably Oskar Kraus, a disciple of Brentano's, prominent in the Louvre circle, who alerted him to Marcus Aurelius. 'I am pushing Marcus Aurelius aside,' he wrote on 10 January 1904, 'pushing him aside with difficulty. I don't believe I could go on living without him, for two or three sayings of his are enough to make me feel more composed, more under control.' [45] Later on in the month he read all four volumes of Hebbel's diaries. [46] He wanted to answer a letter of Oskar Pollak's, but the diaries, he said, made him feel like a caveman who had rolled a block of stone in front of his cave and then, finding himself shut off from light and air, has to push at it.

> But it does one good when the conscience receives extensive wounds, because they make it more sensitive to each prick. I believe one should read only the books that bite and sting. If a book we're reading doesn't wake us up with a punch on the head, what are we reading it for? . . . We need the books which affect us like a disaster, which pain us deeply, like the death of someone dearer to us than ourselves, like being lost in the woods, far from everyone, like a suicide, a book must be the axe for the frozen sea in us. [47]

He had made a similar point, though without expressing it so forcibly, when he was reading Fechner and Meister Eckhart ten weeks earlier:

'Books often work like a key to unknown rooms in one's own castle.'[48] The books that gave him this feeling were mostly mystical, psychological or autobiographical.

His friendship with Max Brod developed slowly, partly because Brod was more sociable than Pollak, and, despite his spinal deformation, charismatic enough to attract a circle of friends glad to be in his company, while to Kafka, who found even a one-to-one relationship taxing enough, it seemed Brod was letting himself be diluted and vulgarized. Insofar as his companions were dependent on him, Kafka complained, 'they surround you like responsive mountain scenery with a ready-made echo. . . . But insofar as they are independent, they damage you even more, because they distort you, through them you are put in a false position. To the listener they make it seem as though you're contradicting yourself.'[49] Kafka could see that Brod was sometimes disinclined to exert himself mentally: he enjoyed the feeling, especially when tired, that other people were tiding him along approximately in the right direction.[50] Kafka was probably the only one to notice he was slightly off course. That Kafka expressed his feelings as honestly as he could was, as Brod understood, a gesture more friendly than hostile.

According to him, their friendship began with the pact they made, at his instigation, not to let their Greek go rusty. 'We read Plato's *Protagoras* together, with help from a translation and our school dictionary, but often with great difficulty. . . . What we chiefly enjoyed was the colourful and scurrilous account of the Sophists' activities, and the Platonic–Socratic irony.'[51] Kafka's suggestion was that they should read Flaubert together in French. They met two or three times a week, mostly in Kafka's small room, sometimes in Brod's. Years were to elapse before Kafka confided in Brod, as he had in Pollak, about his writing, but Brod soon found himself jotting down phrases which occurred in what Kafka said. The first was about a garrulous man: 'Talk comes out of his mouth like a stick.'[52]

Hanging over Kafka's writing table was a large *Kunstwart* reproduction of the picture 'Der Pflüger' ('The Ploughman') by Hans Thoma. On the wall at the side was a yellowing plaster cast of a small antique relief – a maenad holding a leg of beef. 'The graceful folds of her dress danced around the headless figure.'[53] The room was furnished simply in a way that struck Brod as 'almost miserly'.[54] But Kafka was so attached to the furniture – bed, wardrobe, ancient desk, not quite black[55] – that, when he eventually moved out of his parents' flat, he took it with him. He had been subscribing to the periodical *Neue Rundschau*, where he read Thomas Mann's story 'Ein Glück' ('A Piece of Good Luck', written in 1904). The opening sentence made a tremendous impression on him: 'Quiet! We want to look into a soul.' 'Again and again he repeated this sentence, each time laying his finger pantomimically on his lips as he let the melody resound. About the story itself he said nothing.'[56]

Though six years were still to elapse before 'Das Urteil', the late summer of 1904 formed a turning point in his development as a writer. In the letters, as in the stories and fragments that survive, a highly original style is being precipitated from the acid mixture of precision with vagueness, strength of feeling with ambivalence. In his attitude towards the routine of his own life, there was a deep uncertainty about how much change he wanted. He had settled down almost comfortably into the discomfort of splitting time between the compulsory study of law and the voluntary activities which interested him. Unable to occupy the whole of his life, he had surrendered the larger part of his territory to the enemy, but he never studied after seven o'clock,[57] and then he could enjoy himself – writing, reading, chatting with Brod, listening to discussions at the Louvre circle or at the house of Berta Fanta, the wife of a chemist with a shop in the Altstädter Ring and herself a member of the circle, as was her anthroposophist sister Ida Freund. The Mme Récamier of Prague, Berta Fanta lectured about her travels, and organized literary-cum-philosophical discussions at her home. So Kafka was often surrounded by people who stimulated him intellectually while reflecting an image at variance with the one he had of himself. He took part in charades and masquerades; in 1904 he dressed up as a red-sashed diplomat from the time of Goethe.[58]

In the emotional turbulence which the beginning of summer brings to a man in his early twenties, he had felt quite hopeful. 'One expects oriental marvels, while repudiating one's optimism with a comic bow and bumbling speech, and this animated game makes one feel both snug and flurried.'[59] Despite the 'daily prayer that, in outward appearance, the continuity of our life should graciously be preserved',[60] we 'tunnel through ourselves like a mole and emerge quite blackened and velvet-haired from our sandy underground vaults, our poor little red feet sticking out pitifully in hope of sympathy'.[61] The image occurred to him after he had watched a desperate mole trying to escape from a dog. At first Kafka was amused.

And then it struck me that – No, nothing struck me. I was merely under the delusion it did because on that day my head was drooping so heavily that in the evening I noticed with amazement that my chin had grown into my chest. But on the next day I was again holding my head upright again, quite prettily.[62]

This indicates the same scrupulous truthfulness that compelled him to reveal his misgivings about Brod, and in the vacuum created by the refusal to simulate, a humorously surreal image pops up. If he felt he had failed in his human duty towards the mole, no analysis of the inadequacy could have been as revealing as the comic image. Kafka is using the awkwardness he felt about his height and his posture but more imaginatively than in the letter about Shamefaced Lanky. In 'Beschreibung eines Kampfes' ('Description of a Struggle', first version, started 1904), the earliest of his stories to survive his holocaust of juvenilia, it occurs to the narrator that his long body is upsetting his companion by making him feel too small. This idea

tormented me so much that I bent my back enough for my hands to touch my knees while walking. But so that my acquaintance should not notice my intention, I changed my posture only very gradually and with great caution, trying to distract his attention from me with remarks about the trees of Schützen Island and the reflections of the bridge-lamps in the river. But with a sudden turn he pressed his face into mine, and said indulgently: 'So why are you walking like that? You're quite crooked now and almost as small as I am.'

Since it was said kindly, I answered: 'That may be so. But I like this posture. I'm rather frail, you know, and it's too much of a strain to hold my body upright. It's no trifling matter, I'm very tall.'[63]

The feeling of frailty was partly a matter of feeling puny beside his burly father and partly a matter of not having a firm grip on life. One afternoon, waking up from a nap, he heard his mother calling out from the balcony: 'What are you doing?' And a woman answered from the garden 'Having a little snack on the lawn.' ('Ich jause im Grünen.') Kafka was 'astonished at the strength of the hold people have on life',[64] and the exchange impressed him sufficiently to be reproduced verbatim in 'Beschreibung eines Kampfes'.

His study of philosophy and psychology had sharpened his awareness of how moods could be virtually independent of either mental events or external events, and it was in the summer of 1904 that his prose accommodated itself to the change of outlook, which was also partly a change of life style. He had begun to lose faith both in explanations and in good resolutions. Life was a jumble of experiences, uncontrollable. All he could do was slide along and snatch at passing sensations or events. If a girl falls in love with him, perhaps there is no more to be said about it than about her putting on a white dress.[65]

Another day I took excitedly painful pleasure in the agitation of a day, which was overcast. Then a week or two blew past, or even more. Then I fell in love with a woman. Once there was dancing at the inn, and I didn't go. Then I was depressed and very stupid, so that I stumbled along the country roads, which are very steep here.[66]

The vagueness and the detachment admit a comic non-commitment, as if he were only an unprivileged spectator of his own experience.

The letters and the fiction overlap. In a sense, the fiction is even more private and diary-like than the letters, not being intended, as yet, for anyone else's eyes. Nor is it merely that incidents such as the conversation between the two women are used in both letters and fiction or that the style developed for one finds its way into the other. He was trying in both not so much to understand as to savour the inconsequentiality in his attitudes to other people and in theirs to him. In the letters he may resort to fiction or fable, and in the stories to self-analysis perfunctorily disguised by splitting himself into two characters, each ambivalent towards the other, each oscillating between wanting his company and wanting to be left alone. In 'Beschreibung eines Kampfes' the mixture of self-love and self-hatred prefigures that of 'Das Urteil' when the narrator casually condemns his acquaintance to death:

> 'You'll have to murder yourself,' I said, and smiled too. . . .
> 'Right,' he cried, and hit the bench with his tight, little fist, but left it lying there. 'You go on living though. You don't kill yourself. No one loves you. You're achieving nothing. You have no control over the moment that comes. But that's how you talk to me, you vulgar creature. You're incapable of loving. Nothing arouses you but fear. . . .'[67]

Kafka's whole life was a series of hesitations in the process of condemning himself and carrying out the execution. The violence of his antagonism towards himself is played out in this story between the two men, and the physical climax comes where the acquaintance plunges a knife into his own upper arm. The narrator sucks at the deep wound, grateful to recognize that it is for his sake his friend has stabbed himself. And if the action is approximating to the Rimbaudesque, so is the style:

> Just think, in the spring we'll drive into the orchard – no, not we, unfortunately, but you and Annie, happily, at a trot. Oh yes, believe me, I beg you, and the sun will show you off beautifully to everyone. Oh, music is playing, hoof-beats heard far off, nothing to worry about, shouting and barrel-organs playing in the avenues.[68]

In the party sequence at the beginning of the story the two men were almost strangers, having exchanged only a few words as fellow-guests. Like many a later *alter ego* of Kafka's, the narrator lets himself be drawn abruptly into intimacy with a male stranger, having at first resented the intrusion on his privacy. 'If you weren't so confused you'd realize how inappropriate it is to talk about an affectionate girl to a man who's sitting alone drinking schnapps.'[69] Like Brod, he takes reproof only as an invitation to intimacy, and when other guests crowd around, hoping to overhear the conversation, the narrator keeps his new friend to himself by proposing a midnight climb up the freezing Laurenziberg. It is when they are outside that the influence of Brentano is evident in Kafka's awareness of mood-changes that can catch one by surprise:

Scarcely had we walked out into the open air when I obviously started to feel high-spirited. I lifted my legs sportively, and let my joints crack cheerfully, I shouted out a name down the street as if a friend of mine had just gone round the corner, I threw my hat high in the air and ostentatiously caught it.[70]

The narrator seems to have no girlfriend, and the story is quite subtle in its suggestions of intermittent jealousy and ambivalence. Feeling almost proprietorial towards his new friend, he is also wishing he could be alone. 'But I was too timid to go away without saying goodbye, and too weak to shout out to him, so I stood still, leaning against the moonlit wall of a house, and waiting.'[71] Sincerely disliking his own behaviour in such situations, Kafka can pinpoint both the shyness and the narrator's vicarious pleasure in the other man's love affairs. 'His life became more precious to me than my own. I found his face beautiful, I was proud of his success with women and I participated in the kisses he'd received from the two girls.'[72] Kafka was later to say he loved Brod more than himself. But what has to be balanced against the narrator's vicarious satisfaction is anxiety over what his friend may say about him to the girls. Having no clear image of his own identity, Kafka is especially prone to speculation about images other people may form of him, and, as in the Shamefaced Lanky letter, he camouflages his anxiety with cruelly comic hyperbole.

He looks like – how should I describe him? – a dangling stick with a yellow-skinned, black-haired skull rammed rather clumsily on top. His body's hung with a lot of rather small, gaudy, yellowish bits of cloth, which completely covered him yesterday night because there was no wind and they were lying flat.[73]

Alongside the caricature, which makes a claim to detachment, there is a hyper-subjectivity, which assumes that the whole external environment can be transformed by the individual perception or will. 'It seemed to me as though rising and falling with his flat chest was the hard vaulting of the starry sky.'[74] And in the second section of the story, which is entitled 'Divertissements, or Proof That It Is Impossible to Live', the narrator is able to manipulate the landscape:

But because I, as a pedestrian, was worrying about the strenuously mountainous road, I let the path become flatter and flatter, finally sloping away into a valley. The stones vanished at my will and the wind dropped and disappeared into the evening. . . . I let a high mountain rise, its peak, covered with bushes, bordering on the sky. . . . I forgot to let the moon rise, and it was already behind the mountain, probably furious at the delay.[75]

This ironically solipsistic landscape painting is one of the means by which Kafka abolishes perspective. The device can be compared with Gustav Klimt's trick of merging an opulent but imprisoning dress into patterned wallpaper, or compounding women with water-snakes and body-contours with ripples in a stream. Outer space is invaded by the quivering expectancy of an excited young man, not yet quite certain of whether control can be exerted over perceptions or actions, one's own or other people's.

My acquaintance, indifferent and merely surprised to see me still here – so it seemed to me – turned to me, and said: 'You see, that's how it always is. As I came down the steps to go for another evening walk before having to be sociable, I was surprised to see how my reddish hands were swinging to and fro in the white sleeves and how they were doing so with unusual gaiety. I was expecting an adventure. That's how it always is.'[76]

Can the idea of violence provoke violence? The acquaintance is doing nothing more sinister than flick his hand out to make his cufflinks jingle when the narrator starts expecting him to pull out a knife. 'Yes, if the mood took him – a happy man is so dangerous, that's indubitable – he'd kill me like a street-murderer. That's certain, and since I'm a coward, I wouldn't dare to scream.'[77] The unprepared intrusion of this idea suggests a masochistic pleasure in the idea of becoming a sacrificial victim. This is already the Kafka who will enjoy writing the end of *Der Prozess*.

The only injury actually incurred by the narrator is the one he does to his knee by slipping on the ice, and this leads to a delicately erotic episode between the two men: 'I didn't see any sign of surprise as he bent sympathetically over me and stroked me with a soft hand. He let it go up and down my cheekbone, then lay two thick fingers on my low forehead. "You've hurt yourself, haven't you?"'[78]

The story remained unpublished during Kafka's lifetime; he allowed two fragments of it to appear in a literary magazine, taking them out of their context and not even making it clear that the 'Gespräch mit dem Beter' ('Conversation with the Suppliant') is not narrated by the principal narrator but put into the mouth of a fat man who is being carried in a litter across a river by four naked men. That the story suffers so little from being taken out of context means that it gains little from being read in context. Again the characters are transparently self-projections, and the main interest is in the confession of a man tortured by self-consciousness.

There's never been a time when I was convinced in myself that I'm alive. I form such uncertain impressions of things around me that I always feel they were alive once, but now are fading. Always, my dear sir, I have this tormenting desire to see things as they may have been before they presented themselves to me. They must have been beautiful and peaceful. [79]

Because his interlocutor fails to react, except by involuntary facial twitchings, he then launches into the story about his mother and the woman just having a snack on the lawn. Like Kafka, his character wants to believe there is no reason to be ashamed. Why should he not be one of those who stride along with an upright carriage and a ponderous gait, hitting at the pavement with a cane? Why does he have 'to scamper alongside the houses like a shadow with hunched shoulders, often disappearing into the glass of shop-windows?'[80] His existence, he feels, is less solid than the next man's.

In the other story which Kafka published, 'Gespräch mit dem Betrunkenen' ('Conversation with the Drunk'), part of the point is that the man is too drunk to understand what is being said to him. Much of the narrative is about contact or lack of contact between people in the streets of a city like Paris:

They're all truly curious but also apprehensive of disappointment; they breathe quickly and stick their heads forward. But if they brush up against one another, they bow deeply and ask pardon: 'I'm very sorry – it was accidental – it's so crowded, please forgive me – clumsy of me, I admit. My name is – my name is Jérome Faroche, spice merchant in the rue du Cabotin – allow me to invite you to lunch tomorrow.'[81]

Never having been to Paris, Kafka was free to fantasize about what life must be like in a romantic cosmopolis – later he'd set a novel in America without having been there – but the focus is on the personal relationship. Contact is so fraught with difficulty that the only possibility is violent oscillation between extremes. And at the end of the story, when it is clear that nothing has been communicated in the conversation between the two men, the narrator offers the drunk his arm.

Kafka himself would probably have behaved in the same way. When he met Oskar Baum, the man who had been blinded in one of the battles between the German and Czech schools and the cousin of Max Bäuml, he behaved with extraordinary considerateness. It was an autumn afternoon in 1904 when Brod took Kafka to meet Baum, who later wrote:

He knew he was in the presence of a blind man. And made a *silent* bow while Brod was introducing us. That was, it might be thought, a pointless formality so far as I was concerned, not being able to see it. His smoothly brushed hair touched me lightly on the forehead, probably because my simultaneous bow was too violent. I felt an emotion, the reason for which I could not at first understand. Of all the men I'd met he was the first to indicate that my disability was something that concerned no one but me. [82]

48

Brod read a story he had just completed, 'Ausflüge ins Dunkelrote' ('Excursions into Dark Red') and in the discussion that followed Kafka said: 'It's when there's no need for stylistic devices to distract from the flow of incident that the temptation's at its greatest.'[83] From then on Kafka, Brod, Baum and Felix Weltsch would meet fairly regularly at weekends to read from their own work – all except Kafka, who was still concealing the fact that he wrote – and to discuss it. Brod also introduced Kafka into a novella he wrote in 1904, 'Die Insel Corina', using his friend as a model for Carus, who maintains 'that we have our freedom, that we can make experiments with our life, that we don't need to live it away (*hinzuleben*) so joylessly'.[84] Still seeing a good deal of Oskar Pollak, too, Kafka collaborated with him on a parody of Wagner's *Die Meistersinger*, satirizing the doctrines of Brentano, and it was performed at a New Year's Eve party in Berta Fanta's house.

What attracted Kafka to Brod was his energy, his enterprise, and his self-confidence. He had the qualities Kafka lacked, the qualities that made for success. He established himself quickly, not only as a speaker at student meetings but as a writer, while Kafka's genius would not eclipse Brod's talent until after his death in 1924. He must have sensed from the beginning that Brod, who was nothing if not generous, would be encouraging and helpful, but it was his admiration for Brod's writing and their common interest in other writers that drew them together. Kafka loved to infect Brod with his own enthusiasms, and as Brod has written – (disguising Kafka as Garta in his novel *Zauberreich* (*Magic Kingdom*) – he

does not persuade – that's not his way – and he never evolves systems ... what he does is read out again and again one passage or another from his favourite authors in his rapid, unemotional delivery, while creating a sense of rhythm and momentum, with subdued melody vibrating in his voice. His eyes flash, as he submits totally to joy in human greatness, only now and then does he mildly screw up his mouth, not at all maliciously but gleefully sceptical – well, well! – when something strikes him as awkward or forced or not quite successful ... he always sees clearly, there is clarity even in his boundless enthusiasm.[85]

Brod was fascinated by 'the aura he gave out of extraordinary strength, something I've never encountered elsewhere, even in meetings with great and famous men ... the infallible solidity of his insights never tolerated a single lacuna, nor did he ever speak an insignificant word'.[86] Everything that came from him was tinged with his individual outlook – 'patient, life-affirming, ironically tolerant towards the idiocies of the world, and therefore full of sad humour. ... In a thousand quite easy ways, it seemed, he observed interconnections no one had ever noticed ... minute but accurate *perceptions*, which gave one a strong desire to build up a whole new system of knowledge.'[87]

49

He was highly regarded, too, at Beata Fanta's house, despite his diffidence in discussion. 'If for example eight people are sitting on the fringe of a conversation, when and how is one to take the floor in order not to be considered uncommunicative? For Heaven's sake, surely it can't be done at random, even if one is as impartial as an Indian. I should have asked you this earlier!'[88]

If the narrator in *Beschreibung eines Kampfes* yearns intermittently for solitude, so, no doubt, did Kafka, who was alone relatively little during his university years. From the autumn of 1903 until the summer of 1905 he had to attend lectures on civil law, commercial law and law of exchange, civil litigation, criminal law and its procedures, administrative law, political economy, economics, the history of legal philosophy, and statistics. The Professor of Austrian civil law was Horaz Krasnopolski, who lectured for two hours every day. According to Bruno Kafka, 'His delivery was fiery and lively, and he interpolated into theoretical explanations examples from real life, stimulating the attentiveness of his audience with humorous comments and many sharp, satirical words.'[89] In his fifth, sixth and seventh terms Kafka had to spend sixteen hours a week listening to the lecturer on criminal law, Hans Gross, formerly an examining magistrate, who maintained that punishment is aimed not at the crime but at the criminal, and that the lecturer should therefore discuss not just the law but life. He had written a book on criminal psychology and a handbook for examining magistrates and police officers.[90] During lectures Kafka would while away the time by drawing in the margins of the lecture texts that were circulated among the students. Thanks to Brod, many of these drawings have been preserved. Despite their crudity, the emaciated linear figures have some affinity with Giacometti's, and show that Kafka's imagination was already working its way into the territory that his later novels have made familiar.

The desperate, isolated figures seek refuge or perform onerous tasks against sparse backgrounds. If the law is present as an undertone, it is oppressive but incomprehensible, unreachable. The drawings are mostly on a very small scale, but, as in the later drawings, there is a strong suggestion of empty space and silence. The lecturers were authoritarians, authorized by the university authorities to discourse in public about the legal system. His own authorship was already being directed, at least partially, towards the discovery of the rules that governed existence, but he was operating at the opposite extreme – in privacy, lacking both fervency and self-confidence.

The lectures Kafka often attended during the evenings at the Lese- und Redehalle must have seemed extremely different. Writers such as Meyrink, Hugo Salus and Detlev von Liliencron read from their own work. Brod and other students spoke about such writers as Grillparzer, Heine, Gottfried Keller, and Nietzsche. While the literary orientation was strongly German, what Kafka saw of student life increased his sympathy for the Czechs. The Union was the biggest one for German-speaking students in Prague, and most of its members were Jewish. There was another non-Jewish union, which had a hall next door, and two other unions, both exclusively Jewish, one for students who wore fraternity colours, one for those who did not. Though the Lese- und Redehalle was theoretically neutral, politically it was affected by the German nationalism of the colour-wearing students. Kafka never participated directly in the feuding, but he sometimes attended the election meetings of Czech politicians such as Dr Kramář, a National Democrat, Dr Soukup, a Social Democrat, and Klofáč, a National Socialist.

In 1905, already finding it hard to cope with the multiple strains of his existence, Kafka began the twenty-third year of his life with his first visit to a sanatorium. A month before the end of term he left Prague for Zuckmantel, a small town in Moravian Silesia. He did not write to Brod until his fourth week there, and then only tersely on a picture postcard. 'Certainly I'd have written to you if I'd stayed in Prague. But here I am light-headed – already in my fourth week in a Silesian sanatorium, socializing a lot with men and females, and I have become rather lively.'[91] It was here that he had an extremely satisfying relationship with an older woman. Eleven years later, staying at Marienbad with Felice Bauer, he said: 'Basically I had still never been really intimate with a woman, with the exception of two occasions, the one in Zuckmantel (but then she was a woman and I was a boy) and the one in Riva (but then she was half a child and I was totally confused and sick in every conceivable way).'[92] The woman in Zuckmantel seems to have been the model for Betty in 'Hochzeitsvorbereitungen auf dem Lande' ('Wedding Preparations in the Country', 1907–8), who is described as 'an oldish pretty girl'.[93] She has often told Raban, her fiancé, 'what a nuisance lecherous men had been, and how she'd had to rebuff their advances'.[94] Kafka was at least playing with the idea of becoming engaged: 'See whether something nice can't be bought cheaply at the exhibition. Perhaps even as a wedding present.'[95]

At the end of August he travelled from Zuckmantel with his sisters to stay for several weeks with an aunt in Strakonitz, on the Wotawa, thirty-three miles to the north-west of Budweis. Returning finally to Prague, he felt 'almost glad to be studying again'.[96] But he was working, nervously and under pressure, for the law examination he had to take in November, Rigorosum II. Even now he read no law books after seven in the evening, but he went less often to the Café Louvre,[97] finding that 'this kind of relaxation undermines my work on the following day'.[98] The examination, which was in Austrian civil law, commercial law and law of exchange, civil litigation and criminal law, began on 7 November. He was graded as 'satisfactory'. But the reprieve was only temporary. In February 1906, the month before he had to take the examination in political and international law, he thought of persuading a doctor to certify that he was too ill to be examined: 'While my knowledge is not yet even trifling I've let myself be misled into accepting a premature date.'[99]

In about December 1905 Kafka and Brod together subscribed to the periodical *Der Amethyst. Blätter für seltsame Literatur und Kunst*. The 'unfamiliar literature and art' was pornographic. The editor was Franz Blei, whom Kafka later described as 'enormously clever and witty.... World literature parades past our table in its underpants.'[100] Kafka was not living without sexual activity, but he appears to have had little pleasure from it. A letter written probably in May 1906 lists reasons for not having had time to visit Brod: 'some girl, very little studying, your book, prostitutes, Macaulay's *Lord Clive*', but the list begins with 'carrying crates and dusting', for his father's fancy-goods business was moving from Zeltnergasse 12 to the ground floor of the Kinsky Palace, where Kafka had been to school on the first floor.

The one advantage of agreeing to examination dates in the near future was that his legal studies would be brought quickly to an end. After borrowing some of Brod's notes to memorize, Kafka sat for the Rigorosum III on 16 March. 'I should have written to you while the examination was still going on, for it's certain that you've saved three months of my life, for some other purpose than studying finance. Only your slips of paper saved me.' Once again Kafka was graded as 'satisfactory', with three of the five judges voting in his favour.

With the second examination behind him, he was qualified to work, as he did for six months, drafting legal documents for Dr Richard Löwy, a lawyer with offices in the Altstädter Ring. (He was no relation.) Kafka had no intention of becoming a lawyer, but it was a way to make full use of his time, or perhaps overfull use, for he still had to study German, Roman and canonical law for the final examination. He worked hard, but without any real interest in the subjects. But he now had less time and energy for anything outside the routine of work. 'Since I find it a strain to take off my rags during the day and change into clothes for going out, I have to live like some nocturnal animal.'[101] He did not even have the energy to plead for more time when Professor Frankl, the director of studies, brought the date of the examination forward to 13 June. 'I was ashamed to be more cautious than he was.'[102] So, besides having to work in the office, Kafka had less than three months between the two examinations. In the last few weeks he scarcely went out at all, concentrating on memorizing material, rather in the way that he had worked at school. But he was successful. When he sat the examination on 13 June, the examiners were unanimous that he was 'satisfactory', and on 18 June he was awarded his doctorate in law.

During the second half of June he went on working in Löwy's office, but for part of July and August he went back to the sanatorium in Zuckmantel, where he resumed his relationship with the 'oldish pretty girl'. He invited Brod to stay either in the annexe of the sanatorium or in a hotel two minutes away, close to the woods,[103] but Brod did not go.

Raban's exhaustion in 'Hochzeitsvorbereitungen' probably reflects Kafka's: 'One works so exorbitantly in the office that one's too tired even to enjoy one's holidays properly.... So why don't I stay in town over these short holidays to recuperate? How irrational I am.'[104] He even incorporates into Raban's interior monologue a comment on how much easier it is to tell a story about oneself in the third person than in the first: 'So long as you say "one" instead of "I", there's nothing to it, and the story can be told, but as soon as you admit to yourself that it's you, yourself, you feel transfixed and horrified.'[105] Raban is not involved in telling a story to anyone, but the word 'story' occurs when he sees a woman looking at him indifferently, or perhaps not even looking at him – only in his direction. It seems to him that she is surprised, and he wishes he could explain everything to her. What he wants, of course, is her love. 'But all the work one does gives one no right to expect loving treatment from everybody, on the contrary, one's alone, quite remote, and only an object of curiosity.'[106] This helps to answer the question: 'Who was Kafka writing for?' Neither publishing his stories nor even showing them to his friends, he was writing for himself – though not in the same way as he did later, when he began to keep a diary – but he was also writing to the people (and especially to the women) who looked at him with an indifference he found intolerable. Like the letter to his father, these letters to strangers would remain undelivered: communicative gestures that he sketched and left uncompleted. But at least they were taken one step beyond the level of idle fantasy, and they would make it easier for him to tolerate the inevitable uncertainty about how much the stranger saw or wanted to see. They satisfied his need to believe that everything could be explained, that if only the woman could have been made to listen, nothing about him would strike her as odd. Later this need would drive him to write over a quarter of a million words in his letters to Felice Bauer. The compulsion was to win her love by making her understand everything about him; what he didn't really want was her physical presence.

Kafka's extreme insecurity in dealing with friends is refracted in Raban's musings. 'For one isn't at all sure even of long-standing acquaintances,' he tells himself.[107] And he proceeds to a nervously detailed review of Lement's friendly behaviour. 'He started talking to me, and then walked along with me, although there was nothing he wanted to find out from me, and even had something else still to do. But he went away abruptly, though I couldn't have said a single word that upset him.'[108]

The persona again becomes transparent in the frightened discussion of how everything that is to be dreaded will be dispersed by the passage of time. Like a child, Raban is reassuring himself that he will manage to get through the next fortnight.

> For it's only fourteen days, which means a limited period, and even if the vexations grow worse and worse, the time they have to be endured grows smaller. . . . The people who want to torment me and who have now occupied all the space around me, will quite gradually be forced back by the good-natured passage of these days without my having to help them in the slightest. And I can, as it will turn out quite naturally, be weak and silent and just let everything happen to me, and everything just has to turn out all right simply because of the passing days. And besides, can't I do what I always did as a child in face of dangers? I don't even need to go to the country myself, it isn't necessary. I can send my body with clothes on. If it totters out through the door of my room, the tottering betrays not fear, but its nothingness. Nor is it excitement if it stumbles on the steps, travels sobbing into the country, and eats its evening meal there in tears. For I myself am all this time in bed, tucked up cosily under the yellow-brown blanket. . . . For I am still dreaming. Coachmen and pedestrians are shy and each time they want to step forwards, they ask me by looking at me. I encourage them, they find no obstacle.[109]

So in fantasy he has abolished the situation in which hostile powers occupy all the surrounding space. Just as when he could remodel the surrounding scenery or postpone the moonrise, he is in total command of the space: instead of being dangerous, other people are subject to his control. But at the same time, because reality is so terrifying, the only refuge is in the pretence that everything is happening to someone else, an *alter ego*. This is how he had held his ground against his father; this is how he graduated in a subject he did not want to study. It is only one step from the belief that the clothed body is someone else to the equation of Kafka with Raban – of jackdaw with raven. Raban's belief that everything could be explained is a projection of Kafka's need to explain everything, by means of a story about an *alter ego*. The story is not intended or expected to make strangers love him: it is enough if he can convince himself that they would if only it were possible – as it never could be – to explain everything and make them listen. But the stratagem involves self-annihilation. Abdicating from the real self, he identifies it with the child that stays huddled safely in bed. The self that goes through the door is a nothing, and it is Kafka who has negated it.

He goes on, prefiguring one of his most famous stories, to identify with insects: 'I have, as I lie in bed, the form of a large beetle, a stag-beetle or a cock-chafer, I believe. . . . Then I'd pretend it was a matter of hibernating, and press my little legs to my paunchy body. And whisper a few words, instructions, to my sad body, which is close by me, and crooked. I have soon finished. It bows, goes hastily and it will do everything as well as can be, while I rest.'[110] He has split himself like an amoeba: the self to be asserted is detached from the self that abdicates. This clean dichotomy cannot be irrelevant to what impressed acquaintances and attracted women: by choosing never to assert what power he had, he had gained considerably in power.

5 Good Conduct

'I'm familiar with indecision, there's nothing I know so well, but whenever something summons me, I fall flat, worn out by half-hearted inclinations and hesitation over a thousand earlier trivialities.'[1] With no more desire to become a civil servant than to become a lawyer, Kafka must have come immediately under paternal pressure to exploit his new qualification. 'It was taken as settled', writes Brod, 'that he would not live at his parents' expense for a day longer than necessary,'[2] but in fact he did not yet start contributing to the family finances. Lawyers who wanted to work for the state had to give their services, unpaid, for a year. This Kafka planned to do, though he did not want to work for the state. He also had a secret savings bank account, feeling, privately, that it improved his status within the family.[3] He kept the bank book in a locked bookcase, carrying the key about with him.

In September 1906, after returning from the sanatorium, he applied to the police for the certificate of good conduct (*Wolverhaltungszeugnis*) that was indispensable if he was to be employed by the state. His application form was completed by the police with data about him ('single, Jewish, good conduct'), and about his parents, his dead brothers and his sisters. The attached sheet, bearing the official stamp and dated 19 September, is marked 'No grounds for objection'.[4] From this it can be inferred that Kafka had not been seriously involved in the activities of the young socialists and anarchists. Lectures organized in clubs and hotels were invariably visited by police observers, who listed the names of those who attended regularly. In 1905, when the Klub Mladých, the Generation Club, which had been founded in 1900, moved to the Karolinenthal area, police surveillance became more intensive, and if Kafka's name had been on the list, there probably would have been 'grounds for objection'. In October 1906 Kafka started a year of unpaid work at the district court and the criminal court, in spite of all his misgivings about being a lawyer and about state service. On 5 October, at the request of the district court, the Prague police once again investigated his records, and again the verdict was positive. But the work, inevitably, was futile and frustrating. 'I've certainly accomplished nothing – this is clear – during my year at the courts ... and I'd incessantly make a fool of myself during working hours.'[5] The one consolation was that there were only six of these.

Though the experience of courts and officialdom seemed useless, the foundations were being laid for *Der Prozess* and *Das Schloss*, which both point satirically to the arbitrariness and injustice in the behaviour of powerful officials. This theme is later developed in the short story 'Die Abweisung' ('The Rejection', 1920), which makes provinciality seem more pernicious than it ever does in Chekhov: the narrative is inflamed with a feeling of helpless remoteness from the centre at which the crucial decisions are taken. The village is a long way from the frontier and even further from the capital. 'For centuries, no political change has occurred that was initiated by one of the citizens themselves.' The highest rank of officials come from the capital, the middle rank from other towns, and only the lowest are native villagers. The highest official, the colonel, is the chief tax collector, but while no one questions his authority, no one appears to have seen evidence of his authorization. At formal occasions he stands holding two long bamboo poles in his outstretched hands: 'It's an ancient custom which roughly speaking means that he supports the law and it supports him.'[6] Presented with a request which was probably for a year's moratorium on taxes, and for cheaper firewood from the imperial forests – the narrator remembers only dimly – he lets go of the bamboo poles at the moment of refusing and becomes a man again 'like the rest of us', sinking into an armchair, sticking a pipe into his mouth.[7] As in *Das Schloss*, officials behave differently when not speaking *ex cathedra*: the viewpoint is very much that of the provincial boy stultified by his non-relationship with the centre of imperial authority. The soldiers' dialect is incomprehensible. Standing around in shops, listening to conversations which are probably incomprehensible to them, they intimidate the shoppers, who disperse. It is no fun to be under surveillance, but it is only the young people, between the ages of seventeen and twenty, who are potentially rebellious.[8] Kafka's attitude was at the opposite pole from Karl Marx's. 'Marx keeps his head like a God,' wrote Bernard Shaw. 'He has discovered the law.' Freud's father, who was hardly less contemptuous than Kafka's about his son's failings, and hardly more considerate of his feelings, provoked an inexorable scientific drive towards the discovery of laws that motivate human behaviour. Kafka reacted differently: his discovery was that he would never discover the law.

In about 1906, the year Brod published his first book, the Vienna newspaper *Zeit* was holding a short-story competition, and Kafka mentioned that he had pseudonymously entered a story.[9] Brod retained no memory of reading any work by Kafka until 1909, but at the beginning of 1907, reviewing Franz Blei's play *Der dunkle Weg* (*The Dark Way*) for the 7 February issue of the Berlin daily *Die Gegenwart*, Brod played a practical joke by naming Kafka as an important writer, together with Mann, Wedekind, Meyrink and Blei.

What was printed in the *Gegenwart* should only be said in a whisper. Well, it's carnival, pure carnival, but the nicest kind – good, so after all I've danced a measure this winter. . . . The only pity is – I know this wasn't your intention – that it would now be indecent if I were to publish something later, for the delicacy of this début would be ruined. And I'd never be able to achieve an effect on the same level as that attributed to my name in your sentences. [10]

In Germany, he went on, probably no one reads reviews with any care. 'The focal points of my fame are therefore Dar es Salaam, Ujiji, Windhoek. But for the reassurance of these eager readers (it's all right: farmers, soldiers) you should have added parenthetically: "This name will have to be forgotten."'

There was plenty of evidence that other people – male and female – were remembering it. In the spring of 1907 a twenty-three-year-old girl 'provided me with a miracle of a Sunday. What a Sunday it was.'[11] But none of this was enough to counterbalance his self-contempt. Brod's friendship was invaluable, but he felt unworthy of it, and, neurotically, tried to subvert it, failing to keep appointments and compounding the ensuing confusion. 'Here in the tobacco shop on the Graben I ask you to forgive me for not coming tonight. I have a headache, my teeth are rotting away, my razor is dull; it adds up to an unpleasant sight.'[12] He sent the card by pneumatic post, but with Oskar Pollak's address on it instead of Brod's. His next letter ended: 'Please be angry about it and don't speak to me any more. My future's not rosy and I'll surely – this much I can see – die like a dog. I too would be glad to avoid myself, but since that's impossible, I can at least be glad to have no self-pity.'[13] This self-contempt conditioned not only his writing but his view of its function, while Brod received little gratitude for his interest in the beginning of *Hochzeitsvorbereitungen*: 'Tell me, why do you keep pestering me about the two chapters? You should be happy – as I am – that you too write incomprehensible things, and you should leave the other stuff in peace.'[14]

Brod not only admired Kafka but let himself be influenced by his attitudes: 'Breadwinning and literary art must be rigidly separated: Kafka rejected any combination of the two, such as journalism.'[15] But when Brod was about to work for the courts, Kafka felt guilty and apprehensive: 'Your situation and mine are quite different. . . . You need a lot of activity: your needs in this respect are clear to me, even if I can't understand them.'[16] Though even if Brod started out on the same dreary legal routine, he could probably establish a literary reputation so rapidly that by the end of the year he would need no other employment. [17]

On 20 June the Kafka family made yet another move. After eleven years in Zeltnergasse they took a flat in No 36 Niklasstrasse, a more imposing corner-house near the Moldau. From the window of his room Kafka could

Good Conduct

see the river and the Belvedere Park on the other side of it. There were double windows in his room but he neither had any heating, nor any privacy. 'My room is a passage or rather a thoroughfare, between the living-room and my parents' bedroom',[18] and not only was he disturbed each time they wanted to pass from one to the other, he was unable to leave exposed anything he did not want them to see. Even letters were liable to be read. Yet this was how he chose to live. He did not move into a flat of his own until he was nearly thirty-two.

In August he escaped for a few restful weeks in Triesch with his uncle. Riding around on a motorbike, swimming, lazing about, nude, on the grass by the pond, playing billiards, going for walks and flirting with a local girl, he enjoyed the present, though he dreaded the future. 'If there's no improvement in my prospects by October, I shall take the matriculation course at the Handelsakademie, and learn Spanish as well as French and English.'[19] He was succumbing once again to the fantasy that his Uncle Alfred would find a job for him in Spain. This time he even tried – not altogether ironically – to involve Brod in the fantasy. Wouldn't he like to come to the Handelsakademie too? Either Uncle Alfred could find jobs for both of them in Spain, or they could go to South America or Madeira or the Azores.[20]

He spent most of his time in Triesch with two girls:

> very bright girls, students, very keen Social Democrats, who have to keep their mouths shut or they come out with their convictions, their principles at every opportunity. One is called A. [Agathe]; the other, H. W. [Hedwig Weiler] is small, with cheeks that are invariably red all over. She's very short-sighted – not merely as an excuse for her pretty gesture of adjusting spectacles on her nose, whose tip is really beautifully composed of tiny facets. Tonight I dreamed of her short, plump legs, and in these roundabout ways I recognize the beauty of a girl and fall in love.[21]

Hedwig, a blonde Jewish girl of nineteen who had completed her first term of studying languages at the University of Vienna, was visiting her grandmother in Triesch. Within four days of returning to Prague, Kafka wrote: 'Now I've opened the shop and by writing to you in the office I'm trying to make the room a little pleasanter. And everything around me is under your spell. The table nuzzles up lovingly against the paper, the pen lies like a docile child in the hollow between thumb and forefinger, and the clock chimes like a bird.' But, far from trying to sound impressive, he confided in her about his self-doubt:

> I transfer my headaches from one firm decision to another, no less firm, but the opposite. And all these decisions inform themselves with new life, receive upsurges of hope, of belief in a satisfied life. . . . By the way I've no social life, no

59

distraction, the evenings I spend on the small balcony above the river, I never read the Social Democratic newspaper and I am not a good man. [22]

By the end of September he had written eight letters to her, throwing himself for the first time into the kind of long-distance love affair he was later to conduct with Felice Bauer and Milena Jesenská. 'How useless it is to meet only in letters,' he wrote in the first, 'it is like splashing by the shore when two people are separated by an ocean.' [23] 'But I didn't say', he added in the next letter, 'that the splashing could be heard.' [24]

Too strong to be quenched by her love, his self-dislike only blazed more fiercely, like burning oil when water is thrown over it. On a solid base of depression, the exhilaration of reciprocated love made him feel suicidal. Hedwig was five years younger, vivacious, outgoing, a believer in action. He was aggravated by her attempts to help and to comfort him, just as he was by Brod's. It felt as if she were trying either to deny his existence or drive him to suicide. [25] If he was unhappy it must mean either that he was groundlessly dissatisfied with his situation – which would imply that his whole pattern of reactions was unbalanced – or that he had valid reasons for dissatisfaction. Perhaps his situation is so bad that if he were to examine it as thoroughly as she is doing, now that she has become interested in it, he would see that it is unendurable. In reply to his first letter she quoted from Jens Peter Jacobsen's novel *Niels Lyhne*:

But every castle of happiness that is erected rests upon a foundation that is partly sand, and the sand collects and runs out under the walls, slowly perhaps – it may be, imperceptibly – but it runs and runs, grain by grain. .... And love? Neither is love a rock, however ready we are to believe it. [26]

Kafka retorted:

But the observer of the sand is not inside the castle, and which direction is the sand running in? What am I to do now? How am I going to stay intact? I am also in Triesch, I am going across the square with you, someone is falling in love with me, I am still receiving this letter, reading it, scarcely understanding it, now I must say goodbye, hold your hand, run away, and vanish in the direction of the bridge. Oh please, it is enough. [27]

But he was not planning to throw himself into the Moldau. He wanted to join her in Vienna, to study for a year at the Exportakademie, and he was disconcerted when she announced that she was coming to Prague. 'I'd have left my parents here, a few friends and other things I'd miss; now you'll be in this damned city, and it seems I won't be able to force myself through the many narrow streets to the station. But I need to be in Vienna more than you need to be in Prague. [28]

Though not always aware when he was deceiving himself, Kafka knew that 'more courage is involved in not hoping than in hoping'.[29] Corresponding with her was a way of keeping hope alive, so it would have been braver to stop, but instead he demanded details about the last party she'd been to: 'What time did you arrive, when did you leave, what were you wearing, which wall did you sit by, did you laugh much and dance much, whose eyes did you gaze into for a quarter of a minute, were you tired at the end, and did you sleep well?'[30]

He was expecting her to arrive in Prague on the first Thursday in September, and on the Wednesday night he 'was running around the streets by starlight to get everything ready for you (I'd had to study during the day)'.[31] Happily he went to meet the morning train; later, less confidently, the train due to arrive at three. On Saturday he received her letter saying she'd decided against coming: 'At which point I could think of nothing better to do than go to bed.'[32]

We've danced a bit of a quadrille between Prague and Vienna, with so much bowing that one hasn't made contact, however much one wanted to. But the round dances must follow, sooner or later. I don't feel at all well. I don't know what's going to happen. If one gets up early and a lovely day's dawning, it's tolerable, but later. . . .[33]

Letters formed the only outlet for his disappointment. He couldn't confide in his parents or even expect sympathy from them, when, at night, they were taking his ink away to stop him from writing. Two of his letters to Hedwig were in pencil.[34]

Possibly she might come to Prague later; probably he would stay there. Instead of helping him to employment in Spain, Uncle Alfred had advised him to apply for a job with an Italian insurance company, the Assicurazioni Generali, which had its head office in Trieste and its Prague office in Wenzelsplatz. The company's general representative in Madrid was the son of the American Vice-Consul in Prague, Arnold Weissberger, who knew Kafka's father and 'warmly recommended' the son.[35] He was uncertain what to do. 'Other people rarely have to take decisions and enjoy it when they do, but I'm incessantly having to decide, like a boxer, except that then I don't box, it's true. . . . But of course I must be careful not to make Providence nervous, now that it's concerning itself with me.'[36] He didn't want the job any more than he had wanted to work in the law courts for a year, but he applied. His mind was focused on Hedwig, and he felt like an exile 'reading news about important changes in the homeland but unhappy at being unable to intervene'.[37] If she was helping to nurse the sick, he felt no sympathy for them. 'You're misunderstanding me prettily if you believe that striving towards ideal usefulness appeals to my nature, which can be summed up as indifference towards all practical

61

usefulness.'[38] He was in love with her to the extent of feeling that he wanted everything he possessed – even his pencil – 'somehow or other to be involved with you',[39] and that his letters came alive with impatience to reach her as soon as he wrote the word 'love' on them,[40] but there were plenty of openings for misunderstandings and suspicion between them. 'How you misjudge me, and I don't know whether a degree of disapproval is the prerequisite of such misjudgments.'[41] Unable to tell when he was being ironic, she was incredulous that someone so intelligent should genuinely – naïvely – want answers to the questions he posed.[42] 'The purpose of those very sentences you call ironic was only to imitate the tempo at which I was permitted to stroke your hands on a few beautiful days.'[43] She may have suspected this sentence, too, of containing irony.

He was not in suspense to hear whether the Assicurazioni Generali would offer him a job, but when it did, he settled down conscientiously to study insurance, which he found quite interesting.[44] He also tried to procure teaching engagements for Hedwig: if she came to Prague she would need money. He advertised in the Sunday edition of two newspapers:

A young woman, undergraduate, formerly a student of French, English, Philosophy and Education at the University of Vienna and now at the University of Prague, available to give lessons to children, with whom she believes, on the basis of past experience, she can achieve excellent results, or available as companion or reader.[45]

Not knowing whether she would be in Triesch or in Prague when the replies came in, he arranged to collect them himself.

Already she was feeling less sure that she wanted to come; in his next letter he did his best to persuade her.[46] Writing again the same day, he forwarded the only two replies that had been sent. 'One of them looks reassuringly Jewish, and I'll find out what sort of people they are.' The other, which he translated for her from the Czech, was for German conversation three times a week with a young lady of twenty-one.[47]

On 1 October he started his job, and on his first day he was given a prolonged medical examination. Apart from a slight congestion in the upper lobe of the lung, 'in consequence of rachitic deformation', Dr Wilhelm Pollak found nothing that might have given an early indication of tuberculosis.[48] In a six-page report he described Kafka as a 'delicate but healthy man . . . 1.82 metres in height, 61 kilograms in weight . . . slim . . . fragile . . . unquestionably well-suited' for the work.[49] But he was called back for another medical examination at the end of October.[50] His salary was only 80 kronen a month, and he had to work from 8.00 a.m. till 6.15.

'If my troubles previously walked on their feet, they're now, aptly, walking on their hands.'[51] In the evenings he was studying Italian, hoping to be sent to Trieste. 'I wasn't in the habit of limiting my private life to six hours every day ... and I don't emerge from my crowded leisure hours feeling relaxed.'[52] Sunday always seemed a very short day: 'morning for sleeping, afternoon for washing hair, evening for strolling about like an idler.'[53]

The work was dreary, the main consolation being the prospect of getting sent abroad. He pictured himself 'sitting in armchairs in very remote countries, looking out of the office windows at sugar-cane fields or Moslem cemeteries'.[54] The other consolation was in fantasies about Hedwig: 'It's often pleasant to lay down my pen and imagine, for instance, that one's placing one of your hands on top of the other, gripping them and knowing that one would not let go, even if one's own hand were unscrewed at the wrist.'[55] Even while fantasizing about her, he could not help postulating violence that would diminish him.

But soon their correspondence became less frequent. 'Don't think the beautiful weather has driven you out of my mind. It's only my pen that has been displaced.'[56] It still seemed possible that he would be sent away from Prague, but probably not during the next twelve months.

I'm not complaining about the work so much as about the swampy viscosity of time. The fact is that office hours can't be divided up: even during the last half hour the pressure of the eight hours can be felt just as much as during the first. It's often like a train journey that goes on overnight; finally, dispirited, you no longer think either about the labour of the engine or about the scenery, hilly or flat, but you blame everything on your watch, which you hold constantly in the palm of your hand.[57]

He had little in common with his colleagues – 'Cheerful, undemanding. ... The springboard for their cheerfulness is the last minute of the working day.'[58]

Intentionally or not, Hedwig roused Kafka's jealousy by describing a young writer she had met in Vienna. She even enclosed one of his poems, which failed to impress Kafka, but provoked him to send her his recent story 'Die Abweisung'. 'I'll be very pleased if he laughs at me derisively.'[59] Kafka's only stipulation was that his name should not be mentioned.

Her reply reassured him, but full of self-contempt, he again visualized himself as disfigured, dehumanized – 'gradually turning to wood from my frozen fingertips upwards – I wear no gloves – and then you'll have a fine letter-writer in Prague and my hand will be a beautiful possession. And because I live such a brutish life I must doubly beg your forgiveness for inflicting myself on you.'[60] He then forgot to post the letter. 'But it's not just laziness but fear, generalized fear of writing, of this horrible occupation, though my entire unhappiness now consists in having to sacrifice it.'[61]

Before the end of the year he was looking for another job which would leave more space for it. In some offices the working day ended at two or three o'clock. Both Kafka and Brod would have liked to find a job that ended at two, but these were rare, except in government offices, where Jews were hardly ever employed unless they had specially good connections.[62] Kafka was hoping for a job in the post office.[63]

He oscillated haphazardly between solitude and gregariousness. Late in November he 'suddenly became involved with a crowd of people. Army officers, Berliners, Frenchmen, painters, cabaret singers.'[64] Then in December he told Brod: 'I'm feeling so low I think I can survive only by not speaking to anyone for a week – or as long as turns out to be necessary. If you don't try to reply in any way to this card, I'll know you care for me.'[65] He felt constantly tired, and fatigue penetrated like fog both into his craving for human contact and into the terse stories or prose poems which express that craving.

The forsaken solitary who still wants now and then to attach himself somewhere, the man who, depending on the time of day, the changing state of the weather, of his business, and so on, may need to catch sight of a friendly arm he could cling to – he can't hold out for long without a window looking out on the street. And if he feels no desire for anything at all, and only, as a weary man, leans on his window-sill with his gaze shifting between sky and passers-by, if he wants nothing and his head's slightly thrown back, even then the horses below will draw him down into their traffic of carts and noise, so ultimately into human concord.[66]

He wasn't altogether half-hearted in wanting to attach himself somewhere, but it was becoming increasingly clear that Hedwig would not come to Prague, and he was not yet ready to settle for nothing more than epistolary intimacy.

I beg you, my dear, dear Max, even if you'd already made other plans for the evening, wait for me, so that I don't have to pick anyone up from the theatre or ride around in a cab with rubber tyres, or sit in the balcony of some coffee house, or go into some bar or other or gaze at that striped dress. If only you had time for me every evening![67]

Brod's closest friendship was with Max Bäuml, who had been his classmate for eight years at the Gymnasium; Kafka had to survive without any such intimacy. He went on writing to Hedwig, but less frequently, and with more indulgence in elaborate jokes against himself, which she could hardly be expected either to enjoy or to answer:

Good Conduct

You neglected to compliment me on my energy in wanting to bury my head in any old road gravel and not pull it out again. So far, if only intermittently, I've been living decently, for in normal times it's not too difficult to build oneself a sedan-chair and to feel carried across the streets by good spirits . . . but then if one wooden strut breaks, especially in bad weather, one's left standing in the country road, unable to cope and still a long way from one's phantom destination. Allow me to pull stories like this one over me, in the way a sick man snuggles into the sheets and blankets. [68]

This sedan-chair image, which also occurs in his drawings, expresses a feeling of unhealthy dependence on other people, who could not be relied on to help him. Still debilitated by his uncertain position within the family, he was unsure of his right to exist, to occupy space:

I stand on the platform of the tram, completely uncertain in retrospect of my status in this world, in this city, in my family. Not even casually could I explain what claims I could be entitled to make in any direction. I cannot justify standing on this platform, holding on to this strap, letting myself be transported by this vehicle. Why should people make way for the tram or walk along quietly or look in shop-windows? – It's true but irrelevant that nobody asks for explanations. [69]

Not that he was constantly depressed. Sometimes he admitted in his letters to feeling very happy, and in one of the prose poems the mood is euphoric:

I stride along and my tempo is the tempo of the pavement, the whole street, the whole district. I am responsible, and rightly so, for all knocking on doors, on the surfaces of tables, for all the toasts that are drunk, for couples in their beds, in the scaffolding around new buildings, pressed close to each other against walls in dark alleys, on brothel divans.
I weigh my past against my future but find both admirable. [70]

As in the fiction that arrogates godlike domination over all the space that surrounded him, the act of writing conveys no sense of contributing anything useful to the society that provides the trams, but it allows full play to the empathetic capacity for riding beyond the frontiers formed by skin. Imaginatively he can identify with all the lovers, the buildings, the mountains.

Kafka's capacity for empathy was strengthened by the low view he took of himself: everyone else's situation seemed preferable; Hedwig's for instance.

All right it's ridiculous you have to study so hard. . . . But look, you're visibly making progress, you have an aim that can't run away from you like a girl, and it will make you happy, even if you try to resist, but I'm going to remain an eternal humming-top, and briefly perhaps torture the eardrums of a few people who come too close, but nothing else. [71]

65

He'd had an abominable week, 'a frightful lot to do in the office, perhaps it'll always be like that, yes, one must earn one's grave . . . in short I've been hunted all over the place like a wild animal'.[72] He had started the letter to her in the office, resumed it at home, and not finished it until a letter arrived from her. His letter was in three colours of ink, like a flag with stripes of blue, grey and black.[73]

At the beginning of March 1908, thanks to Brod, eight of Kafka's prose poems were published in the first issue of a bi-monthly, *Hyperion*, edited by Franz Blei and Carl Sternheim. Blei, who had been enthusiastic about Brod's first book, *Tod den Toten* (*Death to the Dead*), often came to Prague, and on one of these visits, Brod introduced Kafka to him. The prose poems were published under the collective title *Betrachtung* (*Meditation*) and did not receive individual titles until later – 'Der Kaufmann' ('The Tradesman'), 'Zerstreutes Hinausschauen' ('Absent-minded Window-Gazing'), 'Der Nachhauseweg' ('The Way Home'), 'Die Vorüberlaufen-den' ('Passers-By'), 'Kleider' ('Clothes'), 'Der Fahrgast' ('The Passenger'), 'Die Abweisung', and 'Die Bäume' ('The Trees'). The magazine's first issue also contained work by Rilke, Hofmannsthal and Heinrich Mann. Either before or after it was published, Brod was in Willy Haas's house with him and Franz Werfel. When Brod read out some of Kafka's prose poems, Werfel's reaction was: 'They won't get any further than Boden-bach.'[74] Bodenbach was the frontier town, and he meant Kafka's writing would be of no interest outside Bohemia. Some readers took the name Kafka to be a pseudonym for Robert Walser. In the summer Blei announced: 'Kafka is not Walser but really a young man of that name in Prague.' Kafka had discovered the work of Walser, his senior by five years, in 1907, and certainly he had a strong affinity with the Swiss writer, as Robert Musil noticed when he reviewed their work together in August 1914. Both cultivate a narrative style which helps to blur distinctions between mental events and external reality. Inspiring the reader's confidence with their quiet matter-of-factness, and with their scrupulousness in chronicling moment-to-moment changes in awareness and mood, they tangent into nightmarish absurdity, unobtrusively shifting perspective, making consciousness behave like a clown while proceeding, with no loss of seriousness, in its passionate quest for self-knowledge. But it should not be assumed – as it often is – that Walser influenced Kafka. This style was already developing in the letters and stories he was writing three years before he read Walser.

Nearly two pages long, 'Der Kaufmann' is the longest of these texts, and the only one to draw on his ability to empathise with his father, who worried a great deal about his business. 'Der Kaufmann', which is more like a story and less like a prose poem, takes the form of a monologue from a man whose small business fills him with so much anxiety that his forehead and temples ache. Each season he has to forecast the next season's fashions not among people of his own circle but in the inaccessible provinces. 'My money's in the hands of strangers; I've no means of knowing how they're placed or what misfortunes are likely to overtake them, and there's nothing I could do to help them.'[75] At the end of his working day the man must remain passive – prey to the anxiety which activity had dispelled. It 'floods back like a returning tide, but it can't be contained inside me and it sweeps me away with it, not in any direction'.[76] With his face and hands dirty and sweaty, his boots scratched by nails on crates, he goes home, snapping the fingers of both hands, and stroking the hair of any children he meets in the street.[77]

The exhaustion Kafka felt at the end of the working day made it easier to identify with the mood his father came home in, but at this point in the story the businessman comes to resemble the son more than the father. He doesn't have far to go home. Alone in the lift, he goes down on his knees in front of the looking-glass, addressing the multiple spirits inside himself. Do they now want to make for the shadow of the trees or the arbour in the garden or merely to lurk behind the window, looking out? (Kafka seems to have spent a lot of time gazing out of windows.) He daydreams of travelling to Paris, of looking out of Parisian windows at processions converging on each other, at a beautiful lady driving past. He thinks of sailors on a distant battleship, of trailing a small man and robbing him in a doorway, of mounted police and empty streets. Then he has to step out of the lift, ring at the door of his own flat and say 'Good evening' to the maid who opens the door.[78]

For Max Brod's birthday on 27 May Kafka sent him two books and a pebble.

I've always made great efforts to find something for your birthday so immaterial that it can't change or get lost, spoilt or forgotten. . . . Therefore I'm now sending you a pebble and will send one as long as we live. Keep it in your pocket, it will protect you, leave it in a drawer, it will not be inactive there either, but throw it away, that's best of all. For you know, Max, my love for you is greater than I am, and I live in it more than it lives in me, and it has only a poor grip on my uncertain nature, but it now has a home, safe as rocks, in the little stone. . . . In short I've discovered the most beautiful birthday present for you and send it to you with a kiss which is the gauche expression of my gratitude for the fact that you're there.[79]

With so little satisfaction to be had out of work, so little opportunity to settle down to writing, so little communication with his parents or even – judging from the paucity of references to them in his letters – with his sisters, who were now in their late teens, Kafka had few gratifications apart from those afforded by the friendship with Brod and by the night-life of Prague. His first experience of sex had made him prepared to tolerate – if not to expect – an element of tawdriness in sensual pleasure, and the casual relationships with women who were available had little in common with the relationship he had imagined himself having with Hedwig, if only she had come to Prague, or if he could have escaped to Vienna. He sometimes patronized the brothels, which were plying such a lively trade in Prague, and he sometimes took prostitutes to hotels. 'I like hotel rooms. In hotel rooms I'm immediately at home – more than at home really!'[80] He explained to Brod how he sometimes felt 'the urgent need to find someone who will just touch me in a friendly way'.[81] The prostitute he described was 'too old to go on being melancholy and though not surprised that men aren't so nice to prostitutes as they are when having an affair, she regrets it. I didn't comfort her, because she didn't comfort me either.'[82]

For nine months he worked eight to nine hours every weekday, taking Italian lessons in the evening and sometimes working on Sunday. Then in July 1908 he finally found a job with a working day that ended at two o'clock. He left the Assicurazioni Generali on 15 July. 'Tendering my resignation, I explained to the director, not quite truthfully but not entirely falsely either, that I couldn't tolerate the abuse, which inciden-tally hadn't been aimed directly at me: I'd been made too painfully allergic to it at home.'[84] The resignation was recorded as due to 'enervation connected with extreme cardiac excitability'. But Kafka was able to remain on friendly terms with the director, Ernst Eisner, corresponding with him about Robert Walser's writings. After nine months in the job Kafka felt uncertain whether he was incapable of working or merely incapable of doing work that bored him. In 1915, when he had to spend time in a factory, although free to get on with his own work, he was unable to: 'However detached I feel inwardly, direct contact with working life makes it impossible for me to take a bird's eye view of things, as if I were in a ravine, and couldn't even hold my head up straight.'[85]

6 The New Job

It was thanks to his old friend Ewald Příbram that Kafka found his new job. Dr Otto Příbram was chairman of the Arbeiter-Unfall-Versicherungs-Anstalt für das Königreich Böhmen in Prague, the Workers' Accident Insurance Institute for the Kingdom of Bohemia. Business was carried on in both German and Czech: Kafka had to submit an application in both languages. In May, at the Prague Handels-akademie, he had taken a course on workers' insurance, tutored by officials of the institute, and he had been graded as 'excellent', but there was only one other Jew on the staff, although Příbram was Jewish, and it was thanks to him that Kafka got the job.[1] Instead of 80 kronen a month he was paid 3 kronen a day plus a bonus of 10 per cent.[2]

At the office in Proschitscherstrasse his boss in the 'technical' department was Eugen Pfohl, a senior inspector. Kafka had to take three more courses, an enrolment course, one on statistics, and one on ministerial departments, but he soon made an extremely favourable impression on the head of the department and secretary of the Institute, Dr Robert Marschner.

For almost twenty years the institute had steadily been losing money, and in the late summer Marschner was appointed to succeed Privy Councillor Dr Haubner as director. At the celebration party it was Kafka who made a congratulatory speech on behalf of the staff. Marschner's brief was to reorganize the institute, and Kafka paid tribute to him as being 'a zealous friend' of the workers at the same time as 'respecting the boundaries imposed by the law and the economic situation'.[3] Kafka was lucky to have joined the institute at a time of radical reorganization: despite his youth and inexperience he was entrusted with writing in the bulletin for 1907–8 on compulsory insurance in the building trade and on motor insurance. He was soon transferred to another department concerned with the protection of workers against accidents. This involved him in writing a great many reports. On the one level the work bored him; on another he obviously took pleasure in unearthing issues that might have remained partly buried if the report had been entrusted to someone else. At the same time he was – without being aware of it – writing preliminary drafts for future work. It is not only the subject-matter of 'In der Straf-kolonie' but also the detached objectivity of the narrative that is anticipated in:

An extremely cautious worker could probably take care not to allow any joint of his fingers to project over the timber either during the work or when moving the wood away from the cutter head, but caution is irrelevant to the main danger. Even the most careful workman must be drawn into the cutter space when it slips or when the timber is thrown back, as happens quite often, while with one hand he is pressing the piece he is planing against the machine-table, and with the other feeding it to the cutter spindle. It is impossible either to foresee or to prevent the wood from rising and sliding back, for this would occur when the wood was gnarled or knotty in particular places, when the blade was not moving fast enough, or moved itself out of position or when the pressure of the hand on the wood was unevenly distributed. Such accidents would seldom occur without the amputation of several finger joints or even whole fingers.[4]

Even if Kafka felt more compassion for injured factory workers than he had professed to feel for the patients Hedwig was nursing, he could not have given voice to moral outrage in an official report, and the obligation to sustain emotional neutrality seems, in some ways, to have given him pleasure, involving, as it did, an extraversion of the masochistic gratification he had in thinking about damage done to his own body or its destruction or degeneration. In forcing him to preserve detachment in his reports, the job may have been giving him an alibi for something that came naturally. Just as the boring job in the law courts prepared the ground for *Der Prozess* and *Das Schloss*, the cultivation of apparent neutrality would serve him in good stead. In the life of a great artist nothing is wholly wasted, but like many great artists, Kafka never had the satisfaction of knowing himself to be one.

He was now working in an office building which, according to Gustav Janouch, was 'so massive and dignified that the poor invalids and workmen summoned to collect pensions or receive compensation for injury usually looked bewildered and intimidated from the first moment of glimpsing the porter with his enormous beard'.[5]

If Kafka had at first been intimidated, he had soon found enough self-confidence to impress his colleagues as being the right man to make the speech at the celebration. He also impressed his superiors sufficiently for them to send him on two business trips within his first two months. At the beginning of September he went to the industrial region of northern Bohemia, inspecting factories to check whether they were insured under the correct classifications. 'Drinking down with milk the boredom of six hours' work,' he wrote on a picture postcard of Tetschen.[6] But he enjoyed the food, the hotels, and the scenery. After returning to Prague on 3 September he was sent away again to Černošic, a village ten miles to the south-west. Before the end of September he was given a week's holiday, which he spent in the Bohemian forest: 'the butterflies there fly as high as the swallows do at home'.[7] 'I'm protecting my feet from the cold floor-tiles',' he informed Brod, 'by putting them on a ledge under the table, yielding only my hands because I'm writing. And I write that I'm very happy, and that I'd be glad if you were here, for in the woods are things one could think about for years while lying in the moss.'[8]

On 7 or 8 April Brod's friend Max Bäuml had died suddenly. Since wryly expressing the wish that Brod had time for him every evening, Kafka had been uninhibited in showing his affection. Judging from Brod's novel *Zauberreich*, what ensued now was almost like a proposal of marriage:

A few days after the funeral, Christof goes for an evening walk with Richard Garta, profoundly melancholy. The Kleinseite, dark castle stairways rising upwards. 'Will you – take his place for me?' he asks, stammering, knowing in the deep oppression of his heart that he is asking the impossible, understanding when Garta does not reply, realizing that even a less sensitive man would find this question unanswerable, but also that there was something justifiable, brave, and good in the question, which was also fully acknowledged by Garta. But it can be acknowledged only with a long, deep silence.

Side by side they walk through many narrow winding streets, still in silence, and Christof believes he can feel the presence of his good, loving, dead friend. Really the whole of his boyhood died with him, memories of countless experiences at school, moments of perception and moments of suffering, narrow yet deep scars in the heart. . . . Nothing more is ever said about the question that remains unanswered. But from this night onwards the handclasp when the two friends say goodnight is tighter and more prolonged.[9]

Kafka could never have written as badly or as sentimentally, but to recognize the gaping discrepancy in sensitivity and style between the two men is not to deny the depth of their intimacy or its importance. Brod's loyalty, warmth, tolerance and accessibility must, to Kafka, have more than compensated for his sentimentality. If Brod had had more of the qualities essential to a good writer – irony, humour, discernment, critical stringency – it might have been more difficult for the friendship to survive. Walter Benjamin, who is rightly critical of Brod's inability 'to gauge the tensions which permeated Kafka's life',[10] calls the friendship 'primarily a question mark which [Kafka] chose to put in the margin of his life'. But he did not put it in the margin. Benjamin is still harsher, but in some ways closer to the truth when he wrote: 'Kafka as Laurel felt the burdensome duty of looking for his Hardy – and that was Brod.'[11] Habituated to being bullied, and to escaping into literature, Kafka needed a friend who would bully him to write, and to publish. The friendship now became more intimate. Brod wrote: 'We saw each other every day, sometimes even twice a day. As long as Franz stayed in Prague (it wasn't until later that his illness forced him to stay in the country, in sanatoria) we kept up this habit.'[12] Brod had also by now succeeded in finding himself an office job that ended at two o'clock, and he waited for Kafka every day, staring up at the double-headed imperial eagle on the gable of the tax collection building.

Franz invariably arrived later than I did. He'd had extra work to do or been drawn into conversation with colleagues. My stomach rumbling, I paced up and down, but the irritation was quickly forgotten as the tall, slim figure of my friend emerged, usually with an embarrassed smile which was meant more to parody than to express extreme fear or even horror at being so very late. He also held his hand pressed to his heart. 'I'm innocent' was what this gesture signified. Besides, he arrived at the run, so it was really impossible to say anything angry to him. On our way home through Zeltnergasse to the Altstädter Ring there was always a tremendous amount to discuss. And it was a long time after our arrival outside Franz's home that we stopped talking. Then in the afternoon or evening we were together again.[13]

But the new intimacy had scarcely begun when Kafka found his freedom of movement curtailed. 'One of the clerks is ill and Father himself isn't feeling well. It would be murder if I didn't stay in the shop till eight, and probably if I came out in the evening.'[14] But he took generous pleasure in Brod's literary successes – 'I congratulate you and myself and all of us.'[15] 'You'll soon be coming up in the world.'[16] He had his own moments of elation: 'Today I feel fine, as though I were just beginning to live.'[17] But the happier moods seldom lasted for long: 'For, as I realized early this morning before washing, I've been depressed for two years and it's only the greater or smaller extent of this depression that determines the momentary mood. . . . On getting up in the morning I've been unable for the last two years . . . to remember anything that comforts me – adept as I am at comforting myself.'[18] This effectively denies the whole relationship with Hedwig and everything good that had happened to him since he started work in the law courts in October 1906.

There are things we've never seen, heard or even felt, and we can't prove they exist, though no one has yet tried, but we run after them, without knowing which direction to run in, and we catch up with them without reaching them, and, still complete with clothes, family souvenirs and social relationships, we fall into them as into a grave that was only a shadow on the road.[19]

The year 1908 ended with a depressed refusal to visit Brod on New Year's Eve. He'd been intending to go, but when, at four o'clock, he heard there were to be other guests, he went to sleep instead. 'How do you know they want me to come or even that they would find it tolerable? Besides, for four days now, each time I've been awake, I've comforted myself with the prospect of sleeping today.'[20] And if he went to Brod's while other people were there, he'd get tea but no opportunity for reading Flaubert with him or the novel Brod was working on, *Die Glücklichen* (*The Happy Ones*).

A week later he received a postcard from Hedwig. She was in Prague, and she wanted him to return all her letters to him. He complied immediately, enclosing the postcard, beginning the letter formally (Geehrtes Fräulein), and addressing her in the second person plural. He wanted to see her, but did she want to see him? 'Perhaps the prospect of disgust or boredom will deter you.'[21] She was invited to the Kafkas' house for lunch, but he wanted to see her alone, if at all. 'I'm no obstacle to your accepting the invitation. I never arrive home until 2.15, and if I hear you're coming, I'll stay away till 3.45.'[22]

This was not quite the end of their relationship. She wrote again, probably about three months later, to say how lonely she was and how hard she was having to prepare for her examinations. He replied sympathetically, comparing her experience with his. 'It feels – I remember it well – as though one's endlessly stumbling through unfinished suicides, one keeps feeling it's all over, but then has to go on, and all this studying seems to be the centre of the whole miserable world.'[23] It was worst in winter; in the spring and summer

windows and doors are open, and the same sun and air are in the room where you work as in the garden, where others are playing tennis. . . . It must be possible to break through whatever hellishness remains. And surely you will, if I could, I, who do everything while literally disintegrating.[24]

The division in his life between work and social pleasure was less watertight than it seemed, and so was the division between insurance and literature. Had he thought of writing reports as totally unliterary, he would not have sent Franz Blei a copy of the institute's annual report containing his piece on car insurance. He had been asked to review Blei's book *Die Puderquaste. Ein Damenbrevier* (*The Powderpuff: a Female Breviary*) for the paper *Der Neue Weg*, and after the review appeared on 6 February 1909 – Kafka's second literary publication – he sent a copy to Blei together with the report.

Certainly Kafka must at least have gained some comfort and some confidence from the esteem of his insurance colleagues. Pfohl loved him 'like a son'[25] and in April reported that he 'combines constant interest in all memoranda with very great zeal. He has also been doing work for the institute outside office hours. Excellent adaptability. I have come to know the above-named employee as an excellent member of the staff.'[26]

In March Brod changed jobs. He was taken on as a probationary worker in an administrative position at the post office. 'The post office,' Kafka wrote, 'a government job without ambition, is the only thing that suits you.'[27] He was seeing less of Brod because he was having to work in the shop. 'Father and Mother aren't well, Grandfather's sick, the dining-room's being painted, and the family's living in my room as if it were a gipsy caravan.'[28] By the middle of April it was clear that his mother would need an operation. 'There's literally a battle going on in our family, my father's getting worse, my grandfather collapsed unconscious in the shop.'[29] The operation was successful,[30] but, busy in office, shop and home, the exhausted Kafka felt sure his brain 'won't get better quickly if it ever gets better at all. I wanted to sleep for a quarter of an hour on the sofa after supper yesterday, but though Father made several futile attempts to wake me about ten, I slept with the light out until half past one, and then transferred myself to bed.'[31]

In July he was still complaining of sleepiness at the office:

I don't know what I did a moment ago, or what I'll be doing in a moment's time and I've no idea at all of what I'm doing now. For a quarter of an hour I untangle the problems of one Board of Administration, and then, with surprising presence of mind, put away a file which I've long been searching for, which I need, and which I haven't yet used. And on the armchair there's such a heap of unfinished work that I can't even open my eyes wide enough to look at it.[32]

The obscurities and the vagueness of his unfinished novel *Hochzeitsvorbereitungen auf dem Lande* derive from the same mental state. One letter treats the disorder of the manuscript as no more controllable than the disorder in the office. If the copy he sent Brod was incomplete, so much the better,

it's even more effective than if I'd torn it up. Do be reasonable. This girl means nothing. So long as she has your arm around her hips, back or neck, she'll either say yes to everything in this heat or to nothing. What's that got to do with the centre of the novel, which I know very well and feel somewhere inside me when I'm very unhappy. And now not another word about it, we're agreed.[33]

His writing was the one area in which he could preserve control, just as a man sitting at an untidy desk in an untidy study can write neatly constructed sentences in neat handwriting laid out neatly on the page. And while disliking himself, he could feel less hostile towards his writing because he generally had the impression of being able to exclude himself from it. He could send an *alter ego* into it, just as he could send out his clothed body while keeping his real self in bed.

Receiving a letter from Brod, who wanted to convince him that a girl was fond of him, he responded by setting up a barrier of elaborate ironies:

She loves me but it doesn't occur to her that she could ask who was with me in Stechowitz, what I am doing, why I can't go out on weekdays etc. . . . From which we can draw a simple geometrical diagram. What she feels for me is the greatest friendliness. Nothing could be more incapable of growth, and it's as remote from strong emotion as from weak, having nothing to do with either. Naturally I don't need to insert myself into the diagram, if it's to remain clear.

Now I've really earned my sleep.[34]

He knew that inaccuracy was involved in keeping himself out of the diagram, but perhaps he enjoyed knowing that he would be the one to suffer if he persisted in ignoring his own feelings for the girl. And, as in the correspondence with Felice and Milena, there was always consolation to be had from writing masterfully controlled sentences about uncontrollable situations.

Reality itself seemed to be pushing him away from realism. In reports he was obliged to be neutral and objective, but it was at about this time that he was taking part, with Brod, Franz Werfel and Paul Kornfeld in séances, consulting spirits that communicated by moving a table,[35] while there were humorous deviations from realism in Kafka's letters about his insurance work:

In my four administrative districts – quite apart from my other work – people fall off the scaffolding like drunkards, or into the machines, all the beams collapse, all the ramps work loose, all the ladders slip, everything they carry up falls down and everything they pass down they fall over. And the girls in the china factories are giving me a headache – they keep throwing themselves down the stairs with piles of crockery.[36]

For Brod the rewards of the friendship were enormous, but so were the strains. Kafka would often cancel arrangements to meet or fail to turn up, but besides being a charming, witty and delightful companion, he was a supportive and useful critic. 'Only the first paragraph is perhaps rather unreal, for today, at least. "Everything smells good" etc. You're reaching for a depth in the story that doesn't yet exist.'[37] 'For a rather incompletely informed reader this passion is possibly introduced a little too suddenly and too close to his face, so that perhaps he'll see nothing at all.'[38] Kafka also tried to protect Brod's writing from interfering girlfriends: 'it was good news that Fräulein Prima Donna has left the novel in peace for a fortnight since even the best novel wouldn't be able to survive for long against uninterrupted assaults, internal and external, from the same girl'.[39]

On 19 August Kafka applied for a week's leave of absence from the insurance institute, submitting a letter from a doctor saying he needed rest. On the following day permission was granted. The previous year

Brod's brother Otto had been to Riva, a bathing resort on Lake Garda, and on 4 September the three of them went there together for a week's holiday. Kafka was a good swimmer, and they had often swum together. At Riva there was a small spa under the cliffs, and Otto Brod took them to see all the sights he had discovered.

They did no reading except in the Italian local newspaper, *La Sentinella Bresciana*. On 9 September they read in it about the flying display at Brescia sixty kilometres away. None of them had ever seen an aeroplane, and Kafka, who was 'interested in everything new, topical, technical',[40] was especially keen to go.

Brescia was crowded with visitors from Venice, Tuscany, Rome, Naples, France, England and even America.[41] Arriving late in the evening, they found the railway station teeming with people 'shouting as if the ground were on fire'.[42] Short of money, they had a long argument with a cab-driver who demanded three lire but refused to show them the tariff,[43] and they spent the night in a cheap room above a bar which was visible through a large hole in the floor.[44] At the airfield a 'Grand Buffet International' had been installed, big enough to serve two thousand people, and the army was in attendance to preserve order.[45] With closed curtains draped at the entrance, the hangars looked like 'the closed theatres of strolling players'.[46] There were national flags on their roofs, above the names of the aviators – Rougier, Curtiss, Moucher. But they could not find the name they knew best – Blériot. Eventually they found him working with his mechanics on a plane that looked too frail to carry him. His young wife, dressed too warmly for the day, and their two children watched while the men struggled to get the noisy engines started. Among the fashionable spectators in cane armchairs Kafka saw Gabriele d'Annunzio, 'small and feeble, shyly dancing attendance on the Conte Oldofredi. . . . In front of the grandstand, the strong face of Puccini, with a nose that could be called the nose of a drinker, looks out over the handrails.'[47] In preference to sitting, the fashionably clothed ladies strolled about, showing off their dresses. 'The bodice lies low, almost out of reach, the waist seems broader than usual, because everything is narrow; these women want to be embraced further down.'[48]

The prize, 30,000 lire, was won not by Blériot but by Curtiss.

Already he's flying away from us, flying over the airfield, which seems enlarged in front of him, to the distant woods, which now appear to rise. He flies for a long time over the woods, he vanishes, we look at the woods, not at him. From behind houses, God knows where, he emerges at the same height as before, dives towards us, climbs, then the underside of his biplane looks dark, dives, then the upper surfaces glisten in the sunlight. He circles round the control tower, turns indifferently away from the applause in the direction he came from, quickly becoming small and solitary again. He completes five such circles, flying fifty kilometres in forty-nine minutes and twenty-four seconds.[49]

Kafka had been persuaded by Brod to take notes on everything he saw. The idea was that they should both write articles about the aeronautical display and then judge who had made the best comments. Meanwhile, to avoid influencing each other, they should be careful to conceal their feelings and reactions. Brod writes:

> I was pursuing a secret plan. Kafka's literary art was lying fallow at that time: for months he'd completed nothing, and he often complained to me that his talent was obviously leaking away, that he'd totally lost it. He was living for months on end in a kind of lethargy, very depressed; in my diaries I find recurrent entries about his melancholy. *Le coeur triste, l'esprit gai....* Even when he was in his deepest depressions, the effect he had on other people was stimulating, not depressing, except in moments of closest intimacy.[50]

Brod's encouragement was effective. Kafka enjoyed writing 'Die Aero-plane in Brescia',[51] which Brod then showed to the editor of the daily paper *Bohemia*, Paul Wiegeler, who published a cut version of it at the end of September. Brod wanted to incorporate an uncut version into a book of his own, *Über die Schönheit hässlicher Bilder* (*On the Beauty of Ugly Pictures*), but the plan fell through.[52] 'Often I was like a scourge, drove him and pushed him, not directly of course, but always using different methods and tricks. . . . He often found my encouragement irksome.'[53] As a literary Hardy, Brod was persistent and successful: the satisfaction Kafka found in recording his experiences at Brescia prepared the ground for the diary, which he began in the spring of 1910.

The note-taking at Brescia may have made Kafka more aware of how much depended on writing about events while they were fresh. In a postcard from Maffesdorf, a small spa in northern Bohemia, he declared himself unwilling to report on the few days that had just passed. 'Even at the time it would have been a strain to write about them properly.'[54] He was growing more aware, too, of how much depended on viewpoint. He had been learning to ride and had been visiting Kuchelbad, the race-track six miles to the west of Prague; if the view is considered from the saddle of a horse leaping the hurdle, the experience is de-familiarized. Or is this 'the most extreme, immediate, quite truthful essence of racing'?[55]

> The oneness of the grandstand, the oneness of the living spectators, the oneness of the surrounding countryside at this season of the year etc, also the orchestra's last waltz and the way they like to play it today. But if my horse turns back and won't jump and walks round the hurdle or runs away or gets excited inside the arena or actually throws me, the overall view would naturally seem much better. There are gaps between the spectators, some are flying, others

falling, hands waving here and there in every possible direction, momentary relationships rain down on me, and, sensing it, some of the spectators feel for me as I lie on the grass like a worm.[56]

In this unfinished letter, as in the fiction, relish for a hypothetical humiliation and thirst for contact – of any kind – with others stimulates his capacity for empathy with them. The identification with animals or insects is present here only in embryonic form – as a simile.

On 15 September Kafka started work again in the office, and two days later he was transferred back from the accident to the technical department, which had been reorganized according to a scheme conceived by Pfohl,[57] who had once again testified during Kafka's absence to his capacity for hard work, his ability and his loyalty,[58] and on 1 October he was promoted from being an 'assistant' to being a 'probationer'. His salary was increased to 1,000 kronen plus an allowance of 300 for lodgings and 130 as a bonus,[59] but this was low for a probationer. There was a staff of seventy in the department,[60] and of Pfohl's three clerks Kafka was the one who dealt with the most important matters. But one of his superiors, Dr Fleischmann, was hard to satisfy. Kafka was urged to write scholarly papers, and by the middle of October, he was nervous that he would be reprimanded 'for letting his, our business go unattended'.[61] Nevertheless he applied successfully for permission to arrive late twice a week in order to attend lectures on mechanical technology by one Professor Mikolaschek at the German Technische Universität.

In about the middle of September he had got to know the Czech anarchist, Michal Mareš, who was working at an office in Niklasstrasse. Seeing each other almost every day, they used to exchange smiles. According to Mareš they both wore broad black felt hats, 'like the Italian Carbonari at that time, and we both deviated from the male norm of wearing a grey tie by wearing a black silk butterfly bow à la Verdi, very fashionable then among artists and men of letters, but also a badge of anti-militarists, free-thinkers and Young Socialists'.[62] One morning Mareš pressed into Kafka's hand a leaflet inviting him to a meeting at the Klub Mladých. Kafka may have attended the meeting, which was broken up by the police, and a few subsequent meetings at the club.[63] He also went to meetings held by Masaryk's party, the Realists.[64] But he was going less to cafés, night-clubs, cinemas, operettas, and generally socializing less, except for his visits to Berta Fanta's house, and for his weekend expeditions into the country with Felix Weltsch and Brod, who wrote: 'Kafka and I were living under the strange belief that you hadn't taken possession of a landscape until your contact with it was physically consummated in its living streams.'[65]

A typical itinerary is outlined by Kafka in a letter persuading Brod not to renege on the arrangement to be at the Franz Josef station in time to catch the train at 6.05 a.m. 'At 7.15 we make our first step towards Davle, where at 10.00 we'll eat a paprika goulasch at Lederer's, at 12.00 we'll lunch in Stechowitz, from 2.00–3.30 we'll go through the forest to the rapids, and we'll go rowing on the river. At 7.00 we'll go back to Prague on the steamer.'[66] He loved boating and walking in the forest. 'We looked at the forest,' wrote Brod, 'enjoying its nearness and its infinite size.'[67] Not that Kafka was always confined to Prague during the working week, but his tours of inspection – classifying businesses according to the insurance risk involved – gave him progressively less pleasure. 'It's good that it's nearly over,' he wrote in December 1909 about a tour of western Bohemia, 'I've felt bad all the time, and there's no therapy in classifying all the time from drinking one's morning milk to rinsing one's mouth out in the evening.'[68] It may have been the same malaise that made him decide, a month later, to have his stomach pumped: 'My feeling is that disgusting things will come out.'[69] His mother's absences and his father's efforts to encourage and discipline his son's eating had fomented a neurotic fastidiousness about food. Ideally he'd have managed without any.

On 28 January 1910, lecturing in Kafka's presence to the Prager Verein Frauenfortschritt (Progressive Women's League) on the limits of artistic representation, Brod read from *Hochzeitsvorbereitungen* without mentioning the author's name. Kafka took part in the ensuing discussion.[70] Six weeks later he was still working on the story,[71] but after reading the revised version to Brod on 14 March, he said he was going to destroy it.[72] He let Brod take the manuscript home with him, afterwards writing: 'What pleases me most about the story, dear Max, is that I've got it out of the house.'[73] The episode prefigures his ultimate ambivalence in asking for all his fiction to be destroyed but entrusting it to Brod, who had said he would not destroy it.

Feelings about his writing were inseparable from the malaise that was persistently sapping his energy. In January and February 1910 he wrote few letters, though he went on doing exercises.[74] He was using a system devised by the Danish gymnastics instructor Jörgen Petersen Müller, who in 1903 had published a book prescribing exercises for daily home use. Kafka gave them up in the middle of March. 'In fact I had rheumatic pains in my upper back, then they slid lower down, then into my legs, but instead of continuing into the ground, they went up into my arms. It fits in quite well with all this that my rise in salary hasn't come, also won't come next month, and not until one's bored enough with it to spit on it.'[75] He found it hard to distinguish between physical pain that was involuntary and mental pain that seemed partly self-inflicted:

Just at the right moment stomach pains etc. begin, and with an intensity suitable for a body fortified by Müller. Throughout the afternoon, long as it was, I lay on the sofa, with some tea inside me instead of lunch, and after dozing for a quarter of an hour I had nothing to do but feel annoyed that it would not get dark. . . . Sometimes I feel like saying 'God knows how I can possibly feel any more pain, because my sheer urgency to originate it in myself stops me from perceiving it. But often I have to say: 'I know that truly I am feeling no pain. I am really the most pain-free man imaginable.'[76]

Though he distanced himself from it ironically, he did not repudiate the idea of divine powers that made him suffer, just as he believed, however distantly, in a God who did not want him to write. Mahler, who also had to contend with anti-Semitism, had a similar attitude towards his own creativity, comparing himself with Jacob, 'who wrestles with God until he's blessed. Even if the Jews had produced nothing but this [image] it would have been obvious that they were a marvellous people.'[77] At the same time Kafka's attitude to pain – and especially the sense of being able to negate it by originating it himself – is reminiscent of Nietzsche, who found pain easier to tolerate than his inability to control it. By concentrating on the voluntary element, the cruelty necessary to self-conquest, he could forget what was beyond his control.

This secret self-ravishment, this artistic cruelty, this lust to impose form on oneself as on a tough, resistant, suffering material, cauterizing into oneself a will, a criticism, a contradiction, a contempt, a negation; this uncanny, weirdly enjoyable labour of a voluntarily divided soul making itself suffer out of pleasure in causing suffering, finally this whole, *active* 'bad conscience' – you can guess already – is the true womb of all ideal and imaginative experience.[78]

Unlike Nietzsche, Kafka did not think of his work as a distillation of everything that was best in him, as an alternative self which could survive the one subject to rapid deterioration, but he did think in terms of two selves, and there is an affinity between Nietzsche's idea of cauterizing a will into a suffering self and Kafka's image of a machine that engraves the law on the flesh of a disobedient body.

7 The Ladder in Mid-Air

Virtually all Kafka's writing, like Nietzsche's, proceeds directly or indirectly out of self-examination. On one level he was always addressing himself, even in his letters, but the diary, which he began in the spring of 1910, gave him a pretext and a medium for talking to himself when he felt incapable of producing fiction. He could even write about his inability to write – even overcome it, if he questioned himself about it rigorously enough:

> I always answered if I really asked myself, there was always something left to be beaten from me, from this heap of straw I've been for five months, whose fate it seems is to be set ablaze during the summer and burn up faster than the onlooker can blink. . . . My condition's not unhappy, nor is it happy, not indifference, nor weakness, nor exhaustion, nor another interest, so what is it? . . . Everything that occurs to me occurs not from the root up but from somewhere about the middle. [1]

What he lacked was a sense of rootedness: he seemed to be living off-centre in relation to his own identity. He used the image – both in his diary and in his drawings – of an acrobat climbing a ladder that's resting not on the ground and not against a wall but only on another acrobat's feet. He felt precariously situated inside his body. 'If I lacked an upper lip here, an earlobe there, a rib here, a finger there, if I had bald spots on my head and pockmarks on my face, there still wouldn't be enough of a physical correlative to my inner imperfection.' [2] 'Why don't I stay in myself?' he asks contritely, appalled at the insolence of his behaviour towards a bus conductor or someone who had been introduced to him, more appalled that other people may confuse his behaviour with his personality. [3]

In April, together with two colleagues, who had also been promoted, he had to appear in a formal black suit to thank the President, Otto Příbram. One of them – not Kafka, who was the youngest – had to make a speech. Příbram listened 'in the pose he normally assumed for formal occasions, a little reminiscent of our Emperor's when giving audience . . . legs lightly crossed, the left hand clenched and laid on the outermost corner of the table, the head sunk, so that the full white beard bends on his chest, and on top of this the not excessive but nevertheless prominent paunch sways a little'. [4] Irresistibly impelled to giggle, Kafka did his best to pretend that he was coughing. His colleague went doggedly on with his speech, eyes fixed straight in front of him, but when Příbram looked up, he saw from Kafka's face that it had not been a fit of coughing which had produced the half-smothered sounds. For a moment Kafka was terrified, but when the President made a speech in reply, the urge to laugh again became irresistible, despite the admonitory glances from his colleagues. Trying to restore the dignity of the occasion, the one who had not made a speech made an impromptu one when Příbram finished, but this only made Kafka laugh unrestrainedly, though his knees were shaking with fear at the same time. 'Beating my breast with my right hand, partly to expiate my sins (thinking of the Day of Atonement) and partly to drive out the quantities of repressed giggles from my chest, I made all kinds of excuses which might all have been very convincing if new outbursts of laughing, constantly renewed, had not rendered them totally incomprehensible.'[5]

Here he was at the mercy of a weakness closely related to one of his greatest strengths as a writer. Giggling in his dark suit he must have felt as if the laughter were an irresistible external force, but when his pen was in his hand, it was advantageous to put emotional and mental events on the same plane of objectivity as external events. An avid and excitable theatregoer, he responded to performance as to actuality and to his own reactions as to a performance. 'Listened to myself for a time from outside myself – like the occasional whimpering of a young cat.'[6] When he saw Albert Bassermann as Hamlet, 'For whole stretches of fifteen minutes I had, by God, another man's face, from time to time I had to look away from the stage into an empty box in order to compose myself.'[7] Scampering away from the circle of his authentic self, he sends all these images flying up. When he pictured himself as disfigured – with a hand that unscrewed at the wrist, for instance – he was imaginatively demolishing a part of himself; the same energy is present in the similes and metaphors that make him into an animal. The whimpering cat is preparing the way for the insect, the ape, the dog and the mouse.

In May 1910, when the Russian Ballet performed at the German theatre in Prague, Kafka started dreaming about the dancer Eugenie Eduardova. In one dream he asked her to dance a Czardas just once more, but 'someone with the disgusting movements of an unconscious intriguer' interrupted to tell her the train was about to leave.[8] The flowers stuck into her girdle had been sent, she said, by all the princes of Europe.[9] But her features were less attractive in daylight than on the stage. With her pale complexion and cheekbones that drew her skin so taut that her face seemed immobile, 'she looks like one of my aunts, an elderly lady'.[10]

At the beginning of the month a Yiddish theatre troupe from Lemberg had made its début at a shabby café, the Savoy, in the former ghetto. The plays were melodramas, but Brod was enthusiastic about them and on 4

May he took Kafka to the Savoy. 'Franz, after the first time I took him there, entered right into the atmosphere.'[11] Brod later confused the troupe, which stayed only twelve days, with another one that came in 1911 and stayed much longer. Kafka may have seen only one performance in 1910, but a year later he still remembered the male impersonator, Salcia Weinberg: 'It was Frau W's standing joke to bump into her fellow actors with her large behind.'[12]

Kafka used his diaries both to record events or impressions and to sketch out fictions or descriptions. Some entries consist of fragmentary phrases or sentences. 'The seamstresses in the showers of rain.'[13] 'My ear-lobe felt fresh, rough, cool, juicy as a leaf.'[14] There are also prose poems like the ones he had published in *Hyperion*, and there are stories, some abortive, some complete. 'Unglücklichsein' ('Unhappiness') is written out in the diary for 1910 after a prose poem describing how badly men, when they are in danger, treat beautiful strange women, pushing them up against walls if they get in the way. 'Then our garrulous women fall silent, their ceaseless talk arrives at a verb and a full stop, the eyebrows climb above their resting places, the respiratory pulse of thigh and hips stops, more air than usual enters mouths only half closed for fear, and cheeks seem a little distended.'[15]

The first paragraph of the story can equally well be described as a prose poem. It is about the panic of an isolated man turning away from the window and screaming at what he finds in the depths of the looking-glass. Nothing replies to the scream, nothing can check it, even when it ceases to be audible, but a child blows in like a small ghost from the dark corridor. After some inconsequential conversation with the young ghost, he goes out of the room and confides in a fellow-tenant he meets on the stairs. 'The real anxiety is about what originated the apparition. And this anxiety remains. It's still going strong inside me.'[16]

The other fragmentary story in the 1910 diary also involves a conversation between two men who, without being friends, enter into intimate discussion of existential anxieties. The fitful rapport makes the narrative reminiscent of both 'Gespräch mit dem Beter' and 'Beschreibung eines Kampfes'. Again there is a meeting outside a church and again the aggressiveness of the narrator (who in both abortive drafts begins by shoving his knee against his companion) seems to function as an objective correlative to the uncontrolled insolence in Kafka's behaviour. In both fragmentary versions of the narrative *Der Verschollene* and *Das Schloss* are sketchily prefigured in the uncertain prospect the narrator has of going to another place which is higher and possibly better. His interlocutor concedes: 'Down here things are going badly for us, indeed it's a dog's life . . . nothing ever happens to me that people would notice, how could it happen in the framework of the ceremonies necessary for me, in which I can only go on creeping, no better than vermin.'[17] He does nothing to detain the narrator, who says he wants to go up, but stays talking.

At the end of August 1910 Kafka applied for his salary to be raised to 2,400 kronen. There was no immediate reaction from his superiors, but it was indicative of their confidence in him that at the end of September he was sent to give a public lecture in Gablonz on behalf of the institute. He also visited Brod's grandmother there. And in the middle of October his salary was increased to 2,100 kronen.[18] But by then he had left Prague with Max and Otto Brod as his holiday companions. After spending the night in Nuremberg, they went on to Paris. Kafka and Max Brod had been taking French lessons together in preparation.

But in Paris he felt ill at ease, depressed, and to avoid infecting his friends with his glumness, spent most of the time on solitary walks. He visited the guignol theatres in the Jardin du Luxembourg and he went to a horse-race, but when he came out in boils, and found the Parisian doctors unable to help, he left after only nine days. During his first night back in Prague he had a dream: 'I was billeted for the night in a large house which consisted of nothing but Paris cabs, cars, buses, etc. that had nothing to do except drive hard into each other, over each other, under each other, and nobody talked or thought about anything except fares, junctions, connections, tips, currency exchanges, counterfeit money, etc.'[19] Writing to the Brods on three successive picture postcards, he described a fainting fit that had forced him to lie down at the doctor's surgery. 'During this time I felt – it was very odd – so much like a girl that I was at pains to adjust my dress with my fingers. My idea, which naturally I didn't confide to the doctor, is that the international pavements of Prague, Nuremberg and above all Paris have caused the eruption.'[20] He consoled himself for the failure of his abortive holiday in Paris by telling himself he would make efforts to go back soon.[21]

Six weeks after returning to Prague, Kafka visited Berlin for the first time, but, with a kind of comic perversity, the three postcards he sent to Brod give no indication of his reactions to the place. He bought tickets for two plays, but on his second day there he wrote: 'nothing is as good as the food here in the vegetarian restaurant. The locality is rather dreary, people eat cabbage with fried eggs (the most expensive dish), the architecture is nothing much, but the contentment one feels here.'[22] His silence about any other architecture was a form of comment, but it was more a matter of self-absorption than of unwillingness to be impressed.

I listen only to what's inside myself, at the moment, admittedly, it's still very bad, but how will it be tomorrow? It's so vegetarian here that even tipping is forbidden. . . . I am now being served with semolina pudding and raspberry sauce, but I still intend to eat lettuce with cream, a gooseberry wine will taste good with it, and I'll end up with raspberry leaf tea.[23]

He returned from Berlin on 9 December in time for the twenty-one-year-old Elli's wedding, and he didn't have to start work again until the 19th. He was so unsettled in his familiar surroundings that he felt almost capable of 'behaving like an animal . . . I never felt afraid of the office till yesterday evening, but so afraid then I'd gladly have hidden under the table.'[24] It was advantageous to have the diary as an alternative channel to his letters: 'I won't give up the diary any more. I must hold on to myself here, for it's only here that I can.'[25] The previous day he had made parallel attempts in it and in a letter to Brod at analysing an emotional state, and the improved domestic situation. His parents were in better health, and quarrelling with him less, except when his father found him writing late at night and told him off for damaging his health.[26] For the rest of the family the wedding had been a major event; it may have sharpened Kafka's anxieties about protracted bachelordom, but his laconic comment to Brod was: 'At home it was almost completely peaceful. The wedding is over, new relatives are being digested.'[27]

The main emphasis in the letter is on eupeptic peacefulness. The vegetarian food had gone deeply and peacefully into his stomach 'as if good fortune had been feeding me up specially for this week'.[28] But in the diary entry, written the same day (without apparently giving a thought to his sister) he debated whether his inner state was the same as it had been throughout the year, or at a new nadir:

Almost no word I write goes well with the rest, I hear the leaden sound of friction between consonants, while the vowels sing like nigger minstrels. My uncertainties stand in a circle round each word, I see them before the word, but what then! I don't see the word at all, I make it up. Which wouldn't be so bad if only I could make up words that could blow the smell of corpses away from my face and the reader's. When I sit at my desk I feel no better than a falling man who breaks both legs in the middle of the traffic of the Place de l'Opéra. In spite of their noise all the cars move silently in all directions from all directions, but that man's pain keeps better order than the policemen, for it closes his eyes and empties the square and the roads without making the cars turn back.[29]

It was not only that in the diary he could write about himself at greater length and in greater depth than when writing to Brod: he could analyse his feelings without needing to consider whether his friend would be propelled into corrective action. But, continuing his letter to Brod two days later, he began to write as if the state of affairs he had described was a long way from being 'almost completely peaceful'.[30]

I'm in such a whirl of feeling that I'm flying. I'm simply drunk with myself. . . . In two days little has changed, and the little is for the worse. My father's not quite well, he's at home. When the noise of breakfast stops on the left, the noise of lunch starts on the right, doors are now being opened everywhere as if the walls were being demolished. [31]

He had been trying to write but producing nothing that satisfied him.

On the other hand I've struck out everything – it wasn't much – I've written since Paris. My whole body warns me against each word, each word, before it lets me write it down, first looks round in all directions; the sentences literally disintegrate for me, I see their insides and then quickly have to stop. [32]

Instead of helping him forward, destruction of old material was having more of a negative effect than the positive one he had expected: the mass of scrapped writing was like a mountain. 'It's five times as much as I've ever written before, and already its weight is dragging everything I write away from my pen towards it.' [33]

Recently he had been unable to look anyone in the eye – not even Brod. [34] The diary had added a new dimension to his activity as a writer, but even if he could have been sure that his parents, passing through his room, never read his diary, it would have been impossible for him to write in it about the noises he heard through the wall at night. Later he complained to Felice Bauer that he could hear if his father turned over violently in bed. [35] It would have been out of character for Hermann Kafka to restrain any noises he felt like making during coupling; it would have been out of character for Kafka, who was ultra-sensitive to noise and had grown up with these noises, to mention the suffering they caused him. The most he would ever say was that the sight of his parents' pyjamas and nightdress, laid out in readiness on their bed, filled him with disgust. [36] He was now earning enough money to move out, and his guilt about not marrying must have been partly guilt at a sense of unhealthy implication in his parents' marriage. He must have thought a great deal about what he knew of their sexual relationship, and perhaps the noises help to explain the eccentricity of his sleeping habits. 'I now sleep so much and so deeply during the day, I weigh more when I'm asleep.' [37] It is also possible that his austere habits of sleeping with the window open and sitting in an armchair with a blanket round his legs were induced by an irrational faith in cold air as an anti-sexual antiseptic.

This central imbalance helps to account for the peripheral idiosyncrasies. He was compulsive about personal cleanliness, habitually late for appointments, hesitant about going into rooms where someone was waiting for him, and liable to leave letters unopened for a long time. An unopened envelope 'offers itself to me continuously, continuously I receive it but without taking it'.[38] He was often late for work, but Marschner protected him.[39]

·If he set himself ambitious disciplinary objectives, the conscious motive was to compensate for everything that made him dissatisfied with himself, but since the objectives were usually beyond him, there may have been an unconscious desire to bolster the dissatisfaction. Intent on writing more, he ordered himself to be at his desk for three hours from eight o'clock every evening, but the decision merely forced him into a clearer awareness of how much energy was draining into his job.[40] The desire to think badly of himself was so strong that he felt guilty both when he wrote (in defiance of God's disapproval) and when he failed to write enough to satisfy the self sitting in judgment over the self which wrote. 'What excuse is there for still having written nothing today? None. Especially as my state of mind could be worse. Constantly in my ear is the invocation: "Were you to come, invisible judgment!"'[41] His father's anger when he caught him writing late at night[42] may have been only ostensibly through anxiety on account of his health: he may have sensed that the writing was a weapon that could be used against him.

As Christmas approached, with its chilly reminder that time was passing, his depression deepened. What had been achieved? Thanks to the diary, he knew himself better than ever before, but, disliking what he had discovered, he could hardly regard this as progress. He was losing faith both in the prospects of gaining more liberty and in his ability to use it. His capacity for self-recrimination was almost unlimited, but there were days when even that appetite felt jaded.[43]

For two and a half days over Christmas he was almost completely alone. 'Solitude has a power over me that never fails. . . . A slight tidying of my interior gets under way, and I need nothing more, for in small talents nothing is worse than disorder.'[44] Taking stock of himself, he was still depressed. 'I have now studied my desk more closely and recognized that nothing good can be done on it. So much is lying about on it forming a disorder without any regularity and without that sociability disordered things can have to make disorder bearable.'[45] On the stage or in the pit of old theatres, any amount was tolerable, but Kafka's writing-table reflected the untidiness he disliked about his own personality:

Only the shaving-mirror stands erect in the way it's used for shaving, the clothes-brush lies with its bristles downwards, the purse lies open in case I need money, from the key-ring a key sticks out, ready for work, and the tie is still partly twined around the collar I was wearing. . . . In this pigeon-hole lie old papers I'd have thrown away long ago if I had a wastepaper-basket. Pencils with broken points, an empty match-box, a paperweight from Karlsbad, a ruler with an edge bumpier than a country road, collar studs, blunt razor-blades (these have no place in the world) tie-clips and another heavy iron paperweight.[46]

There is a similar passage in which Meyrink catalogues the disorder on his desk, but in following suit Kafka was creating something structured. 'The burning electric lamp, the silent house, the darkness outside, the last moments of wakefulness, they give me the right to write, even if it is only the most wretched stuff. And this right I hastily use. That's what I'm like.'[47]

Sharpening his self-awareness, the diary habit also sharpened his ambivalence. Collecting self-criticisms, he felt the acquisitive joy of a collector each time a butterfly perception could be netted, poisoned, pinned down. But he knew there were dangers of falsification and self-betrayal. Unless he was scrupulously truthful and specific, 'what is noted down will, in accordance with its own purposes and with the superior power of what is fixed, displace what has been felt only vaguely, in such a way that the authentic feeling vanishes while the worthlessness of the note becomes apparent only too late'.[48]

Another deterrent was his critical stringency when looking at his own work. Listening to Brod's he was incomparably more tolerant:

How can I, as I am today, get anywhere near this? I'd have to search for a year before I found a true feeling in me, and I'm expected somehow to feel entitled, when faced with such a great work, to remain seated in my chair in the café, plagued by the stray winds of a digestion which is still bad, in spite of everything.[49]

The fluctuation in his moods was becoming more violent. On 7 January external and internal circumstances struck him as being friendlier than they had been for a year,[50] but twelve days later he felt as if he had never during the past year been able to stay awake for more than five minutes at a stretch.[51] The same self-condemnations recur in diary and conversation. 'Every day – since I seem thoroughly finished . . . I'll have either to wish myself off the face of the earth, or, without being able to see the slightest hope in it, to start from the beginning like an infant.'[52] A week later he told Brod: 'Every day I wish myself off the face of the earth.'

'What do you need?'

'There's nothing I need except myself.' Pressed to explain what he meant, he said: 'I have a hundred thousand false feelings, it's frightful. The right ones don't come out, or only in shreds, very feebly.'[53] Discussing their common predicament of having jobs that drained away time and energy, Brod urged him not to neglect his writing:

He didn't answer. . . . He keeps his distance, walking next to me in silence for ten minutes at a stretch, giving no answer to questions that don't suit him.

'What are they, the false thoughts that occur to you?'

'It's impossible to say.'

'But if you have a hundred thousand of these false feelings or thoughts, you must be able to think of at least one you could tell me.'

He falls silent again.[54]

There is a hint towards an answer in the diary, which explains why externally it would be easier now than it would have been before to start all over again like an infant. 'For at that time I was still striving naïvely for a way of describing which would connect up, a word at a time, with my life, a way I could take to heart and which would transport me away from where I was.'[55] He had lost this naïve optimism and, with it, he feared, lost spontaneity. Inevitably, comparing himself with the dauntingly prolific Brod, he felt desperate. What he could not yet know was how much he would build out of his despair.

At the end of January he had to go on an inspection tour to Friedland and Reichenberg in northern Bohemia. After his silence about the appearance of Berlin, he described this scenery briefly in postcards and at length in travel diaries.[56] In Friedland the view is dominated by the Renaissance castle that had belonged to Wallenstein. Kafka sent Brod a postcard photograph of it. 'This castle's smothered with ivy, which climbs half-way up the loggias. It's only the drawbridge that looks like bric-à-brac, with chains and wires you want to ignore, just because they're bric-à-brac, and although you've taken trouble over everything else.'[57] Depending on whether you viewed it from the plain, from a bridge, from the park or from the woods, the castle presented different aspects.

Even after you've stepped into the courtyard, the castle, with the surprising way its parts are built one above the other, makes no unified impression, for its multiplicity is compounded by the dark ivy, the grey-black walls, the white snow, the ice covering the slate-coloured slopes. The castle's built not so much on top of a plateau as around a rather sharp peak. Constantly slipping, I walked up the path, while the castellan, whom I met further up, climbed effortlessly up the steps.[58]

The castle was surrounded by a beautiful park, laid out terrace-fashion.[59]

The only entertainment Kafka found in Friedland was a lantern-slide show called the Imperial Panorama. Arriving with snow on his boots he felt embarrassed by the elegance of the interior. Until two elderly ladies arrived he was the only patron. An old man, who had been reading a volume of the *Illustrierte Welt*, showed slides of Brescia, Cremona, Verona.

People in them like wax dolls, glued to the pavement by the soles of their shoes.... The pictures more lifelike than in the cinema because they allow the repose of reality to the gaze. The camera imparts its own restless motion to the observed object.... Between hearing about something and seeing a lantern slide of it there is a greater gulf than between the latter and seeing it in reality.[60]

At the end Kafka wanted – but did not dare – to tell the old man how much he had enjoyed the show.[61]

Generally he was finding it difficult to implement the simplest decisions before changing his mind. Displayed in the window of the only bookshop in Friedland was the Dürer Society's *Literarischer Ratgeber*. Hesitating over whether to buy it, he went away, came back. What drew him inside the shop was its desolation. 'All desolation gives me a feeling of warmth, so I quickly sensed the happiness of this bookshop.'[62] An old lady was sitting under a green-shaded electric lamp. He offered to take the book out of the window for her, but, though she insisted on taking it out herself, she could not, in her husband's absence, tell him the price. He promised to come back later, but did not.[63]

His next stop was Reichenberg, a large town fifteen miles south of Friedland. In the evening, seeing people hurrying with lengthened strides through the square, which looked even smaller than it was because of the disproportionately large town hall, he felt alienated and puzzled. Citizens who lived outside the town would have to use the tram, but, the town being so small, residents of the interior could have no great distance to go, so why should they be in such a hurry?[64]

The Arbeiterkrankenkasse (Workers' Sickness Benefit Office) was holding an exhibition, but one policeman knew nothing about it, another did not know where the Office was, a third could not direct Kafka to Johannesgasse. 'They explain that they have been in the service only a short time.'[65] He finally went to the police station, 'where enough policemen of different kinds were taking it easy, all in uniforms, which were surprisingly beautiful, new and colourful, for otherwise only dark winter coats were to be seen on the streets.'[66]

He paid three visits to the theatre in Reichenberg, and several times found tears in his eyes, as at the end of Grillparzer's *Des Meeres und der Liebe Wellen* (*The Waves of the Sea and of Love*) when Hero and Leander could not take their eyes off each other.[67] But the backdrop representing the wall of the tower chamber turned up again a few evenings later in an operetta by Fritz Grünbaum and Heinz Reichert, *Miss Dudelsack*.[68]

It was on 19 February, about a week after his return to Prague, that exhaustion caught up with him, and he used his diary to draft a letter of resignation to Herr Pfohl: 'This morning when I wanted to get up I simply collapsed. The reason is simple enough – I'm terribly overworked. Not by the office but through my other work.'[69] The pressure was at its worst on

Friday and Saturday because he was preoccupied with his own ideas, anticipating the weekend break, and because the cumulative effect of working six hours a day for six days a week was at its worst. He had been leading 'a frightful double life from which, probably, the only escape is into insanity'.[70] The smallest piece of good luck in one profession became a disaster in the other. 'If one evening I write something good, I'm on fire the next day in the office, and achieve nothing. This to-ing and fro-ing constantly gets worse. In the office I outwardly fulfil my duties, but each unfulfilled inner duty becomes a burden I can never throw off.'[71] The draft letter to Pfohl contains the phrase 'you love me like a son', and even if he had not simultaneously been made into one of the institute's fully accredited legal representatives, there would have been no more likelihood of his delivering the letter than of delivering the later one to his father.

Already, eighteen months before writing 'Das Urteil', he was close to equating his father's disapproval with a death sentence. In some respects the story 'Die städtische Welt' ('The Urban World') which is written out in the diary, serves as a first draft for 'Das Urteil', a first attempt at translating his guilt-ridden relationship with his father into fictional terms. Oskar M. is described as 'an elderly student – if you looked at him closely, you were scared of his eyes'.[72] His father, 'a clean-shaven man with a heavily fleshy face',[73] greets his return home with a burst of rage: 'Please stay by the door. I'm so furious with you I don't know what I might do.' Oskar's sense of being suffocated in the parental home is conveyed by the blocking of the light from a window when the father stands up. 'I'm just not going to put up with your good-for-nothing life any longer. I'm an old man. I thought you'd be a comfort in my old age, but you're more trouble than all my illnesses put together. Shame on you! You're driving your old father to his grave with your laziness, your extravagance, your wickedness, and (why shouldn't I be frank with you?) stupidity.'[74] Kafka's letter to his father makes it obvious that this is a sample of the nagging that had become so familiar. If the paternal hyperbole is taken literally, it contains an accusation of murder, which is in line with the fictional death sentence later to be passed on the son. Oskar tries to explain himself. He has always meant well; embittered by his invariable failure to please his father, he has been going out of his way to upset him. And now he has had an idea, he says: he will be able to make himself into an industrious person beyond all his father's expectations. In the past he had found that the relentlessly reproachful voice of his father had the power to drive ideas out of his mind, but now it is having the opposite effect, consolidating his confidence. His father knows how to express his scepticism in the most mortifying way. Oskar moves his head as though someone is gripping him by the throat. 'You're getting under my skin more than you need to.'[75]

The father, compulsive about destroying the son's self-confidence, involves the mother in her absence. If he shouts at Oskar, he says, he does it only in the hope of improving him, and only for the sake of his 'poor good mother who may not yet feel any immediate distress because of you, but she's slowly going to pieces under the strain of fending off that distress, because she thinks that's a way of helping you.'[76]

Still entangled in neurotic forces just like the ones he was writing about, Kafka could see some aspects of the problem objectively, but he had never before written about it in his diary. Even now, treating it fictionally, he introduced a character called Franz as Oskar's friend, perhaps needing to pretend, if only to himself, that Oskar's situation was not identical with his – or perhaps nervous that the diary might fall into his parents' hands.

In his father's flat, living with no privacy and sleeping with only a wall to divide him from his parents' bedroom,[77] he would remain infinitely vulnerable. Yet he had moments of feeling strong. Going to sleep one night at two o'clock he felt intently aware of what was special about his talent. 'If I indiscriminately write down a sentence, for instance "He looked out of the window", it is perfect.'[77] He was 'the happiest and unhappiest of men'.[78] 'For a moment I felt bulletproof.'[79]

The difficulty Kafka experienced during March 1911 in completing his diary entry about Brod's novel *Jüdinnen* (*Jewesses*)[80] evidences his current ambivalence on the Jewish question. In *Selbstwehr* (*Self-Defence*), the independent Jewish weekly which had been published in Prague since March 1907 and taken over in 1910 by Leo Herrmann, a leading member of the Jewish students' association, *Bar Kochbar*,[81] the novel was criticized for failing to put the complex manifestations of Judaism in the perspective of an individual viewpoint.[82] Kafka was apparently in touch with Bar Kochbar from 1910 onwards and may have joined in discussions about the book and the review,[83] which patently influenced his own reaction to his friend's novel. Surprisingly, he attacked it for failing to suggest a solution to the Jewish question. 'With the existence of Zionism, the possibilities of solution stand so clearly ranged around the Jewish problem that the author needed to take only a few more steps to find the possibility of a solution suitable to his story.'[84] Kafka complains, too, about the absence of non-Jewish observers to put the Jewishness into perspective, and unflatteringly he compares Brod's Jewesses to lizards. However happy we are to watch a single lizard on a footpath in Italy, we would be horrified to see hundreds of them crawling over each other in a pickle-jar.[85] The reptile image is less offensive in view of his later work, but where was the non-Jewish observer in his everyday impressions of his social life?

Rudolf Steiner came to deliver a series of lectures in Beata Fanta's house, where he founded the first theosophical community in Prague. 'I remember', testifies the Fantas' daughter, 'that I watched during the lectures how Franz Kafka's eyes sparkled and gleamed, and a smile brightened his face.'[86] Some of Steiner's claims struck him as absurd. 'A Munich doctor's curing with colours Dr Steiner prescribes. He's also sending patients into the art gallery with instructions to concentrate on a particular painting for a half hour or longer. . . . He communicates with absent disciples by means of thought-forms he sends out to them without having to think about it once they have been emitted.'[87]

But Kafka was not too sceptical to consult Dr Steiner in his room at the Viktoria Hotel in Jungmannstrasse. Steiner's black jacket was dusty and spotted, especially on the back and elbows. Not knowing where to put his hat, Kafka placed it with consciously exaggerated deference on a small wooden stand intended for lacing boots.

'So you are Dr Kafka? Have you been interested in theosophy for long?'

A cold in the head was making Steiner's nose run. He kept working his handkerchief deep into his nostrils.

Kafka said that a great part of his being was striving towards theosophy, though he was afraid of the confusion it might cause him. His only talents were literary.

And here I have indeed experienced states (not many) which in my opinion come very close to the clairvoyant states that you, Herr Doktor, have described, states in which I fully inhabited each insight, and filled it out, feeling at the outer edge both of myself and of humanity. Only the calm of enthusiasm, which probably belongs to clairvoyance, was missing from those states, though not entirely. I deduce this from not having written the best of my works in those states.

What Kafka wanted from the doctor was quasi-paternal encouragement to believe that the triangular pull of forces between theosophy, writing and job would be easier to handle than the tug of war between the last two. Steiner listened without looking at Kafka, but nodding from time to time as if the movement of his head helped him to concentrate.[88] The meeting effectively killed Kafka's enthusiasm for theosophy.

In the second half of April 1911 he had to make another tour of inspection. From Zittau, an industrial city in the Kingdom of Saxony, he made an excursion to Mount Oybin,[89] and in Warnsdorf he consulted another father-figure, a rich industrialist, Moriz Schnitzer, an amateur naturopath, who interpreted the Bible in vegetarian terms. Moses had led the Jews through the desert for forty years to make them give up eating meat. Manna was divinely vegetarian. Quail-flesh was evil, and so were the fleshpots of Egypt. In the New Testament Jesus had identified his body with bread.[90] When Kafka submitted himself to examination, Schnitzer looked only at his throat, first in profile and then from the front, before diagnosing poison in his spinal marrow. Already it reached almost up to his brain – a result of living badly. Schnitzer prescribed sleeping in front of an open window, sun-bathing, working in the garden, joining in the activities of a naturopathic club, and subscribing to a naturopathic magazine, presumably the one he published.[91] This time scepticism failed to save Kafka: he acquired a lifelong habit of sleeping with the window wide open and a lifelong idealization of sun-bathing and gardening. Vegetarianism was already deeply implanted in him.

After returning to Prague he was depressed and withdrawn. He applied unsuccessfully for his salary to be increased to 2,600 kronen.[92] He confided less in Brod, who on 25 May came to the conclusion that nothing interested him any longer except his dreams.[93] His birthday letter to Brod said:

> I'm not even sending you the usual book, for it would be merely a form; the truth is that I'm not even in a position to give you a book. I'm writing only because I so badly need to be in your presence for a moment today, if only by means of this card, and I've begun with this lament so that you recognize me straight away. Yours, Franz.[94]

Three weeks later Brod wrote in his diary: 'Constantly trying to talk him out of his depressions.'[95]

He was writing neither stories nor letters. Even his diary was abandoned, but at least his image of himself was changing for the better. 'The time that's passed without my writing a word has been important for me because I've stopped being ashamed of my own body in the swimming schools of Prague, Königssaal and Czernoschitz. At the age of twenty-eight I am tardily making up for my education – a delayed start, as they say at the race-courses.'[96]

As he saw it, his inability to make himself into a success was not the worst consequence of his education.

> This is only the still visible, clear, healthy core of the progressively dissolving disaster, which is becoming boundless and it's driving one back to the inside of the circle when one should be running around the outside. . . . I've no time for the slightest bit of good work, for I really have no time for a story that would expand me in every direction in the world – which is what I'd need.[97]

His relationship with the tolerant Brod had not deteriorated too badly for them to go on holiday together, and Kafka tried to prepare himself, believing 'that my trip will turn out better, that I'll take more in if I'm relaxed by a little writing.'[98] What follows in the diary is an eight-line fragment of the story he had begun the previous year in the first person. In the new fragment the narrator is no longer aggressive but churlish and suspicious towards the man who is offering help. 'Indeed I stood stubbornly here in front of the house, but, just as stubbornly hesitated about going up.'[99]

The story's relevance to his relationship with Brod is illuminated by the next entry, written *à propos* something he had read about Dickens: 'One experiences a story from its beginning inside oneself, from the point in the distance to the locomotive's approach – steel, coal, and steam – but instead of abandoning it now, one wants to be pursued by it, and one has time to be, so one is pursued, and runs away with one's own momentum in any direction it pushes and in any direction one lures it.'[100] The self-contradiction is a fairly accurate translation of the paradoxical tension between controlling and being controlled, taking the initiative and submitting to one that seems to come from outside. And while analysing the sensation Kafka was experiencing it with the heightened sensitivity he always gained from the activity of writing. 'I'm alive only here and there in a small word, losing my useless head momentarily in an accent above it, the Umlaut above *stösst* [pushes] for instance. First and last letters are the beginning and ending of my fishlike sensation.'[101]

At the end of August 1911, nearly eighteen months after starting the diary, and the day before he was due to leave on holiday, he brought himself for the first time to write directly and non-fictionally about the situation at home. Hermann Kafka's business worries had been exacerbating his illness. 'On his heart a wet cloth, vomiting, breathlessness, sighing as he paces up and down. In her anxiety Mother finds new solace. He'd always been so energetic, overcome every difficulty and now –'[102] Kafka joined in the domestic drama, remarking that the business troubles could not last for more than another three months. 'He walks up and down sighing and shaking his head. It's clear that from his point of view, we won't be able to relieve him of his worries or even alleviate them, but even from our point of view, all our good intentions conceal a residue of the sad conviction that he must provide for his family.'[103] At moments of insecurity, as in the conversation with Steiner, Kafka could try to regain his balance through sceptical observation of other people's behaviour. 'By yawning frequently or by picking his nose (not repulsively, by the way) Father offers us slight, almost subliminal reassurance about his condition, though he generally doesn't do this when he's well.'[104] Observations like these must have been more comforting when he was recording them than when he was making them: he must have felt dwarfed by his father as a breadwinner just as previously he had felt physically dwarfed. 'Poor mother will go begging to the landlord tomorrow.'[105] And poor Kafka will go off on holiday with his friends, suppressing his guilt at leaving the family in the lurch.

8 Holiday and Malaise

To prod Kafka into writing, Max Brod again proposed a competitive exercise: they should both keep diaries, describing both events and their feelings towards each other. The impracticality of the scheme was immediately apparent when a wagonload of peasant women passed by. One was laughing, while another, from sleeping in her lap, woke up and waved. 'If I described the way Max greeted them, a spurious hostility would invade the description.'[1] Nor could he write truthfully about what happened when a girl got into the carriage at Pilsen. When her hat fell from the luggage rack on to Brod, he felt obliged, as a man of honour, 'to say something that would neutralize the danger in the situation'. At Munich a lady who had noticed the girl was unchaperoned offered her a lift in a car. She accepted with alacrity.

They were on the train overnight, and, arriving at Zürich, walked up and down a bridge, 'undecided about the order in which to have cold and warm baths and breakfast'.[2] Some of Kafka's notes were perfunctory. 'Altstadt: narrow steep road which a man wearing a blue blouse descends laboriously. Down steps. Memory of the lavatory in front of St Roche in Paris threatened by traffic. Breakfast in a temperance restaurant. Butter like egg yolks. *Zürcher Zeitung.*'[3] They went to see the cathedral; they swam in a pool for men only. After going to a free concert presented by the *Offiziersverkehrsverein* (Officers' Tourist Club), they lunched in the town hall on pea soup with sago, beans with baked potatoes and lemon creme. They drank sterilized wine made from fresh grapes.

In the afternoon they left for Lucerne. At the casino a notice asked Swiss citizens to give foreigners precedence, 'as the gaming is intended for the amusement of our visitors'.[4] Kafka was impressed by the dexterity of the croupiers with their nickel-plated rakes on wooden handles. They could 'pull the money on to the right squares, sort it, pull it to them, catch the money they throw on to the winning squares'.[5] Kafka and Brod decided to gamble five francs each. 'You feel as though you're alone in the room. The money vanished down a gently sloping incline. . . . Anger at everything.'[6]

In the morning they took the train to Flüelen. At the Hotel Sternen they were given a room with a balcony. In the hall two girls and a man with alpenstocks reminded Kafka of *Miss Dudelsack.* He and Brod both devoted a lot of time to writing in their diaries. 'From four till eleven in the evening at the same table with Max, first in the garden, then in the reading room, then in my room.'[7] Brod came to pity 'travellers who took "only" cameras with them',[8] or as Kafka put it, 'Irresponsible to travel or for that matter to live without taking notes. It precludes the deathly feeling that the days are passing monotonously.'[9]

From Tuesday 29 August, they spent a week in Lugano, staying at the Hotel Belvedere au Lac, bathing a great deal, going for long walks and idling away the evenings on the hotel terrace.[10] Kafka's diary does not yet mention any constipation. He 'was very sensitive about all irregularities in his health – any physical imperfection tormented him, whether it was scurf or a toe that hadn't grown fully. Suspicious of medicines and doctors, he demanded that nature herself should restore the balance: he despised all "unnatural" remedies.'[11] Refusing laxatives, he 'ruined my good mood with his moanings'.[12] Laxatives are mentioned in Kafka's diary four weeks later, when he contrasts the beneficent effects of powdered seaweed with 'the unhealthy chemical effect of other laxatives which simply tear their way through the excrement, therefore leaving it hanging on the walls of the bowels'.[13]

Having to economize, they evolved a compensatory fantasy about a lucrative series of guidebooks to be called 'Billig' ('On the Cheap'). They would write a volume for Switzerland, one for Paris, and so on. 'Franz, who was inexhaustible, took childish pleasure in detailing the principles that were to make our fortunes, and liberate us from our frightful office jobs.'[14] Brod could never tell whether he was joking, or even whether he knew himself.[15] In discussing posters to go on the walls of Paris métro stations alongside advertisements for Byrrh, he was 'simply surrendering himself to the creative fantasies of a great teller of fairy-stories'.[16] The series must protect its readers from all the difficulties of making decisions, 'so it needed compulsory routes, only *one* hotel in each town, only *one* method of transport, the cheapest'.[17] In the brochure Kafka wrote: 'Neither hurried nor slow tourists, but a medium-paced category. Variations are more easily arranged, because they can always be related to something specific.'[18]

Their 'guide to conversation' would allow for the impossibility of mastering a foreign language completely. 'We therefore prefer to instruct you in making mistakes. It is less trouble and quite sufficient for being understood. A kind of Esperanto, our version of bad French or English. Also dialects and sign language according to local custom.'[19] They would write sections on 'What to do on rainy days', 'Travel souvenirs', 'Suitable clothes', 'Free concerts', 'Where and how to get free tickets for the theatre like local inhabitants', 'Seeing only the few most important paintings in galleries but studying them thoroughly'.[20] Later Brod tried in vain to find a publisher for the series.[21]

Kafka's diary jottings give vivid impressions of his observations: 'Telegraph poles: cross-section of clothes-hooks.'[22] 'Telescope. Jungfrau in the distance, rotunda of the Monk, dancing waves of hot air making the picture move. The Titli like the outstretched palm of a hand. A snow field sliced like a loaf.'[23] Brod was less observant but produced more literary snapshots of himself and Kafka:

We're sitting under bushes in the cliff, our feet in the water, amid the overgrown landscape. Passers-by point us out as examples of Italian youth. Sitting down here, ourselves invisible, we hear voices from the road above, and see people where the road bends, but then they vanish into the shrubbery above us. . . . Kafka's worries, a bit exaggerated. Conversation about the beauty of toes, and their seaweed-like movement under water. Among other complaints Kafka says: 'And then my appearance! This is how I come of age! I'll go on looking like a boy till I'm forty, and then suddenly a withered old man.'[24]

They were still in Lugano when they read newspaper reports of a cholera epidemic. They thought of going to Paris instead of staying in Italy, but it seemed fairly safe to go on via Porto Ceresio to Milan. They ate apple strudel in the courtyard of the Mercanti.[25] They saw a performance at the Teatro Fossati. 'In no other way can such unity be formed between stage and auditorium as for and against the spectator who doesn't understand the language.'[26] Sitting at the table of a café in the Piazza del Duomo, Kafka found the cathedral 'tiresome with its many spires'.[27]

They went to a brothel after seeing a woman leaning against the lattice of a top-floor window. 'I was uninhibited then in every way, and resolute, and felt my body grow weightier as it always does in such moods.'[28] Once inside, Brod seemed nervous. Alertly observant, Kafka inspected the prostitutes:

The girl whose belly was unquestionably shapeless between the spread legs under the transparent dress while she was sitting down, but when she stood up it disappeared behind veils like a piece of stage scenery, and a tolerably feminine body came into view. The French girl whose sweetness, to the judicious eye, was evident above all in the round but precise, eloquent and affectionate knees. An imperiously monumental figure shoving the money that had just been earned into a stocking. . . . The one by the door with the evil Spanish face and the Spanish way of putting her hands on her hips stretching herself in her bodice-like dress of condom silk. In the brothels at home it's the German girls who manage to make clients momentarily forget their nationality, here it's the French girls.[29]

The next day they went inside the cathedral, which struck Kafka as consisting of mere architecture. There were few benches, few statues on the pillars, and few pictures, visible only dimly.[30] From the roof they looked down on the slow-moving trams. 'A conductor, stunted and crooked from our point of view, hurries along to his tram and jumps in. A fountain shaped like a man, spinal column and brain removed for the rainwater to find its way through.'[31] They spent the afternoon in Stresa. Here Kafka felt an unusually strong urge to write: 'My whole self felt like a fist whose nails are digging into its flesh – I can put it in no other way.'[32]

They decided – partly because of the cholera danger, partly to compensate themselves for their anxiety about it, partly to save time and money – on a visit to Paris.[33] They arrived on Friday 8 September after being on the train all night. Once inside their hotel rooms Kafka said:

'Now quick. No unpacking. We're only here for five days. Just wash your face a bit.' I comply, wait for him, go up again. He's washing with soap and a flannel, has unpacked every possible luxury out of the trunk and doesn't go out until he's tidied everything away. My trunk's still unopened.[34]

Annoyed, Brod

sat down on my bed to wait with all the dirt of the night's journey on his clothes. It's Max's habit, when grumbling, as now, to pull his mouth and in fact his whole face into an expression of sweetness, as if on the one hand he is trying by that means to make his complaints more readily understandable, and, on the other hand, to show that he has nothing but this facial sweetness to restrain him from slapping me. That I am forcing him into a dissemblance alien to his nature is another cause for reproach, which he appears to me to be making when he falls silent, and his face, in order to recover from the sweetness, relaxes in the opposite direction, away from the mouth, that is, which naturally has a stronger effect than the first expression. In contrast, I know how to withdraw so deeply inside myself out of weariness – this is how it was in Paris – that such expressions exert no influence at all on me, which is how I can control my misery sufficiently to apologize to him straight away without any feeling of guilt, and speaking out of the most complete indifference. That appeased him then . . . or seemed to, so that he stepped out on to the balcony with me, talking about the view, and above all about how Parisian it was. All I saw was how energetic Max was, and how well he fitted into some kind of Paris I wasn't aware of, how now, stepping out of a dark room at the back on to a sunny Paris balcony for the first time this year, he could feel he deserved to be there, whereas I, unfortunately, felt distinctly wearier than when I'd first stepped out on the balcony a little while before Max came to my room.[35]

To Kafka it sometimes seemed that Brod liked him most when he was being most difficult.[36]

He made up for his failure to see the sights on his first visit to Paris. They spent two days looking at pictures in the Louvre, where Kafka found that however slowly he walked around the Venus de Milo, its appearance altered rapidly and surprisingly. At different angles the bended left knee seemed to have a different effect on the rest of the figure.[37] They walked down the Champs-Elysées, and visited the Bois de Boulogne and Versailles.

They went to see *Carmen* at the Opéra Comique. Waiting in the narrow street outside was the donkey who would appear in the first act. In the dance at the smugglers' inn, a ballerina substituted for Carmen, but when she had to dance herself it looked as though she had found time only for a few hasty lessons from the ballerina. 'The footlights whiten her soles when she leans on the table, listening to someone and letting her feet caress each other under the green dress.'[38] Too tired to watch the last act, they sat in a bar on the other side of the road. 'Max in his exhaustion squirts soda water over me, while I in mine can't stop laughing and get grenadine up my nose.'[39]

Before going to see Racine's *Phèdre* at the Comédie Française, Brod bought a text, and read it under a street-lamp outside the Aristède while Kafka was having supper. In the Opéra Comique the previous evening the fat usherette had accepted their tip condescendingly, and Kafka had made up his mind not to tip at the Comédie. He even ventured the remark that in his opinion tipping was redundant. But when the usherette, who was thin, explained, hanging her head, that the management paid her nothing, he tipped her generously. Though Œnone moved from one rigid pose into another, and Hippolyte recited his verse looking proudly at the audience, Kafka sometimes felt it was all taking place for the first time.[40]

Going to a brothel he was impressed to find not a man but a well-dressed woman in the concierge's office. She rang her electric bell, but detained them while two other clients made their way down the stairs. Brod and Kafka were then received by two respectable-looking women. When the light was switched on in the adjoining room, girls, waiting in calculated poses, were in a circle, which was not complete till they moved into it. The madam led Kafka towards a girl who stepped forward with 'long paces',[41] but his desire to escape was becoming irrepressible. 'Impossible to imagine how I reached the street, it was so quick.'[42] But the street outside was equally full of prostitutes. With so many crowding around, he got no clear impression, except of one, who 'had gaps between her teeth, stretched herself to her full height, held her dress together over her pudenda with her clenched fist, rapidly opening and shutting her large eyes as well as her large mouth.'[43] His instinct was to raise his hat. 'One has to tear one's hand away from the brim. Lonely, long, ridiculous walk home.'[44]

The regularity of his bowel movements was easily upset, and in Paris he was eating too much spongy pastry and too little fruit. Sometimes, with Brod sitting in a café waiting for him, he would scour the side streets for fruit. Sometimes they would buy apple strudel in a baker's shop and eat it in a café.[45] At Duval's in the Boulevard Sebastopol Kafka ordered one yoghurt after another, enjoying the semi-darkness, and when the waitress removed the cutlery he would not need, he thought he could 'sense tolerance and understanding of my sufferings in a woman who was so silent'.[46]

Having succeeded with his idea of parallel diaries, Brod went on to propose collaboration on a novel about two friends who go on holiday. The title was to be *Richard und Samuel*. According to Brod the idea was conceived in Lugano; in Kafka's diaries the names are first mentioned in the Paris section. He wrote a sequence in his diary, introducing a quartet of friends, Robert, Samuel, Max and Franz. Franz is a bank clerk, Max a civil servant. The four of them meet once a week to drink beer and compare notes about office experiences since they last met. They laugh so much at these meetings that Max complains: 'Seriousness naturally makes greater demands on people, and since it's obvious that one's capacity's greater in the company of one's friends, laughing should be done in the office, where nothing better can be achieved.'[47]

Brod returned to Prague on 13 September but Kafka, who had another six days of holiday, went on to rest at a nature-cure clinic in Switzerland. Most of the journey was by train, with a short trip in a small steamer. The clinic was in Erlenbach on Lake Zürich. He enjoyed being examined by the doctor, who listened to his heart, tapping the area around it. 'It lasted so long it seemed to be done almost unthinkingly.'

In the reading-room, finding himself in the company of a lady, Kafka introduced himself to her, but he realized she was deaf. He tried to make conversation about the weather by pointing to the rain outside. With the aid of an instruction book she was using a pack of miniature cards to tell fortunes.[48]

The schedule for the patients included therapeutic baths, massage sessions, and gymnastics, with rest periods before and afterwards. He characterized the clientele as

People with thin skin, rather a small head, looking exaggeratedly clean, with one or two anomalous characteristics (with Herr F [Fellenberg] missing teeth, an incipient paunch) greater leanness than would seem appropriate to their bone structure, i.e. corpulence rigidly suppressed, they handle their health as if it were a disease or something that had been meritoriously acquired (I've nothing against that) with all the other consequences of an artificially induced healthiness.[49]

Apart from vegetable and fruit juices, the diet consisted mainly of nuts, apple sauce, mashed potatoes, wholegrain bread, omelettes and puddings.[50] With his intestines still clogged, he had little appetite, but he took a mild pleasure in the family feeling that had grown up among the patients, despite the formality of the social arrangements. During evening programmes of gramophone records the gentlemen were seated separately from the ladies. There were also organized games.

Seeing that the deaf lady carried around a portfolio of writing-paper, cards, pencils and pens, Kafka, who had written almost nothing about Paris while there, was stimulated to write about it. She had a son with her, and it crossed Kafka's mind that being deaf, she would not object if he, too, addressed her as 'Mutter' – a thought that would occur only to a man starved of maternal solicitude. But he did not join in the organized games, partly 'because of my ineptitude',[51] partly because he went on trying to write, though everything he did left him dissatisfied. 'It didn't seem to me as though there were anything ugly or degrading, anything sad or painful in this solitude, which is incidentally organic – as if I consisted only of bones.'[52]

In health he did feel some benefit from the week at the clinic, and, on the day he left, he reported that 'one of my diseases is beginning to loosen its grip under the astonished gaze of my others'.[53] But his constipation persisted after his return to Prague. A new acquaintance, the painter Alfred Kubin, turned out to be a fellow-sufferer, and he recommended Regulin, the laxative made from seaweed. Kafka portrayed Kubin as 'very strong but rather monotonous in his facial movements, he describes the most dissimilar things with the same muscular expression. Varies in his apparent age, size and strength according to whether he's sitting or standing, wearing just a suit or an overcoat.'[54] 'Listening to his many anecdotes you can forget his importance. Reminded of it suddenly you're scared.'[55] But not too scared to discuss constipation. 'Throughout the evening he spoke often – and quite seriously in my opinion – about constipation, mine and his. But towards midnight, when I was letting my hand dangle over the edge of the table, he saw part of my arm and called out: "But you're really ill." '[56] After that he was noticeably more indulgent in his treatment of Kafka, and defended him when the others were trying to coax him into going with them to the brothel. Kubin had already said goodnight when, from some distance away, he called out once again the word 'Regulin'.[57]

By articulating so many observations in his diary Kafka was habituating himself both to greater precision in perceiving and to a tighter correlation between observation and formulation. At the same time he became more aware of the way memory failed to retain what the sensitivity registered.

He might, for instance, remember that a girl's hair was beautiful, but forget in which way.[58] He was progressively alerted not only to the relevance of viewpoint but of the rate at which it changed. Goethe's observations on his travels had been made from a mail-coach, which meant that changes in landscape occurred slowly.

> A calm, literally provincial thinking sets in. Since the landscape offers itself unadulterated in its original character to the passengers in the coach, while the roads cut through the countryside much more naturally than railways, standing perhaps in much the same relationship to them as rivers to canals, no violent exertion is required from the onlooker.[59]

In contrast the jockey thrown off his horse found his viewpoint changing dizzyingly fast.

Though Kafka had never been touched deeply by Judaism as a creed, he was aware, going to the Altneu synagogue on the Day of Atonement, of feeling less involved than he had been at the Pinkas synagogue. As in describing his meeting with Rudolf Steiner, he recorded only observations that encouraged scepticism. 'Muted stock-exchange muttering. . . . Churchlike interior. Three orthodox, presumably Eastern Jews. In socks. Bent over their prayer-books, prayer shawls pulled up over their heads, becoming as small as possible.'[60] At least two of them were weeping; the other might have been dabbing his eyes with his handkerchief because they were sore. A small boy, who could have no idea of what it was all about, was pushing his way through the congregation. Kafka recognized the family of a brothel-owner. A man who looked like a clerk was shaking himself briskly while he prayed, 'which can be construed only as an attempt to put the strongest possible emphasis – incomprehensible though it may be – on each word, and as a means of economizing with the voice, which wouldn't in any case, be able to effect much emphasis against this noise'.[61]

Why was Kafka attending the service? It may have been to please his father, but, without feeling any positive identification with the West European Jews, he seems to have shared their negative feelings towards the East Europeans, who were much less assimilated in manners, habits, clothing, hair-style, and language. Most of them spoke Yiddish; the more orthodox still wore long sidelocks. Probably Kafka's hostility to Buber was partly a hostility to Eastern Jews, for what Buber was doing in his books was presenting them to the West by translating into literature the oral tradition of Hasidic stories which merged religion, mysticism and folklore. 'The word *Hasid* implies intense piety, ardour, fervour, ecstasy.'[62] Many of the stories centre around a miracle-working rabbi, the Baal Shem Tov; many were originated by his great-grandson, Rabbi Nachman of

Bratzlav. Kafka felt ambivalent towards the whole tradition, as he did towards the experience in the Altneu synagogue, but, as in the consultation with Steiner, he may have felt less sceptical at the time than he did in describing retrospectively. When he did not feel ready to analyse ambivalences in the diary, he would use it to build up a barricade of words against awareness of them.

The diary was helping to increase both his acuity of observation and his eidetic power: hearing a girl's voice in an adjoining room he could visualize her in detail.[63] This worked hand in hand with what he called 'a considerable talent, which nobody notices, for transforming myself. Often I couldn't help imitating Max.'[64] Later he used this talent on transforming himself into an insect or animal.

Kafka goes on to compare himself with Szafranski, an artist whose grimacing, while observing and drawing, had a connection with what he was drawing. On the day he described the writer Kurt Tucholsky, Kafka felt that if he could have seen himself from outside, he might have mistaken himself for Tucholsky. 'The alien being must be as distinct and invisible in me as the hidden object in one of those puzzle pictures in which you'd be unable to find it if you didn't know it was there.'[65] Tucholsky was twenty-one and 'all of a piece. ... From the powerful, measured swing of his walking-stick, which gives his shoulders a youthful lift, to his calculated mixture of pleasure and contempt he feels towards his own literary work.'[66]

Either the energy that was going into observing, formulating and recording was over-stimulating Kafka's imagination, or both the physical and the imaginative hyper-activity were symptoms of a deeper malaise. At night about an hour after falling asleep, he would wake up 'as if I'd laid my head in one of the wrong holes. I'm wide awake, have the feeling of not having slept at all, or only under a thin skin, have the whole labour of falling asleep in front of me, and feel rejected by sleep.'[67] He would make himself feel as heavy as he could by crossing his arms and resting his hands on his shoulders, lying there like a soldier with his pack.[68] Until about five in the morning, he would have the feeling of being awake and asleep at the same time, of being kept awake by the strength of dreams, which were already sending out rays into wakefulness before he fell asleep,[69] of having to struggle with the dreams while sleeping alongside himself. When he finally woke, exhausted, he felt surrounded by dreams it would be dangerous to think about.[70] If he wrote about them later the process of writing would stir the mixture of memories and fantasies. One dream was about a blind or half-blind child, apparently the daughter of an aunt who in fact had only sons. One of the girl's eyes receded; the other was milky-grey and bulbous. She wore spectacles of a special kind: the receding eye needed a lens close against it, so her cheek had been pierced and a lever had been attached to her cheekbone, while another small wire rod, which came out of the cheek, went back over her ear.[71] Kafka felt so debilitated by the dream that he confided it to Pfohl and, while talking about it, associated the special spectacles with his mother, 'who sits next to me in the evening and, while playing cards, looks across at me not very pleasantly from under her eyeglasses'.[72] He must have observed that the right lens was closer to the eye than the left, but the observation had not been available previously to his conscious memory. He had always been horrified by the idea of metal twining itself into a living thing – flowers on wire made him almost shudder[73] – and the early image of unscrewing his hand from his wrist involves a similarly unpleasant confusion of organic with mechanical.

It seemed to him that his sleeplessness was directly due to his writing. Far from being a comfort to him, his inescapable consciousness of creative powers was frightening because it seemed, on the one hand, as though he could extract from himself anything he wanted, and on the other as though he couldn't control the forces he called up. Behind the conflict between dreams and wakefulness was a conflict between unconscious and conscious forces. Towards evening and even more strongly in the morning, he felt tremors of an approaching movement which, it seemed, could tear him open or make him liable to do anything. A suppressed harmony, perhaps, which could have expanded him if he had let it, but, keeping it in check, he was weakening himself. 'In the daylight the visible world helps me; at night it cuts me to pieces, unrestrained.'[74] He felt like Paris during the revolution, when the suburban population, previously strangers to the Parisians, occupied the centre of the city.[75]

The discomfort exacerbated the tension between writing and office work. He was being paid to put words together in writing reports. To hold back on this would be to rob the institute, but to channel creative energy into insurance reports was to steal from himself. Besides, he hated dictating in an office full of colleagues: if he hesitated or got stuck, the restlessness of his typist attracted their attention. Even when he found the word that had been eluding him, he could still go on hesitating, 'still hold everything in my mouth with disgust and a feeling of shame as if it were raw meat cut from my body'.[76]

The tension produced physical symptoms, mostly when he was trying to sleep. A vertically moving pain in the centre of his forehead, as if a wrinkle were being sharply pressed into it;[77] a tension over his left eye; what felt like a small cool flame running up the left side of his head.[78] He felt restless and vicious. In the office he could usually retain a superficial calm, doing what he was told or expected to do, but when he restrained his irritability at home, he felt as though something would explode. Sometimes one of his sisters would come in while he was writing, sit down at the table with a book, eventually taking a card from the tray, and fiddling around with it between her teeth. 'With departing rage, from which only a pungent vapour remains in my head, and with incipient relief and confidence, I begin to write.'[79] His syntax reflects the relief or release after frustration. German grammar, with its rigid postponement of the verb to the end of the sentence, tends anyway to produce this effect, but no writer has exploited it more subtly than Kafka.

9 The Yiddish Actors

If the experience in the Altneu synagogue on the Day of Atonement had strengthened his negative feelings towards Jewishness, a powerful antidote was administered by the troupe of six Yiddish actors he saw on 4 October 1911 at the Savoy Café. Many companies of Yiddish actors were touring in Eastern Europe, operating on small budgets and putting on plays – produced simply and fairly crudely – in cafés or wherever they could find space, and this one was to settle in Prague for several months.

It was called the Polish Yiddish Musical Drama Company, but the only accompaniment to the singing was provided by one pianist. The stage was in a corner of the restaurant. For changing and making up, the actors were given space in the cellar and to the right of the stage. The audience was at two angles – to the front and to their left – so the curtain had to rise and fall simultaneously at two angles. There was no scenery, and only the most basic furniture – a table and a few chairs.[1] When the actors embraced, they had to hold each other's wigs in position.[2]

With his awareness of his own protean tendencies, and with his ability to identify with the other sex, Kafka was immediately interested in the male impersonator, Frau Klug. She wore a caftan, short black trousers, white stockings, a black waistcoat and a white woollen shirt with a wide loose collar. Her hair was held under a skull-cap, concealed by a soft black hat with a turn-up brim. She and her husband appeared to be 'workers for the community, servants of the temple, notorious idlers accepted by the community, privileged beggars' – Kafka uses the Yiddish word *Schnorrer* – 'for some religious reason, people who as a result of their being set apart, are quite close to the centre of community life, and as a result of their futile wanderings, know a great many songs'.[3] Going to synagogue so seldom and exposed to his father's mockery of everything Jewish, Kafka had never employed Yiddish words (except when quoting his father) and never felt any sense of community, but when he wrote that the Klugs had 'a deep insight into relationships between all members of the community, though, as a result of being cut off from business activities, they don't know what to do with their knowledge', he was not only identifying with them but also assuming himself to be one of the community. 'In us', he was later to tell Gustav Janouch, 'the ghetto still lives – the dark corners, the secret alleys, shuttered windows, squalid courtyards.'[4] The Yiddish theatre troupe reversed his attitude to the Eastern

Jewish tradition. He now wanted to familiarize himself with Yiddish literature, which was 'obviously dedicated to a continuity of national struggle that determines every work. An attitude not found in such a thoroughgoing way in any other literature – not even that of the most oppressed people.'[5] The actors he described as

Jews in a specially pure form because they live only in the religion, but without weariness, understanding or upset. They seem to make fools out of everyone, laugh straight after the murder of a noble Jew, sell themselves to a renegade, dance with their hands held delightedly to their earlocks when the unmasked murderer poisons himself, calling on God, and all this only because they are so volatile, sinking to the ground at the slightest pressure, and so sensitive, readily dissolving into dry-eyed weeping (they do all their weeping with grimaces), but once the pressure is taken off, they haven't the slightest weight to keep them from bouncing into the air.[6]

He saw them as reflections – at once caricatured and caricaturing – of himself, but also of his father: they were clownishly arrogating the right to ridicule everyone. By the end of the year he had attended at least fourteen of their performances,[7] and probably about twenty. The leader of the troupe, Jizchak Löwy, was to become a close friend; the name of Frau Tschissik, the actress who most attracted Kafka, is first mentioned in the diary on the same day as Löwy's, 14 October.

The two assistants in his novel *Das Schloss* may derive partly from the two choric characters wearing caftans in Lateiner's play *Der Meshumed* (*The Apostate*). Entering the villain's empty room, collecting for the synagogue, they look around, feeling ill at ease. Clownishly incredulous at finding no *mezuzah* – the small metal or wooden cylinder containing a roll of parchment inscribed with verses from Deuteronomy – on the doorposts, they jump up and down as if catching flies, slapping the tops of the door-frames. They have not yet spoken a word.[8] Kafka was fascinated by the way they could occupy the front of the stage, 'large as life and often on tiptoe with both legs in the air',[9] not so much undercutting the suspense as cutting it to pieces, while the plot was kept healthily and meaningfully alive further upstage.[10] 'Despite their outspread arms and snapping fingers, the murderer is visible behind them, tottering towards the door, poisoned, his hand at his collar, which is really too large.'[11]

In the Yiddish theatre, as in synagogue services, rhythm and sung melody were basic to the excitement generated, and in the audience, as in the congregation, the inclination was to join in by swaying the body. Kafka, who was not immune to the urge, was reminded of the šlapák, a Czech folk dance.[12]

The plays were mostly passed orally from one troupe of actors to another. Christian roles would be doubled or even trebled to show how one Jewish actor could cope with them, and if he played them badly it was only the Christian element that was being debased. [13] God's hand would sometimes be seen in the action, as when a villain was struck blind. In the trial scene of *Der Meshumed* the two characters in caftans are involved as witnesses, instructed by the villain in what to say, as well as being used chorically to register joy when things begin to go badly for him. He has become a Christian and a murderer. Repenting as the poison takes its effect, he again prays to the Jewish God.

It might sound as though the plays and the performances were too crude to have any influence on Kafka's feelings about assimilation or Judaism. But his experiences in the shabby café were like a revelation. He saw that Jewish theology, Jewish ritual, Jewish folklore, Jewish culture were intertwined in a tradition that was cut off neither from artistic expression nor from him. He could not have known yet how the plays were going to help him towards self-realization as a writer, but he felt inexplicably elated by them. In his diary he gave them more space than he had ever given to German theatrical performances.

But his malaise persisted. He had a recurrent tension over the left half of his skull.

It feels like an inner leprosy, and when I merely consider it, disregarding its unpleasantness, it makes the same impression as a cross-section of a skull in student textbooks or as an almost painless dissection, when the knife, rather cool, cautious, often stopping and retracing its tracks, frequently lying still, slices into the integument, already thin as paper, near the working parts of the brain. [14]

Again and again we get this image of the knife – often a butcher's knife – cutting into his flesh. This relish for the destructive blade follows like an obscene corollary on the equation of living with suffering.

Possibly the Yiddish performances influenced Kafka's nightmares. The troupe had arrived when dreams were taking a stronger grip on him – none of his previous dreams had been given so much space in the diary as the one about metal attached to a cheekbone. It was a coincidence that the style of Yiddish theatre was dreamlike in being simple, emotional, unrealistic, liable to abrupt and illogical jumps in narrative sequence, tinged with bizarrerie. He even began reviewing his dreams as if they were plays, praising one for 'a small comic scene consisting of two ripostes I've forgotten, which resulted in that tremendous pleasure dreams can give'. [15] What he could remember was walking through a long row of houses, rather as one walks through carriages in a tram. In one room a bed stood against a dark or dirty sloping wall. The cover, crumpled by the sleeper's feet, was hanging down in a point. Embarrassed at walking through bedrooms, Kafka took long strides on tiptoe, trying not to look around. Interspersed between the houses were brothels. In the last one the furthest wall was either made of glass or broken through, and prostitutes were lying towards the edge of the floor. One of them had her head dangling over the edge into the air. After fingering her legs, Kafka rhythmically pressed the upper parts of her thighs, deriving so much pleasure from it that he couldn't understand why he didn't have to pay. But when the girl turned her back on him, it was covered in scarlet circles with paling edges. They were all over her body, and there were tiny particles of red in his fingers, like powdered sealing-wax. Brod, who had been occupying himself with the neighbouring girl, was sitting on the ground, eating a thick potato soup. When the potatoes peeped up like large balls, he either pushed them down or just turned them around.[16] These images seem to merge Kafka's brothel experiences with his parents' sexuality and his mother's cooking. The suggestion of dried blood on the Christian girl's body – Kafka had seldom if ever had sexual relationships with non-Jewish girls except in brothels – may derive from memories of the accusations about ritual slaughter.

On the evening before the dream, Kafka had seen the Yiddish troupe in Zigmund Faynmann's *Die Sedernacht* – the Seder is the ceremony performed in Jewish homes on the first two evenings of Passover. 'At times ... the only reason we failed to intervene in the action was not that we were just spectators but that we were too moved.'[17]

On 18 September the *Tetschen-Bodenbacher Zeitung* had carried an anonymous leading article describing the crisis-ridden developments in the Prague office of the Arbeiter-Unfall-Versicherungs-Anstalt and attacking the Bohemian entrepreneurs for extensive fraud over contributions. It fell to Kafka, who had now been working at the institute for more than three years, to reply in print, and on 10 October he wrote what he called 'a casuistical article for and against my insurance institute'.[18] It was about five thousand words, and it appeared on the front page of the supplement to the newspaper on 4 November under the title, 'Die Arbeiterunfallversicherung und die Unternehmer' ('Workers' Accident Insurance and the Entrepreneurs').

Elli's husband, Karl Hermann, was trading in asbestos, and Kafka was invited to become one of the partners in what was to be 'Prague's first asbestos factory'.[19] This involved him not only in applying, once again, to the police for a certificate of good conduct, which was issued in October, but also in consultations with a tiresomely talkative lawyer, who had a poor opinion of the supreme court. He maintained that its decisions were contradictory, and that it was overburdened. The court of appeal, he said, was better, and the court of administration better still.[20]

In the evening Kafka went to see the Yiddish actors in Avraham Goldfaden's *Sulamith*, 'really an opera, but every play that's sung is called an operetta'.[21] At the end of the performance, when Löwy should have appeared to make a speech announcing the play to be performed the following evening, the curtain was still held tightly closed. Eventually it was drawn wide enough apart for him to be seen trying to fend off someone who was attacking him from behind. To keep his balance he took hold of the curtain, putting so much weight on it that the wire supports gave way and it fell down on top of him. M. Pipes, who had been playing a savage servant, was grabbing at Löwy, who was on his knees, and trying to push him sideways off the stage. There were shouts of 'Close the curtain', but the curtain was unusable. On the naked stage Frau Tschissik 'stood pitiably in her pale *Sulamith* face'.[22] Standing on tables and chairs, waiters rearranged the curtain, which was hastily drawn, while the café-owner tried to placate the police official who sat in on each performance, but he seemed more annoyed at being detained than at the disorder. Behind the repaired curtain Frau Tschissik's voice could be heard: 'If we're trying to preach morals to the public from the stage. . . .' Later the head waiter was seen propelling Löwy towards the door.[23]

Brod had mentioned Löwy by name in a *Prager Tagblatt* article about the Yiddish theatre, and this was the first time Löwy had ever been treated to a review.[24] The company director arranged for Löwy to present himself to Brod. They went to a restaurant. With Brod were Kafka, Franz Werfel, Hugo Bergmann, Otto Pick and Oskar Baum. In making friends with Löwy it was Kafka who took the initiative without any feeling of condescension. The friendship was more important to him than any he had begun since meeting Brod. Within three days Kafka was thinking of Löwy 'incessently'.[25] But he was unable to keep their first appointment to meet because a crisis blew up at the shop.

On Saturday the whole staff gave notice. Talking to them, separately or together, Hermann Kafka managed – 'by cogent arguments, cordiality, effective use of his ill-health, his size and former strength, his experience, his cleverness'[26] – to persuade most of them to stay on, but one clerk wanted till Monday to think it over, and on Sunday the bookkeeper wrote that he could not stay after all. When Kafka went to see him at his home in Žižkov, it felt strange to be wanting something from a man he had known for ten years without ever paying much attention to him. Arguing in Czech, Kafka found himself putting on an actorish performance and enjoying it. 'I look silently around the room with a rather elongated face and narrowed eyes, as if I were pursuing something significant into what was unmentionable.'[27] But the man had already signed another contract, and been too intimidated by Hermann Kafka to say so earlier. Neverthe-less Kafka was self-critical. 'In places my arguments were too abstract and formal. Mistake not to have called the wife into the room.'[28]

In the afternoon, instead of meeting Löwy, he took the train to Radotin, where he pleaded on his father's behalf with the clerk. He also went to see the man who had introduced the clerk: perhaps he would be able to intervene. Talking to him in the yard, surrounded by children and chickens, Kafka realized he was being watched by a young girl, who was alternately leaning on the railing of a balcony and hiding behind a door. She was a nurse, looking after a child. 'Under her gaze I don't know what I am, whether I'm unconcerned, ashamed, young or old, arrogant or meek, whether I'm holding my hands in front of me or behind me, whether I'm hot or cold, an animal lover or a businessman.'[29] Returning to Radotin the next day, he saw her again when he was walking alone in the garden, feeling very cold,[30] and again, a few days later, when she did not have the child with her. This time he invited her to come down. Pre-viously she had giggled readily and flirted with him. Without the child she was not so quick to relax, but soon they were laughing together.

Though I was freezing down below, and she above, at the open window. She pressed her breasts against her folded arms, and, with her knees apparently bent, her whole body against the window sill. She was seventeen years old, and took me to be fifteen or sixteen – a notion the whole conversation failed to dispel. Her small nose wasn't quite straight, and therefore threw an extraordinary shadow on her cheek, but this wouldn't have helped me to recognize her again.[31]

Afterwards he went for a walk with the clerk, who would not have left anyway. They could hear the scuffling of rats as they strolled along a path trodden by townspeople across an unused field in the middle of the town. It belonged to one of the factories which surrounded it, 'starkly but only partially illuminated by electric lights'.[32]

Again and again Kafka rebelled inwardly, impotently, against the job that took so much of his week: 'Nothing gets finished, because I've no time, and it builds up so much pressure inside me.'[33] When he had a free day, he could let his restlessness go on mounting till midday, and wear itself out in time for him to sleep peacefully. Most often the restlessness could be unleashed only in the evening. Still at its peak during the night it leaked all over his sleep without fuelling any work that satisfied him.[34] On the surface he was quite unlike Wallace Stevens, who also worked in an insurance office but believed that his poetry depended on 'the grind day after day which keeps me well, cheerful, prosperous, overweight and sober'. But, underneath the surface, the dissimilarity was less extreme: release from office pressures was not always going to increase Kafka's productivity. Writing was one way of releasing tension that accumulated in the job, while much of Kafka's raw material comes from office experiences.

It was not only his writing that seemed to misfire. Each time he took an initiative, he felt, it precipitated a minor disaster.[35] On Monday 16 October he took Löwy to the National Theatre to see *Dubrovačka Trilogija* by Ivo Vojnović. The seats were expensive, and by the end the penurious actor was even more bored than his benefactor, who felt the money could have been better spent.[36]

It was only through the achievements of others that Kafka could enjoy the impression (or illusion) of having all his abilities concentrated. Browsing in the *Aussprüche Napoleons* (*Napoleon's Sayings*), he could swell empathically with pride. 'How readily one becomes momentarily a small part of one's gigantic conception of Napoleon.'[37] Or, listening to a gipsy dance by Bizet, he could feel overpowered by an inner wildness that had been decoyed, compressed into the music. 'At the beginning and ineluctably throughout, a strong affinity to gipsydom, perhaps because a people that dances so wildly shows its tranquil aspect only to friends.'[38] And on the evening of the 17th, when Löwy gave an evening of Yiddish readings, Kafka came into his own. It was not until three days later that he described the performance in his diary, but his recollections were not stale:

Natural to the actor is a recurrent widening of the eyes, which remain for a while in that position, framed by raised eyebrows. Complete truthfulness of the whole reading; the feeble, passive-looking movement of the right arm, raised from the shoulder; the jerking of the pince-nez, which seems borrowed for the occasion, so badly does it fit his nose; the position (under the table) of the leg, stretched out so that the weak joints between thigh and shin are particularly active; the curvature of the back, which looks weak and wretched.... On my way home after the reading I felt all my capacities were co-ordinated, and so, when I arrived, I could speak sharply to my sisters and even to my mother.[39]

Two days later hostility flared against a relation he knew less well, when he found himself face-to-face with Karl Hermann in the presence of a garrulous lawyer. The need to draw up a contract made the brothers-in-law mutually suspicious. Walking diagonally up and down the room, the lawyer tried to relax the tension with anecdotes.[40] The meeting was all the more difficult for Kafka because he was unwell. His body was itching all over. In the afternoon, having his hair cut, and studying the reflection of his hot, blotched face in the barber's mirror, he was nervous the man would think him seriously ill. 'Also the connection between stomach and mouth is partially disturbed, a coin-sized flap moves either up or down or stays down, exerting a light but expanding pressure upwards over my chest.'[41]

The actress who attracted Kafka, Frau Tschissik, had a large mouth, a big bony body, and long, restless arms, Singing the Hebrew national anthem, she gently rocked her large hips, the arms moving up and down, 'hands cupped, as if playing with a slow-moving ball'.[42] It was thanks to Brod that on 21 October he sat next to her when they ate together in a large party after the performance of Scharkansky's *Kol Nidre* – the name of the main prayer said on the Day of Atonement.[43] 'Frau Tschissik (I so enjoy writing the name) likes nodding her head at table even while eating roast goose, you believe you can get in under her eyelids with your gaze if you first look carefully along the cheeks, and then, making yourself small, slip in, without having to raise the eyelids, for they're raised, letting out a bluish gleam, which tempts you in.'[44] But even in his diary he never wrote Mania: she would remain Frau T. As an actress, she depended mainly on a frightened look while searching for a way of escape from her antagonist, on the softness of her voice, which, aided by an inner resonance, could mount heroicially without being raised, on a joyful expression that spread from her face through her high forehead into her hair, and on the erectness of her stance, which forced the audience to concentrate on her whole body.[45] He could hear her voice without feeling 'the ghost of a shudder on my cheekbones',[46] even when she fluffed her lines badly enough to turn upstage in agitation. Beside her muscular mouth, the smoothness of her cheeks was remarkable. Her young daughter struck Kafka as 'rather shapeless'.[47] Her husband was a socialist whose commitment affected the value judgments he passed on literature. He had heated arguments with Löwy about which writer was the best,[48] and shortage of space in the dressing-room inflamed their acrimony. An actor would come off stage, exhilarated by the performance he had just given, only to have his foot trodden on.[49] The dressing-room behind the stage was so narrow that if an actor was standing in front of the mirror, no one could pass by without pushing aside the curtain and showing himself to the audience.[50]

But what Kafka felt towards the whole troupe was nothing less than love, based on identification. Like him they were talented, idealistic, hard-working, but received little money, gratitude or recognition.[51]

On 24 October he saw Yakov Gordin's play *Der wilde Mensch*, and the following day Löwy read to him all afternoon – from Gordin's play *Gott, Mensch, Teufel* (*God, Man, Devil*) as well as from his own diaries. Gordin struck Kafka as superior to the other Yiddish playwrights: 'he has more detail, more order, and more sequentiality in this order'.[52] In *Der wilde Mensch* a young widow, who marries an old man, with four children, brings her lover into the family, and, with him, ruins it. The daughter takes to prostitution. One son leaves. Another starts gambling and drinking heavily, while the third, Lemekh, becomes so crazed with hatred and love for his stepmother that he murders her. 'The conception of this woman and her lover,' Kafka wrote, 'a conception which asks no one for his opinion, has given me a vague self-confidence of a different kind.'[53] He may have been thinking of borrowing something for his own writing: the father and Lemekh seem to have given him most ideas. As Lemekh declined into insanity, Löwy had to find increasing difficulty in remembering what he had just said – a problem that afflicts Georg in 'Das Urteil' – and the lecherous old father plays the fool, dancing and drinking. This may have inspired the antics of Georg Bendemann's father on the bed, while Kafka may have identified with Gordin, who was quoted in a book he read as calling himself one of those 'who remain isolated and see nothing around them except ignorance, envy, enmity and rancour!'[54]

Lemekh's deterioration is due, apparently, to the way he is treated at home. As the housekeeper says, 'They kill him if he comes in here, so he lies in his own room days on end, with his eyes open, and stares, like an animal waiting to be sacrificed.' In Kafka's 'Die Verwandlung' the animal simile becomes an insect metamorphosis.

At the same time Kafka was being pushed towards such equations by dreams that merged the human with the non-human. A few weeks after the one about the girl with spectacle frames attached to her cheek-bones, he dreamed about an Englishman whose clothes covered not only his body but his face, with slits in the material for mouth and eyes.[55] And sometimes Kafka would dream about human deformation. On the night the Klugs left Prague to rejoin the four children they had not seen for eighteen months, Kafka, who had only just realized how much Frau Klug liked him, dreamed about her as being unnaturally short and almost legless. Two weeks later he had a waking dream about the upper half of a wax woman lying on top of him, her face bent back over his, her forearm pressing against his chest.[56]

In his diary he wrote at length about *Der wilde Mensch* in spite of having to sit at the same table where the rest of the family was playing cards 'specially noisily . . . O [Ottla] laughs with her whole mouth, stands up, sits down, reaches across the table, talks to me.'[57] Miserably convinced that he was writing badly, he felt overshadowed by Brod, and he compared himself with Bernard Shaw, who let his parents support him for nine years. Kafka's parents had to listen when he quoted: 'But although I was a strong young man and my family found itself in poor circumstances, I did not throw myself into the struggle for a livelihood; I threw my mother in and let her support me. I was no support for my old father, on the contrary, I hung on to his coattails.'[58]

Kafka's digestive troubles made it harder for him to take pleasure in eating, but sometimes his window-shopping was masochistically greedy, especially in front of pork butchers' shops:

If I see a sausage labelled as old and hard, I bite deeply into it in my imagination, and swallow quickly, regularly, ruthlessly, like a machine. The despair immediately induced by this action, albeit imaginary, increases my haste. I shove the long hunks of rib-meat into my mouth, devour them unchewed, and pull them out again behind, tearing through stomach and intestines. Dirty delicatessen shops I eat completely empty. Stuff myself with herring, pickled cucumber, all the bad old acid foods. Sweets from their tins are shaken into me like hail. So I enjoy not only my health but also a suffering which is painless and soon over.[59]

Löwy was sometimes coming to the flat, staying for perhaps three hours at a stretch,[60] and sometimes accompanying Kafka and Ottla on long walks.[61] He loved the force of Löwy's enthusiasm, and sometimes found himself imitating it.[62] His father naturally disliked the shabby actor, and one day, in his presence, launched into an insulting tirade about the strange people who were being admitted to the house, and the uselessness of entering into such relationships.[63] Kafka, who often let his father abuse him, was outraged;[64] Löwy, for his part, was accustomed to being insulted as if he were a tramp or a beggar: this was the way Yiddish actors were treated, even by Jews.[65] But a few days later when his father quoted the proverb: 'If you lie down with dogs you get up with fleas,' Kafka lost his temper. His outburst was received in silence. Eventually Hermann Kafka said: 'You know I mustn't be upset and I need to be treated with consideration. So that's how you speak to me. Now I've had quite enough upsets for one day, more than enough. So don't speak to me like that.' Kafka answered: 'I make great efforts to restrain myself.' But he sensed in his father 'as always at such moments of extremity, the existence of a wisdom which I can no more than scent'.[66] He realized neither that he was idealizing his father nor that he was reacting as to an unjust parental attack on a younger brother. In a sense he would be emulating this younger sibling in all his animal identifications: empathy as literary acting.

The friendship with Löwy, who had studied abortively at a *Yeshivah*, a rabbinic college, and the growing familiarity with Yiddish literature, deepened Kafka's interest in the Hasidic tradition, and at the beginning of November he read Heinrich Graetz's *Geschichte des Judentums* (*History of Judaism*), stopping periodically 'to let my Jewishness collect itself'.[67] Gordin's play *Schechite* (*Slaughtering*) which Kafka saw on 24 November, contained quotations from the Talmud, and in the next few days he noted down rulings from the Talmud and the Kabbalah in his diary.[68]

Guilty about hearing noises in the night, Kafka seldom protested about daytime noises; though he was tormented by the opening and shutting of doors, the slam of the oven door in the kitchen, the sound of ashes being scraped out of a stove, Valli's shouted enquiry whether Father's hat has been brushed, someone else's attempt out of consideration for Kafka to shush her, a shouted riposte, the unlatching of the front door, its slam as Father went out, the singing of the two canaries. As so often, aggressive impulses boomeranged back against him and, translating himself into a reptile simile, he wondered 'whether I shouldn't open the door a narrow crack, crawl like a snake into the next room, and beg my sisters and their companion for quiet'.[69]

His dissatisfaction with his writing came into sharp focus when one of his stories was read by Brod at Oskar Baum's house. Kafka felt as though the sentences in the story were disordered and full of holes. He even felt guilty of imitating Brod's prose. 'I explain it to myself as the result of having too little time and tranquillity to dig the possibilities of my talent fully out of myself. That's why only broken beginnings see the light of day. . . . Each tiny fragment of story runs homelessly around, driving me in the opposite direction.'[70] He felt more relaxed in Baum's house when Brod was away in Breslau. 'I felt free, could carry each movement to its completion.'[71]

On 6 November the Yiddish troupe was giving its last performance, and he took flowers for Mania Tschissik, but he was worrying so much about whether the flowers would wilt before they were presented to her that he had them unwrapped by a waiter, and then, seeing kitchen staff and 'several dirty regular guests' handling them, felt too anxious to concentrate on her performance.[72] Having brought a non-Jewish friend from the office, he was uncertain how much to explain. The play was Goldfaden's *Bar Kochbar*, and the Klugs had been replaced by unpaid extras who barely managed to avoid giggling on stage. One actor's false beard shook so much with concealed laughter that it slipped out of position. The Roman soldiers who had to arrest Frau Tschissik were so nervous of touching her that she had to pull them to her, and in the prison scene, when she had to remove the helmet of a drunken Roman governor who was visiting her, she found a crumpled towel inside it, presumably because the helmet had been hurting the actor's head. The play did not end until after two in the morning, and when the head waiter presented the flowers to her, no one seemed to pay much attention.[73] She did not even find out who had sent them until just before she left Prague.[74] Löwy, who had promised to tell her, had let him down, but would not admit it.

Kafka had wanted 'to appease my love a little; it was quite useless. It could be done only through literature or sleeping together.'[75]

The actors did not know where they were going. Löwy wanted to play in Brünn, but by sleeping till four he had made them miss the train; Pipes preferred the idea of Nuremberg. Kafka sat down with them in the café while they argued across a table. He would have liked to impress Frau Tschissik, who was sitting opposite him, but when she smiled at him, he looked away, not wanting to seem amused at Pipes's excitement, and not wanting to make it obvious that he was in love with her.[76] Eventually he brought himself to intervene. 'Why go as far as Nuremberg in one jump?' he demanded. 'Why not give a few performances at a smaller town in between?'

When she asked whether he knew of one, he had to look at her. 'All that was visible of her body above the table, all the roundness of shoulders, back and breast was soft, despite her bony, almost rough build, which was apparent when she was on stage in European clothes. Absurdly I suggested Pilsen.'[77] The regular customers who were sitting at the next table suggested Teplitz. Her husband favoured Teplitz, and she agreed. They asked about train fares. As long as they could earn enough to live on, they said, it would be all right. Kafka offered to write a letter of introduction for them to an acquaintance in Teplitz, a doctor. Pipes, his heart still set on Nuremberg, asked for lots to be drawn between the three towns, and in this way they decided on Teplitz. Excitedly Kafka sat down at another table to write the letter, and then left, saying he would find out the exact address of his acquaintance. The name would have been sufficient by itself, and anyway no one at home would know the address. 'In embarrassment, while Löwy got ready to accompany me, I played with the hand of the woman and the chin of her daughter.'[78]

The day after they left he had a dream which featured an imperial castle besieged and occupied by a revolutionary crowd. Stage events were confused with reality. In one act the set, which represented the Altstädter Ring, was so large that it engulfed the auditorium. The audience had become an on-stage crowd. The stage floor was rocking slowly. It was the most beautiful set of all time. Dim sunlight was fragmentarily reflected in the stained glass window on the south-east side of the square, which was very steep, the pavement almost black. In the courtyard of the small castle were monuments which normally stood in the square. The French revolution was being enacted in Prague because of the set. The mob occupied the castle while the court was away at a fête. Kafka ran out into the open over the moulding of a fountain that was usually in the square but now in the castle courtyard. Hung with garlands of flowers, the court carriages were coming at a gallop from Eisengasse, but, braking a long way from the castle, they slid across the pavement with locked wheels, horses rearing. A crowd streamed past Kafka out into the square, among them a girl he knew, accompanied by a well-dressed man. The castle in the dream may have been based on the Lieutenant-Governor's castle, which Kafka used to call Mount Zion. Sometimes when he walked to it, it seemed to him that the gates matched the colour of the sky.[79]

10 Bachelor Life

There was nothing Kafka wanted more than to marry and have a family. In a meeting at the lawyer's office to discuss the draft partnership agreement for the asbestos factory, he was sidetracked into a daydream when the lawyer came to the provisions about the wife and children he might have in the future. 'Facing me I saw a table with two big chairs and a smaller one. At the idea of never being in a position to fill these or any similar three chairs with self, wife and child, I was overcome with such despondency that I sidestepped my excitement by asking the lawyer the only question I still had after his long reading.' The question revealed his failure to take in what had been read.[1]

In bed one night, a week later, he thought before falling asleep about the hardships of bachelor life – solitary evenings, having to carry one's meals home, having no wife to go upstairs with, nobody to look after one when ill, awareness of having cut the chain of marriages that led to one's own birth, envious admiration of other people's children.[2] The diary entry is reproduced almost verbatim in 'Das Unglück des Junggesellen', which is more like a prose poem than a story. It was published in *Betrachtung*, the collection he made in 1912, and the line of thought continues into the story he wrote early in 1915, which Brod later titled 'Blumfeld, ein älterer Junggeselle' ('Blumfeld, an Elderly Bachelor'). Having no one to watch him climbing the six flights of stairs to his room, putting his dressing-gown on, lighting his pipe, sipping his home-made kirsch, or going to bed, and not wanting to feel secretive about any of these activities, Blumfeld thinks of getting a small dog.[3]

Unease made its way freely from Kafka's mind to his body. He felt he was 'intended' (*bestimmt*) – he could not have said by whom – to correct evil conditions in other people's lives, and inability to relieve the tedium of Elli's married life gave him a momentary sensation of numbness in the muscles of his arm,[4] while inability to exploit his own talents produced more pronounced physical symptoms. Lying in bed, he would think of his faculties as if they were objects he could hold in his hand. When his chest tightened, they were tightening it; when his head ached, they were setting it on fire. To protect himself from himself he would think of pulling a cap with a visor down hard over his forehead. But awareness of blood pounding inside the tight head was inseparable from awareness of waste.[5]

Seldom able to sleep at night, except intermittently and nightmarishly, he would sleep on the sofa during the day, or lie there trying to sleep. When the old housekeeper called, wanting to see him, he sent a message that he was out, and went on lying there, listening to the conversation she had about him in the next room with the cook and his sisters' companion. He had been good and obedient, she said, with a quiet disposition. The other two women were equally laudatory. The cook said he would go straight to heaven. But there he lay on the sofa, feeling 'booted out of the world. . . . My joints are sore with exhaustion, my scraggy body trembles its way towards destruction in convulsions whose nature it dare not recognize, my head twitches amazingly.'[6] Later the same day he wrote: 'With a body like this nothing can be achieved. I must expect constant frustration from it.'[7] After several almost sleepless nights, it was so hard for him to see beyond the painful present that he would gladly have died. 'My body is too long for its weakness, it hasn't the least bit of fat to engender a beneficent warmth, to keep inner fire alight, no fat to nourish the spirit beyond its daily need without damage to the whole. How could the weak heart, which has often been troubling me lately, pump blood all through these legs?'[8]

The return of the Yiddish troupe gave him some pleasure. He was glad to see Löwy again, but Frau Tschissik had quarrelled with the others, and left the troupe, together with her husband. They had been replaced by a couple called Liebgold. Seen in full face the wife was pretty, but her profile was ruined by her long, sharp nose, and she was illiterate.[9] Frau Tschissik was working in Berlin, where a company had taken her in 'out of pity . . . initially setting a low value on her and making her sing duets in an old-fashioned dress and hat'.[10] At least, that was what Löwy said; soon Kafka saw her with her husband in the Graben. She was wearing the dress she had worn in *Der wilde Mensch* after the girl turns to prostitution. Kafka turned away without greeting them, and he was too nervous to turn round until they were out of sight. She had seemed smaller. Her left hip had been thrust forward, her right leg bent, the movements of throat and neck very quick. Her head had been close to her husband while she tried, with her arm crooked outwards, to take his. He had been wearing his small summer hat with the brim turned down. Guessing they had gone to the Café Central, Kafka followed, waiting for a long time on the other side of the Graben until she appeared at the window. When she sat down, he could see only the rim of her hat.[11] Afterwards he dreamed that he was walking next to her down a long, narrow, blank-walled passage inside a tall glass-domed house with two entrances. She was apologizing, imploring him not to believe what people were saying about her. At the second entrance her husband was whipping a shaggy blond St Bernard, standing on its hind legs.[12]

Kafka liked to believe he could exteriorize all his anxiety by writing, and could formulate something he could interiorize.[13] It was comforting, anyway, to compare his frustration with Löwy's dissatisfaction and indifference towards everything the troupe did. Though Kafka considered homesickness to be Löwy's main affliction, he could identify even with that.[14] The actor's friendship often seemed indispensable.[15] By Christmas they were seeing each other regularly every evening, Löwy, to avoid an encounter with Kafka's father, waiting outside in the cold. Usually Kafka kept him waiting about half an hour.[16] One evening he looked down from a window to see Löwy, who suffered from severe headaches, leaning against a wall, clutching his forehead.[17]

The reason Kafka gave himself for unpunctuality was immunity to the pains of waiting, coupled with ignorance of what they were like. 'I wait like an ox.'[18] Waiting an hour for Brod, pacing up and down, glancing occasionally at the clock, was almost as pleasant as lying on the sofa.[19]

Six days before Christmas Frau Tschissik acted again at the café. Her body was now more attractive than her face, which looked narrower than before, drawing too much attention to her forehead, which wrinkled when she spoke. The disparity between head and beautifully rounded body made him think of a centaur. There was a stain on her short-sleeved blouse. Talking to her again he could not stop himself from asking why she had gone to Dresden, though she would not want to talk about her quarrel. 'My love hadn't really caught hold of her, only fluttered round about her, now nearer, now further away. It can find no resting place.'[20]

When Kafka's father grumbled at him for taking so little interest in the factory, he listened in silence, but started going there after finishing work at the office. Unaware of the trouble this cost him, his mother was making less and less effort to defend him against her husband's onslaughts. Talking to her briefly one morning at breakfast about children and marriage, Kafka saw that she viewed his malaise, his commitment to writing, and his indifference to the factory as minor problems which would vanish as soon as the right girl came along. He would marry, have children, take more interest in business and less in literature.[21]

His growing interest in Eastern Jewish traditions made him no more tolerant of Jewish rituals, which 'are on their very last legs . . . have only a historical character'.[22] He watched his sixteen-day-old nephew being circumcised. The short, bow-legged *mohel* (circumciser) already had 2,800 operations to his credit. 'One sees blood and raw flesh, the *mohel* works briefly with his long-nailed, trembling fingers, pulling skin from somewhere like the finger of a glove over the wound. . . . Now only a short prayer remains to be said, while the *mohel* drinks wine and with his finger, which isn't yet quite unbloody, puts some wine on the child's lips.'[23]

When his assistant said the grace after meals, the two grandfathers were the only people present who weren't day-dreaming or bored or failing to understand the Hebrew.[24]

Even if Kafka's New Year's Eve dinner had not consisted of parsnips and spinach, the awareness that another year had passed would probably have prompted another bout of psychological stock-taking and self-criticism. He had arrived, he felt, at maturity of self-knowledge, but with so much time and energy channelled wastefully into office work, he could not come fully alive. This must be why there were no signs of age on his face. If he made progress with his real work – his writing – his features would reflect it. Other propensities should be allowed to atrophy. He did not have enough energy to cultivate his capacity for listening to music, making love, eating, drinking, or philosophical reflection.[25] But he so enjoyed reading to his sisters that he would sometimes even sacrifice writing time. 'I give way totally to the rage for proximity to the good writing I read, melting into it not through any merit of my own but through my listening sisters' attentiveness, which has been stimulated by the reading and is unresponsive to inessentials, while my vanity has enough of a hushing-up tendency to let me participate in the sense of having created the effect that the work is having.'[26] But it was only to them that he could read unhampered by self-consciousness. With Brod or Baum he was more aware of his performance and less confident of its quality: 'I flutter around the text with my voice, trying to force my way in here or there, because they want me to.'[27]

To feel relaxed he needed to feel possessed by something stronger than himself. Sometimes he could arrive at 'coolness and detachment. Out walking, yesterday evening each little street sound, each glance directed at me, each shop-window photograph more important than I was.'[28]

But the simple act of going out for a walk might provoke parental resistance. If the weather outside was bad and if he had been sitting in an indoor jacket with no apparent intention of going out, he could not, even at the age of twenty-eight, change his mind, without an argument. Not feeling either free or strong when inside the house, he would, once outside, feel a surge of energy. Merely escaping into the street could feel like a minor adventure.[29]

One of the pleasures – subordinate but important – in theatregoing was in observing the actors as human beings in action. Watching Frau Klug at a benefit performance, he was completely held only by her first song:

after that I have the closest involvement in every aspect of her appearance, in her arms, which are outstretched with snapping fingers as she sings, in the tightly twisted curls at her temples, in the thin shirt, innocently flat under her waistcoat, in the lower lip, which pouts in relishing the effect of a joke ('You see I can speak all the languages there are, but in Yiddish'), in the plump little feet in white stockings, held down by her shoes to behind the toes.[30]

He appreciated her self-confidence and her self-consciousness. When Frau Tschissik was on stage, he enjoyed watching her body. 'One of her important gestures moves outwards like a shudder from her hips, which are trembling but held rather stiffly.'[31] He still felt confused in her presence.

> Her large mouth, which was so close to me, took on surprising but natural shapes. The conversation seemed likely – and it was my fault – to peter out hopelessly, and then, making a hasty effort to express all my love and devotion, I managed only to remark that things were going badly for the troupe, that their repertoire was exhausted, that therefore they wouldn't be able to stay much longer, that the indifference of Prague Jewry to their work was inexplicable.[32]

Without wanting to be involved in family life, Kafka hated to feel excluded. He neither liked to let himself be drawn into arguing with his argumentative father nor to feel ignored by him. The flow of provocations seemed incessant, but he could not be sure which were real and which were imaginary. When Elli's young son Felix came to stay, he slept in the girls' room with the door left ajar, while the door of Kafka's room was closed. Irrationally he took this as meaning that the family wanted to lure Felix into it and to exclude him.[33]

The relationship with Brod was functioning less compensatorily than usual. Collaboration on *Richard und Samuel* merely highlighted their temperamental differences. Without ceasing to admire Brod's energy, Kafka disliked his 'calculating pettiness and hastiness', resenting the domineering behaviour that was calculated to ginger him out of wasting his literary talent. The tension made him condemn himself as 'unfit for friendship'.[34] On New Year's Eve, next to Brod in the crowded Graben, Kafka pressed his hand without looking him in the eye.[35] A week later he was finding it easier to look at Brod 'when his face was in the dark, although mine in the light can give itself away more easily'.[36] When Brod failed or refused to acknowledge Kafka's mood, he could not acknowledge it himself, which led to insincerity. 'On the way home after saying goodnight, regret at my duplicity and pain at its inevitability.'[37] He decided to start a separate notebook on his relationship with Brod. 'What isn't written down wavers in front of one's eyes, and optical accidents determine one's judgment.'[38]

At the office he lost his temper with Pfohl, the head of his department, and made peace only by dint of writing an apologetic letter.[39] In the middle of January he was spending little time either with his diary or with Brod, but a lot with the Jewish actors. Impatient to arrive at an understanding of Jewishness, he was reading books on Yiddish literature and on Judaism.[40] He tried to help the actors, drafting a circular for them, and he speculated about Jewish speech patterns. Admiring and envying their ability to exteriorize moods – was this characteristic of Eastern Jews? – he wondered whether some of the recurrent Yiddish phrases – 'Weh ist mir', for example, and 'S'ist nicht', were intended less to cover embarrassment than to stir up the stream of speech which was too sluggish.[41] He went for the first time to an event organized by the Bar Kochbar society, an evening of folk songs, with a lecture, and at the beginning of the next month he attended a lecture in the Jewish Town Hall by Dr F. A. Theilhaber, who argued that German Jewry was doomed.[42]

When he felt well and self-possessed, he was almost euphoric. On his way to see *Orpheus in der Unterwelt* in February, 'My inner being tasted like honey. Drank it at a single draught!'[43] Inside the theatre he had to stand, and the euphoria vanished. The performance was so bad and the audience so uncritically enthusiastic that he left after the second act.[44] A few days earlier he had seen Frank Wedekind and his wife Tilly in his play *Erdgeist* (*Earth Spirit*). Kafka was impressed by the clarity and precision of her voice, by her 'narrow face, shaped like a crescent moon',[45] and by her stance, the calf of one leg forking sideways.[46] 'Clarity of the play even in retrospect, so that one returns home calm and self-possessed.'[47]

Though not always accurate, his self-observation was relentless, especially when he was repressing irritation or simulating more goodwill than he felt. The trick was to generate extra energy.

I tear myself out of the armchair, stride round the table, move head and neck, make the eyes sparkle, tense the surrounding muscles. Go against each feeling, greet Löwy cordially if he arrives, amiably allow my sister to stay in my room while I write, swallow in long draughts everything said at Max's, despite the pain and the exhaustion.[48]

But all this involved reducing himself to something like an inert mass, letting himself feel 'blown away', not allowing himself a single unnecessary step, staring out at other people with an animal gaze. 'A characteristic gesture in such a condition is to run one's little finger along the eyebrows.'[49]

Going dutifully but pleasurelessly to the asbestos factory, where twenty-five workers were employed,[50] he was uncertain of how to behave towards the girls

in their intolerably dirty and befouled clothes, hair as dishevelled as in bed, expressions on their faces held rigid by the incessant din of the transmission belts and of the individual machines, which break down unpredictably for all their automation. They aren't people, you don't greet them, you don't apologize if you bump into them, if you call them over for some small errand, they perform it but return at once to their machines, a nod of the head's enough to tell them where to begin, they stand there in their petticoats, subject to petty-minded domination, without having enough relaxed understanding to acknowledge it and appease it with subservient looks and movements. But when it's six o'clock, and they tell each other, untie the scarf from around neck and hair, dust themselves down with a brush that's handed around and impatiently called for, pull their dresses on over their heads, wash their hands as clean as they can – so finally they're real women, who despite paleness and bad teeth can smile, shake their stiff bodies, they're not to be bumped into, stared at or ignored, you step back against greasy crates to let them pass, keep your hat in your hand as they say good evening, and don't know how to react when one of them holds out your winter coat for you to put on. [51]

Remembering the one-man show Löwy had given last year, Kafka had the idea of putting one on for him in front of a larger audience in the banqueting room of the Jewish Town Hall. Kafka would make all the arrangements – book the hall, organize the tickets, arrange for the pro- gramme to be printed, advertise the performance in the newspapers, persuade the Bar Kochbar Society to take a block booking, inform the police, who would arrange for a censor to attend – but he wanted Oskar Baum to deliver an introductory lecture on Yiddish, and when Baum, after agreeing, changed his mind, Kafka decided to give the lecture himself. This caused him more misgivings than any of the other work he was taking on. 'I was completely at the mercy of uncontrollable twitch- ings, the pulsing of the arteries jumped all over the body like little fires, if I sat down, my knees trembled under the table, and I had to press my hands together.' [52] Struggling to write notes for the speech, he made no headway until the evening before the performance, but with help from Brod's parents he arranged everything else – not without anxiety but without much difficulty. His own parents not only failed to help but refused to attend. [53]

During his introductory speech, Kafka felt proud, abnormally alert and confident, cool towards the audience. [54] He said it would have less trouble than it expected in understanding Yiddish: 'Yiddish is everything, words, Hasidic melody, and the essence of this Eastern Jewish actor himself.' [55] Only inexperience restrained Kafka from gesturing enthusiastically with his arms. He was in good voice, had no trouble with his memory and felt self-confident enough to deal peremptorily with three town hall porters who were demanding twelve kronen. He gave them six. [56] 'Powers appeared to which I'd gladly entrust myself, if only they remain.' [57] According to the Jewish weekly *Selbstwehr* (*Self-Defence*), Kafka's speech was 'lovely, charming', and Löwy 'showed himself to be a powerful and effective performer'.[58] One of the poems he recited, 'Die Grine' by Morris Rosenfeld, was about greenhorns – penurious Jewish immigrants arriving in New York and being mocked by the crowd that gathers round them.

The gain in self-confidence had its effect – at least on his fantasies. Writing sleepily and effortlessly,[59] he described himself standing in the doorway, watching the passers-by, seizing a ribbon hanging from a girl's skirt, letting it slide through his fingers, playfully stroking the shoulder of another passing girl and challenging the man who reprimanded him by striking him over the fingers.

I pulled him behind the bolted half of the door, my threat consisted of raised hands, glances out of the corners of the eye, a step towards him, a step back, he was glad when I shoved him away. From now on I naturally summoned people to me, a signal with the finger was enough, or a brisk glance with no hesitation in it.[60]

In actuality Kafka could not so easily overcome his shyness. Introduced to Hofmannsthal after a reading, he said nothing,[61] just felt envious of Hofmannsthal's freedom from the office routine: he had 'the satisfied face – resistant to all disappointments – of a man who's doing the work he chooses.'[62] But a month later when a boy aimed a large ball at the bottom of a servant girl walking defencelessly in front of him, Kafka grabbed the boy, half-choked him, and pushed him aside, swearing. Then he walked away without even looking at the girl.[63]

So long as he went on living in his parents' flat, he was easily tilted towards thoughts of suicide. His father shouted a great deal, provoking the others to shout back. There are recurring complaints in the diary about din in rooms on either side of him. Often he was unable to write or so distracted he could write only pages he would afterwards destroy. One reason for writing was that it partially insulated him from the noises, and one of the reasons he was later to write so often and at such length to Felice Bauer – the collection of his letters to her is three times as long as *Das Schloss* – is that in writing a letter (as in writing a diary) he did not have to shut himself off from the distracting sounds. He could complain about conversations in neighbouring rooms or sounds made during card games – the slap of cards on the table, the laughter, the jeering, the screams, his father's attempts at mimicry.[64] Nor was failure with his writing his only source of guilt. The baleful presence of his father in the house was like a constant reproach, while Kafka's indifference to the factory was now the focal point in a complex of grievances. In March Hermann Kafka resumed the attack he had begun in December. Why couldn't Franz go there more often? He submitted, sacrificing writing time, feeling guilty about it, and thinking seriously of suicide.[65]

In one sense, keeping a diary was a confession of failure, reaffirmed daily. He was writing but not writing a novel. He was making perfunctory skirmishes in a battle that could be won only by a full-scale attack. Re-reading was therefore painful – a survey of recurrent failures.[66] He could only intermittently feel completely involved, even when he went beyond the autobiographical towards the fictional, as in the episode of the confrontation in the street or in an account of a summer seduction in the Iser mountain. 'Incomprehensibly, as is often the way with lung cases, he threw the girl down on the grass of the river bank, and after a brief attempt at persuasion, took her as she lay there, unconscious with fear. She was the daughter of the landlord and she liked to go out for walks with him in the evening after work.'[67] The sentence in which Kafka felt most involved was: 'Later he had to bring water from the river in his cupped hands and dash it over the girl's face, just to revive her.'[68] He also felt momentarily interested in his description of the indifferent landscape: 'The river spread calmly from the meadows and fields to the distant mountains. Sunshine was left only on the slope of the opposite shore. The last clouds were withdrawing from the clear evening sky.'[69] It is curious that he should already be identifying with a 'lung case'.

But in none of his writing could he feel that he was doing more than 'sticking finger-tips into the truth' – the phrase he used after the publication of his collection *Betrachtung*.[70] In March 1912, believing he was catching hold of himself 'the way one catches a ball on its way downwards',[71] he made up his mind to start work immediately on 'a larger-scale work that will adjust to my abilities without being forced. I won't abandon it if I can possibly hold out. Better live without sleep than survive the way I am.'[72]

In the juvenile novel he had exposed to his uncle's mockery one of the brothers had escaped to America while the other remained in a European prison. Kafka may have been thinking of his cousins, Otto and Oskar, the sons of his Uncle Philipp. Otto probably ran away from home when he was sixteen, and, after studying at the Export Academy in Vienna, emigrated to America; Oskar attended a cadet school in Prague.[73] In March 1912 the *Neue Rundschau* began to publish a series of articles by Arthur Holitscher describing an American journey. His book *Amerika heute und morgen* (*America Today and Tomorrow*) was published later the same year, and Kafka, who owned a copy, repeated one of the spelling mistakes – 'Oklahama' – in his unfinished novel *Der Verschollene* (*The Missing One* – it was Brod who retitled it *Amerika*). And at the beginning of June Kafka attended a lantern slide lecture on America and its bureaucracy by the Czech Social Democrat František Soukup. Soukup explained that all officials in America were elected.[74] The novel contains a highly unrealistic account of an open-air election meeting held by a candidate for a position as judge.[75]

For Kafka the governing idea was of escape from his father, who often appeared in his dreams together with symbols of imprisonment. In one dream the city of Berlin was nothing but a forest of turnpikes. After stepping with his father through a gate, Kafka was confronted by a sheer wall, which was no obstacle to his father, who scaled it with a dancer's agility, but without making any effort to help his son, who had to clamber up on all fours, though there was human excrement all over the wall.[76]

On 11 June Kafka was examined by Dr Siegmund Kohn, whose report was sufficiently unfavourable for a week's sick leave to be added to his holiday: the patient 'has been suffering for some considerable time from a nervous indisposition which manifests itself above all in almost constant digestive troubles and in sleeplessness.'[77] Doctors had this power to procure stints of freedom for him, but with his naturopathic inclinations, he was consistently suspicious of them: 'If only I had the strength to found a Nature Cure Association.'[78]

Together with Brod he left Prague on 28 June for a holiday in Weimar. They spent the first two nights in Leipzig, sharing a hotel room. The noise of horses on the asphalt, trundling carts and bells on trams made Brod close the bedroom window at four in the morning of their first night. This woke Kafka who, without fresh air, felt 'buried alive'.[79] Daylight did not dispel his dissatisfaction with the city. He noticed a great many monocles in the streets and many heavily bandaged students,[80] wounded presumably in duels.

On the morning of their second day Brod went to see the publisher Ernst Rowohlt, taking specimens of Kafka's writing, and in the afternoon he took Kafka. Rowohlt was four years his junior: 'young, red-cheeked, beads of sweat between nose and cheeks, he moved only above the hips.'[81] With him were Walter Hasenclever and Gerd von Bassewitz, a count who had written a book called *Judas*. 'All three flourished sticks and arms.'[82] Rowohlt was eager to publish something by Kafka, who agreed to collect prose pieces for a book. Once again Brod was helping him into print.

At five o'clock they left for Weimar. It was a short journey, and though it took them a long time to find their hotel, it was not too late to swim from the public beach on the Kirschberg, but night had fallen before he caught his first glimpse of Goethe's house: 'Immediate recognition. Yellowish brown colour all over. Perceptible involvement of all our previous experience in the momentary impression. The darkness of the windows of the disused rooms. The light-coloured bust of Juno. Touched the wall.'[83] In the morning they went to Schiller's house. 'Locks of hair no longer human, yellow and dry as grain.'[84] Returning to Goethe's, they inspected the drawing-rooms, the study and the bedroom. 'A sad sight, reminiscent of dead grandfathers. This garden continuously growing since Goethe's death. The beech tree darkening his study.'[85]

The curator had a pretty daughter. Brod and Kafka were sitting on the landing when she ran past with her small sister. Thinking he heard her voice in the garden, he went out, but too late. He caught sight of her on a balcony, but she came down only later, together with a young man. Kafka thanked her for having called their attention to the garden, and when her mother, Frau Kirchner, came up, they got into conversation with her. Margarethe was standing next to a rosebush. Encouraged by Brod, Kafka went over to her. She was about to leave with her parents on an excursion to Tiefurt, and Kafka was invited to accompany them. He went without Brod, chatting with the coachman and then with her father. They took photographs. 'Finally, on the way home, definite contact without any real communication.'[86]

In the evening, when he met her walking with a girl friend, he and Brod escorted them to the Goetheplatz, and he was told he could come to the garden any time after six in the evening. He did not see her the next day, but went back the day after. She was leaving to do some sewing with a friend, but after visiting Liszt's house in the afternoon, Kafka and Brod went back. Her father showed him the photographs taken at Tiefurt. 'She smiled at me meaninglessly, uselessly behind her father's back. Sad.'[87] He saw her again at the strawberry festival in front of Werther's garden, where there was a concert. 'The mobility of her body in the loose dress.'[88] The next day, Wednesday, she agreed to meet him on Thursday afternoon,[89] but failed to turn up. In the evening he went back to the Goethehaus, where he spoke to her. He looked for her again in the morning, unsuccessfully,[90] but saw her later in the day. 'She certainly doesn't love me, but has some respect.'[91] He gave her a box of chocolates with a little heart and chain entwined about it. She promised to meet him at eleven in the morning in front of the Goethehaus, but, knowing she had to do the cooking, he did not expect her to be there. In fact she spent an hour with him. She was wearing a pink dress and the little heart he had given her. 'No contact with her at all. Conversation kept breaking off and starting up again. Sometimes walking especially fast, sometimes especially slowly. A strain not at any cost to let it become evident that we haven't the slightest thread of anything in common. What keeps us together all through the park? Only my stubbornness?'[92] He said goodbye to her in the evening in front of the kitchen door. She was wearing a ball gown less attractive than her everyday dress, and her eyes were red from weeping after an altercation with the young man who was to partner her to the ball.[93] Kafka never saw her again, but he wrote to her, asking whether she would like to go on receiving cards from him. She replied that it would be a great pleasure for her and her parents to hear from him.[94] She also sent him three photographs of herself.[95]

On 7 July, when Brod returned to Prague, Kafka travelled on alone to a natural therapy sanatorium at Jungborn in the Harz mountains. On the way he visited Halle and Halberstadt, spending his first night in Jungborn at the railway hotel. 'Never have I seen people leaning so beautifully in windows.'[96] At the sanatorium some of his fellow-patients liked to sun-bathe in the nude. 'In the park, reading-room, etc., pretty little fat feet are to be seen.'[97]

The doctor was an ex-officer. 'Affected, insane, tearful, undergraduate laughter. Buoyant gait. . . . He steps out of his consulting room, you go in, passing him. "Kindly step inside", he laughs after you.'[98] He forbade Kafka to eat fruit, but added that there was no need to obey him.[99] He recommended atmospheric baths at night. 'Only don't expose yourself too much to the moonlight, which can be injurious.'[100] Credulously Kafka would slip out of bed at night into the meadow in front of the cabin. Three evenings a week the doctor gave lectures expounding his theories. One was that diaphragmatic breathing stimulated and expanded the sexual organs. It was for this reason, he said, that female opera singers were so sensual.[101]

Persistently wearing his swimming trunks for group gymnastics, which the others performed in the nude, Kafka was dubbed 'the man in the trunks'.[102] The naked bodies made him feel slightly ill.[103] The pleasures of hay-making were not enhanced by 'old men who leap naked over haycocks',[104] and it was disconcerting that naked feet made no sound. 'People creep up on you so inaudibly. Suddenly one of them's there and you've no idea where he came from.'[105] Secretly he may have envied their lack of inhibition, but he was aware only of irritation when a friendly naked stranger stopped at his door to enquire whether he lived there.[106] At night, walking across the meadow to the lavatory, he would find naked bodies asleep in the grass.[107] When it rained he would see an old man 'charging like a wild animal across the meadow', taking a rain bath.[108] Some of the bodies provoked non-human similes: a Swedish widow was like a leather-strap.[109] One night Kafka dreamed he heard Goethe reciting 'with infinite freedom and spontaneity';[110] another dream was that the nude sun-bathers were divided into two hostile groups when a man shouted: 'Lustron and Kastron!' Fighting broke out almost immediately.[111]

Every evening Kafka sat for an hour and a half in the writing room, where no talking was allowed.[112] His progress on *Der Verschollene* was slower, and his evaluation of it lower than in Prague. 'The novel is so big, as if outlined against the whole sky (also as colourless and indefinite as it is today) and I get knotted up in the first sentence I want to write.'[113] But the independence of life in the sanatorium was conducive to the mood he needed: 'an idea of America intimated to these poor bodies.'[114] He persevered, even when it was dreary to re-read what he had written.[115] If anything, sanatorium life encouraged the hostile view he took of himself: 'This opinion is my only good point, it's what, after I've decently contained it in the running of my life, I must never, never doubt, it gives me a discipline, and since I easily go to pieces in face of the unpredictable, it makes me calm enough.'[116] He was determined to complete his book, so it was important not to show it to Brod in its unfinished state. He was trying to create only small units, 'worked on to each other rather than into each other'.[117]

One day he was accosted by the handsome, sun-tanned, bearded, happy-looking man he had noticed lunching with a small child on cherries and dry bread, or lying in the grass with three Bibles open in front of him, taking notes. He introduced himself as a land-surveyor, and gave Kafka evangelical tracts. 'I read a little and then go back to him and try, tentative because of the respect I hold him in, to explain why there's no prospect of grace for me at present.'[118] They went on talking for an hour and a half. 'He sees that I'm close to grace. −How I interrupt all his arguments and refer him to the inner voice. Effective.'[119]

Kafka came nearer to making friends with the atheistic Dr Schiller, a forty-three-year-old local government official from Breslau, who showed him some of his oil-paintings,[120] and Kafka posed for him.[121] They went together to a dance at Stapelberg, where there had been a shooting competition. Picking up a girl he had noticed with two others, eating frankfurters and mustard, Kafka danced with her. She was a farm-girl due in just over three months to go into a convent, but she enjoyed dancing, 'which was especially apparent later on, when I lent her to Dr Schiller'.[122]

After his first two weeks at the sanatorium, Kafka wrote: 'Having come here for social reasons, I'm satisfied that at least this wasn't a mistake. Look at the way I live in Prague. Holidays provide the only outlet for this urge I have to be in other people's company, an urge which changes into anxiety as soon as it's fulfilled.'[123] On the way back to Prague he would avoid Weimar and spend a night in Dresden, where he would 'visit the zoo, in which I belong'.[124]

11 Felice

Back in Prague Kafka found it difficult to select texts for the book. How could he send Rowohlt pieces that needed more revision? 'One isn't entitled to let bad things remain permanently bad unless one's on one's deathbed.'[1] He hated the 'harmful, absurd self-consciousness that goes with reading old things for the sake of publication'.[2] Finally he added only nine texts to the nine that had already appeared in *Hyperion* – enough to fill thirty-one pages. But he still had not decided on the sequence when he took the texts to Brod on 13 August, two weeks after his return from holiday.

It was about nine in the evening when he arrived.[3] Sitting at the Brods' table was a girl who 'looked like a maid. I wasn't at all curious about who she was, immediately taking her for granted. Bony, empty face that carried its emptiness openly. Bare throat. Blouse flung on anyhow. Her clothes gave her an air of domesticity.... Almost broken nose, blond, rather stiff, unappealing hair, strong chin. When I sat down I looked at her more carefully for the first time; as I was sitting there I'd already arrived at an irreversible judgment.'[4] He handed his holiday photographs around, and when the girl got up, he saw she was wearing Frau Brod's slippers. She had got her shoes wet in the rain.[5] She was four years younger than Kafka but took him to be younger than she was. When she casually asked where Kafka lived, he thought she wanted his address so that she could write to him, and the misunderstanding embarrassed him for the rest of the evening, but before they parted they had held hands to confirm their agreement to go to Palestine together next year. They may both have been uncertain whether it was a joke, but Fräulein Bauer told him she wasn't fickle.[6] When Brod offered to show her a picture of Goethe in his underwear, she quoted a line from a play: 'He's still a king even in his underwear.'[7] This irritated Kafka: 'I felt what was almost a displeased pressure in my larynx.'[8] When she left, Brod walked with them towards Felice's hotel, doing most of the talking. Four years later, after becoming engaged to her for the second time, he would still remember 'that spot on the Graben, where, for no reason, but deliberately, because of uneasiness, desire and helplessness, I stumbled several times from the pavement to the street'.[9] At the hotel he crowded into the same section of the revolving door, almost treading on her feet. They said goodbye almost immediately, and she disappeared into the lift.[10]

Two days later he wrote: 'Thought a great deal about – what embarrassment over names – F.B.'[11] Not that she had disturbed the state of 'frightful calm'[12] he was in. Selecting texts for *Betrachtung* had upset his routine. After posting the typescript on the 14th, he found himself re-reading old diaries instead of going back to writing. 'I couldn't live more unintelligently than I do. . . . Instead of shaking myself I sit there wondering how to express all this as insultingly as possible.'[13] The next day he wrote a few pages in the Weimar diary, but he was still like a becalmed boat. 'Evening – the moaning of my poor mother at my not eating.'[14] Pfohl was away till the end of the month,[15] but instead of taking the opportunity to push ahead with his own work, Kafka spent a lot of time asleep or day-dreaming. He read Lenz 'incessantly',[16] but everything seemed to reflect his own mood. Even a street symbolized dissatisfaction: 'each foot is lifted because someone wants to get away from where he is'.[17]

The visit of his Uncle Alfred from Madrid failed to rouse him out of his inactivity, and Werfel's reading of his 'Lebenslieder' ('Life Songs') and 'Opfer' ('Sacrifice') at the Café Arco had only a short-term effect. 'A monster. But I looked him in the eye and held his gaze the whole evening.'[18] Afterwards Kafka felt 'shattered and exalted'. He went to a party where he behaved 'almost wildly and without making any mistakes'.[19] What he remembered most clearly from his uncle's visit was his way of ignoring remarks addressed to him on his way to the lavatory.[20] Though he claimed to be dissatisfied with his life, he behaved with the confidence and curtness of a man who could feel at home anywhere. He enjoyed dining at exclusive restaurants in the company of high-ranking diplomats and military men, and if, going home, he regretted his celibacy, the mood would pass.[21]

During phases of prolonged inertia Kafka felt he would never manage to prod himself back into action. 'Have I finally got stuck, a big thing lumbering along a narrow alley?'[22] One afternoon, lying in bed, he heard a key turn in a lock. 'For a moment my whole body had locks on it, like fancy dress, and at intervals, here or there, something would be unlocked or locked up.'[23]

At Jungborn he had enjoyed playing with children: he took six girls on a merry-go-round and a Big Dipper.[24] At home, hearing his loud-voiced mother and her women-friends dealing with children of the same age-group, he could not bear to stay inside the flat. 'Don't cry! Don't cry! etc. That's his! That's his! etc. Two grown-up people! etc. He doesn't want to. . . . Now! Now!. . . . And how did you like Vienna, Dolphi? Was it nice?. . . . Now just look at his hands.'[25]

Though the inertia was not directed strategically at his unconscious, this was eventually coerced into helping him with the novel. A dream provided the atmosphere and much of the detail for the opening chapter. He was on a long jetty made of square-cut stones. Rows of battleships were at anchor. He was in New York harbour. Instead of rafts there were long bundles of logs, roped together, tilted by the enormous waves or turning right over. 'I sat down, pulled my feet close to me, quivered with pleasure, nearly dug myself into the ground with delight and said: "That's really even more interesting than the traffic on the Paris boulevard."'[26] As in the ending of 'Das Urteil', which was written only a few days later, the phrase's significance depends on the double meaning of the word *Verkehr* (traffic and sexual intercourse). Possibly his uncle's visit had revived the long-buried idea of living in Madrid. New York was an equally unknown quantity. Both represented escape from captivity in Prague.

When Valli's engagement was announced on 15 September, it must have made him think even more about Fräulein Bauer. 'Love between brother and sister,' he wrote cryptically, 'the repetition of the love between mother and father.'[27] Valli was the prettiest of the three sisters, and, without ever being as close to her as he was to Ottla, he may have entertained sexual fantasies about her when the sounds of love-making came through the wall.

Five days later, sitting at a typewriter after six hours in the office, he wrote his first letter to Felice. It was the eve of the Day of Atonement, when the synagogue service began with the prayer Kol Nidre. Last year he had attended the service; but in a 1913 letter he was to tell her that in the past few years he had been to synagogue only twice – for his sisters' weddings – so clearly he did not go on the Day of Atonement in 1912.[28] He begins the letter by introducing himself, as if she might have forgotten him, and suggesting that they should start making arrangements for the trip to Palestine. His more immediate objective is to enter into correspondence with her – 'this is all there'd be for the moment'.[29] He is therefore, charmingly, at pains to recommend himself as a correspondent. He never expects a letter to be answered by return. 'Even when I'm waiting for a letter in suspense that's renewed daily, I'm never disappointed if it doesn't come, and if it finally does, I enjoy being taken by surprise.'[30] He describes himself as an erratic letter-writer, but if his mood falls short of letter-writing, there are always his fingertips to type one. He thought of typewritten letters as belonging to a different species.[31]

It may have been this letter that released him from his inertia. Two days later he wrote 'Das Urteil', having used the word 'Urteil' in his diary for the judgment he had reached while sitting next to Felice at the Brods' table. It could refer to a favourable verdict on her, but why in that case should he have called it irreversible? Could he have been sentencing himself to become engaged to her? His description of her in the diary is unromantic and unflattering. Obviously he was not attracted to her as he had been to Margarethe or to Mania Tschissik. But Felice was available, and sufficiently interested to tell him that she was not fickle. It is obvious from the story that he was already thinking of becoming engaged to her, and one advantage of passing an irreversible sentence on himself was that it gave him the right to fantasize, fictionally, about using the ultimate weapon against his father – the threat of marriage. Elli had made it and implemented it, Valli had made it and would implement it, Kafka, who had not made it, would never be able to implement it. The story is an imaginative attempt at working out the consequences of making it. While writing it he thought of his earlier story 'Die städtische Welt',[32] but Oskar had fought unarmed against his father.

When Kafka sat down to write, his intention was 'to describe a war'.[33] It had been a miserable Sunday. He had spent the whole afternoon 'silently circling around my brother-in-law's relations, who were at our house for the first time'.[34] The story was to be written from the viewpoint of a young man whose window looked out over a river. He was to see 'a crowd of people advance over the bridge, but then everything changed under my hands'.[35] The story is set on a Sunday afternoon, but the hostility of the advancing group was replaced by a hostility between father and son, and, as never before, Kafka found himself taking sides against himself. Kafka lets the son use the ultimate weapon but he lets the father win, and he may have been surprised by the extent to which the son's love for the father shines through the hostility. The Oedipal pattern is reversed not only when the son obediently carries out the death sentence his father has passed on him, but also in removing the mother, who has died some time before the action of the story, making it possible for son and father to come closer together. In reality, most likely, Hermann Kafka had no more desire for his son to arrive at maturity and independence than Kafka had to manage without parental protection, but in the first part of the story maturity is made to seem compatible with harmonious co-operation between father and son who work together in the business. It was only during the mother's lifetime that the son had been held back by the father's despotism in the business, and in the two years since her death the staff has been doubled and the turnover multiplied by five. In Hermann Kafka's shop business had actually been going better since the move.[36]

The father sits in a dark room – in the story 'Die städtische Welt' the father blocks the window by standing up – hung with mementoes of his dead wife, and, as if rejecting Georg's love before he has a chance to express it, the old man complains: 'Mummy's death prostrated me more than it did you.'[37] He also complains that things are being done in the business without his knowledge. But Georg lovingly offers to give his father the brighter room he has been sleeping in. 'There's no hurry, now I'll put you to bed for a while, what you need is rest, come on, I'll help you to get undressed, you'll see, I can. Or would you rather go straight into the front room, then you can lie down in my bed for now.'[38] The sexual overtones become still stronger when Georg picks up the big man in his arms to carry him into the other bedroom. But the old man won't be put down: he clutches firmly at his son's watch-chain, as if to interfere with the natural time-process which changes the balance of power between the generations. Though he does not offer not to become engaged, all Georg's attempts to propitiate his father suggest that he would make any sacrifice to win the old tyrant's love. Without even mentioning it, he decides to take the father with him into his new home.

If Kafka had decided to become engaged to Felice, his main object was to escape from imprisonment in his parents' flat. Once, outside the house, he told Janouch that it only looked as if he were going home: 'Really I'm going up into a prison specially constructed for me, all the more oppressive because it looks like a perfectly ordinary bourgeois home. . . . One can't break one's chains when no chains are to be seen.'[39] But the irreversible commitment brought guilt-feelings of its own. To marry a woman who did not attract him was despicable. He would be resigning his involuntary membership of his parents' marriage, but at least they loved each other, while his love for his sisters was closer to that love than his feeling for Felice. So even if Georg's father gets the facts wrong about what attracts his son to Frieda Brandenfeld, he's still voicing Kafka's self-contempt, condemning his self-condemnation:

'Because she lifted up her skirt like this, the horrible goose', and, to demon-strate, he lifted up his shirt high enough to expose the scar of the war-wound on his thigh, 'because she lifted up her skirt like this and this and this, you made a pass at her, and to satisfy yourself with her undisturbed, you've disgraced the memory of our mother.'[40]

Years later Hermann Kafka launched a similar attack on his son's second fiancée, calling her one of those Prague Jewesses who seduced men by putting on some special blouse:[41] Kafka knew his father well enough to anticipate this reaction. In the story, as the old man kicks his legs out on the bed, Georg shrinks back, remembering what he once resolved – 'to observe everything with great precision so that he could never be out-flanked, surprised from behind or above.'[42] Even his success in the business is dismissed when the old man claims to have prepared the deals that Georg has merely concluded.[43] Georg feels a murderous hope that his father will topple off the bed, but, keeping his balance, he completes the emasculation of his son by threatening to take his bride away from him. Already he has taken away his closest friend, who has been corresponding with him. The son has been abjectly defeated before the death sentence is pronounced.

Writing to Felice on the eve of the Day of Atonement and staying away from the Kol Nidre service, in which the orthodox look forward to the Day of Judgment, thinking of rewards and punishments that God will decree, Kafka must have put the sentence he had passed on himself into a perspective of divine judgment, and he must have remembered Scharkansky's play *Kol Nidre*, in which a Grand Inquisitor is obliged to pronounce judgment on his own daughter. He condemns her to death at the same time as condemning her Jewish lover. They both escape execution by leaping prematurely into the flames.

Another Yiddish play that influenced 'Das Urteil' was Gordin's *Gott, Mensch und Teufel*, which leads more subtly to a similar climax, one human being effectively condemning another to death. Herschele, the Faust-like hero who succumbs to the influence of the Mephistophelean Mazik, loses all respect for his ancient father, formerly a jester, ruins his best friend, Khatskel, whose son is forced to work in Herschele's factory, where he loses an arm – and later his life – as the result of an accident: a coincidental overlap with Kafka's professional preoccupations. When Herschele, learning of the accident, pronounces the traditional benediction ('Blessed be the True Judge'), Khatskel challenges him: does he still believe in the True Judge? Will he be able to settle his account with him, a mere man, let alone with God? Accepting his guilt, Herschele hangs himself with the blood-soaked prayer-shawl of the dead man.[44]

In the first act of *Gott, Mensch und Teufel*, when the father gets drunk, his son carries him to bed. In the second the old man climbs on a chair and declaims in the manner of a jester at a wedding, joking about the way marriage puts an end to youthful irresponsibility. In the story, after the father has been prancing on the bed, Georg calls him a 'comedian', and the word 'devilish' features in the death sentence: 'Once you were an innocent child. But you were a devilish man. Therefore I condemn you to death by drowning.' And insofar as Kafka is condemning himself in the story, it is for the same reason that he will go on condemning himself for the rest of his life: he cannot obey one of the central precepts in Judaism. In his diary he had copied out a phrase from the Talmud which he had heard in Gordin's *Schechite*: 'A man without a woman is not a human being.'[45]

Not that the Yiddish plays were the only possible literary influences. Grillparzer's story 'Der arme Spielmann' ('The Poor Musician'), which

Kafka had read aloud, presumably to his sisters, five weeks before writing 'Das Urteil', [46] is about a powerful, domineering man's ineffectual son, whose decline culminates in the loss of his girlfriend and in becoming a street-musician. [47] In Dostoevsky's *Crime and Punishment* the guilt-ridden Raskolnikov thinks of throwing himself into the river. And in Wedekind's *Frühlings Erwachen* (written 1891; staged 1906) repressive paternalism leads to the suicide of one boy, Moritz Stiefel, who tries to lure another, Melchior, into suicide. Inter-generational conflict was to become one of the main themes in Expressionist plays from Reinhard Sorge's *Der Bettler* (written 1912; staged 1917) onwards. Often, as in Walter Hasenclever's *Der Sohn* (written 1914; staged 1916 in Prague) the conflict between father and son would end in a death. Kafka could not, obviously, have been influenced by these playwrights, but he was familiar with the work of their local precursors such as Gustav Meyrink and Paul Leppin. As J. P. Stern points out, he came close to being 'stuck in the literature of provincial sensationalism', and never met writers outside the Prague circle. [48]

One of the oddities of 'Das Urteil' is that nearly a third of the narrative is devoted to a letter Georg has just finished writing to his bachelor friend who has emigrated to Russia, having been dissatisfied with the prospects at home. Brod has suggested that the friend in Russia can be equated with Löwy, who was unmarried and Russian. [49] Later, writing to Felice, Kafka tells her he has been receiving letters from him which (like Georg's letters from his friend in Russia) are 'all monotonous and full of complaints; there's no way of helping the poor fellow'. [50] But Kafka may also have been thinking of Brod, who had just become engaged; in spite of the compact he had proposed, he would now have much less time to spare for Kafka: 'To me he'll be disengaged.' [51] In other ways the figure of the friend relates to Kafka's bachelor uncle, who 'knows all of Europe except Russia', [52] and in still others to Otto Kafka and to the twin in the juvenile novel who had gone to America. If the polarity between Georg and his friend reflects a polarity between two opposing aspects of Kafka himself, Georg is the businessman who doesn't write but becomes engaged, while the friend is the writing self who remains a bachelor. This would explain why Georg feels he is betraying his friend by becoming engaged, and why he is so shaken when the father claims to have formed an alliance with his friend and to have informed him already about the engagement. That, says the father, is why he hasn't been here for such a long time. Nothing is more likely to have made Kafka suicidal in reality than loss of the ability to write.

Despite the smallness of Frieda Brandenfeld's role in the action, Kafka called it 'your story' when he wrote to Felice about it, and he inscribed 'a story for F' in the line below the title. He had written only one letter to her, addressing her as Fräulein Bauer, but he was already thinking of her as Felice. In his letter of 24 October he tells her that the dedication was written a month ago. When the story was published in Brod's yearbook *Arkadia* (1913) the dedication was 'Für Fräulein Felice B.'.

Kafka's second letter to Felice, written on 28 September at ten o'clock in the morning, immediately after reading her first letter to him, is largely about writing his first to her. This was to be a very literary correspondence, and essentially less private than most of Kafka's writing, which was done not for publication but for himself. From now on much of the literary energy that had gone into the diary would be diverted to the letters, and after the entry of 25 September 1912 the diary is blank for nearly five months. In this second letter he surveys the space between the intention of writing and the action. For ten days he had been drafting the letter mentally. Unable either to memorize all he drafted or use the fragments he did remember, he kept pondering and procrastinating. But he had been so hopeful of receiving a reply that he arrived at the office singing on the Feast of St Wenceslas, a public holiday, when the only reason for going there was to see whether she had written,[53] the office address being the only one on the writing paper he had used. There was nothing he wanted more, now, than another letter from her, and falling into the pattern of Brod's proposals to him, he asked her to keep a diary for him. 'This is less troublesome and more rewarding. . . . Make entries, for instance, about when you arrive at the office, what you had for breakfast, the view from your office window, your work there, the names of your friends, male and female, why you get presents, who tries to sabotage your health by giving you confectionery, and the thousand things of which I know nothing.'[54] From the outset he was determined to stop her from baulking, as Hedwig had, at his interest in the minutiae of her daily life.

Though the certainty of having written well in 'Das Urteil' brought a concomitant certainty that his novel was 'on the atrocious lowlands of literature',[55] he went back to it, reinvigorated almost to the point of euphoria. On 29 September Brod noted: 'Kafka in ecstasy. Goes on writing all night.' On 1 October: 'Kafka in incredible ecstasy.' On 2 October: 'Kafka still very inspired.'[56] By then he had finished the first chapter, which he read to Brod on the 6th, together with 'Das Urteil'.[57]

The chapter, which is brilliantly written and, unlike subsequent chapters, rich in foretastes of Kafka's mature style, is called 'The Stoker' ('Der Heizer'). Eight weeks earlier, having to spend two hours in the gas-filled air of the engine-room at the factory when the engine would not start, Kafka had been impressed by the 'energy of the foreman and the stoker in dealing with the engine'.[58] His feelings towards the two men may have been in line with childhood feelings towards Czechs subordinated to his parents in shop and home, and with adult feelings towards underprotected workmen injured in factory accidents. The stoker in the novel has vague but valid-seeming grievances against his superior, and a passenger tries to obtain justice for him by appealing to the highest authority, the captain. But the passenger, a sixteen-year-old immigrant to America, alone and with little money, allows himself to be led away by his influential uncle, a senator, abandoning the stoker to the rough justice he is likely to receive at the impromptu hearing in front of the captain.

As in Kafka's dream, the boat is at anchor in New York harbour, and a nightmarish confusion runs through the events, infecting the reader with anxiety. Illuminated by a sudden burst of sunshine, the Statue of Liberty seems full of promise, but it is described as a goddess carrying not a torch but a sword. We also feel worried on behalf of the boy, Karl Rossmann, who, jostled by passing porters, is just about to disembark when he remembers the umbrella he has left below decks. (On the day Kafka met Felice, she had left her umbrella on the train.)[59] Karl asks a casual acquaintance to wait by his trunk while he hurries back to search. How long will the man stay? Will Karl lose his trunk as well as his umbrella? The danger increases as he lets himself be drawn into a conversation with a huge man in a tiny room. 'Through some kind of a hole in the ceiling, dingy second-hand daylight, worn out on the upper decks, filtered into the wretched cabin, where a bed, a cupboard, a chair and the man were all packed tightly in together.'[60] Karl has been knocking at the door only because he has lost his way, but the man invites him to lie down on the bunk, saying he'll have more room there. And when, remembering his trunk, he tries to get up, the man pushes him back. 'In a little while I'm going too, and then we can go together.'[61] When he stretches his legs, resting them on the bunk, Karl has to shift closer to the wall, but he has 'almost lost the feeling that he was on the uncertain floor of a ship, on the coast of an unknown continent, he felt so at home here on the stoker's bed'.[62] Like Kafka's father, the stoker is a big man with dark, short, thick hair; the use of the bunk parallels the use of the bed in 'Das Urteil'. Kafka was excited by the idea of a quasi-sexual bedroom rapprochement with the big father. The moment of greatest physical intimacy with the stoker occurs when Karl is on the point of abandoning him. He pulls the man's right hand out of his belt and holds it gently, asking him why he simply puts up with everything. Later on Kafka was to make a similar remark about workers injured in accidents: why did they simply put up with the way they were exposed to risk?[63] Karl then draws his fingers backwards and forwards between the stoker's, whose eyes shine happily as Karl tells him to defend himself. Finally, bursting into tears, the boy kissed the man's 'chapped and almost lifeless hand, and pressed it to his cheeks like a treasure that had to be abandoned.'[64] This is an inversion of 'Das Urteil': reluctantly and guiltily the son is escaping from the father figure who has no power to keep him.

Karl has been shipped to America by his unloving parents who want to avoid paying alimony to a servant-girl, Johanna Brummer, who has seduced him and given birth to a child. She has helped Karl by writing to inform his uncle that he is on his way to America, but he feels nothing towards her. (*Brummer* means meat-fly or horsefly; Karl's name, Rossmann, means literally horse-man.) Her sexual appetite and her possessive stare are reminiscent of Kafka's shopgirl, and in the lovemaking Karl is both passive and repelled:

Then she lay down next to him and wanted him to tell her a secret, but he couldn't, and she got angry either in jest or in earnest, shook him, listened to his heart, offered her breast so he could listen to hers, but she couldn't make him, pressed her naked stomach against his body, groped with her hand between his legs so disgustingly that Karl shook his head and neck free of the pillows, then thrust her stomach several times against him, as though, it seemed, she were a part of him, and perhaps this was why he was seized terribly by the feeling of needing help. Weeping he arrived finally in his own bed after she had several times asked him to come to her room again.[65]

Kafka himself did spend a second night with the shopgirl, but the fictional episode obviously expresses at least one side of the ambivalence he had felt.

The narrative verges so closely on the autobiographical that writing and re-reading made him emotional. Though he was seldom able to weep, there was one passage which had him 'shaking in my armchair, twice in rapid succession, I was nervous of waking my parents in the adjoining room with my uncontrollable sobbing'.[66]

The burst of inspiration that began after writing to Felice on 28 September lasted until 6 October, when he wrote ten pages. The spate of prolific energy would probably have continued into the evenings of the following week had it not been for the departure of Karl Hermann on a business trip which for ten or fourteen days would leave the factory unsupervised by anyone but the foreman and Karl's brother, unless Kafka offered to fill the gap. His father, who was too busy in the shop to go himself, was worrying about the money he had invested, while his mother, relaying her husband's anxieties, nagged at her son almost every evening about his duty to reassure his father.[67] She was so busy acting as cashier at the shop that sometimes she did not come home for lunch, and she was blaming Franz for both her husband's ill-health and his bitterness. When Ottla, who normally sided with her brother against parental attacks, joined in the onslaught, 'bitterness – I don't know whether it was only gall – ran through my whole body, I understood with perfect clarity that for me there were now only two possibilities, either to jump out of the window after they've all gone to sleep or else to go every day for the next fortnight to the factory and my brother-in-law's office'.[68] The first (which inevitably he was considering in the perspective of 'Das Urteil') would be a means of repudiating all responsibility for the factory and for the interruption to his writing; the second would give him the prospect of resuming his writing but not without loss of momentum.[69] All this suggests that Felice was irrelevant to his premiss that writing constituted his only justification for staying alive. 'I stood for a long time at the window and pressed myself against the pane, and in many ways it would have suited me to startle the toll collector on the bridge by jumping. But . . . it also seemed to me that survival causes less of an interruption to my writing than death.'[70] Brod was sufficiently alarmed to intervene. He wrote confidentially to Julie Kafka, enclosing a copy of her son's letter, suppressing only the postcript written at 12.30 a.m.: 'I hate them all, every one of them, and in the next two weeks hardly expect to find words for bidding them good morning. But hatred – which again gets directed against myself – belongs more outside the window than to quiet sleeping in bed.'[71] She replied to Brod's letter immediately: 'You'll see from my shaky handwriting how much it upset me.'[72] Her husband, because of his illness, had to be protected from shock, she said, but she would tell Franz not to go to the factory.[73]

Though the danger of suicide had receded, his depression was deepened by Felice's silence. One night in bed, half-asleep, he 'wrote letters to you uninterruptedly, the feeling was of a light, uninterrupted hammering.'[74] He wrote two real letters, which remained unposted, and on 13 October, fifteen days after his second letter, he wrote his fifth – the third to be posted.[75] The next day, 14 October, he wrote to enlist the support of Brod's sister, Sophie Friedmann, who lived in Berlin and knew Felice. In fact Felice had written a letter which failed to reach him, but on 23 October he heard from her and replied immediately from the office, informing her parenthetically of interruptions – questions about insurance for convicts and a ministerial appeal by Joseph Wagner in Katharinaberg.[76] He had a restless night, 'contorted only in the last two hours into an enforced, calculated sleep, in which the dreams are far from being dreams, the sleep even less like sleep'.[77] He had an insatiable appetite for the details of her life, wanting to know not only about her theatregoing but about all the circumstances – weather, mood, and when she had dinner – before or after. In answer to his question about presents she received, she had mentioned books, chocolates and flowers, and in one version of the dedication below the title line of 'Das Urteil' he wrote: 'For Fräulein Felice B, so that it's not always only from others that she receives presents.'[78]

Three days later, on Sunday 27 October, he settled down at eight o'clock in the evening to write her a long letter, having oriented everything else during the day towards the moment of writing – even the half-day he had spent in bed, deprived by rain of his Sunday walk.[79] Two days later he wrote again, offering to share the blame for her headaches. 'Have I therefore any right to advise you against taking Pyramidon?'[80] In her answer she asked whether it wasn't disagreeable for him to receive a letter from her every day. Of all the people who came through the door of his office, confident of being in the right place, he answered, only the postman was entitled to be there.[81]

Her queries about his mode of life served as a pretext for addressing her on 1 November as 'Liebes Fräulein Felice', instead of opening with the formal 'Gnädiges Fräulein'. 'I shall probably want to refer to more delicate matters than can be proffered to a "gracious Fräulein".'[82] His account of his dedication to writing wasn't designed to make him attractive to her. 'If there's a higher power that uses me or wants to, then I'm in its hands, at least as a carefully prepared instrument; if not, then I'm nothing and will suddenly find myself in a frightful void, unwanted.'[83]

He described his daily routine: after being in the office from eight till two or two-thirty, he had lunch till three or three-thirty, and then retired to bed till seven-thirty, sleeping or trying to sleep. Then ten minutes of exercises, naked at the open window, followed by an hour's walk, usually alone or with Brod, and then dinner with the family. Between ten-thirty or eleven-thirty he would sit down to write, going on, usually, till one, two or three. 'Then again exercises, as above, though of course avoiding anything strenuous, a wash, and into bed, usually with my heart hurting slightly and my stomach muscles twitching.'[84] Exhaustion did not guarantee deep sleep: he would be too worried about his writing and about whether a letter from her was on its way. 'In one of the corridors between my office and my typist's there used to be a kind of bier for moving documents and files: each time I passed I thought it was highly suitable for me, was waiting for me.'[85]

Since 1909 she had been working for Carl Lindström AG, originally as a shorthand-typist, but earlier in 1912 she had been promoted to a superior position in the Parlograph division, the Parlograph being a rival of the dictaphone. But Kafka still did not know what her work consisted of, or whether the factory produced anything but Parlographs.[86] Nor did she know much about his office work, which he was reluctant to describe.[87]

In his next Sunday letter he wrote to her about the Yiddish theatre company, which had been playing in Leipzig: Löwy had sent him a poster, which had been printed in north-east Berlin, in the Immanuel-kirchstrasse, where she lived. From a later postcard of Löwy's, it looked as though the troupe was playing in Berlin, where, according to him, it was impossible for them to earn any money on weekdays. [88] Perhaps, with her interest in theatre, she would like to see it.

By the end of the first week in November, though they were still addressing each other formally in the plural, there was enough intimacy for them to worry about each other. Felice was taking dictation in the evenings from a professor – wasn't she overworking? [89] She thought he was, but he rebuffed her encouragement to take things more easily: 'Am I wrong to stake myself in the one space on the gaming table where I can stand up?' [90]

After three days of silence he received two letters and the promise that she would write every day. 'My heart, listen, a letter every day!' [91] But he was nervous that the correspondence was harming her. She was restless, disturbed, liable to cry out in her sleep. [92] 'My existence is torturing you. My existence. I'm fundamentally unchanged, go on turning in my old circles, have gained only one more unfulfilled craving, while my former sense of being lost has been complemented with a new self-confidence, perhaps the strongest I've had.' [93] Guiltily he felt he had gained more from her than she had from him, and that, face to face, she would find him and his way of life insufferable.

For months on end, until he got used to it, my father had to hold the newspaper in front of his face rather than watch me eat my supper. For several years now I've taken no trouble with my clothes. The same suit gets worn in the office, in the street and at the writing-desk at home – summer and winter too. I'm almost more hardened against cold than a piece of wood, but even that isn't really a reason for going around as I have now, for instance, into November, wearing no overcoat, light or heavy, on the street, among the carefully wrapped pedestrians I walk around like a fool in a summer suit with a little summer hat and actually no waistcoat (I set the fashion for discarding waistcoats) and I'll say nothing about the peculiarities of my underclothes. How it would startle you to meet a man like me near the church I picture at the end of your street. [94]

Werfel made fun of him for not wearing warmer clothes when they went out walking at night. [95] In fact he possessed only one suit. Though he drank no alcohol, coffee or tea, seldom ate chocolate, never smoked, he was aware of undercutting all his gestures towards healthy living by starving himself of sleep. [96] But he entreated her neither to reject him nor try to reform him. Left suddenly alone in the dining-room the previous evening, he had 'felt such a need for you that I'd have liked to lay my head on the table, just so as somehow or other to feel supported'. [97]

He was so exhausted in the evening that instead of trying to write he walked the cold streets for two hours, returning only when his hands felt frozen stiff in his pockets.[98] Then he had six hours of undisturbed sleep, dreaming of her for the first time. He was woken earlier than usual with the news that Elli had given birth to a girl. Kafka felt 'nothing but raging envy against my sister, or rather against my brother-in-law, for I'll never have a child'.[99]

The arrival in the flat of his nephew, displaced by his sister's birth, intensified Kafka's depression. The next day, Saturday, after hearing the clock strike each quarter-hour through the night, he wrote 'Dearest Fräulein, You mustn't write to me any more, and I won't write to you any more. I'd only make you unhappy by writing, and I'm definitely beyond help. . . . Stop thinking about the ghost that I am, and go on living happily and peacefully, as before.'[100] But then he could not bring himself to post the letter. Out walking with Brod, he was talking about his unhappiness when, not noticing where he was going, he was nearly knocked down by a horse-drawn carriage. 'At that moment I was actually furious at not having been run over.'[101] He stamped his foot with rage, saying something inarticulate. Misconstruing his annoyance, the coachman swore at him.[102]

At meals over the weekend he spoke even less and ate even less than usual. On Monday morning, before leaving for the shop, his mother burst tearfully into his room, wanting to know what the matter was, and caressing him. He comforted her, kissed her, made her smile until she felt sufficiently relaxed to scold him for going without his afternoon snack.[103] After describing the incident to Felice he went on: 'I'm now in the mood to throw myself before you, whether you like it or not, to give myself to you completely, so that no trace and no memory of me remains for anyone else.'[104] But later in the day he wrote again. She must write only once a week: it was intolerable to hear from her daily. 'How I belong to you, there's really no other way of expressing it.'[105] But he did not want to be told she was fond of him.

> For then why am I fool enough to go on sitting in my office or here at home instead of hurling myself into a train with my eyes shut, and not opening them till I'm with you? Oh, there's a bad reason, bad and short and good: I'm healthy enough for myself but not for marriage and certainly not for fatherhood.[106]

By the time he arrives at saying: 'Let's abandon the whole business,'[107] it is obvious he neither expects nor wants her to agree. Sending flowers for her birthday he wrote: 'External reality's too small, too unambiguous and too truthful to contain what there is inside a single man.'[108]

Felice meanwhile had been confidentially in touch with Brod, who tried

147

to reassure her.[109] Kafka was 'a man who wants only the absolute, the
extreme in everything'.[110] His uncompleted novel was superior to 'everything I know in the way of literature'.[111] This is to overpraise it absurdly.
Kafka later refused to publish any more of it than the first chapter,
regarding the rest as written in recollection of strong but totally absent
feelings.[112]

Later he would condemn both 'Der Heizer' and the draft he wrote for
the rest of the novel as derivative from Dickens, and in particular from
David Copperfield: 'Story of the trunk, engaging boy, the menial labour, the
sweetheart in the country house, the dirty houses, etc., but above all the
method. My intention, as I now see, was to write a Dickens novel, only
enriched by sharp highlights, taken from the times, and dull ones, taken
from myself. Dickens's richness and mighty, mindless profusion, but
resulting in passages of ghastly feebleness, where he wearily stirs up
what he's already achieved. Barbaric, the impression of the nonsensical
whole, a barbarism I've actually avoided, thanks to my weakness and my
canny derivativeness. Heartlessness behind the emotionally overflowing
manner.'[113]

On 12 November he finished the sixth of the eight chapters,[114] knowing
that the book was unlikely to be completed.[115] Though it was at least of
anodyne value to feel he was making progress with it, the narrative lacks
thrust and coherence, while autobiographical fragments are introduced
haphazardly. The childhood memory of being shut out on the balcony,
for instance, is incorporated when Brunelda, a rich and self-indulgent
singer – maybe her sexuality has been overstimulated by diaphragmatic
breathing – wants to be alone in her flat with Delamarche, formerly a
vagrant but now her resident lover. Robinson, formerly Delamarche's
mate, and Karl are therefore locked out on the balcony.

If Kafka had sunk to a nadir of depression since his euphoric burst of
creative energy, his spirits were greatly boosted in the middle of
November by the first letter in which Felice used the second person
singular. 'Dearest, dearest! If there's so much goodness in the world,
there's no cause for fear or for anxiety.'[116] The letter brought him the calm
'I've long been wishing for and which three nights ago I prayed for.'[117] He
had ended one of the three letters he wrote on 11 November with characteristic diffidence and self-accusation: 'Did I want to sign myself *"Dein"*?
Nothing could be more misleading. No, I am mine, and eternally bound
to myself.'[118] But her response moved him profoundly. In a relationship
which had words as its only currency, the most crucial word – 'you' – had
changed. 'Can I be sure now of being yours? The *"Sie"* slides away as on
skates ... but the *"Du"* remains, it stays there like your letter, which
doesn't move and lets me kiss it again and again.'[119] He invited her now to

write as often as possible. There was nothing to stop them from talking to each other over the telephone, but the idea filled him more with anxiety than excitement. [120] Before going to bed he wrote again, speculating on whether she was sleeping or reading, rehearsing with the amateurs in her company or dreaming. 'In my thoughts I'm circling round your bed and demanding silence.' [121] Their correspondence should become almost tele-pathic. She must give him the facts and he would measure his guesswork against them. 'Would it then be so incredible if, finally, after many attempts, they coincided and became a single great reality we could always count on?' [122] He now claimed full responsibility for her headaches. Patent medicines like Pyramidon were useless to her. 'Generally there can be no healing except from person to person, just as the transmission of pain is from person to person.' [123] But she must not abandon him now. 'Stay under the delusion that you need me. Think your way still more deeply into it. For look, it does you no harm, if you one day want to be rid of me, you'll always have enough strength for that, but meanwhile the gift I have from you is greater than I ever dreamed of having in this life.' [124]

Within twelve hours the feeling of security had vanished: in the morn-ing, when no letter from her arrived, he was restlessly pacing along corridors, rushing from his fourth-floor office down to the post-room, questioning clerks. [125] That night he dreamed a postman brought two registered letters from her, one in each hand, his arms moving like piston rods in perfect precision, and though Kafka kept pulling out page after page, the envelopes never emptied. He was standing half-way up a staircase which became littered with discarded pages, while the paper produced a great rustling sound. [126]

When Kafka's mother read one of Felice's letters to him, she found he was being advised to confide in his mother, who surely loved him. This impelled Julie Kafka to appeal for Felice's help in persuading Franz to sleep more and eat more. 'He's undermining his health, and I fear may not come to his senses until, God forbid, it's too late.' [127] Felice should question him about his daily routine, his meals. If she wanted to reply confidentially, she could write to the shop, marking the letter 'Per-sonal'. [128]

12 Captive Insect

On Sunday morning 17 November 1912, when a letter from Felice arrived at 11.15, he had slept little and was lying miserably in bed waiting for the postman.[1] He had just had the idea for his story 'Die Verwandlung' ('Metamorphosis'), which begins with the sentence: 'As Gregor Samsa woke up one morning out of uneasy dreams, he found that he had been transformed in his bed into a giant insect.'[2] Not without misgivings about putting the novel aside, he worked at the story throughout the day, and again on Monday evening. 'I'm just sitting down to my yesterday's story with an unbounded desire – obviously accumulated from disconsolateness – to immerse myself in it.'[3] After all the images that had fused the human with the non-human – the arms of the postman in the dream had moved like pistons – after all his fantasies of degradation, after being treated by his father as if he belonged to an inferior species, and abused with animal imagery, Kafka arrived at the image of the insect as a means of expressing the alienation from his body he had so often felt. Gregor cannot control his ceaselessly waving little legs, cannot at first manoeuvre his unfamiliar body to the edge of the bed.

Family interventions are much as they would have been in the Kafka flat, while the Samsa flat is laid out in the same way, with Gregor's room between his parents' bedroom and the living-room. When the chief clerk arrives, his sister whispers to him from an adjoining room, and his father asks him to open the door: his visitor will excuse the untidiness of his room. At one point the mother and the sister call to each other across Gregor's room, and at another the father calls through the hall to the kitchen, clapping his hands.

Kafka draws on his flow of anxieties, siphoning some of them into accusations and insinuations the chief clerk makes against Gregor. Why is he causing his parents unnecessary trouble and neglecting his business duties? When Gregor tries to answer, his voice is recognizably inhuman, but if a locksmith and a doctor are summoned, as the human voices threaten, at least he will no longer have to take any initiative.

On seeing his insect son, the father's first reaction is to clench his fist fiercely; his second is to weep, his great chest heaving. Kafka was caricaturing paternal reactions to less exorbitant deviations from the human norm – the story is almost saying: 'Your behaviour would be reasonable if this were the extent of my abnormality.' When the father uses a newspaper and a walking stick to beat Gregor back into his room, Kafka is crystallizing some of the disapproval he had interiorized. The newspaper his father had held in front of his face at meals had also been a weapon, and Kafka's annoyance at not being run over by the horse-drawn carriage is not far removed from a desire to be squashed like an insect. As he said, the feeling 'I hate them all' was virtually indistinguishable from self-hatred. The identification with vermin connects with the point he would make seven years later about his father's offer of prophylactic advice: 'It was you who were pushing me . . . down into the filth as if it were my destiny.' 'Shoo,' shouts Gregor's father and hisses aggressively. Inexperienced in crawling backwards, the unfortunate son is bleeding profusely before the bedroom door is slammed on him. Like Kafka, the insect does no active harm, but he is unable to retain any goodwill. Even the sister he loves – he wants to pay for her to study the violin – wants to have him driven out of the flat.

The continuity with 'Das Urteil' shows in giving the central character almost the same name (Georg, Gregor). In the earlier story the ramshackle houses that stretch along the river bank are differentiated only by their height and colouring; in this one the hospital opposite is endlessly long, dark and grey. The realistic Prague background counterweights the nightmarish disproportion between punishment and crime. The second *alter ego* is executed more gradually and more cruelly. Kafka was allegorizing his relationship with the family, building out from his sense of being a disappointment, a burden. Walter Benjamin was wrong to say that Kafka's stories were parables which interpret a doctrine that does not exist:[4] what they interpret is his experience. But he could not have used it in this way had it not been for events of the previous thirteen months: the visits to the Yiddish theatre, the conversations with Löwy about Eastern Judaism, the serious study of Yiddish literature, the meeting with Felice, sitting down on the evening of the Kol Nidre service to write a letter that ensued out of the 'irrevocable judgment' he had passed on himself, the breakthrough achieved in writing 'her' story about a judgment, and the new involvement in the Talmud, which acted on him as a catalyst. What he had in common with the Talmudists was the ability to take ideas literally and then pursue them relentlessly. The root idea for 'Die Verwandlung' was a gift from his father – an invitation to think of himself as verminous.

On 20 November he wrote reproachfully to Felice. Why did she have to torment him by not writing? It was intolerable. This would be his last letter.[5] In the evening he wrote again, warning her not to believe any of the enemies who might write to her from inside him as one had this morning.[6] On the second day of writing the story, deeply upset by her silence, which continued even after he had sent a telegram, he had arrived at the 'definite decision' that his only salvation was to contact the land-surveyor in Silesia who had given him evangelistic pamphlets in Jungborn. He would have acted on this decision if Felice's telegram had not been delivered.[7] But he went on oscillating between anger and abjection at the hurt he caused her by protesting so violently. Sometimes he would write proposing they should stop the reciprocal torture, but then he would suppress the letter or leave it unfinished and send it only when it was obviously out of date, when there was no danger of her acting on it.

> When I can't bear something, I pull you into my whirlpool with the irresistible strength of weakness . . . it solves nothing to write when one feels the craving, it's merely an irritant, for the craving to write to you and read your letters is with me every instant that God gives me.[8]

She would have to participate in the treatment he accorded to himself: 'indeed you are my own self and I torture this from time to time, it's good for him.'[9] Kafka's alienation from himself makes Rimbaud's 'Je est un autre' look almost simple. Sometimes Kafka would write of himself (or one of his selves) in the third person, trying to identify the other with the Felice who was eventually going to see him again in the flesh, though the fantasy meeting had no anchorage in probability. 'Perhaps you'll run right away from him. Remember, you've seen him only once and by gaslight, and then without taking much notice of him. He almost never goes out by daylight, and has therefore acquired something of a nocturnal face.'[10] Fictional identification with an insect had developed his capacity for self-detachment. 'Still, perhaps you'll get used to him, dearest, for look, I too, your correspondent, whom you've treated so well, have had to accustom myself to him.'[11] At the same time Kafka was beginning to think in terms of a divine power that determined the conditions of his existence. His consciousness was patrolling the quadrilateral space between God, Felice and his two selves.

In answer to the questions she had put – at his mother's prompting – about diet, he said everything was eaten for her benefit. Breakfast consisted of stewed fruit, biscuits and milk. For lunch he ate the same as the rest of the family, but much less meat and more vegetables. (This food was presumably heated up: the others ate earlier.) At 9.30 on winter evenings he ate yoghurt, pumpernickel, butter, nuts and fruit. He drank little – fruit juice rather than wine.[12]

Later in the day, when he discovered that his mother had read Felice's letter, he gave way to an 'almost completely uncontrolled outburst' of rage[13] but afterwards found he could speak to her more openly than he had for years. 'In no other family I know is there so much coldness or false civility as I've always felt obliged (it's my fault and theirs) to show towards my parents.'[14] Walking through his bedroom and seeing the corner of Felice's letter sticking out from the breast pocket of his jacket, she had fished it out. 'Her love for me is just as great as her incomprehension of me, and the ruthlessness that spills over from this incomprehension of hers into love is, if possible, even greater. . . . Parents want nothing but to drag one back to them, to the old days, from which one is panting to escape.'[15]

He went on working at 'Die Verwandlung' until 6 December.[16] It was 'exceptionally repulsive', he told Felice,[17] it would thoroughly frighten her,[18] but

who knows? – the more I write and the more I liberate myself, the cleaner and the worthier of you, perhaps, I become, but certainly there's still a great deal to drain away, and the nights can never be long enough for this activity, which is incidentally quite sensuous.[19]

Towards his writing the mixture of positive and negative feelings was no less pungent than towards his father. Ideally, he said, such a story should be written with no more than one interruption, in two ten-hour sessions, 'then it would have its natural tension and flow, as it had in my head last Sunday'.[20] But he had to represent the institute at a trial in Kratzau, and he was afraid that when he returned to Prague he would have lost the momentum he needed.[21] But on 27 November it was 'rolling drearily and indifferently along, only momentarily illuminated by the necessary clarity'.[22]

The train journey from Prague to Berlin took only eight hours, and it would have been easy, had he wanted to, to see Felice over Christmas. Before the end of November she was enquiring about his holiday plans. He was to have five or six days free, but would lose a day on his sister's wedding, 22 December, and he wanted to work on his novel. Though he said it was 'pointless to be present in rooms from which you're absent',[23] he was afraid of the confrontation. Besides, writing was becoming an addiction. However badly he needed sleep, he had to go on 'watching the pages of the exercise book being endlessly filled with things which one hates, which cause disgust or at best a dull indifference. . . . If only I could annihilate the pages I've been writing in the last four days as if they'd never existed.'[24]

Sometimes it felt as though all the writing he did on the novel was channelled out of the desire to write to her.[25] Sometimes, too exhausted to write, he would sit in his freezing room, wearing his dressing-gown and a blanket around his legs, trying to relax in the armchair.[26] Sometimes the buzzing in his head stopped him from trying to write,[27] and before Christmas he was close to collapse.

My head was crowded out with desire for sleep (though for nights I haven't written, except to you), whatever I leaned against, there I stayed leaning, I was frightened of sitting in my armchair, in case I'd be unable to get up, and to keep myself awake while reading documents I pressed the bottom of my pen into my temples.[28]

As soon as the holiday started he regretted losing his opportunity to be with her. But we must not measure the almost deliberate self-frustration against the behaviour of lovers in the nineteen-eighties. In the first volume of Musil's *Der Mann ohne Eigenschaften* (begun 1924) Ulrich is

so in love that he wanted nothing more than to go as far and as fast as possible away from what inspired that love. He travelled blindly onwards until the railway-track stopped at a coast-line, had himself rowed to the nearest island, where, living cheaply and uncomfortably, he wrote on the very first night the first of a series of long love letters, which remained unposted.[29]

This 'Kafkaesque' behaviour may well owe something to the influence of Kafka, but both Kafka and Musil belonged to the first generation of writers that grew up in the full glare of Freud's demonstration that it was possible to produce a rational analysis of human irrationality. In this ethos paradox could be cultivated on the basis of a widespread belief in the identity of opposites. Theodor Herzl admired Ravachol as having become 'honest in his crimes', and Wittgenstein maintained that 'Ethics and aesthetics are one and the same.'[30] As Musil wrote, 'Knowledge was becoming old-fashioned,' and Ulrich feels 'like a stride that could be taken in any direction'.

On the night of the 22–23 December Kafka went to bed before nine, woke at about two, fantasizing about 'a possible trip to Berlin. The connections were beautifully easy, trouble-free, motor-cars flew like lovers, telephone conversations were as though one was holding hands.'[31] After two wakeful hours in bed, he got up, did his exercises, washed, wrote two pages of the novel, but felt too restless to go on, started a letter to her but, with his head buzzing, abandoned it and went back to bed, where he slept deeply till about nine.[32] But he was deeply exhausted. 'The need for sleep rolls around in my head, tensions in the upper part of my skull on both sides.'[33] By the end of the year he was feeling better, but 'totally unfamiliar twitchings and the play of muscles inside my head are warning me against excessive wakefulness at night.'[34] In this condition he was especially vulnerable to the noise of conversation through either of his bedroom walls. 'Of course the usual chatter was already going on in the adjoining room, and my exhaustion dragged me downwards into sleep, the noise kept jerking me up out of it.'[35]

He felt entitled to enjoy her proximity in her absence. 'If I don't write for myself, I'll have more time to write to you, to enjoy your nearness, evoked by thinking, writing and with all the strength of my soul.'[36] He felt torn between the two compulsions: to write for himself and to write for her. On Christmas Day, sacrificing the afternoon sleep he would have had if he had spent the morning at the office, he worked – between interruptions – on the novel, but ineffectually, and wished afterwards that he had succumbed to the temptation of writing to her.[37]

He was undecided about whether to accept a New Year's Eve invitation from Felix Weltsch's uncle to spend the evening with the family.[38] He tried to make himself work but spent the time lying on his bed, 'neither exhausted nor energetic but unable to get up, depressed by the general New Year celebrations let loose all round'.[39] Just after the midnight cannon was fired, he was writing to Felice. Looking out of the window he could see hardly anyone in the street or on the bridge, but heard shouting and bells ringing, which made him feel alienated, withdrawn, glad he had not taken the risk of meeting her. Twice in her letters she had promised, as he had, that they belonged together unconditionally, but what if they had been spending a few days together in, say, Frankfurt? Rejecting reality in favour of fantasy, he was free to imagine any development in their relationship. What if they had arranged to go to a theatre together, and to meet beforehand at an exhibition? What if he failed to turn up? What if she took a cab to his hotel and found him lying in bed, neither exhausted nor lively, but listless, unable to get up? He would be abjectly apologetic and contritely affectionate, but unable to guarantee it would not happen again. 'If I were you, standing in front of my bed, I wouldn't hesitate to raise my umbrella in anger and despair, and break it over my head.'[40] Imputing an aggressive act to her, the letter justifies it, but the imputation is itself aggressive. He could not protect her from his self-destructiveness. An image presents itself: a couple led to the scaffold during the French Revolution, bound together.[41]

The first mention of engagement is oblique: it occurs in an account of a dream about an engagement party held in semi-darkness at a long wooden table with a black top. Behind the backs of the guests, a waitress tastes the semi-liquid dish she is about to serve, putting the spoon back into the dish. Furious, Kafka leads her down to the huge offices of the hotel, but his complaints are ineffectual.[42] The dream reverses the pattern of the novel: when Karl works in a large hotel, complaints against him never fail to inflict damage.

The idea of engagement did not stop Kafka abdicating from the right to feel jealous when she described how she had, on his account, fended off the attentions of a rather good-looking paediatrician. 'Who am I then, who dares to get in his way? A shadow that loves you infinitely but can't be pulled into the light.'[43] Of course he would have been jealous if she had given his rival any encouragement, but was he offering enough to claim any rights over her? Neither of them wanted to talk to the other, even over the telephone, but he could lie sleeplessly in bed for two hours 'uninterruptedly in the most intimate conversation with you'. 'What speeches I make to you in bed! Lying on my back, my feet jammed against the bedposts, how I talk silently to myself for my dearest listener!'[44]

Because of the war-scare – Austria and Russia had begun to mobilize at the end of November 1912 – Valli's wedding was postponed to 12 January. Dissatisfied with his sister's bridegroom and with himself for not even trying to intervene, Kafka had nevertheless to wear his old tailcoat, his cracked patent leather shoes, a top hat that was too small, to act as usher at the synagogue wedding[45] and to propose a toast at the wedding reception.[46] He had never felt more in need of the support that Ottla gave him. Without sharing his sadness about Valli's marriage, she was aware of it and tried to justify it. While they were packing the bride's things on the evening before the wedding, first the housekeeper and then Valli herself burst into tears; when Ottla called out: 'She's clever – she's crying too,' Kafka took this as praise for a mood that accorded with his.[47]

His parents were highly satisfied with the wedding, despite the expense. On the next day, sitting in the rocking-chair for his after-lunch nap before going back to the shop – because of his heart condition he was not allowed to lie down after eating – Hermann Kafka said in Czech: 'Someone told me our Valli looked like a duchess yesterday in her bridal veil.' The word *kněžna* ('duchess') was spoken with affection, admiration and tenderness.[48]

The resultant force of the wedding experience strengthened Kafka's taste for a solitude which was unbroken by the two-way traffic in fantasies that went on in his correspondence with Felice. He had picked the right woman for his purposes, a woman he would not want to touch, except with words, a woman who would be content with that. Combined with her actual absence, the illusion of her presence made her the ideal accomplice in the outrages he was perpetrating on himself – the slow self-destruction and the flagrant exhibitionism that centred on the pen.

For writing is opening oneself up excessively, the extreme of open-heartedness and surrender in which a man thinks he is immersed in human intercourse and from which, therefore, he will always shrink, so long as he's sane – for everyone wants to live while he's alive – this openheartedness and surrender fall a long way short of being enough for a writer. . . . So it's impossible to have enough solitude, when writing, or enough silence. The night is never long enough. . . . I've often thought that the best way of life for me would be to have writing materials and a lamp in the innermost room of a spacious locked cellar. Food would be brought, and put down a long way from my room, behind the outermost door of the cellar. My only exercise would be the walk, wearing my dressing gown, through the vaulted cellar. . . . But what I'd write! What depths I'd tear it up from.[49]

On 16 January Martin Buber came to lecture on myth in Judaism to the Bar Kochbar Society.[50] Kafka had heard him speak before and found him boring,[51] but meeting him after his lecture, and again two days later, Kafka liked him: 'personally he's bright and simple and interesting, and seems to have no connection with the lukewarm things he's written'.[52] With 'Die Verwandlung' Kafka had already stepped towards the kind of animal legend he was to write later – a kind which has affinities with the Hasidic tales Buber had translated – but if their influence was merging with that of the Yiddish theatre, he was not yet aware of this.

Merely to attend the lecture had been quite an effort for him. He had not been going out in the evenings. 'It must be a year since I went to the theatre.'[53] But three days after the lecture he went to see the Russian ballet, which had excited him so much two years ago, when Eduardova was dancing. Karsavina was ill, but he saw Nijinsky and Lydia Kyast, 'two immaculate creatures, at the innermost point of their art, and they radiate mastery'.[54]

He had been seeing less of Brod, who was shortly to marry, but went to see him on 23 January, only to be told that he looked as if he had just been roused by a drum out of a deep sleep.[55] Brod was 'rather husbandish, rises above moods, remains superficially cheerful despite suffering and upsets'.[56] They met again on Saturday 25 January, and spent most of the evening in a café. They laughed a great deal,[57] but Kafka had not been feeling well, and, associating the malaise with the novel, felt it would be wiser to leave it alone. He relaxed with some confessional literature – Hebbel's letters. 'That was a man who knew how to bear pain and come out with the truth because he stayed closely in touch with his innermost self.'[58]

After all his advice on how to organize her life, Felice felt entitled to propose a timetable for his. Inevitably it was unacceptable: she had scheduled only an hour or two for writing, with no separate allocation of time for writing to her.[59]

At the beginning of February he spent an afternoon with Werfel, who read some of his poems. As he had told Felice, 'I like the lad better every day.'[60] Werfel was twenty-two.

And the lad has grown beautiful and reads with such ferocity that I have reservations about the monotony of this. He knows everything he's written by heart and, when reading, looks as though he wants to tear himself to shreds – the heavy body, the great chest, the round cheeks all seem to catch fire. [61]

The only room in the flat that was heated was the living-room, and when the bedrooms were too cold, the family slept in it, 'one on top of the other'. [62] On Sunday morning Kafka took refuge in the only other warm room, the kitchen, where, despite the cold tiles and the loud ticking of the clock, he settled down to write his daily letter. [63] He would have to get up at 4.30 the next morning for the journey to Leitmeritz, where he was to represent the institute at a trial. At 10.30 in the evening Ottla decided she would like to go with him, [64] and their father raised no objection. He was always eager to remain on good terms with relations, and there were some in Leitmeritz she would be able to visit. [65] Normally she worked in the shop from 7.15, when it opened – he arrived at 8.30 – until four or five in the afternoon, not even coming home for lunch. Kafka was glad of an opportunity to escort her – 'it's always my secret wish to look after somebody' – but after three or four hours of her company, he felt relieved to be on his way to the court. 'Often, dearest, I genuinely believe I'm useless for human relationships.' [66] What he most regretted about his agnosticism – or the vestiges of it that survived – was the lack of a continuous relationship with 'a comfortingly remote, if possibly infinite height or depth'. [67] 'Anyone with a constant sense of this would never need to roam around like a lost dog, gazing about imploringly but silently, and never feel the desire to slip into the grave as into a warm sleeping-bag.' [68] Worse still, Kafka indulged in the fantasy of being a large piece of wood pressed against the body of a cook 'who's holding the knife in both hands and with all her strength drawing it along the side of this stiff log (somewhere in the region of my hip) slicing off shavings to light the fire'. [69] Behind the cook lurked other images – father, butcher, ritual slaughterer, avenger for massacred animals, murdered Christians.

Sometimes Kafka felt 'so loose inside my skin that it would only have needed someone to give it a shake for me to lose myself completely'. [70] He claimed no rights over Felice: if she wrote at length he blamed himself for making her stay indoors, writing, instead of enjoying the fine weather. [71] But in dreams as well as fantasies he was very close to her: in one dream they were walking along together in Berlin, with not only their arms linked but their legs. He illustrated his letter to explain how. [72] But when she told him he had won her completely, he was not pleased: 'Dearest, I have enough imagination to tell myself that just as I, when I think of myself, must stay with you, holding you tightly and never letting go, when I think of you . . . I must use all my strength to keep my distance.' [73]

Max Brod reviewed *Betrachtung* for the Munich weekly *März*. 'In our age of compromise there is, working silently, deeply, one force with medieval inwardness, with a new morality and religiousness. . . . At last mystical immersion in the ideal can for once be experienced.'[74] Kafka's reaction was: 'he overrates me so much that I feel abashed and vain and arrogant.'[75] Kafka knew that what Brod was really reviewing was not the book but him. 'So where am I? Who can look me over? If only I could take a strong grip on the unstructured construction that I am. . . . When I look into myself I see so much which is unclear and still in flux that I can't even quite justify or consolidate the antipathy I feel towards myself.'[76] Could she believe in someone who was making no more use of his life than he was, 'achieving no more than to run around an enormous hole and guard it'?[77]

Unable to regain his grip on the novel, he was easily distracted by noises through the wall. One Sunday morning he was awoken by his father with a 'mad, monotonous, ceaseless shouting and singing and hand-clapping, constantly repeated with renewed force to entertain a great-nephew', and in the afternoon he put on the same performance for the benefit of his grandson.[78] Kafka thought seriously about moving out,[79] but what he was suffering was long-distance sibling rivalry. Two weeks later, when Elli and Karl brought Felix to have lunch in the flat, Kafka fretfully watched his father 'trembling with joy, and popping his head backwards and forwards through a door to make his responsive small grandson say "Dje-dje" meaning Grandfather . . .'[80]

On Friday 28 February Kafka began a story, but wrote no more than four pages of it[81] before going out to see Brod, who had returned from his honeymoon. If the story was any good, Kafka told himself, he could go back to it over the weekend.[82] He didn't, but, kept awake by a headache on Saturday night, he felt guilty about not getting out of bed to write.[83] Feeling rejected by the story, he wanted neither to feel rejected by Felice nor 'to enjoy the fruits of a compassion that must destroy you'.[84]

Abruptly, a week before Easter, he asked whether she would have an hour to spare for him on Easter Sunday or Monday if he came to Berlin. He did not want to meet her family, he said,[85] and he was not even sure whether he would be able to come.[86] Her response, which was positive, arrived on Wednesday 19 March, but he went on vacillating. On Friday night he sent an express letter to say that he did not know whether he would come, but that if he did, he would stay at the Askanische Hof Hotel.[87] On Saturday morning he sent another express letter: 'Still undecided,' but left later in the day, arrived at eleven in the evening, and in the morning, expecting her to contact him at the hotel, waited there for five hours before sending another letter by messenger.[88] He had been planning to leave again at five, but he arranged to spend another night in the hotel and they went for a walk in the Grunewald. On Easter Monday he left for Leipzig, where he stayed the night and met Jizchak Löwy, who had left the troupe to recruit a new one, which made even less money, shuttling between Leipzig and Berlin in competition with the old one. Exhaustion and anxiety had made him ill, and he had gone into hospital, his headaches worse than ever, and burdened with personal responsibility for the company's debts. Kafka's advice was that he should think of emigrating to Palestine.[89]

After returning to Prague on Tuesday Kafka had to stay up till 11.30 studying papers to prepare himself for a trial in Aussig[90] but though he would again have to get up at 4.30 in the morning, he could not sleep. He thought of jumping through the open window, and imagined his body on a railway track, train wheels running over neck and legs.[91]

Though it was not until June that he asked Felice to marry him, the idea seems to have been forming alongside the suicidal inclinations.

My main anxiety . . . is this – that I'll never be able to possess you. That, like an unthinkingly faithful dog, I'll at best be confined to kissing the hand you absent-mindedly proffer, and this will be a reminder not of being alive but only of the despair of an animal condemned to dumbness and to being kept eternally at a distance.[92]

Kafka's self-degradation – his persistent dehumanization of himself – must have affected his sexuality, but Elias Canetti's suggestion that he had an underlying fear of impotence[93] is hard to reconcile with the diary entry that equates coition with 'punishment for the happiness of being together'.[94] He was in such an obvious state of anguish that his mother, accustomed as she was to seeing him in a depressed condition, found a pretext to come into his room and, for the first time in years, offered to kiss him good-night. 'That's fine,' he told her. 'I never dared,' she said. 'I didn't think you wanted to, but if you do, then I very much want to.'[95] Normally he would exchange only about twenty words a day with her, and greetings with his father. And in May, when he read 'Der Heizer' to them, his father listened with undisguised reluctance.[96] With his married sisters and their husbands Kafka remained silent, not because he had quarrelled with them but because he had nothing to say.[97] 'I believe that conversation deprives everything of its significance, its seriousness, and its truth.'[98]

On Monday 7 April he began a new stint of self-punishment – two hours of manual work daily in a suburban market garden at Nusle, a suburb to the south of Prague. Wearing only his shirt and trousers, he worked in the cool rain. 'It's done me good. . . . My main object was to escape from self-torture for a few hours, in contrast to the ghastly office work, which is constantly slipping out of my grasp – *the only true hell is there in the office, I no longer fear any other.'*[99] After four days of gardening he felt 'rather heavier and more erect', and slightly more self-confident.[100] He spent most of Sunday in bed, worrying. Felice had been in Frankfurt, arranging an exhibition for her firm. Perhaps she had found an eligible young man there, 'especially as you would in this way have been fulfilling the request I have made in innumerable letters'.[101] He heard from her in the middle of the week. 'Exhaustion, a cold and hoarseness, and I've contributed to your exhaustion.'[102] Wasn't it obvious to her that he did not really love her? 'For then I'd think only of you, and write about you, but really I worship you, and somehow expect help and blessing from you for the most unlikely things.'[103] He still felt (like his Raban) that he could enlist sympathy from a woman if only he could make her fully aware of what was going on inside him, but the letters always fell short of 'imparting to you the rhythm of my heartbeat'.[104] With the previous letter, written earlier the same day, he had felt so frustrated that he started to tear it up.

Convinced her attitude had changed, he thought of proposing that they should revert to the formal plural,[105] but wanting to see her again at Whitsun, he offered to call on her family.[106] When he told his mother he was going to Berlin, he could not help laughing. Warned not to rush into anything he would regret, he reassured her: 'It's nothing.'[107] He was already thinking beyond Whitsun to the long stretch of time when he would not see Felice unless she would come with him to Italy or Lake Garda or Spain.[108] And on the same day as writing to ask whether to wear a black suit or a summer suit and whether to bring flowers for her mother,[109] he succumbed to the fantasy that recurred so often – a pork butcher's broad knife slicing into his flesh.[110] He had resumed his diary at the beginning of the month: the letters were no longer suitable receptacles for what needed to be noted down.

At Whitsun (11–12 May) he met her again, and her family. 'They all stood around me so gigantically with such a resigned expression on their faces ... they possessed you and were therefore big; I did not, and was therefore small. ... I must have made a very nasty impression on them.'[111] Dressed entirely in black, her mother struck him as 'mournful, disapproving, reproachful, observant, impassive, a stranger within the family'.[112] Her sister Erna was the only one who seemed sympathetic.

As he packed his bag in the Askanische Hof, his feeling was: 'I can live neither without her nor with her.'[113] He was nervous about the way he had behaved. 'You lose interest in me, look away or into the grass, put up with my silly remarks and my much better founded silences, there's nothing you seriously want to ask me about, but you suffer, suffer, suffer.'[114]

He decided to write a frank letter to her father, and show it to her before sending it.[115] It would explain how, for about ten years, he had been increasingly aware of lacking the sense of well-being most people had. Her father might like to recommend a doctor who would examine him and report on his findings.[116] He made several attempts to write this letter, but never succeeded.

Meanwhile, Felice used the only weapon she had against his endlessly fluent self-laceration – silence. On 26 May, *in extremis*, he telephoned her, but understood little of what she said; his letter written the next day starts: 'So this is the end.' He asked her not to write to him any more, and said he would not write to her.[117] But the next day he received a letter from her which had been in the mail for three days because she had posted it without a stamp.[118] It offered little comfort but did offer a pretext for writing again, self-pityingly. Löwy's presence in Prague, he said, had helped him to survive the last few days. Once again Kafka was uncharacteristically acting as impresario, organizing another one-man show, this time at the Hotel Bristol. He enclosed an announcement from the *Prager Tagblatt*:

> His performances of last year have not been forgotten, his characterizations of hardened rogues and repentant villains, the servants he played as cunning oriental Sampo [sic] Panzas, the fidgety movements of his hands, the fetching smile in his heavily lined face, his gait, the range of his virile, beautiful, singing voice.[119]

The performance did not go well, but at least it made some money for Löwy.[120]

On Monday 1 June Felice wrote that she was resuming her daily letters to him, but that was the only one he received until Sunday the 7th. In response he began to write what he called a dissertation.[121] It was not ready until the 16th, and after asking whether she would like to be his wife, he condemned the question as 'fundamentally criminal', and himself as more lamentable, so far as human relationships were concerned, than anyone else he knew. 'I really know less about most things than young schoolchildren.'[122] Even with Brod, he said, he had never had 'a long, consequential conversation that implicated my whole self'.[123] No proposal of marriage could have been more discouraging; no reply could have been briefer. She sent a postcard saying Yes.[124] She had let a day pass before sending it and two days before the letter that confirmed it. He was still anxious. 'The prodigious world inside my head. But how to release myself or it without being torn to shreds. And a thousand times better be torn to shreds than baulk it or bury it. It's quite clear to me that this is what I'm here for.'[125] Would she befriend his writing? If they ever lived together, would she come to love it? He tried to represent it as an ally: 'Did I not have it, this world in my head, agitating for release, I'd never have dared to think of possessing you.'[126] But was she aware of how little time they would actually spend together? He would have to sleep after coming home from the office and write in the evening.[127] Did she realize how poor they would be?[128] He did not explicitly raise the question of having children but aversion to the idea was unmistakable: his family, he complained, 'lost itself quite mindlessly in the lowest sexuality' when playing with Felix.[129] After giving birth to six children, his mother had become 'bloated and bent'.[130] Elli, who had still been a young woman only two years ago, was, after producing two children, beginning to lose her figure, just like her mother, and so was Valli. 'Dearest, how badly I needed to take refuge with you!'[131] But how was she meant to react? She had had no direct experience of his fastidiousness but a letter hints at the revulsion he would have felt if he had ever had to deal with pots and nappies. He admired his father, he said, for putting up with the disorderliness of family life, with 'a repulsive mixture of all possible things visible on the beds', with Elli's husband sitting next to her on a bed and calling her 'my treasure' and 'my all', with their little boy involved in a game and unable to control his bladder, with Julie Kafka spreading bread with goose-dripping which will trickle down people's fingers.[132] But it was not until October, six weeks after ending the correspondence and the relationship, that he directly raised the question of having children. 'How can I step into a new family, and then start a family, I, who fit so loosely into my own family that I make contact with no one?'[133]

In his diary he tried to weigh the arguments for and against marrying. Solitude was pushing him too close to insanity, but 'Everything raises doubts. Every joke in the comic paper, recollections about Flaubert and Grillparzer, the sight of nightshirts laid out ready for the night on my parents' bed, Max's marriage.'[134] Everything valuable that he had accomplished was the result of having been alone. 'Anxiety about being a couple, flowing into the other person. Then I'm never again alone.'[135] Alone with his sisters he felt 'fearless, exposed, powerful, unpredictable, emotionally involved as I never otherwise am, except when writing';[136] if marriage made him feel like that with other people, life would be incomparably better, so long as his writing was not harmed.[137]

Ottla, who was still working unhappily at the shop, could see he was suffering, but their communication was mostly wordless. One Saturday evening she came home from the shop to find him sitting on the sofa, staring blankly in front of him. Aware he had been eating very little, she asked whether he was going to have supper, but he did not answer, and they just stared at each other.[138] At lunch-time the next day it was his mother's turn to sympathize, but, as usual, she could find only the wrong words. She did not want to pry into his secrets, she said, but she did so want him to be happy, and he had no idea how much his father cared for him. He said it was office problems that were on his mind.[139]

He announced to her his engagement on his thirtieth birthday, 3 July 1913, during her brief return from the shop for lunch. She asked him not to write to Felice's father until she had made enquiries about the family, and he wrote down Herr Bauer's name for her.[140] He sent Felice a postcard photograph of his parents: 'Don't they look incredibly like all other strangers, except that perhaps the strangeness is lightened by the Judaism we have in common?'[141] Three days later he withdrew the permission he had given his mother to make enquiries.[142]

Slowly coming to believe in a future with Felice, he wandered around the uplands outside the city where he thought of living. Some building had been done, but gipsies were still encamped on part of the land. After the rain, the air smelt clean, and he felt hopeful.[143] Sometimes he thought he'd have liked to go south with her and live in seclusion on an island or a lake, eating fruit and grass;[144] sometimes he wished he could 'just tear through the nights with writing. And to end up dead or mad as result, I want that too, because I've long known it's the inescapable consequence.'[145] But he joined a co-operative building society which owned a block of flats, one of which he and Felice would be able to occupy in May.[146] On Saturday 2 August he said they should become officially engaged in the presence of their parents. She could come to Prague on her way back from her summer holidays, and he could then go back with her to Berlin.[147]

The family doctor, examining Kafka towards the end of June, could find nothing wrong, but he was suffering at the beginning of August, from palpitations and stabs of pain around the heart. After abandoning the gardening, he had been exercising energetically – swimming and walking – in order to tire himself out – so as to master his longing for Felice, he told her.[148] He went back to the doctor, but refused to take either his medicine or his advice about not swimming.[149] Believing himself to be verging on madness, he had an experience of near-disintegration in the middle of the night. 'My thoughts became uncontrollable, everything fell apart until, at the worst moment, the image of a Napoleonic field-marshal's black hat came to my aid, dropping over my consciousness and holding it together by force. At the same time my heart was beating furiously and I threw the blanket off, though the window was wide open and the night rather cool.'[150] In the morning, despite pains around the heart, he did not feel too ill for a day at the office.[151] But once again he decided to spend the latter part of his summer holiday in a sanatorium.[152] His concern with Felice's health was hardly less rigorous: would she do him a favour without knowing what it would be? After she had promised, he told her to start on Müller's exercises. In a few days he would send her the manual for women. [153]

During her summer holidays the letters she sent from the island of Sylt left him very dissatisfied, and, reluctant to spoil her vacation with grumbling letters, he confined his misgivings to his diary.

The two of us can't hammer a pathway into rock, it's enough to have wept and tortured each other for a year. My last letters will convince her of this. If not, I'll certainly marry her. I haven't the strength to refute her opinion about our prospects, and I can't afford not to achieve what she believes is attainable – so far as I can. [154]

Had she rejected him, his main reaction would have been relief, but the next day three letters from her arrived. 'I couldn't resist the last. I love her, insofar as it's possible for me, but the love lies buried asphyxiatingly under anxiety and self-recrimination.' [155] The only way to endure marriage would be 'to live more ascetically than a bachelor'. [156] But wasn't she, in spite of all his painfully honest explanations, underestimating what she would have to sacrifice?

She had shown his handwriting to a man in the boarding-house who claimed to be a graphologist. According to him, Kafka was very determined in his behaviour, extremely sensual, good-natured, thrifty, generous, and had artistic interests. Kafka, who contradicted every point except the one about thrift, was most irked by the last. 'I have no literary interests but I consist of literature. I'm nothing else and can be nothing else.' [157] Reviewing *Betrachtung* in *Das literarische Echo* [158] Paul Friedrich had used the phrase: 'Kafka's bachelor art'. She must not expect 'merry chatter arm in arm but a *monastic life side by side with a man who is fretful, melancholy, untalkative, dissatisfied and sickly*'. [159] 'You'll feel abandoned if I live as I must, and you'll really be abandoned if I don't.' [160] She had written that she would get used to him and to his 'literary bent' – another phrase that annoyed him. Could she really survive autumns and winters in which they would spend only an hour together each day? [161]

The next day he woke up feeling suicidal, but an argument with his mother changed his mood. Surely Uncle Alfred deserved a letter. Hadn't he sent a telegram and a letter? 'He cares so much about how you're getting on.'

'Those are just externals. He's a stranger to me, he doesn't understand me at all, he doesn't know what I want or what I need. We've nothing to do with each other, he and I.'

'So nobody understands you? I suppose your father and I are strangers to you too? So we all want to harm you.'

'Certainly you're all strangers to me. There's only the blood relation-ship, but there's no outward sign of it. Certainly you don't mean to harm me.'[162]

He was left feeling that there were 'possibilities in my ever-increasing inner decisiveness and conviction that in spite of everything I could be successful in a marriage'.[163] Later he wrote an imaginary dialogue between a nervous but masterful husband, Leopold, and a wife, Felice, who is not easily cowed, but eventually does as she's told.[164]

Before writing to Felice's father he read a Kierkegaard anthology, which may have influenced the tenor of his letter. Kierkegaard was fascinated by Abraham's willingness to sacrifice Isaac: it paralleled his own father's willingness to propitiate God with the death of his son. Michael Pederson Kierkegaard was an eleven-year-old shepherd boy when, cold, wet, and hungry, he put a curse on God for letting an innocent child suffer. From then on he lived in fear of divine punishment. He was forty when he married the woman who had been his maid, and fifty-six when Søren was born in 1813. 'Through a crime I came into existence', he wrote in 1855, 'against God's will.' Brought up to believe he would die at the age of thirty-three to expiate the curse, he could never believe he was fully alive: 'There's something ghostly about me, something which explains why no one will put up with me who has to see me daily. Fundamentally I live in a spirit world.'[165] When he was twenty-seven he became engaged to a girl of seventeen: within twenty-four hours he regretted it, but more than a year passed before he broke it off. 'There too I'm seized by a mysterious dread of having confused an ideal with a reality.' 'He bears me out like a friend,' Kafka wrote.

Three days later Kafka had his first direct confrontation with his father about the engagement. Interrupting the card-game his parents invariably played – briefly – after lunch: 'Father, so what do you think about it? That I want to get married?' The main gist of the paternal diatribe was that he was financially in no position to marry. Hadn't he caused his father enough trouble by persuading him to invest in an unsuccessful asbestos factory? Wasn't it enough for a sick man already paralysed with worries, to have two sons-in-law coming to him for financial help? As usual the aggression was unresisted; as usual it played itself out. After almost half an hour of grumbling he became gentler: he was prepared to meet Felice's parents in Berlin and explain his objections; if they nevertheless wanted the marriage to go ahead, he would say no more.[166]

After three months of procrastination Kafka drafted the letter to Felice's father and copied it into his diary on 21 August, rewrote it to make it even more off-putting, and posted it on the 28th. He said his life with Felice would be 'monastic' – a word he had already used twice in letters to her.

Undeterred, her parents gave their consent, which palpably disappointed him, and when Felice said her mother would come to love him, he was annoyed. What use could he possibly have for love which he could neither reciprocate nor deserve? 'You must understand, Felice, that I'm lying on the ground in front of you and I beg you to kick me aside, or we'll both be destroyed.'[167] Throughout his relationship with her, the irrational resentment he felt at any limitations she imposed on his claims to her attention had echoed the much more justifiable resentment he had felt during childhood at his mother's inability to concentrate on him – 'Stay with me, don't leave me': the Freudian repetition compulsion was equally operative in this desire that the mother-substitute should parallel the maternal rejection. Towards everything but literature his instincts were overwhelmingly sacrificial: 'Relentlessly cutting through all my muscles is the desire to renounce the greatest human happiness for the sake of writing.'[168] He felt akin to Grillparzer, Dostoevsky, Kleist and Flaubert. Dostoevsky was the only one of these four to marry, and Kleist, who shot himself, was 'perhaps the only one to find the right solution'.[169]

13 Grete Bloch

Robert Marschner and Eugen Pfohl had decided to take Kafka with them to the second International Congress for First Aid and Accident Prevention, where they both made speeches,[1] and on 6 September 1913 the three of them left for Vienna. Kafka had to forfeit several days of his summer holiday, but it gave him the chance – on 8 September – to attend a session of the concurrent Zionist Congress, the eleventh. Earlier in the year he had written to Felice about his 'boundless and inexpressible indifference' to Zionism,[2] and now he wrote: 'I don't have the right sense of belonging.'[3] But he went. And shortly afterwards he joined the newly founded *Verein jüdischer Beamten* (Association of Jewish Officials) which was Zionist in orientation.[4]

In January 1914 he was to list 'Ottla's Zionism' as one of the things that held him 'literally together and give me some resolution and hope',[5] and in February he would contribute to the Jewish National Fund.[6]

On the trip to Vienna he suffered from insomnia, and cold compresses on his head gave him no relief. 'I refuse invitations whenever I can, and still have to see a frightful number of people, and at meals I sit there like a ghost.'[7] When he went for a stroll with the writer Otto Pick, he indulged in 'inane literary chatter';[8] and when Pick complained he was walking too fast, he walked faster.[9]

On 14 September he travelled to Trieste, where he took a steamer for Venice. The crossing was short but rough; he was seasick and his head went on throbbing after he landed.[10]

I'm alone here, speak to almost no one except the hotel staff, am so miserable it almost overflows, but think I feel I'm in an appropriate condition, allotted to me by a supernatural justice, irreprievably and for the rest of my life. . . . I can't move myself forwards, it's as if I were in a trap, if I tear myself forwards, it pulls me back again more forcefully. . . . But what can I do, Felice? We must part.[11]

Venice he found lovely,[12] and he went on to Verona, but he wasn't keeping a diary. 'I wouldn't know what for, I encounter nothing that involves me. This is true even if I weep, as I did yesterday in a Verona cinema. I can enjoy human relationships; I can't experience them.'[13] He went next to Desenzano at the south end of Lake Garda, where his main source of pleasure was that no one knew where he was. 'In every corner of my being I'm empty and futile, even in the knowledge of my unhappiness.'[14]

From Desenzano he left for Riva, where he stayed at Dr von Hartungen's sanatorium and hydrotherapy institute. He spoke little, and felt 'sullied by every conversation'.[15] At table he sat between an elderly general and a petite Italian-looking Swiss girl, who at first seemed dissatisfied with both her table-companions. She was about eighteen and she had a low-pitched voice.[16] He could not stop thinking about Felice, longed for solitude, and felt repelled by honeymoon couples.[17] 'When I want to disgust myself I've only to imagine putting my arm round a girl's waist.'[18] But, as so often, he was attracted by the notions that most nauseated him, and before he left Riva about two weeks later, he had become more intimate with the Swiss girl than with anyone since the 'oldish pretty girl' in Zuckmantel. Ignoring friendly glances from an elegant young Russian woman who told fortunes and would possibly have welcomed him into her bedroom,[19] he communicated with the Swiss girl by knocking on the ceiling of his room, which was below hers, and writing fairy-stories that she would 'hold under the table at meals, read between courses, and blush terribly when the sanatorium doctor has been standing behind her for a little while and watching her'.[20] A Christian, she was unlike any girl he had known, and once – perhaps remembering the moment when he'd almost written to the evangelistic land-surveyor – he let her bless him.[21] In his bedroom he listened anxiously for knocks on the ceiling, heard her coughing, and singing before she went to sleep.[22] The intimacy lasted only about ten days, and they both knew it had no future, but 'I had to take great care that when we said goodbye she did not start crying in front of everybody, and I was almost in the same state myself'.[23]

Despite the fairy-stories, none of his relationships (since the one in Zuckmantel) had ever depended less on the written word. The little there is about her in his diaries was written retrospectively – partly, perhaps, because he intended to show Felice what he wrote, partly because the girl made him promise to say nothing about her, partly because the diary had not yet recovered from being abandoned in favour of the letters to Felice.

Just before the end of October he was surprised to receive a letter from Felice and another from a friend of hers, Grete Bloch, who at her request was coming to meet Kafka in Prague and mediate between them. Before seeing her he replied to Felice's letter, hinting that he might come to Berlin at Christmas. 'I have such a longing for you, that it's pressing against my chest like tears that can't be shed.'[24] He was going against his own convictions. 'It's sheer villainy. At a certain depth – not the deepest – I want nothing but to be torn towards you, and my saying so is another piece of villainy.'[25] The stratagem was more complex than double bluff: he was trying to force honesty to the point where it started backtracking.

Grete Bloch turned out not to be the large, strong spinsterish girl he'd expected. She was a slim, vivacious, twenty-one-year-old shorthand-typist, standing conspicuously at the hotel entrance, wearing a fur stole.[26] She had known Felice only about six months. Unable to present the case he had prepared, Kafka found himself listening to a detailed exposition of Felice's problems with her teeth – dental trouble was, to him, particularly repellent – and to the story of her brother's broken engagement.[27] After meeting Grete again the following evening, he decided not to wait until Christmas, but to visit Felice the following weekend. Despite his experience of waiting five hours for a message, he again failed to make clear-cut arrangements. He wrote telling her he would leave Prague at three on Saturday, stay at the Askanische Hof again, and leave on Sunday between four and five.[28] Not being met at the station and finding no message from her at the hotel, he felt doubtful whether she had received his letter, but did not telephone her. At 8.30 in the morning, when there was still no word from her, he sent a messenger to her on a bicycle. The man returned at nine with a note from her to say that she would telephone in fifteen minutes. She did not telephone till ten. They went for a walk together in the Tiergarten. She had to attend a funeral at twelve. They drove to the cemetery, and he watched her walking through the gates with two men she knew. She had promised to ring him at three and go to the station with him, but there was no telephone call from her. 'So I came away from Berlin like a man who'd gone there without being entitled to.'[29] Or did he want to feel that he had no business there?

He had the impression of knowing four different Felices: the one who met him in Berlin did not particularly like him and did not have much in common with the one he had met in Prague, with the one who wrote the letters, or even with the one he heard of as going about with other people.[30] Back in Prague, before writing to her, he wrote to Grete Bloch. Describing the Berlin incident he was using his literary skill to win her allegiance. Eight days later Felice still had not written, but Grete had and he wrote back, explaining how disappointing Felice's letters of the last six months had been in comparison with earlier letters. 'Letters come from both sides dealing with nothing but writing, empty, time-wasting letters, disguised descriptions of the torture it is – or rather can be – to carry on a correspondence.'[31] This letter was itself largely a letter about letters, though it also contained a detailed account of a dream. After starting with a necessarily intimate conversation, their acquaintance was beginning to fulfil the need that the early correspondence with Felice had fulfilled – Kafka needed to chat intimately through writing about internal events.

Towards the middle of the month the Kafka family – depleted by the two marriages – moved again after its longest stay in one flat. The move was to a four-room flat on the fourth floor of a house on the Niklasstrasse. Outside the front door were pillars with caryatids.[32] There was a lift, and stepping out of it you saw the bars over the maid's window – the only window in her room looked out on the staircase.[33] Kafka's window looked out on the large dome of the Russian church with its two towers, and in the distance he could see a tiny church on the Laurenziberg. The massive tower of the town hall was visible on the left.[34]

Brod's marriage appeared to have put an end to the intimacy between them.[35] 'A married friend's no longer a friend. Whatever you tell him is passed silently or explicitly to his wife, and in the process – unless she's unlike any woman I've met – everything's distorted.'[36] But Elsa Brod was trying to help Kafka: after meeting Felice in Berlin she invited her to Prague for Christmas.

At the beginning of December, though, confusion seemed to be the main obstacle in the way of suicide. To die would be a spurious simplification, a meaningless and therefore inconceivable surrender of an empty life 'to a boisterous nothing whose nothingness consists only in its impenetrability'.[37] He was less fearful of acting foolishly than of being paralysed by indecision. 'To see folly in every feeling that moves straight forwards, inducing oblivion of everything else.' If this was folly, what was 'non-folly'? Non-folly was 'to stand like a beggar before the threshold, to the side of the entrance, decaying till the moment of collapse'.[38] As Blake had said, 'If the fool would persist in his folly, he would become wise.'[39]

At home Kafka was exceptionally irritable towards both his mother and Ottla.[40] And reading the novel *Galeere* (*Galley*) by Ernst Weiss, an acquaintance who lived in Berlin, he baulked at the artificial resolution of the plot. Writers should dispense with 'construction'.[41] 'I almost deny experience. I want either peacefulness, one step after another, or agitation, but not calculated grass-hopping.'[42]

One day, glancing up at Pfohl while reading him a report by Marschner, Kafka noticed an expression – sly, boyish, revealing – which made the face look unfamiliar. Two days later, when he studied his own face in the mirror, it appeared 'better than I know I am. A clear, well laid-out, almost beautifully outlined face. The blackness of the hair, the brows and the eye-sockets press forward like life from the passivity of everything else. The gaze is . . . incredibly energetic, but perhaps it was only observant, for I was observing myself and wanted to frighten myself.'[43]

Unable to bear Felice's long silence, he wrote again by express post on 14 December, wrote to Grete again to ask whether Felice was ill,[44] and on the 17th he asked Ernst Weiss to deliver a letter to her personally at her office. She gave him a note to Kafka promising to write a long letter later in the day, but it did not arrive. After writing again, Kafka received a telegram promise. When it remained unfulfilled, he telephoned. She did not want him to spend Christmas in Berlin, but again she promised to write. Still the letter failed to materialize. He sent a telegram, received one back, saying the letter was written. It still did not come immediately, and when it did, it was disappointingly sad and vague.[45]

Four days after Christmas Kafka had started on a long letter to Felice; when he finished it, five days later, he had produced some forty pages of manuscript. Nothing would induce him to let go of her voluntarily, he said. Given the word, he would write to her parents immediately.[46] He had been hurt by two sentences in her letter: 'We'd both have to give up a great deal in marriage, we don't want to argue about where an imbalance might occur.'[47] She was only saying in her way what he had often said in his, but his reaction was: 'there seems to be no way from that paragraph to a reunion, for it's impossible to argue and to move forward at the same time'.[48] But reunion was what he wanted: he could not live without her. He admitted the infidelity in Riva, stressing the Swiss girl's awareness 'that fundamentally there was nothing I wanted but to marry you'.[49] It was pointless to continue the correspondence and the relationship without marrying.[50] Nor should she try to make him 'live more in the real world' and take things as he found them. It was impossible to change people, and he loved her as she was, loved even the traits he disapproved of. 'I love you, Felice, with everything in me that's humanly good, everything that makes me worthy of staying among the living. If that isn't much, I'm not much.'[51]

Felice did not reply, but wrote to Grete Bloch, apparently calling Kafka a 'poor fellow' who kept beating about the bush.[52] Grete sent the letter to Kafka, who promised not to let Felice know, and he sent Grete a copy of Weiss's novel. Eight days later he wrote again: had he offended her, or was there bad news behind her silence?[53] As soon as her reply arrived he wrote again inviting closer epistolary intimacy: 'And when you write about yourself you should no longer add "the fact that you can't be interested in this".'[54] He asked about her room and about a man in Munich who was important to her.[55] He wrote again the next day, again the day after that, and again, at length, two days later. The main subjects were Felice and the non-committal postcard from her that arrived on

9 February, which he credited to Grete's intervention.[56] He begged Felice not to fall silent again, but she did, and he went on exchanging letters with Grete. By the end of February he no longer needed her as a mediator: 'I only want to hear (if you want it a little) how you are.'[57] The ungrammatical syntax is a symptom of embarrassment. During the three or four days that the letter remained unfinished, she sent him excerpts from Felice's latest letter to her. He promised not to betray the betrayal of confidence.[58]

About the middle of February he decided to go to Berlin at the end of the month without telling Felice he was coming. On the morning of Saturday 28 February, arriving at her office, he handed the receptionist a visiting-card he happened to have on him – the name on it was Gotthart. Felice was surprised but not unfriendly, though she did not invite him in. They arranged to meet at lunch-time, when they sat together in a café for an hour, and then went for a two-hour walk, arm in arm. In the evening she was going to a ball which she did not want to miss – for business reasons, she said – but in the morning they spent about three hours together, walking in the Tiergarten and sitting in a café. His photograph was in a locket she had been given in November, and she would not marry anyone else, she said, but she might be unable to put up with his idiosyncrasies or to live away from Berlin.[59] Most of the talking was done by him. Prostrated by the protracted silences which had blocked his only outlet for writing confessionally, he found himself making exhorbitant promises. 'Say "yes", even if you don't think you love me enough to marry me, my love for you is enough to make up for what's missing and altogether it's enough to take the weight of everything. . . . I love you enough to get rid of everything that could upset you. I'll become someone else.'[60] 'Do stop pleading with me,' she told him. 'You always want what's impossible. . . . That's the way it is. You must believe it. Don't hang on to every word I say. . . . I quite like you, but that isn't enough for marriage. And I don't do things by halves.'[61] When they said goodbye in the entrance hall of her house, she held out her gloved hand for him to kiss. As he pulled the glove open to touch her hand with his lips, he noticed 'the quite hostile grimace she made.'[62] Back in Prague he wrote to retract the promises he would not have been able to keep.[63] In the open air she had looked healthy, but indoors she sometimes looked tired and older, with blotchy skin. Her teeth had deteriorated: she had started a new series of visits to the dentist, who was making gold crowns for her teeth.[64]

Grete Bloch, who was given a detailed account of the conversation, announced that she was coming to Prague.[65] He sent her a copy of 'Das Urteil', and passed on Felice's remark: 'Fräulein Bloch seems to mean a great deal to you.'[66] He wanted, before meeting her again, to explain his relationship with Felice, but he left the explanation incomplete;[67] though, for both of them, the relationship was not irrelevant, 'this shouldn't have the slightest loosening effect on the hands we have clasped as good friends'.[68] Perhaps they could meet somewhere between Prague and Vienna, where she was now working. But when a letter from Felice arrived, Kafka wrote back offering to meet her in Dresden.[69] She declined.

For over a year he had written no fiction except for scraps in the diary. His way of life was consolidating his fixation on Felice. 'I go at everything hesitantly, never completing anything at one stroke.'[70] If he couldn't live in Prague as a married man, he would prefer to move. 'Proceed against the worst disaster that's ever befallen me with the strongest counter-measure at my disposal.'[71] If he lived in Berlin, he could become a journalist – 'a means of earning a livelihood which is half-way suited to me'.[72] Impatient at his own indecisiveness, he interviewed himself in his diary. Could he bear to move out of the family flat? 'But you're spoiled,' alleges the interviewer. 'No, I need a room and vegetarian food, almost nothing else.'[73]

Grete Bloch had misgivings about their correspondence, but in arguing by letter Kafka was at his most persuasive. Her doubts neither did him credit nor reassured him. 'It is always a privilege and even a consolation to have the confidence of someone who's suffering, who matters a great deal to one anyway.'[74] Why didn't they spend a Sunday together in Gmünd, the frontier town, half-way between Vienna and Prague? He had studied the railway timetables. She could arrive at seven on Saturday night, he at 7.30. But his next letter was full of questions about Felice. Would her father not retire soon? If her brother had failed as a breadwinner, would she not feel she must support her parents?[75] Meanwhile Grete resumed her role as comforter: perhaps Felice had turned down the suggestion of meeting in Dresden because she could not afford the train-fare.[76]

Unable to bear Felice's silence, Kafka sent a telegram: 'If you don't come to Dresden, I'll come to Berlin Saturday. Do you agree? Will you meet the train?'[77] Receiving no reply, he wrote again and the same day enlisted the help of his mother who wrote, asking Felice 'to answer Franz's letter immediately, for I can see how much your silence upsets him'.[78] Kafka wrote to Grete saying he was in no state to see her,[79] and to Felice's parents, saying he was in no state to do anything except wait for the silence to be broken.[80]

On 21 March he received three telegrams, a letter and a telephone call, which he took in the anteroom of the president's office, with one of the directors standing behind him, cracking jokes, while Kafka, unable to hear all she said, unable to understand all he did hear, and unable to control his tone of voice, simply insisted that he was coming to Berlin.

Hermann Kafka (1852–1931). 'My writing was about you. All I was bewailing in it was what I could not weep about on your shoulder.'

Prague in 1892.

LEFT The Altstädter Ring (Old Town Square) with the Town Hall and Teinkirche (Tein Church).

RIGHT The house at Zeltnergasse 5: Kafka's home during his schooldays. See p. 11.

Maiselgasse: a view towards the Altstädter Ring.

Kafka at the age of about five.

Kafka at the age of about eleven.

Kafka at the age of eighteen, after obtaining his Abitur (School Leaving Certificate) in 1901. See p. 33.

Kafka at the time of writing *Der Prozess* (1914).

Kafka with his uncle Alfred Löwy, who lived in Madrid.

Kafka with Felice Bauer at the time of their second engagement, July 1917. See p. 222.

Felice's friend Grete Bloch. 'In my relationship with F there is not, dear Fräulein Grete, the slightest thing that you are not just as entitled to know as she is.'
See p. 177.

OPPOSITE Kafka's mother with his sister Valli in Franzensbad. Kafka and Felice travelled from Marienbad on 13 July 1916 to meet them there. See p. 208.

OPPOSITE Kafka in Zürau, 1917–18. See pp. 226–37.

With his sister Ottla in Zürau.

A postcard sent to Ottla in 1918. The ringed caption reads:
'Views from my life'.

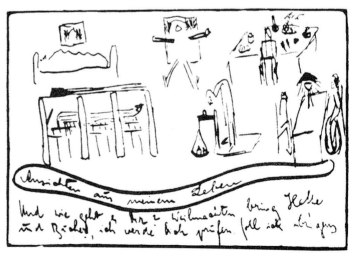

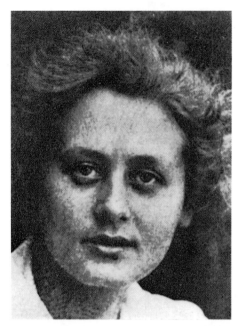

Milena Jesenská-Polák. See pp. 244–61.

The clinic at Matliary where Kafka stayed from December 1920 till the late summer of 1921. See pp. 262–78.

Dora Dymant, who was about nineteen when Kafka lived with her (September 1923 to March 1924). See pp. 290–8.

Dr Hofmann's clinic at Kierling, Klosterneuberg, where Kafka died in 1924. See pp. 301–3. The photograph was taken in 1926.

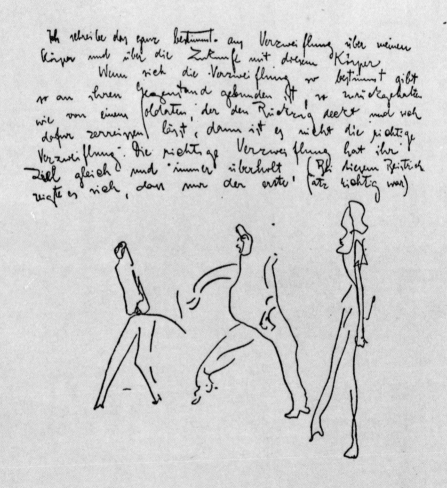

A page from Kafka's diary, 1924. 'I am quite certainly writing that out of despair about my body and about the future with this body.'

Grudgingly she agreed to meet the train. He rushed out into the street, and, despite the rain, he walked up and down, trying to calm down. It was only after going home to find a telegram from Herr Bauer that he made sense of what Felice had said over the telephone – he should not have written to her parents. He decided against going to Berlin.[81]

She had written: 'You told me the love I felt for you was sufficient. So that's fine.' He replied at great length. In conversation he was easily defeated; in correspondence he was invincible – he could turn all her arguments against her. He was doing his utmost to win her back, and his letter culminated in an ultimatum, with a deadline. As he suggested to Grete, 'Perhaps it's the same force that holds me to her and pulls her away from me. There's really no way out.'[82] But he was not too prostrated to continue the long-distance flirtation with Grete: 'You are – now I'm saying something monstrously stupid, or rather what I'm saying isn't stupid but my saying it is – you are the best, dearest and sweetest creature.'[83]

Just as he was at the point of giving up hope of Felice, he received a conciliatory letter. Now secure enough to apologize for 'this immaturity, this instability',[84] he asked her to judge him not by her direct experience of him but by his letters.[85] Her next one was brief and hostile, but he replied ardently, again offering to meet her in Berlin. When she telephoned to discourage him, he promised not to visit her until Easter.[86] 'Our telephonic concord seemed to me pretty good, so far as I can judge this invention, which for me is new and almost impossible to handle . . . even in ordinary telephone conversations slowness of repartee stops me from saying anything.'[87] Meanwhile the epistolary intimacy with Grete Bloch continued; they no longer planned to meet at Easter but she said she might visit the Grillparzer Room in Vienna on his behalf as well as hers.[88]

After his two days in Berlin over Easter (12–13 April) Kafka wrote: 'I can think of nothing I've ever done with such resolution.'[89] He had become unofficially engaged to Felice, who was prepared to marry him in September: before leaving Carl Lindström she wanted to complete her fifth year of work for them. In reply to Grete's congratulatory telegram he said he wished he could be holding her hand. 'My engagement or marriage doesn't make the slightest difference to our relationship, which, for me at least, is full of lovely possibilities I can't give up.'[90] And for the rest of the week he wrote to her every day. On 15 April, 'I feel an undeniable and genuine longing for you.'[91] Could she come to meet him and Felice either in Prague or in Gmünd?[92] When she asked for her letters to be returned, he pretended not to understand why. 'What use are rules to people or in relation to people?'[93] The letters, she insisted, must be burnt as soon as he got married. 'Well,' he replied, 'I'm not married yet.'[94]

His letters to Felice were bristling with reservations about the two days in Berlin. 'I don't want to say they were good days or couldn't have been much better. . . . The nastiest and indeed vilest thing is that we were never alone, except momentarily in the street, and I never had the satisfaction of a kiss from you. You could have given me the opportunity, but you didn't.'[95] Between now and September, she should not do any evening work. 'I'll be your employer outside office hours and send you a salary, as much and as often as you like.'[96] Frau Bauer, whom he addressed as 'Liebe Mutter', was told she was giving Felice 'to a man who certainly loves her no less than you do'.[97] But Felice was warned: 'As human beings we do seem to be at opposite poles, so we must be patient with each other.'[98] He confessed to becoming 'increasingly introverted and unsociable',[99] to feeling discomfort in other people's presence, and to having no capacity 'for establishing close and long-lasting relationships'.[100]

On 21 April Felice announced their engagement in the *Berliner Tageblatt*; Kafka's announcement in the *Prager Tagblatt* appeared on the 24th. He found a flat he liked enough to take an option on it until 2 May, but Felice said she could not come until the 5th,[101] and she did not want to make a trip to meet Grete in Gmünd.[102] Writing to Grete, Kafka pretended that Felice had said nothing about the idea.[103] Would Grete come to Prague? 'I don't yet know quite how to put this, but it often seems to me literally indispensable to have you there when Felice pays her first visit to my home.'[104]

At the beginning of May, thanking Grete for the photograph she had sent – she had broad, Rembrandtesque features which compared favourably with Felice's – he asked for more, and sent her one of him, 'not by way of thanks, which would be funny, but because I want to'.[105] Felice arrived in Prague on 1 May, in good spirits. 'My family likes her almost more than I'd like it to.'[106]

But her ideas about the flat they should live in were quite different from his. She wanted a pleasant, well-furnished home of the type that would be bought by a middle-class couple who could count on their business to go on expanding steadily. Not only was Kafka unable to afford a flat like this, the idea of it filled him with fear and revulsion.[107] He was quite unlike Freud, who sent his fiancée a list of what they would need for their 'little world of happiness' – beds, mirrors, easy chairs, rugs, glasses and china for everyday use and for special occasions, decent linens, artificial flowers, big bunches of keys. 'Shall we hang our hearts on such little things? So long as no high destiny knocks at our peaceable door – yes, and without misgivings.'[108] Kafka told Grete that he 'certainly should have every reason to feel happy, and Felice is certainly the main part of this happiness'.[109] He had so far achieved everything he set out to achieve, never completely, never without detours and great efforts, and always at the last minute – 'in fact usually on the return journey'.[110] And as if to imply that he now wanted Grete, he went straight on to announce that Felice and he had decided she must come and live with them for some time as soon as they were married.[111] It is almost like the situation in Carson McCullers's *The Member of the Wedding*, but with the proposal coming from the bridegroom. 'In my relationship with F there isn't, dear Fräulein Grete, the slightest thing that you're not just as entitled to know as she is.'[112] Still writing to Grete at great length and at short intervals, he told her to reply to him at the office.[113] After she had been to the Grill-parzer Room, he said a physical tie had been established between him and the room.[114] He also confided in her about his reactions to Felice's teeth. At first he had had to avert his eyes from the gleaming gold and the greyish-yellow porcelain; later he took deliberate glances 'to torture myself and force myself to believe it was really true'. Later he had come to find that the undeniable imperfection brought him closer to Felice than a healthy set of teeth, which was 'also, in a sense, horrible'.[115] To Felice he conceded that the basis of their relationship was 'not altogether firm'.[116] 'We may now be gripping hands, perhaps, but the ground beneath us . . . keeps shifting unpredictably.'[117]

Grete came to Berlin for the engagement party at the Bauers' house on 1 June. In a fragment he wrote before the end of the month about an engagement party, the fiancée stands surrounded by friends, while the fiancé leans in the doorway to the balcony until her mother comes over to ask whether they have quarrelled. When he says they have not, she tells him to rejoin her daughter. His behaviour is beginning to attract attention.[118]

Before leaving Prague, Kafka had written to Grete: 'Just hurry to Felice, to whom I've told nothing, regardless of your dress – no more improvements – whatever it's like, it will be seen in the, yes, in the most affectionate way.'[119] And, back in Prague, he wrote:

Quite what you mean to me you cannot know, but even what you do know must make you aware that you do everything for me that one human being can do for another in a situation in which incomplete understanding does not limit the extent of your sympathy for me, and that this everything is always focused in what you do, especially in your gaze, which has its effect.[120]

If Kafka was, as Max Brod came to believe, the father of a child by Grete Bloch, it was probably around this time that the baby was conceived. In April 1940 she wrote to a musician, Wolfgang Schocken, about a visit she paid in Prague to Kafka's grave. 'He was the father of my boy, who when he was nearly seven died suddenly in Munich in 1921.'[121] She was parted from her child, she said, during the war, and never saw him again, except for a few hours. There seems to be no other evidence of the boy's existence or of Kafka's paternity, and the letter is by no means conclusive: she could have become mentally unbalanced. But the boy could have been born some time between the beginning of 1914 and the summer of 1915. Grete can hardly have been pregnant when she, Felice and Kafka made an expedition into the country on 24 May 1915, but it is possible that the baby had by then been placed with foster parents and that both Kafka and Felice remained in ignorance. The editors of his *Briefe an Felice*, Erich Heller and Jürgen Born, argue that his references to her 'sufferings' in letters of August and September 1916 are extremely casual if she was pregnant and he was responsible for it. [122] But if the boy was not born until late in 1916, he would not have been seven until 1923. Kafka may have made love to Grete in Berlin before or after the engagement party, and the 'sufferings' of 1916 may have had nothing to do with the baby.

In May 1914 he was still uncertain about the future of his relationship with Grete, but it had probably been the protracted uncertainty about Felice that had stopped him from writing fiction, and by the end of the month he had written two fragments of stories better than any he had produced for over a year. One is about a man who conceals his trembling hands while, outwardly confident, he strikes a sordid bargain with an ugly, sexually frustrated landlady. [123] The other (which anticipates Harold Pinter's *The Basement*) is about a man who has been wrestling almost wordlessly every evening with a stranger, probably a student, who has moved into the adjoining room. It is useless to bolt the door against him: he breaks it down with an axe. One evening he brings a girl along, and though not as good a wrestler as the narrator, her presence increases his incentive and sharpens his guile sufficiently for him to give her the impression of being better. [124]

Internally something had been liberated in Kafka, but after the engagement party he felt unfree. 'At the time not a moment of the experience seemed safe until it was over. I could think of nothing except how much I'd have liked to be laid low by a good nervous fever or something obvious to everybody, so that I'd have the right to be carried home.' [125] Nothing laid him low, and he felt as though he had been

roped up like a criminal. It would have been no worse if I'd really been put in chains and made to watch everything from a corner with a policeman standing guard over me. . . . Everyone tried to cheer me up, and, failing, to put up with me as I was. Felice least of all, quite justifiably, because she was suffering the most. [126]

If engagement started like this, what lay ahead? 'A marriage founded on the woman's determination? That can't be a steady structure, can it?' [127]

Desperation forced him to write. 'We all have our way of rising out of the underworld. . . . That's why I can stay above, if I must, not by resting and sleeping but by writing.'[128] 'Verlockung im Dorf' ('Temptation in the Village'), a seven-page fragment, looks forward to both *Der Prozess* and *Das Schloss*. A man passing through a village wants to spend the night there. The only inn, he's told, is intolerably dirty, but he decides to sleep for once in a dirty place. A man sitting on a farmyard wall gives him permission to sleep on the farm. Some children lead him up to the attic, where, it appears, he's expected to sleep, as they do. But a dog wakes him up and stays close to him until, rousing himself to carry it away, he trips over one of the children.[129]

Kafka's only luxury was having Grete as his epistolary confidante. It was the letters to her that mattered: the only reason he needed letters from her was that he could not otherwise feel sure that his were being read. Echoing what he had told Felice, he wrote: 'A few lines are enough for me but I do need those. Two sentences and your signature are enough.'[130]

Precarious though his private situation was, Kafka was not too self-obsessed to have premonitions about war. In a June diary fragment, a municipal official locks his front door and checks that the maid is out of earshot before telling his wife that the fighting at Rumdorf 'has gone entirely against us. Already most of the troops have withdrawn from the city. . . . They're all locking up their houses and hiding everything that can be hidden.'[131]

In another fragment, municipal officials look out of a window in the City Hall at the rear guard below waiting for the order to retreat. 'So this is the end,' one of them says. He complains of government policy. 'We're having to atone for sins committed long ago. . . . Total collapse is imminent.'[132] On the last day in June, the Archduke Ferdinand, heir to the Austro-Hungarian throne, was murdered in Sarajevo. War was declared at the end of July, and soon Russian troops would be marching through Austria.

This made it still harder to believe Kafka was soon to be married, and it is possible that he was pursuing Grete and confiding his doubts to her in the semi-conscious hope that she would capsize his commitment by denouncing him to Felice. But even now that she was in Berlin and in close touch with Felice, he does not appear to have assessed the dangers latent in her jealousy. When he complained that the wedding was still three months away, she riposted tartly: 'You'll manage to survive three months.'[133] To him this was 'a crude remark which incidentally as such gave me real pleasure'.[134] He was so desperate for uncritical sympathy that he went on writing to her as if she were providing it. He wrote chattily about insomnia, swimming, doing exercises, drinking sour milk. [135] He reassured her that he was not showing her letters to Felice, and never would. [136] He tried to help her, as once he had tried to help Felice, in business matters, and to arrange for her to be invited to a large firm of underwear manufacturers in Prague to demonstrate the correct use of the machines her company made. [137]

On 27 June he left Prague with Otto Pick. They travelled to Hellerau, a suburb of Dresden where Dalcroze had his eurythmics studio: Kafka, who had seen the dancing, thought it more beautiful than that of the Russian ballet. [138] When he visited the studio, Dalcroze was in Geneva. [139] Kafka went on with Pick to Leipzig, where they met the publisher Kurt Wolff and Werfel. [140] Returning on the 29th to Prague, Kafka wrote four letters to Grete in four days. [141] She could no longer bear the emotional pressure. She regretted 'absurd, irresponsible feebleness in answering earlier letters' and she advised him not to come to Berlin, as he was planning, the following weekend, unless he could be 'clear-headed, resolute and totally happy'. [142] He was disconcerted to learn that she had read Felice passages from his letters. The volte-face was sudden but not at all hard to understand if she was pregnant by him. Nor is it hard to believe that she did not want to tell him about the pregnancy. Ostensibly she was trying to champion Felice, and to demand, on her behalf, a man who was her equal in all respects. Kafka's answer was: 'Either, Fräulein Grete, one is "bright, spirited, intelligent and fundamentally good" or one isn't, but is instead melancholy, depressive, introverted and perhaps well-meaning, but ineffectually.' [143]

Kafka's mother, who still knew nothing of the incipient crisis, wrote a sentimental letter to the Bauers: she had just gone into Franz's room and surprised him 'looking enraptured at dear Felice's photograph'. [144] He left for Berlin on the 11th, and the next day, in the Askanische Hof, confronted what he called a 'law court' consisting of Felice, Grete, Felice's sister Erna, and Ernst Weiss. 'F's face. She passes her hands through her hair, yawns. Suddenly she pulls herself together and launches an attack, carefully thought out, long held back.' [145] The vicious acrimony showed him – even if he did not absorb the message until later – that all his assiduous self-explanation had not generated enough sympathy to outweigh the dislike, impatience and disapproval she felt. He did not defend himself. He saw that catastrophe could still be averted if only he produced some dramatic confession, but he could not think of one. [146] Grete probably said quite a lot. In Kafka's letters to her many of his reservations about Felice are underlined in red – presumably these are passages she read out – either privately to Felice before Kafka's letter of the 3rd, or now at the 'law court'.

Afterwards in his hotel room there was a bed bug, and – reminded perhaps of his short story – he found it hard to make himself crush it. [147] In the evening, suffering from stomach-ache, he sat alone on a bench in Unter den Linden, watching a man selling tickets by standing in front of people and shuffling his tickets until they bought one, if only to get rid of him. How would Kafka feel if he had to do a job like that? [148]

Going to see Felice's parents, Kafka found her mother tearful and her father, who was sitting in his shirtsleeves, understanding. Kafka felt 'diabolical in complete innocence. Apparent guilt of Fräulein Bl.' [149] With tears in her eyes, Erna talked a great deal, telling him about her work, and how she could usually get her own way in spite of a poisonous old white-haired female colleague. [150] When Kafka left, Felice's parents and her aunt waved, but she did not, though afterwards she sent a telegram: 'Expecting you but must leave Tuesday on business.' [151] The engagement had been broken off after only six weeks. What was she expecting?

The next day Kafka wrote to her parents: it was possible to 'remain on friendly terms, even if we've now all seen that the union we all wanted isn't feasible. Felice must have convinced you of this, as she has me.' [152] He considered the letter to be 'dishonest and coquettish'. [153] Eating his evening meal in the garden restaurant outside the hotel he saw an old man watching him while he tried to cut a small unripe peach. He self-consciously pushed it aside and then, defiantly, picked it up and bit into it. [154]

He was intending to spend his summer holiday at Gleschendorf, on the Ponitzer See, a tiny inland lake near the Baltic coast, and he caught a late train to Lübeck, where he took a room at a hotel near the station, but he found dirty clothes in the bed he was given. He took refuge in the garden, where a hunchback was drinking beer. Finally he went back to the bed, and slept despite the incessant noise of trains. The sun woke him by shining into his face. [155] He found another hotel, the Kaiserhof, and made a trip to Travemünde, where he bathed, and in the evening Ernst Weiss and the actress Rahel Sanzara came to see him. They persuaded him to go on with them to the Danish seaside resort Marienlyst. Writing to Brod and Felix Weltsch about breaking off his engagement, he said he was 'not so uneasy as might have been expected about this thing, whose necessity is so obvious'. [156] The beach at Marienlyst was 'rather bleak', [157] and he was in a more upset state physically than emotionally, having started to eat meat. Felice had found his vegetarianism so irksome that perversity had stiffened his commitment to it. Now he was eating 'almost nothing but meat, which makes me ill, and after terrible nights I wake early with open mouth, feeling my abused and punished body in my bed like a strange mess'. [158]

He did not intend to go on living as he had. His father was right: it had been bad for him to grow up in complete dependence and outward well-being. 'Everything's made so easy for me.'[159] He had saved up enough to live for two years without earning, and he would devote those two years to the literary work which 'I can't achieve in Prague with sufficient clarity, fullness and consistency, caught as I am between inner lethargy and external disturbances'.[160]

For stimulus he had been depending more than he realized on girls he did not know well. If sexual desire had played any part in his determination to marry Felice, it was unlike the desire he had felt for Margarethe or for the Swiss girl. Even for casual stimulus he seems to have depended less on Felice than on other girls he would never try to seduce. When he left Berlin, Erna accompanied him to the station, without making conversation, but somehow indicating that she still had faith in him, despite the 'law court' at the hotel.[161] He met her again in Berlin on his way back from Denmark, and they had a meal together. He ate meat, whereas, had he been with Felice, he would probably have ordered a vegetarian meal.[162] Then on the train from Berlin to Prague he sat opposite a woman who gave him 'the first feeling of life I've had for many months in relation to other people'.[163] Her small, ugly body appeared neglected, her dress was cheap, but her freckled cheeks were round and firm, while the liveliness of her gaze looked inextinguishable. She reminded him of the Swiss girl.[164]

The same day Austria–Hungary declared war on Serbia. The war helped to justify procrastination about leaving Prague. 'I've a growing incapacity for thinking, observation, consolidation of certainties, remembering, speaking and empathy. I'm turning into stone. In the office I'm becoming increasingly inept. If I can't immerse myself in some work, I'm lost.'[165] What must have made it all the harder for him to immerse himself in work was the news that 'Die Verwandlung' would not be published in the *Neue Rundschau* unless he was prepared to reduce its length by about fifty per cent – which was unthinkable.[166] And the diary entry for 2 August is: 'Germany has declared war on Russia. Swimming in the afternoon.'[167]

By the end of July general mobilization had begun. Both Kafka's brothers-in-law joined the army, and Elli moved with her two children into Kafka's room – on 3 August he moved out to Valli's flat in Bilekgasse. She and her child were with her parents-in-law in a small town to the east of Prague.[168] The shop stayed open but did virtually no business.

14 Trial

The name Josef K. first occurs on 29 July 1914 in a fictional diary entry. Josef's father, a rich merchant, is insisting his son must give up his dissipated life. For no reason, he goes to the house of the merchant corporation near the harbour. The doorkeeper makes a deep bow, which Josef ignores. He tells himself there is no disparity between what underlings do and what one supposes they do: if he thinks the man is being insolent, he is.[1] The fragment in the third person leads straight into a fragment in the first about a clerk who is being dismissed for stealing five gulden from the till after five years of service. He had stolen the money to take a girl to the theatre, though she did not want to go, and within three days, in any case, he would have had money of his own.[2]

On 6 August, when the artillery marched across the Graben, flowers were thrown and the crowd cheered.[3] But Kafka, who had been feeling suicidal,[4] was still

shattered . . . an empty vessel, still intact but already rejected as broken or already broken but still among the intact. Full of lies, hatred and envy. Full of fecklessness, stupidity, dullness. . . . I discover in myself nothing but pettiness, indecision, envy and hatred of those who are fighting. Passionately I wish them everything evil. . . . My talent for portraying my dream-like inner life has relegated everything else to the incidental, and it's becoming dreadfully and increasingly stunted. Nothing else will ever give me any satisfaction.[5]

Balefully he watched patriotic parades, listened cynically to speeches, slogans, cheering. 'Long live our beloved King, hooray!'[6] Once again Jewish businessmen could feel nationalistic.[7] He shut himself up with his writing, and as soon as he began on *Der Prozess*, his 'routine-ridden, empty, crazy bachelor existence' had a *raison d'être*.[8] At last he was away from the family and was not channelling his energy into letter-writing: he could battle to make the most of his creativity. 'I mustn't abandon myself,' he wrote on 29 August. 'I'm completely alone.'[9] He was telling himself off for failing to continue overnight with a chapter of *Der Prozess* that he had begun 'beautifully'. Had he kept going, he would have succeeded with it; momentum had been lost irretrievably.[10] 'Cold and empty,' he wrote the following day. 'I'm all too keenly aware of my limitations, which, except when I am really inspired, are doubtless narrow.'[11]

The seminal images for the novel derive from the Felice experience. He had been terrified that he was empowering her to make claims on him that would tie his creative hands behind his back. The imagery of ropes and surveillance, used in the diary after the engagement party, is developed in the first chapter of the novel, when Josef K. is told that he is being arrested, but not imprisoned. Admittedly the paradoxical combination of freedom and confinement had deeper roots in Kafka's subjective experience: throughout most of his life he had felt neither entirely free – the cook who marched him to school might have been a warder – nor entirely a prisoner, but the fist of the contradiction had never been so tightly clenched as during his abortive engagement. He saw Felice as the archenemy of his freedom to do as he pleased, to spend as much of his 'free' time writing as he wanted to.

It was coincidence that the word *Hof* (court) featured in the name of his favourite Berlin hotel, and he might in any case have hit on the word 'law court' (*Gerichtshof*) for the confrontation with Felice, Grete, Erna and Weiss. 'You were sitting as a judge over me in the Askanische Hof', he told Grete,[12] but he was accustomed to having the chief witness for the prosecution doubling in the role of judge, like the father in 'Das Urteil'. The memory of being carried out on to the balcony when he was about four was a memory of arbitrary punishment at the hands of an unchallengeable authority, while the whispering and laughing with Ottla in the bathroom, the conversations that looked like the plotting of 'cheeky conspirators',[13] were discussions about the 'frightful trial pending between you and us ... this trial in which you consistently claim to be judge, though you, for the most part ... are just as fallible and biased as we are'.[14] The only relief from the sense of being on trial would come when the death sentence was passed.

He had always sided against himself. At the Askanische Hof, he told Grete, 'I was sitting in your place, and still haven't moved out of it.'[15] In the first chapter of the novel, one of the warders who arrests Josef K. is called Franz, and they describe themselves as 'the ones who of all your fellow-creatures are closest to you'.[16] The first sentence tells us that he has done nothing wrong, and the warders do not know whether he is charged with an offence. The imputation of guilt probably has no more importance than he accords it. As he tells his landlady, 'if I'd behaved sensibly, nothing further would have happened'.[17] Listening to his father's explicit allegations, Kafka knew they were damaging only insofar as he accepted them.

Josef K. does not sit in the hostile judge's place, but he is a master in the art of making things worse for himself, like the Josef K. in the sketch who steals without needing to, and like Karl in *Der Verschollene*. In the dreamlike second chapter of *Der Prozess*, he takes a great deal of trouble to

present himself for interrogation, when, given no time and no precise
address, he could have absented himself, but once he is in the presence of
the examining magistrate, complaisance turns suddenly into its opposite.
Asked whether he is a house-painter, he ridicules the question as 'characteristic of the whole style of the proceedings being taken against me'.
After he has gone on to denounce the authorities and their methods, the
examining magistrate says: 'Today – though you may not yet realize this –
you've deprived yourself of the advantages an interrogation always gives
the accused.'[18] Kafka was doing the opposite of what he had done, at
inordinate length, in his letters to Felice; they constitute an elaborate
apologia for his way of living. He felt, guiltily, that his life was useless, but
he did not feel, even in his relationship with Grete, that he had done
anything wrong. Not that he felt innocent – 'diabolically innocent' was his
paradoxical verdict on himself. At the 'law court' in the hotel he had
remained silent or stammered incoherently, and the verdict – in effect –
had been 'guilty'. With perverse *esprit d'escalier* Josef K.'s defiant eloqu-
ence compensates for Kafka's inarticulacy. When he read the first pages to
his friends, he could not control his laughter.

The novel had its effect on his relationship with Felice. When he wrote
to her again after a three-month silence and after heralding the letter with
a telegram,[19] he described his internal conflict in terms of wrestling
between two selves. One of the selves, he said, was much as Felice would
wish it to be, and this self could develop sufficiently to close the gap
between the man he was and the man she wanted him to be.[20] (Again he is
contradicting his earlier contention that people could not be changed.)
The other self was obsessive about writing: 'the death of his best friend
would strike him as primarily a temporary obstacle in the way of working'.[21] But the first self would never overpower the second, would kneel
down to help him whenever necessary, oblivious of everything else.[22]

He still believed that his only chance of ever feeling free was through
literature. In the battle against the strongest internal enemy, torpor, he
was retreating whenever he failed to advance the book. On 1 September
he was angry with himself for writing barely two pages in spite of having
slept well.[23] Another internal enemy, in his opinion, was cold-
heartedness; his willingness to tolerate humiliation was both an advantage and a worrying symptom of hopelessness.[24]

As an official of an important national institute he was exempted from
military service, but not immune to anxieties about the war, which were
'like my old worries about Felice, tormentingly gnawing into me from
every angle. I can't bear anxiety, and perhaps it's my fate to be destroyed
by it.'[25] The Russian army was advancing into East Prussia. Austria–
Hungary had declared war on Russia on 5 August, and within a week

both France and Britain had declared war on Austria–Hungary. On 13 September, when Kafka again failed to produce more than two pages, 'At first I thought it was depression over the Austrian defeats and anxiety about the future.' But it was sluggishness, he decided. [26] Incessantly assessing the value of his own life, he was incessantly questioning whether he was entitled to stay alive. Other people's existences he never challenged in the same way, but in October, when he took a week off to work on the novel and found on Wednesday evening that he had made little headway, he was already asking himself whether the evidence proved he was unworthy of living without an office job. [27]

His guilt-feelings would go on edging him towards transcendentalism until the need to feel authoritatively condemned made it impossible for him to remain agnostic. Nothing was more integral to Kafka's vision than his awareness of himself as a failure, an awareness that burns its way into his narrative style. 'He couldn't fully prove his value, nor was it for him to do all the work of the authorities: the failure for that lay with whoever had denied him the remnant of the requisite strength.' The premiss of failure implies a viewpoint which is necessarily external, preferably extraterrestrial.

After putting himself on trial for an additional week by extending the holiday and staying at his desk, most nights, until five in the morning, and one night until 7.30, [28] he reprieved himself. He was still considering suicide, [29] but at least his output had been considerable, despite persistent headaches, [30] and he had not only had flashes of insight into his private situation but found how to brew positive artistic work out of suicidal inclinations and speculations about what experience might be like after death if consciousness survives. The last chapter he completed of *Der Verschollene*, the chapter Brod titled 'The Nature Theatre of Oklahoma', was written early in October, and it is more allegorical than any of the earlier narrative. Karl sees a placard announcing that the Oklahoma Theatre offers an engagement to everyone who comes along. Like death, it welcomes everybody. No one will be refused a place. [31] Karl, who has disgraced himself or at best failed in all his jobs and relationships, is eager to be accepted in a place where he will no longer feel ashamed. His motives are therefore negative – close to those behind Kafka's suicidal inclinations. The recruitment meeting is held on a racecourse, where hundreds of women are dressed as angels. They work for two-hour shifts. 'Then we're relieved by men dressed up as devils. Half of them blow trumpets and the other half plays drums.' [32] Some passages are quite funny, but the satire on conventional ideas of heaven and hell is blurred – perhaps by the underlying ambivalence towards death.

On Thursday 15 October a surprise letter from Grete Bloch intimated that the possibility of marriage with Felice was still open.[33] Though he remembered moments of aversion – Felice patting her hair at the Askanische Hof, Felice dancing 'with disapproving eyes lowered'[34] – the temptation was to submit. 'Indeed that was the only thing I wanted to do.'[35] But he wrote an unyielding reply, knowing it would be better for all three of them if it ended the correspondence. And knowing that it would not.[36] For two months he had been corresponding with Erna, but not with Felice. He had been dreaming about her as if she were dead,[37] but now she was 'again the centre of everything. She's probably disturbing my work, too.'[38] The novel did come virtually to a standstill for two weeks, though from August till 3 November there were only four days when he wrote nothing at all.[39] Impatiently he waited for Grete's reply, and, when it came he did not know how to answer it.[40] 'Thoughts so base I'm completely unable to write them down.... Totally incapacitated by sadness.'[41]

At the beginning of November Josef Pollak, who had been wounded in the hand, came home on sick leave. He would not have survived the trench-fighting, he believed, but for a mole. Seeing it burrowing under him, he thought heaven was signalling him to move away. As he started crawling along the trench, the man crawling behind him was hit by a bullet.[42] Pollak's captain had been taken prisoner, and the next day his naked body had been found in the woods with bayonet wounds all over it. Perhaps he had had money on him, and had refused to be searched, 'just like an officer'.[43] And some soldiers – to punish them – had been bound to a tree and left until the cold turned them blue. Stories of trench warfare may have contributed to the story 'In der Strafkolonie' ('In the Penal Colony') which was completed by the end of November; thanks to the Dreyfus affair and German war propaganda he would have already known about the penal colonies of French Guiana and Devil's Island. Kafka read it to Brod, Werfel and Pick on 2 December.[44] 'Not wholly dissatisfied, except at the ineradicable faults which are all too clear.'[45]

He had been working simultaneously on the story, on *Der Prozess* and on the chapter of *Der Verschollene*. One device used in both the chapter and the new novel is transposition of action associated with one locale to another. In setting the recruitment for the Nature Theatre on a racecourse, Kafka is giving himself both an ambience he liked and a base for introducing counterpoint. We are told that the umpire's platform is being used by the leader of the theatre, some of the bookmakers' booths are serving as offices for signing on recruits, some as employment bureaux, so that each recruit can be given a job similar to the one he has previously done. There is a mechanically controlled board normally used for announcing the names of horses that have won races, but now the names of recruits are flashed up as they are accepted. So, as in a dream, Kafka combines incongruous elements. Despite the associations of posthumous existence with theatre, with race-meetings and with employment bureaux, the action does not fit consistently into any of these frames. The dream-like anxiety of the writer infects the reader, who keeps trying to fit the story into an interpretative frame, and always fails.

Among Kafka's concerns are identity, bureaucracy and provincialism. Dissatisfied with the evidence of identity that his past failures constitute, Karl wants to find somewhere – on this side of the grave or beyond it – where they will not matter. He had not expected to be asked for his papers or be questioned about his past; he is, but he gives a false name, and his answers to questions are not checked by cross-examination. This pre-figures the way that K. in *Das Schloss* will claim to be a land-surveyor.

Karl never meets the leader of the theatre. Like Josef K. he has to deal with officials, employees with titles that make them sound important. But the theme to be explored in the late story 'Die Abweisung' is developed more clearly in *Der Prozess* and *Das Schloss* than it is in *Der Verschollene*. Karl is not personally threatened by the confusion that results from the introduction into one locale of associations belonging to another, but both Josef K. and K. will later be handicapped by mystification at the series of interrogations and juridical phenomena which are conducted or dis-covered in incongruous places. The two warders come into Joseph K.'s bedroom and eat his breakfast; the inspector questions him in the bed-room of another lodger, a desirable woman; to reach the room where the enquiry is held you have to pass through a dingy flat in the most tumbledown district of the city; in a lumber room at the bank where he works he finds the two warders being whipped because he complained about them at the enquiry. If the proceedings had all been made to take place in a courtroom, the danger would have appeared to be circum-scribed; as it is he can find a new threat at any moment, in any corner, behind any door, while his insecurities in relation to women are insepar-able from the guilt-feelings, which make increasingly painful inroads on him as the investigation proceeds. Its ubiquity implies that every area of his competence as a man is being challenged; the only area where Kafka felt secure is closed to his character – Josef K. is not a writer.

Mainly because he had interiorized so much of his father's aversion to him, Kafka was highly vulnerable to the critical hostility he believed to be present in other people's awareness of him. For him, as for Sartre's Garcin, *l'enfer c'est les autres*. In the third chapter of *Der Prozess*, the wife of the law court attendant allows K. – Kafka's identification with him seems to increase when he drops the Christian name – to see the books on the Examining Magistrate's table. Everything in the room is dirty, and the tattered old books are pornographic novels with crude illustrations.

Emotionally Kafka envied his father's confidence and competence, while, intellectually he placed more value on the intellectual qualities which he had and his father lacked. But any analysis such as this leaves sexuality out of account, and there is a dream-like insistence in the narrative on bringing sexuality into the foreground. In the first courtroom scene proceedings are interrupted by a shriek. A woman with sparkling black eyes is being clasped by a man: it is he who has uttered the shriek.[46] Later she will offer herself to K., who wants her, in spite of anxiety that she may be trying to trap him. But her molester, a bow-legged student, Bertold, who is always fingering his straggling reddish beard, is watching them from the corner of the courtroom. She promises herself to K. but says she must talk to Bertold first. It is now that the narrative parallels what occurred when Kafka had his first sexual experience. K., who has to watch while the student embraces her, registers impatience by pacing noisily up and down. Each of the rivals tells the other to go away, but the decisive factor is that Bertold has been sent – or so the woman says – by the Examining Magistrate, another suitor for her sexual favours. There is an unmistakably Oedipal flavour not only to K.'s interest in her but to the whole sequence, which has an affinity with Klimt's *Jurisprudence*, in which the rebellion against judicial authority also seems Oedipal in origin. The hopeless, bowed, ageing male victim, imprisoned in a womb which has tentacles, is as helpless as a foetus. The three Furies who surround him, voluptuous and indifferent, bulk much larger than the judges, who are represented only by impotent, withered, disembodied heads.

Kafka's Examining Magistrate is a 'small, fat, wheezing man'[47] and Josef K. feels eager to dispossess him of his woman. Later, in the office of the lawyer, Huld, K. will see an imposing picture of a judge on a high, throne-like seat, but the actual man, Leni says, is 'almost a dwarf'. Still later the painter Titorelli will be seen at work on another portrait of a judge. Retouching the figure of Justice in the background, he makes it look 'just like the goddess of the Hunt in full cry'. When the woman in the courtroom lets Bertold carry her off, K. feels that this is

the first indubitable defeat he'd suffered from these people. There was nothing, of course, to worry about; he had been defeated only because he had joined battle. If he had remained at home, leading his normal life, he would have been a thousand times superior to these people, and could have kicked each one of them out of his way.[48]

Kafka the writer is wrestling with Kafka the would-be fiancé. As the woman is carried up a flight of wooden stairs towards a garret – a surprising place for the Examining Magistrate to use – she waves to K., as Felice's parents had waved to him. Or as the shopgirl had in 1903.

K.'s first encounter with Leni is even more strikingly Oedipal. K.'s Uncle Karl, an aggressive father-figure, takes him to meet the attorney, Huld, an invalid who is being nursed by a girl with a round, doll-like face. The Chief Clerk of the Court in charge of the case, who is visiting Huld, seems amiably disposed to K., and Huld seems both influential and willing to help, but hearing a noise of breaking crockery, K. discovers that Leni has thrown a plate against the wall to bring him out, and he lets her take him into another room. He stays with her so long that when he goes back the Chief Clerk has already left, and his uncle is waiting outside in a car, fuming. 'How could you do a thing like that? You've badly damaged your case, which was going quite well. Creeping away with a dirty little thing, who's obviously the lawyer's mistress, and staying away for hours!'[49] K. has begun a new love-affair at the cost of alienating three powerful father-figures.

Perhaps there was also something Oedipal in the way Felice's appeal had increased with her inaccessibility, her willingness to let his letters go unanswered for weeks, her tantalizing use of an intermediary. As with Frieda Brandenfeld in 'Das Urteil', Kafka was thinking of Felice's initials when he introduced Fräulein Bürstner, the woman in *Der Prozess* whose room is invaded by the inspector. A white blouse is dangling from the latch of the open window.[50] Elias Canetti associates Fräulein Bürstner with Grete Bloch and this blouse with the dress she wore at the engagement party,[51] but Kafka is more likely to have been thinking of the blouse Felice had been wearing when he first saw her – 'Blouse flung on anyhow.'[52] Fräulein Bürstner resists K.'s urgent entreaties for a meeting first by a prolonged silence and later by using another girl, Fräulein Montag, as an intermediary. Fräulein Montag, whose lame, trailing gait is very well realized, is invited to move into Fräulein Bürstner's room, apparently as a means of defending the territory against K.'s encroachment.

As in *Der Verschollene*, the hero abandons a low-ranking acquaintance to injustice. Leaving the stoker in the lurch, Karl lets himself be led away like a child; when Franz is being whipped in the lumber room, K., who is not too young to take responsibility, could intervene either by offering money to the man who is whipping him or by offering himself as an alternative victim.[53] The adult *alter ego* does no more than the child had done to protect Czech employees from the injustices of his belligerent father.

After working prolifically through most of November, Kafka thought he had come to a stand-still. 'I'm at the ultimate boundary, where I'll stay perhaps for years, and then perhaps begin another story that won't get finished. This destiny dogs me. Also I'm cold and atrophied again, nothing remains except a senile desire for complete peace.'[54] But he did not stop writing. In December he produced another chapter, which is far more profoundly death-oriented than the Nature Theatre chapter in *Der Verschollene.* K. has been told that no one is ever acquitted by the court, that its final decisions are never recorded, that the best he can hope for is either ostensible acquittal – which is temporary – or postponement.[55] All this suggests the death sentence we are all condemned to, and in a passage Kafka wrote at the beginning of December, the priest, talking to K. from the pulpit, says that the proceedings gradually develop into a verdict. He is still in the pulpit when they argue about whether all men are innocent – 'We're all men here,' says K., 'one's much like another.' But the priest comes down before telling the story about the man from the country who asks for access to the Law. 'But the doorkeeper says that he can't let him in now. The man thinks it over and asks whether he'll be admitted later. "It's possible," says the doorkeeper, "but not now."'' He provides a stool for the man, who sits waiting for days and years, often asking to be allowed inside, often trying to bribe the doorkeeper, never trying to force his way in, deterred by the furred robe, the huge pointed nose, the Tartar beard, and the man's stories of even more powerful guards inside the building. In the last moments of his life, realizing that in all these years no one else has applied for admittance through this door, he asks why. 'No one else could have been admitted here, for this door was intended only for you. I'm now going to shut it.'[56]

As the priest points out, there is no reason to assume that the door-keeper is lying. Between what he says on the first day and what he says on the last the contradiction is only apparent, which could be taken to imply that the doorway to the Law is the doorway to death, that the law of life is the law of death, but the law against suicide makes it illegal for the man to choose his moment. It must be chosen for him. This will be his punishment, even if he has done nothing wrong. No one is acquitted.

The story is more like a parable than the final chapter of *Der Verschollene* or 'In der Strafkolonie', and the cathedral context arouses expectations that it may have a religious meaning. There is no description of the building in which the gate (Tor) is situated; all we are told is: 'Before the Law stands a doorkeeper,'[57] and what he says about other doorkeepers implies that the building is as large as a castle or a palace. In the upper world, according to some Kabbalistic parables, there are seven palaces, each guarded by hosts of gatekeepers, and God sits at the highest point, surrounded by awesome mystery. The phrase 'man from the country' is also Judaic in origin. Kafka's diary shows that he was familiar with the phrase *am ha' aretz* (one from the land),[58] and according to a book he possessed on Judaism during the lifetime of Jesus,[59] the phrase was used pejoratively by the Pharisees for an ignorant or sinful man.[60] A man, in other words, who is out of touch with the Law. So there is something in common between the man from the country and the soldier in the story written the previous month – the law he had ignorantly broken was to be engraved on his body by the machine that would kill him. One of the warders in the first chapter of *Der Prozess* tells K. that according to the Law 'our officials' are attracted to guilt. And when K. retorts, 'I don't know this law', he is told, 'You'll get to feel it.'[61] The Muirs translate this as 'You'll come up against it yet',[62] but *fühlen* implies that in these proceedings the process of learning is as much physical as mental.

What does Kafka mean by Law? In Judaism the Torah symbolizes cosmic law, and it is held in the Kabbalah to have pre-existed the creation of the world. The divine mysteries could be partially revealed through interpretation of the Torah according to what Scholem calls the 'unlimited mystical plasticity of the divine word',[63] and in writing the parable of the doorkeeper Kafka found what he had been reaching for – tentatively in the chapter about the Nature Theatre and more confidently in the story about the penal colony – a narrative dramatization of paradox. Interpretation can be grafted into the narrative, as in the priest's conversation with Josef K. about the meaning of the story, which Kafka wrote later, on 13 December, but the meaning is like an elusive cluster of seaweed which can never be brought to the surface intact. The context associates the Law with the authority that is accusing K., but if he is guilty, the guilt seems to consist partly in his inability to find out what law he is alleged to have violated. Guilt-feelings are fomented by uncertainty and this is how the proceedings develop into a verdict. On one level the Law can be equated with the laws of Judaism: according to these, Josef K., like Kafka, is guilty of failing to procreate. ('Be fruitful and multiply' is a commandment.) The Law is also the cosmic law or the human condition which condemns all of us to death. No one is acquitted, and each of us has his own doorway to death, but the law against suicide forbids us to make our own choice about when to go through it. At the same time the parable can be interpreted in relation to the Kabbalistic tradition 'that the Torah turns a special face to every single Jew, meant only for him and apprehensible only by him, and that a Jew therefore fulfils his true purpose only when he comes to see this face and is able to incorporate it into the tradition'.[64] Here Hasidism is at one with Kierkegaard: *Fear and Trembling* urges that the individual's relation to the Absolute must be personal, unique.

Kafka's fear was that he was himself a man from the country, a provincial who would never be summoned to the royal presence, never see the face of God or the face that the Law turned towards him. Less than a year earlier he had defined 'non-folly' as standing 'like a beggar before the threshold, to the side of the entrance, decaying till the moment of collapse'. Behind the parable's development of this image is Kafka's terror of being paralysed by indecision. It might have been folly to ignore the doorkeeper's warning about the hierarchy of still more formidable doorkeepers, but non-folly was worse.

Determination to put his precepts into practice explains the non-sequitur in the diary entry for 30 November: the observation that nothing is left except a senile desire for peace is followed by the resolution that if self-disgust does not prevent him, he will try again to have Felice back.[65] Apparently the only alternatives were suicide and a marriage that might paralyse him as a writer. Her father had died at the beginning of November after a heart attack, and a month later, when Erna, who was due to take a Christmas trip with him, described the family situation, he blamed himself for making Felice unhappy and for driving a wedge between the sisters. He even tried to share the blame for the final heart attack.[66]

Even the tiniest of worries acted on him punitively, but the fear of death was a source of pleasure. Unless he was in great pain, he said, he would lie very contentedly on his deathbed. All the best things he had written had their basis in

this capacity for dying in a satisfied way. In all these fine and convincing passages someone's dying, and they're about his extreme difficulty in dying, how unjust or at least cruel he finds it. . . . Such descriptions are secretly a game, I enjoy dying with the dying man, can therefore calculate my exploitation of the attention that the reader focuses on the death, keeping a clearer head than he, who'll presumably complain when he's on his deathbed.[67]

In the story he wrote on 18 December Kafka comes closer to parodying Talmudic commentators on the Bible. 'Der Dorfschullehrer' ('The Village Schoolteacher')[68] describes a businessman's ill-conceived attempts to vindicate a village schoolmaster who has published a pamphlet about a giant mole. Without having seen the mole, a reputable savant dismisses the phenomenon; without having read the pamphlet, the businessman writes one of his own in defence of the teacher, who then writes another pamphlet. Printed words, confusion, suspicion, envy and bitterness all accumulate, eclipsing the animal.[69]

Kafka's father had again become reproachful about the asbestos factory, which was steadily losing money. He blamed his son for inveigling him into the investment: 'Then went home and wrote peacefully for three hours, in the awareness that my guilt is indubitable, if not so great as father makes out.'[70] He was doing his best to live in the interstices of the lawsuit being conducted against him, but he could not pretend that his freedom of movement was unaffected. The next day, Saturday, he did not go into the living-room for dinner, partly from fear of his father, partly to have more time for writing.[71] For about two months he had been keeping his watch an hour and a half fast.[72]

He spent Christmas with the Brods at the Hotel Morawetz in Kutten-berg. He was given a bedroom which, like the maid's room in his flat, had a window that looked inwards. It was hard to write in the room. Con-stantly reproaching himself and resolving to make better use of his time, he was thinking about deliverance, and almost equating it with extinc-tion: 'It won't come from this notebook, it will come when I'm in bed, and will lay me on my back, so that I'm lying there beautiful and light and bluish white, another kind of deliverance will not come.'[73]

Still working on *Der Prozess*, he was still paralleling K.'s experiences so closely that fictional entries in his diary are almost indistinguishable from factual entries. A merchant is dogged for so long by bad luck that he consults a legal expert. This man always has the Law – *die Schrift* can mean scripture – open in front of him, and all his clients are greeted with the words: 'I'm just reading about your case.' Extravagant though it is, the assertion suggests that help may be possible, while assuaging the fear of being harmed secretly by processes which no one else could under-stand.[74] This is allegory domesticated to a diary function. Josef K. on the other hand, tormented by a similar fear of proceedings continuing secretively against him, is not reassured when he keeps meeting people who know about his case.

15 Exodus

Like the three months September–November 1912, the period June–December 1914 had been extremely productive. This pattern would persist through the remainder of Kafka's life – after several months of hyper-activity he would lie fallow for two or three years.

At the beginning of the new year he was resisting the temptation of starting a new story.[1] In spite of his appetite for self-conquest and ruthlessness in battling against insomnia, headaches and pains around the heart, he still had not finished *Der Prozess* or *Der Verschollene* or the stories 'Der Dorfschullehrer', 'Erinnerungen an die Kaldabahn' ('Memories of the Kalda Railway') or 'Der Unterstaatsanwalt' ('The Assistant Attorney').[2] He believed that each story, if it was any good, secreted its whole structure long before it was fully developed;[3] but he also found that stories could disintegrate and get lost if he failed to chase after them by working all through the night.[4] He went on trying to sleep a great deal in the afternoon to store up energy for later, but he found that if he stayed awake after one o'clock he could not sleep at all, and felt ill all through the next day.

When Karl Hermann's brother was called up, Kafka had to go to the factory almost every afternoon. 'Thoughts of the factory are my non-stop Day of Atonement.'[5] And thoughts of happiness with a woman – he had seen an attractive girl from Lemberg at a lecture by Brod – were like 'hopes of eternal life. Viewed from a certain distance they hold their ground, but one daren't approach closely.'[6] Putting 'Der Dorfschullehrer' and 'Der Unterstaatsanwalt' aside, he began a new story on 18 January.[7] 'Now standing up right before me are four or five stories like horses in front of the ringmaster Schumann at the beinning of a circus performance.'[8]

Going to the factory gave him a feeling of 'direct contact with breadwinning',[9] and this was as inimical to writing as it had been when he was at the Assicurazioni Generali. He was also feeling guilty about Ottla. 'I've really suppressed her, and ruthlessly, through indifference and ineptness.... It's my fault her social instincts have remained undeveloped.'[10] She was now in Berlin, where he hoped she would recover from him.

As the ability to work receded – the next period of hyper-activity would not begin till November 1916 – the desire to see Felice grew stronger. For the first time since breaking off the engagement, they met on 24 January in

Bodenbach. She had been up all night travelling;[11] he again found that in her presence he could not stop himself from holding out hope for a shared future, though he still insisted it must centre on his writing, while she was thinking of comfort based on an active interest in the factory, central heating, and going to bed at eleven.[12] Symbolically she put his watch right. She called Elli and Valli 'shallow', failed to enquire about Ottla, failed to inspire anything but boredom and despair. Though they were alone together for two hours, 'We still haven't shared a single good moment when I could breathe freely.'[13] With the girls in Zuckmantel and Riva he had felt loving and loved; Felice made him feel 'boundless admiration, submissiveness, pity, despair and self-contempt'.[14]

Listening to him read his work, she lay back on a sofa with her eyes closed. 'The sentences came out in a repulsive confusion, no rapport with the listener.'[15] But when he read the doorkeeper story, she was attentive and responsive. He had already written the interpretative discussion between Josef K. and the priest, but he now felt he had only just under-stood the story, though she had grasped it immediately.[16] 'Then of course we pitched in with crude comments, I began it.'[17]

The next day, starting on a letter to her, he immediately felt closer to her than when they had been together.

Perhaps it's a pity that I can't quarrel, I literally wait for cogency to emerge, demanding it from inside myself. . . . We walk peacefully side by side, but under-neath that, there's a twitching as if someone were constantly trying to slice up the air between us with a sword.[18]

On the whole, the letter was conciliatory, though he still felt tetchy at being pressed to make more effort over the factory.[19]

Soon he found he did not have to go there so often: Karl Hermann's brother, Rudl, who was stationed in Prague, managed to spend an hour or so there every day.[20] After meeting Felice, Kafka found he was coping better with office life,[21] but worse with the stories that were still claiming attention, like the clients waiting at the bank for Josef K., when he was too preoccupied with his own affairs to realize how badly he was treating them. After two weeks of being unable to write, Kafka started on the story that was later titled 'Blumfeld, ein älterer Junggeselle' ('Blumfeld, an Elderly Bachelor'). Inspired partly by the fear of what might become of him if he failed to reach agreement with Felice, the story failed to please him. He found it 'evil, pedantic, mechanical, a fish on a sandbank, scarcely breathing. I'm writing my *Bouvard et Pecuchet* very prematurely. If the two elements – at their most pronounced in 'Der Heizer' and in 'Strafkolonie' – don't come together, I'm lost. But why should they come together?'[22]

Having found out, accidentally, through the war, how much better he felt living away from the family, he decided to rent a room of his own. Looking for it was more depressing than looking for a flat to share with Felice. 'People bury themselves in dirt ... they confuse dirt – I mean overcrowded sideboards, rugs in front of windows, profusions of photographs on misused desks, linen heaped up on beds, parlour palms in corners – they confuse all this with luxury.'[23] He settled on a room in the same house in Bilekgasse where Valli lived, so he was not moving entirely away from his family. To his elderly landlady's distress, his first action on moving in was to stop the striking clock.[24] But the walls were thin. He could hear the clock in the neighbouring room, and however considerate she was, however little time the other lodger spent in the flat, Kafka could hear doors opening and shutting, as well as coughing, the doorbell, low-toned conversations between landlady and lodger. 'For reading, for studying, for sleeping, for nothing does anyone need the silence I need for writing.'[25] There was less noise in the room than in his parents' flat, but unfamiliar sounds disturbed him more. Though the landlady, who wanted him to stay with her for the rest of his life,[26] even offered to hang a heavy curtain outside the door of his room, he was already thinking of giving notice on the first day,[27] and he actually gave it after three weeks. He had been suffering from headaches that persisted for days, and had done no work that satisfied him, mainly

because of my own disquiet. I want to torment myself, to keep changing my situation, believe in the hunch that my salvation lies in change, and, what's more, believe that through such small changes, which cause violent activity in all my faculties though other people can make them while half asleep, I can prepare myself for the great change I probably need. I'm moving into a room that's certainly inferior in many ways.[28]

It was on the fifth floor of a house in Langengasse, a pleasant, comfortable corner room with a door onto the balcony, and he moved at the beginning of March. The new room was 'about ten times as noisy as the other room, but incomparably better in every other way. I thought the location and appearance of a room didn't matter to me. But they do.'[29] A large expanse of sky was visible from his window, together with the roofs and towers of the Altstadt and, across the river, the Laurenziberg. The room was higher than the surrounding rooftops; the morning sun woke him by shining directly on him.[30] And the noise of carts in the street started in the early morning. Usually there was silence only after eleven at night.[31] He felt incapable of working and in danger of losing 'everything I've painstakingly achieved during the last half year'.[32] On 16 March he resumed work on 'Der Unterstaatsanwalt', and happily went back to it the next day, only to be disturbed by the sounds of a party next door or underneath. 'Struggled with the noise a little while, then lay on the sofa with my nerves almost torn to shreds.'[33]

The engine that operated the lift reverberated through the attics above his room as if someone had installed 'a purposeless noise-machine that imitates the sound of a skittle-game. A heavy ball's rolled rapidly over the entire length of the ceiling, hits the corner and bumps slowly back.'[34] He sent to Berlin for some 'Oropax', an ear-wax coated with cotton-wool. 'It's a nuisance, having to block one's ears up while one is still alive.'[35]

Beyond the damage that the war was doing to the asbestos factory – the salary rise he had in March of 100 kronen which was derisory in comparison with his liabilities if the factory went bankrupt[36] – he felt guilty at taking no part in the fighting. He had decided against volunteering for active service, though he might later be enlisted.[37] He would have felt out of place in the army, as he felt out of place in Prague. He was still too violently in conflict with himself, he thought, to drag anyone else into the battlefield.[38] 'Before feeling entitled or being entitled to another human being, one must either have advanced further than I have or not choose the path I'm totally committed to following.'[39]

In April he escorted Elli on a visit to her husband, who was serving in Hungary. They travelled by train through Vienna to Budapest, where they saw an old couple weeping as they were about to part.[40] Outside Budapest, among the ploughed fields, Kafka and Elli saw sandbagged shelters and barbed wire entanglements.[41] At Ujhel he tried in vain, first at the squad headquarters and then at the rear headquarters, for permission to travel on a military train. In the town a one-armed soldier was walking around ostentatiously, while a crowd surrounded the crudely coloured poster announcing a German victory.[42] Kafka and Elli spent a night in Sátoraljaújhely, and went on through Hatvau to Nagy Mihály. Travelling back without his sister, Kafka spent a couple of hours in Budapest, and arrived in Prague on 27 April.

At the beginning of May he was feeling apathetic, lethargic, impotent. 'The present is ghostly, I don't sit at the table, I flit around it.'[43] The best anti-depressant was Strindberg. 'I read him not to read him but to lie at his breast. He holds me like a child on his left arm.'[44] One reason Kafka felt frustrated when passive was that writing could give him the illusion of inching his way towards his objective of being understood, of bringing the reader to know him as well as he knew himself. To have a wife who knew him and supported him from every angle would be like having God – having the possibility of loving approval from outside. Brod and Weltsch understood a good deal about him, Ottla even more. Erna Bauer understood only a little, but with great intensity; 'F. perhaps understands nothing at all.'[45]

She had sent him a copy of Flaubert's *Salammbô*, inscribed as if the relationship were hopeless. This he denied. 'Nothing is over. . . . We must begin anew.'[46] But he added that 'we' referred only to himself and the relationship. 'For you were and are in the right.'[47] This phrase *im richtigen* is a translation of Flaubert's phrase *dans le vrai*. Kafka often quoted this phrase, which Flaubert had used about a woman and her children. Like Kafka, Flaubert had sacrificed almost everything to literature, and in her *Souvenirs intimes*, his niece, Caroline Commanville, raises the question of whether, towards the end of his life, he regretted it. Walking home along the banks of the Seine one day after a visit to the woman and her children, he said: 'Ils sont dans le vrai. Oui, ils sont dans le vrai.'[48] Perhaps Felice might be able to procure for Kafka an entry permit to *le vrai*. The other possible way in for him was through the army. He would be called up at the end of May or the beginning of June. 'You should hope, as I do, that I'll be accepted.'[49] Meanwhile her silence was worrying him, as it had when she had been in Frankfurt, just over two years earlier. Suddenly she had appeared to have no time for him. He reminded her of the desperate letters he had written. 'Believe me, I'm basically not at all far from writing them again now. They're lying in wait at the tip of my pen. But they won't be written.'[50]

They spent Whitsun (23–4 May) together in Switzerland with Grete Bloch. Kafka still felt that he and Felice's fiancé were two different men, but on the train back to Prague the two men sat on the same seat. 'In my opinion he's completely addicted to F., you should have seen him chasing after memories of F. and her room all the way back along the lilac (this is the only time he's ever taken anything like that on a journey).'[51] The next day he was still writing in the third person: 'Look, he says he's frightened. . . . After two days there are ties. . . . Sleeping under the same roof, eating at the same table, living twice through the same daily routine . . . he's asking for the bilberry snapshot, wanting to hear about her toothache and waiting impatiently for news.'[52] If his health did not satisfy the military authorities, he would like to travel with her to the Baltic coast.[53] The tone of the postcard is fairly bright, and he explicitly denies being unhappy, but in his diary he wrote: 'Am going to pieces. To break up so pointlessly and unnecessarily.'[54]

Depression was his norm, but having drifted away from his anchorage in the family, and failing to consolidate his relationship with Felice or crystallize his anxieties into fiction – or even to bottle them in his diaries – he was at a new nadir of self-loathing and self-torment. He was rejected by the call-up board. During June he joined her in Karlsbad, but could not relax in her company, and when he was back in Prague 'it became intolerable for me, I had to get away. I was being driven away, and since sleeplessness and everything that goes with it joined forces with the pressure, I gave in.'[55] He would have liked to go a long way, perhaps to Lake Wolfgang, but, deterred by the seventeen-hour train journey, he opted for a sanatorium near Rumburg in northern Bohemia. 'My worst disease is – I don't know – impatience or patience.'[56]

By the end of July he was calmer, at least some of the time. 'Great, beautiful forests. Simply hilly but not mountainous countryside, so it is just right for my present frame of mind.'[57] Why had he come to a sanatorium? 'Is there no night-time in a sanatorium? It's worse than that, day-time is just like night-time.'[58]

Back in Prague he felt close to madness. 'Neither in the office nor in conversations elsewhere can I take in more than the most superficial details, and this only between all the pains and tensions in my head.'[59] He found himself treating Felice as she had once treated him – not writing,[60] or sending a postcard or a telegram to promise a letter, which would then get written long after it was due.[61] It seemed absurd to go on living in Prague. Though unable to concentrate on other people, he dreaded being alone in a room; though plagued by insomnia, he found sleep was no better, for dreams were delirious.[62] Worst of all was the knowledge that as time passed, grounds for optimism were slipping away. Could anything improve his situation? Even if she joined him in Prague, it would solve only some of the problems and only at the price of exacerbating others.[63] Writing to her he was still alternating between first and third person, but now the device seems more desperate, more schizoid. 'He's feverish, completely out of control and distracted. . . . Ultimately I couldn't put him in the wrong for not writing? Aren't his letters more hurtful than silence?'[64]

The worst despondency was from May to September. By the middle of May he had 'lapsed from all regularity in writing'.[65] Re-reading parts of 'Der Heizer' he felt incapable of equalling it. The pains around his heart were more troublesome.[66] After the two-line entry in his diary for 27 May[67] there is silence until he begins a new manuscript book on 13 September, saying he no longer needs the diary as much as he used to.[68] The question 'when is it coming'[69] probably refers to death: 'how can a heart, a heart which isn't quite sound, survive so much dissatisfaction and the incessant devastation of so much desire? The distractedness, the forgetfulness, the stupidity!'[70] Nor was he tormented less by headaches or insomnia, and in the middle of September he experienced a new kind of headache – short stabbing pains above the eye and to the side of it.[71]

He did not go to synagogue on the Day of Atonement, but far from feeling immune to divine judgment he called his behaviour 'suicidal',[72] while his fantasy of being sliced up by a butcher's knife shifted into one of wielding the knife himself:

The best place to stab seems to be between the throat and the chin. You raise the chin and stick the knife into the tensed muscles. . . . You expect to see a splendid gush of blood there, and to cut into a network of sinews and little bones, similar to what is found in the thighs of roast turkeys.[73]

When he opened a Bible he happened on the episode of the unjust judges. 'So I come up against my own opinion, or at least the opinion I have previously found in myself.'[74] He felt ill, but was so used to feeling ill it was pointless to complain, and another attack of stabbing pains in his head seemed like an answer.[75] But he deflected his suicidal tendencies by killing his characters. 'Rossmann and K., the guiltless and the guilty one, finally both struck punitively down without discrimination, the guiltless one with a gentler hand, more pushed aside than struck down.'[76] The opening statement that K. had done nothing wrong might have seemed to mean that he, like Rossmann, was guiltless, but Kafka's narrative does not dissociate itself from the judgment passed on him. It is partly that he has been contaminated by the proceedings against him, partly that he has failed to react to them as he should have done, partly that guilt was latent from the outset. 'Whoever seeks does not find, but whoever does not seek is found.'[77] K. had not sought.

Der Prozess is the only novel of Kafka's to arrive at an ending. As J. J. White notices, he was especially reluctant to complete the stories that envisage death as a possible conclusion: of about seventy-five finished stories, only five end in death,[78] while he never got around to killing Karl Rossmann. Although he did not destroy the ending of *Der Prozess* (as he did other endings) he achieved within it a mesh of ambiguity and negation which effectively cancels any meaning that can be seen in Josef K.'s death. Probably Kafka did not himself understand why his character connives in his execution but refuses to kill himself. On the evening before his thirty-first birthday – thirty-one was the age at which Hermann Kafka became a father – two top-hatted, frock-coated men, who look to K. like tenth-rate actors, pale and plump, lead him from his room to the street, where they 'wound the full length of their arms around his, and clasped K.'s hands in a disciplined, practised, irresistible grip'.[79] Kafka must have been drawing on the memory of the happy dream about walking along with Felice, arms and legs tightly intertwined. At one point a policeman with a bushy moustache appears, his hand on the handle of his sabre, 'the sabre entrusted to him by the state', Kafka wrote at first, but suppressed the phrase.[80] In a passage which is crossed out, K. threatens to turn over the proceedings to the law of the land;[81] in the final version he pulls the two men forcibly forwards just as the policeman is about to open his mouth. Kafka does not want to be over-explicit about the divergence between the Law of the Trial and the Law of the Land.

On 20 July 1916 Kafka would write in his diary: 'If I'm condemned, I'm condemned not just to death but to struggle until death comes.'[82] This is the law of *Der Prozess*: part of the sentence is that the suspect remains on trial. There is no line to divide end-result from process, and this is one of the reasons for the inadequacy of the ending. Another is that Kafka had the mixture of strength and weakness to answer affirmatively three questions which K. wants to answer negatively. Am I going to reveal that a whole year of struggling with my case has taught me nothing? Am I to quit this world as a man who fights shy of all conclusions? Is it to be said of me after my death that at the beginning of the proceedings I wanted them to end and at the end wanted them to begin all over again? In Scharkansky's play *Kol Nidre* the lovers escape execution by leaping prematurely into the flames; when K.'s executioners produce the double-edged butcher's knife which has featured so often in Kafka's fantasies, they keep handing it to each other, and as it passes backwards and forwards above him, K. realizes he is intended to grab it and stick it into his own chest.[83] (Once again the underlying subject is suicide and his failure to commit it.) 'He couldn't fully satisfy expectations.'[84] On the top floor of a nearby house a window opens, a faint human figure leaning abruptly outwards, reaching out its arms. K. will see nothing more godlike than this figure. But there's no help to be had from on high: at most there's a witness, whether helpless or merely unhelpful. 'Logic is indeed unshakeable, but it doesn't resist a man who wants to live. Where was the judge he'd never seen? Where was the high court to which he'd never been summoned? He raised his hands and spread out all his fingers.'[85] This is the moment at which the knife is stuck into his heart and turned twice. ' "Like a dog", he said, it was as if the shame should outlive him.'[86] Is there any connection between the human figure and the judge? Is there any compassion in the gesture of the figure, any prayer in K.'s? What is it that is shameful? Nor, in this case, is the ambiguity lessened by the two sentences in the first person which Kafka suppressed: 'I have to speak. I raise my hands.'[87] Most perplexing of all is the 'should' (*sollte*). This implies both intentionality and a moral code. Is this hunger for shame integral to the Law of the process and to the Law that remains unavailable to the man from the country who dies, shamefully enough, at the threshold? Is the force that intends the shame to survive the same as the force that intended the door to be used exclusively by the man from the country? Can the whole novel be read as a parable about the

accessibility of death and the inaccessibility of the authority that pronounces the death sentence? Can the shame lie in the lack of congruence?
Or is the shame merely shame at being unable to commit suicide, to
complete the process or complete the task? Can both now be identified
with self-destruction?

The impossibility of answering these questions does not point to a
weakness in the novel. Nor was it disadvantageous that Kafka had no gift
or inclination for novelistic mimicry, and no distinctive narrative voice.
He succeeds in turning personal material outwards: it is helpful that the
narrative voice is neutral. Kafka had discovered what is both a means of
dramatizing his self-accusations and an accurate fictional correlative to a
pattern of self-frustration which dogs a great many lives besides his own.
He was right to abandon a chapter about Josef K.'s visit to his mother and
an episode in which he penetrates to the court where the warrant for his
arrest had been issued. These would have reduced both his isolation – a
mother cannot be alienated as an uncle can – and his confusion about the
extent to which knowledge of the proceedings against him must be
subjective. As it is, isolation and uncertainty combine to propel him
towards execution. Kafka partially redeems the failure of the ending by
introducing two executioners who disappoint their victim: the court
should have been able to do better than employ men like old-fashioned
actors to finish him off. Kafka will be similarly disappointed that God
employs nothing more sophisticated than tuberculosis.

In October 1915, Kafka heard that Ottomar Starke, the theatrical
designer and illustrator, was to do a drawing for the title page of Kurt
Wolff's new edition of 'Die Verwandlung'. Kafka, who had seen some of
Starke's work, was afraid he wanted to depict the insect. 'Not that, please
not that!... The insect itself cannot be illustrated. It cannot even be
shown from a distance.'[88] The picture could be of the parents with the
head clerk outside the locked door, or with the sister in the light, with the
door of the adjoining room opening into darkness.[89] The resultant drawing shows a folding door in the background with one section ajar. In the
foreground a man in a morning coat is clasping his hands to his face.

In November Kafka thought excitedly about investing 2,000 kronen in
war bonds, and calculated how much time he could spend writing.

Despite heart-pains, ran over the stone bridge, felt the all too familiar misery of
the devouring fire that must not break out, made up – to express myself and calm
myself – the phrase 'Gush forth, little friend,' sang it again and again to a special
tune, and accompanied the song by squeezing and releasing the handkerchief in
my pocket as if it were a bagpipe.[90]

But nothing could curb his compulsion to evaluate his life, to balance it
critically against other people's. Comparing himself with Abraham

Grünberg, a tubercular refugee who had written an account of the pogrom in his home town, Siedlce, Kafka asked: what if one of them had to die now? And what if the choice was his? The answer was obvious: Grünberg's life was incomparably more valuable than his.[91] Feeling he must either kill himself or justify himself, he constantly adduced defensive arguments which then struck him as inadmissible. This was the torture he had devised for himself.

His headaches were as bad as ever, with throbbing and gnawing pains,[92] or sometimes a pain like burning.[93] He was wary of self-pity,[94] but it was impossible not to postulate a divine perspective on his sufferings: 'Who can be looking down on this from beginning to end with open eyes?'[95] Even if he had felt well enough to meet Felice, he could not have travelled to Berlin – or she to Prague – without an official permit, which would not have been granted for a journey that was not considered necessary.

'If the stabbing in the head goes no deeper', he wrote on 5 December, 'I'm glad. . . . But I don't want to thrust a man like this at you. . . . Even the authentic voice of an angel from heaven, I believe, would fail to help me now, so low have I sunk.'[96] He kept thinking in terms of being observed or offered help, notwithstanding the admonition to Josef K. about relying too much on other people. Kafka still blamed his malaise largely on Prague: he should have left three years ago.[97] He could not move while the war lasted, he said, but as soon as it was over he would settle in Berlin.[98] Frightened he was near to breaking down, he asked Pfohl whether his exemption from military service could be cancelled. Instead he was given a week's leave.

On Christmas Day 1915, looking back at his diary, he realized that over the past three or four years he could have made thousands of entries all more or less identical with the last one, all complaining ineffectually.[99] But, at thirty-two, he could no longer believe, as he had ten years earlier, that it was within his powers to solve the problems that made life so difficult for him.

16 Hopeful Interlude

Kafka had not been looking forward to the changes peace would bring. 'My first task will be to creep into a hole somewhere and check myself over.'[1] It was now Felice who complained about protracted silences, but he was reluctant to inflict pain: 'Isn't every word a strain on the nerves of both writer and reader?'[2] Nor could he make any practical proposal: 'I see no remedy except to wait, even if it means being ground to dust . . . I'd like to open a trap door and let myself sink through to anywhere.'[3] He did not want to see her until he felt free. 'On all sides I'm so hemmed in by ghosts, and the office stops me from escaping them.'[4] A minor misfortune like a cold in the head could seem disastrous. 'I'm desperate, like a caged rat, sleeplessness and headaches raging through me, I really can't describe how I get through the days.'[5]

The office was unusually busy, and he was working from eight till two, and from four till six, besides putting in appearances at the factory.[6] But whenever he half-heartedly tried to leave the institute, he always let himself be persuaded to stay. Pfohl said the department would collapse without Kafka.[7] It was enough that he said it.

He had planned to spend Easter in Marienbad, a spa near Karlsbad, before representing the institute there on the Tuesday,[8] but the trip was postponed until May. He thought of taking his vacation then, to stay in Marienbad for three quiet weeks.[9] He had just consulted a nerve specialist, who diagnosed cardiac neurosis, which, he said, could be treated electrically.[10] 'Went home and wrote cancelling. What's the point of treating a symptom?'[11]

A dream about a gigantic naked man may have referred to his father. Kafka was with a group of men fighting a rival group. After capturing the naked giant, five of them held him down, but had no knife to stab him. Nearby was a large oven, with its cast iron door red hot. 'We dragged the man over, held his foot close to the oven door until it began to smoke, pulled him back till the smoke cleared, only to drag him back and soon to hold it close again. We went monotonously on like that until I woke up, not only in a cold sweat but with my teeth really chattering.'[12] As in so many of his fantasies, living human flesh was treated like meat.

He used elements from the dream almost immediately, starting a story in which the butcher's two children, Hans and Amalia, are playing outside a large fortress-like warehouse with a double row of heavily barred windows. Suddenly one of the panes breaks to reveal a man's thin face, smiling. 'Come on, children, come on. Ever seen a warehouse?'[13] Amalia is curious; Hans more reluctant, trailing along behind as the man smashes pane after pane of glass, guiding them along the side of the building till they come to a small, low door of galvanized iron, resembling the door of a large oven. Behind it they hear him opening a series of inner doors, one apparently set closely behind another. (This is reminiscent of the point about the hierarchy of doorkeepers.) The stranger hisses, both when he's speaking and when he isn't – he blames this on the dampness: 'I wouldn't advise you to stay here long either, but for a while it's quite extraordinarily interesting.'[14] The narrative breaks off after Hans has been dragged inside by force while Amalia ignores his shouted command to fetch their father.[15]

In May Kafka made a serious bid to escape from the office.[16] Rewriting the letter three times from beginning to end, he applied for a long leave without pay in the autumn if the war was over by then, or, if it wasn't, for cancellation of his exemption from military service.[17] Marschner assumed that what he really wanted was the normal three weeks' holiday, to which he was no longer entitled, because of the exemption. Kafka would have liked at least six months of freedom, but he did not insist. 'I can't help it. If I want to turn right, I first turn left, then sadly edge rightwards (the frustration then infects all concerned and this is the worst part). The main reason may be anxiety: there's no problem over turning left because I don't want to go in that direction anyway.'[18]

In the middle of May the institute sent him back to Karlsbad and on to Marienbad, which he found 'incredibly beautiful'.[19] In spite of overcast skies and persistent winds, he wandered about in the woods. 'I think that if I were a Chinaman about to go home (fundamentally I am a Chinaman and about to go home) I'd have to make sure of coming back here soon.'[20] He stayed only a few days, and then, in Prague, was 'chased hither and thither with nothing constant except the headaches'.[21] During the last week in May a particularly bad one lasted for five days,[22] and subdued him into accepting the three-week holiday, which he could spend in Marienbad.[23] When Felice suggested they should go together to a sanatorium, his answer was: 'People who are ill, and I now seriously feel I belong in this category, should keep away from sanatoria.'[24] Why didn't she come to Marienbad with him?[25] They agreed to meet there, at the Hotel Neptun, on 2 July.

Not that he had been immune – even in his depression – to the attractions of other girls. 'At least six since the summer,' he noted in his diary. 'I can't resist, it's like having my tongue torn out of my mouth if I don't give in, admiring anyone admirable, and loving to the point where admiration is exhausted. Towards all six my guilt is almost entirely inward, but one of them complained about me to someone.'[26] Suicide seemed like the only means of eradicating the mess, confusion and vacillation. 'To forget everything. To open the windows. To empty the room. The wind blows through it. You see only emptiness, you look in every corner without finding it.'[27]

Later on in the month he was reading *Genesis* and excerpting it in his diary with notes: 'God's rage against humanity. The two trees, the unexplained veto, the punishment of all (serpent, Woman and Man), the priority given to Cain, whom He provokes by addressing him.'[28] During his first days in Marienbad with Felice he read nothing but the Bible,[29] at least half aware he was learning about how to tell what struck him as the truth. 'Only the Old Testament can see – say nothing about it yet.'[30] As in *Der Prozess*, where Huld has books by his bedside, Kafka went on linking illness with a quasi-legal or scriptural book which may give information about a source of help. In one fragmentary story the doctor at the sick man's bedside, after consulting a large medical tome, announces that help is coming from Bregenz in Vorarlberg. 'That's a long way away,' says the patient.[31]

When Kafka arrived in Marienbad, Felice was at the station to meet him. In the hotel they had separate rooms, 'door to door, keys on either side'.[32] But they were ugly rooms on a courtyard, and he slept badly.[33] The next day they moved, and he found his new room 'extraordinarily beautiful'.[34]

It was strange and by no means easy to be living in sudden intimacy with her after the long exchange of letters, the brief meetings, the brief engagement. 'I'm poorly. I have two little pieces of wood screwed against my temples.'[35] The prospect of a permanent liaison seemed dim. 'Strains of living together. Enforced by unfamiliarity, sympathy, lust, cowardice, vanity and only on the lowest ground perhaps a feeble stream worthy to be called love, inaccessible, flashing out once in the tiniest part of a second.'[36]

Impossible to live with F. Intolerable to live with anyone. Nothing to regret there. Regret at the impossibility of not living alone. But go on: absurdity of the regret, the compromise, the resignation. Pulling oneself together. Hold on to the book. But back again: sleeplessness, headaches, jumping out of the high window, but on to the rainsoaked ground, where the impact won't be fatal. Endless tossing with closed eyes, on view to any that are open.[37]

The first six days in Marienbad strongly sharpened both sides of his ambivalence towards her. Some diary entries are prayer-like in tone, the only ambiguity being whether it is God or Felice he is addressing.

'Receive me into your arms, they are the depths, receive me into the depths, if you refuse now, then later.' 'Take me, take me, web of folly and pain.'[38] The turning point came on 9 July. The next day they wrote a joint letter to her mother: they were engaged again.[39] Though his head was still aching on the 12th when he wrote to Ottla, things had gone better than had seemed possible.[40] A diary entry on the 13th is: 'So open yourself. Let the man emerge. Breathe the air and the silence.'[41] The previous entry, made on the 6th, 7th or 8th, had been: 'I've never yet, except in Zuckmantel, been intimate with a woman. Then with the Swiss girl in Riva.'[42] After the first four days with Felice in Marienbad there had been no comparable intimacy; from 3–9 July was a series of

frightful days that boiled up into even more frightful nights. The rat seemed to have been driven into the last hole of all. But since it could get no worse, it got better. The ropes binding me were at least loosened, I began to find my way, she, who'd always held out a helping hand into the most utter emptiness, again helped, and I came with her into a human relationship I hadn't yet known – as precious as the one we'd had when our correspondence was at its best.[43]

The comparison with the relationships in Zuckmantel and Riva is made again, but not this time to disparage the relationship with Felice.

I saw trustfulness in a woman's eyes, and I couldn't keep myself closed. Much is being torn open that I wanted to keep shut for ever (not particular things, but the whole). . . . I really didn't know her at all . . . as she came close to me in the big room to accept the engagement kiss, a shudder ran through me.[44]

They arranged to marry soon after the war ended, to rent a two- or three-room flat in the suburbs of Berlin, but to stay economically independent. She would go on working. 'So one can visualize two rooms in somewhere like Karlshorst, in one of them Felice gets up early, hurries away, and in the evening tumbles wearily into bed; in the other is a sofa where I lie, feeding on milk and honey. . . . Nevertheless – in this there's peacefulness, certainty and therefore a modus vivendi.'[45]

On 13 July, the day Felice had to leave Marienbad, he took her to visit his mother and Valli in Franzensbad, where they were both taking a cure, and he felt perfectly happy in his mother's presence. This was 'so extraordinary that it frightened me violently at the same time'.[46]

Later in the year, writing for his uncle Siegfried on the title page of a guide to Marienbad, he seems to have been trying not so much to give advice as to give the impression that he and Felice had spent their whole time eating:

Breakfast at the Dianahof (fresh milk, eggs, honey, butter), quickly to the Maxtal for a snack (sour milk) quickly to Müller, maître d'hôtel at the Neptun for lunch, to the greengrocer's to eat fruit, a quick siesta, to the Dianahof for a bowl of milk (to be ordered in advance), quickly to the Maxtal for sour milk, to the Neptun for supper, then sit down in the municipal park to count your money, to the patisserie, then send me a few lines and get as much sleep in one night as I did in 21.[47]

Cheap fruit – not very clean – could be bought in the Judengasse, and the best dishes at the Neptun were vegetable omelette, Emmenthaler cheese, *Kaiserfleisch* and raw egg with green peas.[48]

Returning from Franzensbad Kafka found that the hotel management had let his double-bedded room to some new arrivals, moving his things into Felice's single-bedded room. 'Through the single door I can hear noise from the corridor and from couples in rooms on both sides.'[49] He spent the next evening roaming about the municipal park, but returned too early for the noises to have subsided. In the morning he went out looking for a room, but no one was willing to rent one for a single week.[50]

In discussions about Hasidism he must have shown sufficient interest for Brod to think it worth passing on the news that the rabbi from Belz, who was effectively the leader of the sect, had been in Marienbad for three weeks. Kafka made contact with him through Jiří Langer, the brother of František Langer, editor of a Czech monthly which had published some excerpts from *Betrachtung*.[51] Jiří Langer was a *Hasid* who had lived for several years in the rabbi's entourage, and, after meeting him, Kafka could join the group that accompanied the rabbi on his evening walks. With his long white beard and exceptionally long sidelocks, he reminded Kafka of a sultan in a Gustave Doré illustration of the Münchausen stories. He was blind in one eye and his mouth was twisted. 'It looks at once ironic and friendly. He wears a silk caftan, open at the front, a wide belt around his waist, and a tall fur hat, which is most striking of all. White stockings and, according to L., white trousers.'[52]

Usually, Langer said, the rain stopped when the rabbi walked in the woods, but this time it did not. A man with an empty soda-water bottle was trying to find water for the rabbi from one of the medicinal springs, but they all closed at seven o'clock. Whenever the rabbi turned round, the members of his entourage scampered aside so that his view was unblocked. One man carried a chair in case he should want to sit down; another carried a cloth for wiping it dry. Each time he wanted to look at something, the whole procession came to a halt. 'His remarks are mostly like the trivial comments and questions of visiting royalty, perhaps rather more childish and jolly ... Langer tries to find a deeper meaning in everything, I believe the deeper meaning is that there isn't any, and in my opinion that's quite enough.'[53] A bathhouse seemed to make a deep impression on him. He asked several questions about it, made a detour to inspect a drainpipe, listened to the noise of the water. 'Several times he says with that characteristic Eastern Jewish wonderment: "A beautiful building." '[54]

The next day, strolling through the woods on his way back to the hotel from one of the springs, Kafka met Marschner, the director of the institute, with his wife and daughter. They spent an hour together, but did not arrange to meet again.[55] Kafka saw them several times, once from a distance of only five yards, but hurried in the opposite direction.[56] Still suffering from headaches and sleeplessness, he was not trying to work, but was feeling 'calm and happy' about Felice.[57] Though the rabbi is described no less ironically than Rudolf Steiner had been, the encounter seems to have had its effect. The diary entry for 20 July is a direct address to God:

> Have mercy on me, I am sinful in every crevice of my being. Had talents, though, not wholly contemptible, some small abilities, but squandered them . . . am now close to the end, just at the moment when outwardly everything might turn out well for me. Do not consign me to perdition. I know that what we have here is a self-love, absurd whether viewed from afar or even from close at hand, but since I'm alive, I also have the self-love of the living and if the living escapes absurdity, so must its necessary manifestations. – Poor dialectic.[58]

With the self-criticism, the language modulates away from liturgical rhetoric:

> On the Sunday morning shortly before my departure you seemed to be supporting me. I had hope. Until today empty hope.
> And whatever my complaint is, there's no conviction, no real suffering even, it swings like the anchor of a lost ship, far from the ocean bed it could fasten on.
> Just give me peace at night – childish complaint.[59]

The day before he left Marienbad, his mother and Valli came over from Franzensbad, and he took them to Egerlander, the restaurant on the edge of the town where he had often eaten with Felice.[60] On his last night he enjoyed six hours of uninterrupted sleep,[61] but back in Prague, depression supervened.[62] In Marienbad he had read Felice some of the Blumfeld story, which he considered – as he had considered 'Das Urteil' – as belonging to her, though he did not send her a complete text: 'it's too complicated.'[63] Despite headaches, nightmares and wakefulness, he felt some benefit from the rapprochement with her, and from the memory of relaxing in the woods. He had gained confidence, but the stronger he felt, the more he rebelled against the office routine, feeling all the more frustrated when he again submitted to it.[64] He worried, as before, about Felice. She should not try to survive on nothing more than cocoa and a roll at lunch-time,[65] he told her, and he was impatient to hear whether she would help Dr Siegfried Lehmann with the home which Buber and Brod had founded in Berlin during July for the children of Jewish refugees.[66] 'Except for walking and gymnastics there's no better way of spending the little time you have to spare.'[67]

In the July sunshine he discovered a new pleasure – lying on the grass 'in fields where the poor sit with their children . . . this year the grass is tall and thick in the ditch.'[68] 'Seeing a well-dressed acquaintance pass by in a carriage-and-pair, I stretched out and felt the pleasures – in fact nothing but the pleasures – of being déclassé.'[69] Sometimes he would walk to a little wood outside the city and lie down there. He could see the river, a group of thinly wooded hills, and a single hill with 'an old house which has mystified me since childhood. It merges softly into the landscape, and all around the countryside is peaceful and undulating.'[70]

On 18 August he consulted Dr Mühlstein, a specialist in internal disorders, 'who's as good as a doctor can be'.[71] Diagnosing nervous strain, Mühlstein advised him not drink or smoke too much, to eat more vegetables than meat, go swimming, get a good night's sleep.[72] The consultation made him feel more confident about his health, but this led straight to renewed doubts about marriage. He balanced pros against cons:

I consolidate my energy.	You stay outside the context, become foolish, fly to all four quarters of the sky, but get no further. I draw all the energy available to me from life's bloodstream.
Responsible only for myself.	All the more infatuated with you (Grillparzer, Flaubert).
No anxiety. Concentration on work.	Increasing in energy, I bear more. Nevertheless there's some truth in this.[73]

But how seriously should he take his doubts? According to Brod's diary, Kafka was fighting 'frightful internal battles'. 'What looks like a sense of responsibility and, as such, would be laudable, is fundamentally the bureaucratic spirit, boyishness, a will broken by Father. . . . Give up the nonsense of making comparisons with Flaubert, Kierkegaard, Grillparzer. That's pure boyishness.'[74]

In the margin of a postcard to Felice he wrote: 'How does Frl. Bloch bear it and what does it mean for her?'[75] And the next day he wrote: 'Fräulein Grete's sufferings touch me deeply; you certainly won't abandon her now as you often did, rather incomprehensibly, earlier. (I can understand this better than anyone. It often happens that while trying with all your might to get somewhere inside, you're pulled out by the back of your collar.) If you can help her, you are also acting on my behalf.'[76] Judging from Grete's letter to Schocken she cannot have been pregnant now, but

211

whatever her troubles were, it seems an odd way for an ex-lover to write about her.

When Felice raised the question of having children, he was glad to have it brought out into the open, and admitted that it was 'prominent in my onsets of despair. It can neither be solved nor be ignored. What a scourge has been made out of this, the greatest of powers!'[77]

He was not becoming any less intolerant towards noise. 'I think silence shies away from me as water does from a fish thrown up on the beach.'[78] It was partly in quest of silence that he went for walks outside the city, sometimes taking Ottla. He found two spots he liked even better than the grass on the edge of the wood. Both were 'as quiet as the Garden of Eden after the expulsion of Man. To disturb the peace I read Plato to Ottla, she taught me how to sing. I must have gold somewhere in my larynx even if it only sounds like tin.'[79] He was taking increasing pleasure in the country-side. 'Without noticing it I've secretly, over the years, been changing from a townsman into a countryman, or something very much like it.'[80]

Ottla, who had become friendly with a non-Jew, Josef David, was looking for a flat she could rent to meet him. She did not yet know she would find the strength to marry him in the teeth of her parents' opposition; she didn't even confide in her brother about why she was looking for 'a quiet place'. Assuming she just wanted somewhere to be on her own, he helped her, believing they might find an attic in one of the old palaces. After searching in vain they found a tiny house in the Alchimistengäss-chen, a narrow road near the castle. The house, which consisted of only one room, a kitchen and a loft, was dirty, in need of repair, and not available until November, but she took it from then.[81]

He was deriving long-distance pleasure from Felice's voluntary work in Dr Lehmann's Jewish home. 'I know of no closer spiritual bond between us than the one this work creates.'[82] He offered to compute each visit she paid to the home as equivalent in value to a letter.[83] And when she wrote: 'I feel very happy among the children and in fact more at home than I do at work,' he said the sentence was like 'the most beautiful music'.[84] Together with Pfohl, he was also active in helping to found a clinic for treating nervous diseases contracted during active service. It was opened at the Frankenstein clinic, Rumburg, where he had been a patient himself the previous year. He dealt with most of the correspondence.

Some of his letters to Felice were mined with subtle propaganda against her desire to have children. It was at his prompting that she went to the exhibition 'Mother and Infant', but when she reported on it favourably, he said that to be complete it ought to include a Chamber of Horrors showing groups like his cousin's family. Her two-year-old child was attractive, with fair hair and blue eyes, but totally supine, lying 'motionless in its perambulator, the eyes moving aimlessly and listlessly. It can't sit up, no smile plays around the mouth, nor can it be induced to utter a word.'[85] Having been reading a biography of Erdmuthe Dorothea, Countess von Zinzendorff, he told Felice about her twelve children: they all died very young, except one, who reached the age of twenty, but died soon afterwards.[86] Even if he had not been afraid of fatherhood, he was so aware of psychological damage that can be done to children in the process of bringing them up that he felt unwilling to join the 'adult conspiracy' against them. 'From romping in liberty we pull them into our cramped house under pretences that deceive us too, but not in the way we pretend.'[87] Long-distance co-operation with Felice on the work she was doing at the Jewish home – recommending books, giving advice and encouragement – represented a kind of vicarious parenthood with limited responsibility, no infringement of his privacy and no contact with childish faeces or urine.

Felice sent Kafka's parents her best wishes for the Jewish New Year (28–9 September), and his mother wrote back immediately after the Day of Atonement: 'We were very busy in the shop before the holidays, so I couldn't write sooner. We observed the Jewish festivals like good Jews. The shop was closed for both days of New Year, and yesterday, the Day of Atonement, we fasted and prayed diligently.'[88] But Kafka did not send New Year greetings to Frau Bauer. 'Your mother must have shaken her head and probably done more than that . . . Incidentally I scarcely said a word about the New Year either at home or to you, because for me the day has no significance.'[89]

Felice's riposte was that sitting with his parents was not going to be a pleasant experience for her.[90] This made him want to analyse the family feeling he had towards his parents and sisters:

I respect it fundamentally more than I realize. Sometimes this too is something I hate; the sight of the matrimonial bed at home, the bed-linen no longer clean, the carefully laid out night-shirts can bring me close to vomiting, can turn my stomach inside out, it is as if my birth had been only provisional, as if from this stuffy life again and again I need to keep coming back through this stuffy room into the world, need to keep coming back there for my existence to be confirmed, need to be indissolubly connected – if not wholly, then partly – with these repulsive things, at least something still sticks to the feet that want to escape, they're caught in the primeval muck.[91]

But he often felt his parents to be 'necessary elements of my own being, which go on giving me strength, not holding me back but essentially belonging to me'.[92]

At such times I want them the way one wants the best things in life; I have always trembled before them in all my meanness, naughtiness, selfishness and unlovingness – and actually I still do, for one never stops – while they have (Father on one side, Mother on the other) almost broken my will – again, this was necessary – so I want them to be worthy of it.[93]

But he would have preferred his mother to be more like Ottla – 'pure, truthful, honest, consistent, with an infallible balance between humility and pride, openness and reticence, submissiveness and independence, timidity and courage.'[94] This letter, uncharacteristically impetuous and illogical, lurches into asserting: 'Now you belong to me, I've taken you to me, I can't believe that any battle in any fairy-tale for any woman has been fought harder or more desperately than mine for you, since the beginning, again and again, and perhaps for ever. So you belong to me.'[95] His parents must never be allowed to claim her as their ally against him or him as having gone over to their side.[96] The battle was still on. 'Because, literally, I stand facing my family, lunging with my dagger both to wound them and defend them. Give me complete responsibility to act on your behalf in all this, without acting on mine with your family.'[97]

By the end of October he had let nearly two years elapse without any serious writing. He felt split: one part nourished itself on the details of Felice's life; the other, which contained nothing but capacity for work, was 'like a spider's web cut loose, freedom from agitation, freedom from headaches are its greatest happiness, achieved none too often'.[98]

He was to give a reading in November In Munich at a gallery attached to a bookshop, where he had arranged to meet Felice. They had been corresponding about the possibility of meeting there. He wanted to be with her on neutral ground, but after staying for two days, he felt guilty: 'I had, after a two-year silence, the fantastic arrogance to read in public, when for eighteen months in Prague I've read nothing to my best friends.'[99] He called the whole evening a great failure.[100] He read 'In der Strafkolonie', preceded by a few of Max Brod's poems. 'I read my dirty story amid total indifference, no empty fireplace can be colder.'[101] He may have met Rilke, though the evidence of the poet's presence at the reading is not conclusive. We know that Rilke said 'something very kind about "Der Heizer"' and 'gave the opinion that neither "Die Verwandlung" nor "In der Strafkolonie" reached the same level'.[102] He must either have made these remarks – which Kafka found discerning[103] – after the reading, or have read the manuscript, which had been sent to Munich six weeks earlier, and discussed it with a friend, Eugen Mondt, who may have passed the comment on to Kafka.[104] After this, in any case, Rilke wanted to read everything Kafka wrote.[105]

With Felice there was more friction than in Marienbad. After a quarrel in a cake-shop, he was left feeling they would seldom be at peace.[106] She kept accusing him of selfishness. 'The only injustice is that it's you of all people who complain, that in doing so you deny me – perhaps much less in actions than in words – any justification for this egocentricity, which focuses less (incomparably less) on the person than on the thing.'[107] He needed her as chief witness for the defence.

With a woman willing to marry him when the war was over, he felt secure enough to renew the search for a quiet room. He had been spending a great deal of time at home. In his room on Langengasse it was 'impossible to feel at peace, complete unsettlement, breeding ground for every delirium, ever increasing debility and pessimism'.[108] He forced himself to call at an agency for furnished accommodation; one of the first flats he was shown was in the Schönborn Palace on the Marktgasse, an eighteenth-century palace which had belonged to a count. For 600 kronen a year he could rent two rooms and a hall, half of which had been converted into a bathroom. The rooms, high and beautiful, decorated in red and gold, reminded him of Versailles. Four windows looked out on a quiet courtyard, one on a beautifully spaced double flight of stone steps and a large garden that swept up to a belvedere. The present tenant, an official who had left Prague, wanted an additional premium of 650 kronen to cover his expenses in installing electricity and telephone, building the bathroom and putting in cupboards. On the second floor of the palace was an empty flat with lower ceilings, and therefore easier to heat, but it had no kitchen or bathroom.[109] Encouraged by the owner of the accommodation bureau, the caretaker of the palace, and the maid at the flat, he chose this one. 'Since yesterday my mother has been joining forces with them, really very good-naturedly.[110] Believing he would be able to get more work done in a new flat, he did not want to take a break in order to meet Felice over Christmas.[111] But his self-control was precarious: 'Perhaps the relative calm is only a reservoir of dissatisfaction, which then overflows as it did last night, when I could have howled. Today I've been wandering about as if I were at my own funeral.'[112] Again and again his imagery derives from the idea of his own death; to feel fully alive he needed to feel simultaneously afraid and unafraid of death.

Ottla had bought some bamboo furniture for the small house on Alchimistengässchen, which they both kept secret from their parents. Though he still spent the night in Langengasse, he ate his evening meal in the house and felt that he was living there. 'There are still some small improvements to be made. . . . But I'm still going home at the beginning of the best time – at first it was at 8.0, later at 8.30, now after 9.0. It's strange to be locking the front door in this narrow street by starlight.'[113] Later he would stay till midnight. His presence must have been a great encumbrance to Ottla, who appears never to have confided in him about her motive for renting the house. Nor does he seem to have speculated about it. Happy at the opportunity to resume writing after the two-year gap, he worked there for several hours each day until his routine was upset by the December coal shortage. He wrote a ten-page dialogue posthumously titled 'Der Gruftwächter' ('The Warden of the Tomb') and brief stories, 'Die Brücke' ('The Bridge'), 'Ein Traum' ('A Dream') and several fragments including the first two sections of 'Der Jäger Gracchus' ('The Hunter Gracchus'), a variant on the Flying Dutchman story, appropriating it for a partly personal purpose, exploring his sense of being dead while still being alive. Gracchus is alive to some extent because his death-boat went off course, but he was killed long ago by a fall from a rock in the Black Forest when there were still wolves there.

In the second fragment, which, both in tone and in substance, strongly prefigures Beckett's trilogy of novels, the narrative voice identifies with the hunter, who, ever since his death, has been lying on a wooden board wearing a filthy winding sheet. It is here that he is writing, not in order to summon help, for no one will read what he has written, and no one would know how to find the empty 'wooden cage', the bark where he is lying. 'The idea of wanting to help me is an illness, people have to recover from it in bed.' He had slipped into his winding-sheet as happily as a bride into her wedding-dress. This is reminiscent of the story written around twelve years earlier about children playing on a country road.

During the winter Kafka went on to write 'Ein Landarzt' ('A Country Doctor') 'Auf der Galerie' ('Up in the Gallery') 'Ein Brudermord' ('A Fratricide') and 'Das nächste Dorf' ('The Next Village'), 'Ein Besuch im Bergwerk' ('A Visit to a Mine'), which may have been suggested by the January strike of the Ruhr miners, 'Der Kübelreiter' ('The Bucket Rider') which was obviously prompted by the ensuing coal shortage, 'Schackale und Araber' ('Jackals and Arabs') and 'Der neue Advokat' ('The New Lawyer').

The old country doctor, whose horse has died in the night, finds a strange groom and two strange horses in his stable. He drives at magical speed through ten miles of snow to a fetid sick-room where the young patient at first seems perfectly healthy but eager to die, and later seems eager to live but to have a huge and incurable wound in his side with worms already crawling about in it. Kafka knew Buber's collections of Hasidic stories,[114] which feature supernatural journeys and miraculous cures.[115] In one story the Baal Shem travels magically fast to resurrect a bride who has been snared into death by an evil spirit; in another uncontrollable horses carry him into the depths of an unknown forest. In both stories the uncannily rapid journey is consequent on a summons from a superior spiritual force, and it represents a transition to a higher mode of awareness, but whereas the Baal Shem could perform miraculous cures (or function on both levels) the country doctor is only forced into humiliating recognition of his limitations, and the reader can infer no moral precept.

At the circus, in relation to the fragile tubercular equestrienne, the spectator in the gallery is in the same position as the spectator from the high window looking out on the execution of Josef K. There is no apparent justification for intervention. If the ringmaster were ruthless and the performance likely to continue without giving her any rest, the young spectator might rush down to shout 'Stop'. But since, like the two executioners, the ringmaster appears to be deferential, considerate, concerned, avuncular, and the girl gives no sign that she is being humiliated, the young man in the gallery can only weep.

'Ein Brudermord' is even more reminiscent of the killing sequence in *Der Prozess*. Pallas, a private citizen, witnesses everything from a second-storey window. Why does he allow it to happen? He stands with his dressing-gown drawn tightly around his plump body, shaking his head. The killer has been holding his weapon, a cross between a kitchen knife and a bayonet, unconcealed in the moonlight. He stands on tiptoe to plunge the knife twice into his victim's throat, once into his stomach. 'Water rats, when slit open, make a sound like the one Wese made.'[116] Again the animal image; again the echo of paternal threats ('I'll tear you apart like a fish').

In 'Der Kübelreiter' the sky is described as 'a silver shield against anyone looking for help from it'. The coal-dealer is deaf to ordinary appeals and his wife pretends not to see the bucket-rider who is begging for a shovel-full of their worst coal and promising to pay later. As so often in Kafka, a metaphor is developed into dream-like narrative action. The coal-bucket is so light he can ride on it, and he does, but when the woman waves her apron to shoo him away, he is driven up into the ice mountains, and he will never return.

17 The Modern Kabbalist

In the spring of 1915, it seems, Kafka had been predominantly – if not totally – sincere about wanting to be called up, and certainly there was no ambivalence behind his excitement in buying war-bonds in November 1915. But by March 1917 his feelings had changed. When a patriot tried to involve him in campaigning, he replied: 'Really I'm not in a position to make my mind up about a spiritually and culturally united Austria, and still less to think of myself as completely belonging to it. I'm very nervous of any such commitment.' In any case he was no good as an organizer, and did not have a large circle of acquaintances, but he would be glad to send a subscription if a membership society was formed.[1]

Determined to achieve independence, Ottla now wanted to study agriculture, and he tried to find out which course she would do best to attend. Partly because of her, he was hesitating about whether to take the second-floor flat in the Schönborn Palace. He enjoyed the walk from his office to the little house, enjoyed the evening meal she cooked for him – she had befriended a hunchbacked flower-girl, who waited on him – enjoyed the midnight walk to Langengasse, feeling that it helped him to sleep. Just occasionally Ottla showed irritation at his encroachment on her privacy, but mostly she was good-humoured, generous, and glad he could make more use of the house than she did. Sometimes she went there at lunch-time; on Sundays she spent most of the day there. But if he took the flat in the Schönborn Palace, he and Felice would have 'the most wonderful flat I can imagine in Prague, all ready for you, though only for a short time, in which you'd have to manage without a kitchen of your own, and even without a bathroom'.[2] At the beginning of March he moved into the flat but went on using the house until the beginning of May, and on 18 April, just after Ottla had left Prague and the fire had gone out, he burned newspapers and some of his manuscripts to get warm.[3]

Ottla had finally managed to break away from the family and the business to run Karl Hermann's fifty-acre farm in Zürau, a small village in the north-west of Bohemia. He was still at the front, and the asbestos factory had finally closed down in March. In April, when Karl's brother Rudl came to say goodbye before going to Bielitz, Kafka's father made a scene, accusing Karl of fraud. When Rudl protested, he was ordered out of the flat. The normally placid Julie Kafka helped to push him out.[4]

In the spring Kafka wrote another story about metamorphosis, 'Ein

218

Bericht für eine Akademie' ('A Report for an Academy'). This time the transition is from the animal to the human: the ape has been a man for nearly five years. The resonance depends partly on the way his individual development satirically encapsulates Darwinian evolution, partly on the ironic, shockingly heretical suggestion that evolution has been retrogressive, and partly on a fierce undercurrent which owes its presence to Kafka's private experience in feeling that he belonged to a different species from everyone else, in making efforts at overcoming his own nature, and in being aware of assimilation as an escape route for the persecuted Jew. The narrator has forgotten what it was like to be free. His memories go back no further than captivity on the boat that brought him from the Gold Coast. He was in a cage too low for him to stand, too narrow for him to sit. There he came to see that the only way out was to stop being an ape. Imitating the crew, he learned first to spit and then to drink alcohol. Human speech became available to him after his first successful attempt at emptying a bottle of schnapps. When you need to find a way out, you learn ruthlessly. 'You stand over yourself with a whip, at the slightest opposition you beat your flesh raw. My simian nature fell away from me in such a headlong rush that my first teacher almost turned into an ape himself, had to give up teaching and go into an asylum. . . . There's an excellent idiom: to cut corners. That's what I've done. Cut corners and slipped away.'[5] But he cannot bear to look into the eyes of his mistress, a half-trained chimpanzee with the insane look of the bewildered half-broken animal.[6]

As with so many of the fictions which derive partly from his knowledge and direct experience of anti-Semitism, it is possible to interpret the story without taking Jewish experience into account. Kafka does not allude to it: he merely uses it. The story was published, together with 'Schakale und Araber', in two successive issues of a monthly edited by Martin Buber, *Der Jude* (*The Jew*). Kafka asked him not to call the stories parables: if he wanted an overall title for them, it would have to be 'Two Animal Stories'.[7]

'Ein Bericht' was finished before Kafka wrote 'Die Sorge des Hausvaters' ('The Troubles of a Householder') during the last week in April. Here, anticipating Borges's *El Libro de los seres imaginarios* (*The Book of Imaginary Beings*) he invents a creature with the name *Odradek*, an invented word with Slav roots.

The creature looks like a flat star-shaped spool, with a small cross-bar sticking out of its middle, and with bits of broken thread wound round it. Asked where it lives, the Odradek says it has no fixed abode, and laughs lunglessly, with a sound like rustling leaves.

Recognizing Kafka as a precursor, Borges analysed the tradition behind him, and found it included Zeno's paradox, the story of Achilles and the tortoise, Han Y, a ninth-century Chinese writer, Kierkegaard, Browning, Léon Bloy and Lord Dunsany. Borges's list does not include the Talmud or the Kabbalah, but George Steiner, describing both Kafka and Borges as modern Kabbalists,[8] points out that the Talmud, 'which is often Kafka's archetype, refers to the forty-nine levels of meaning which must be discerned in a revealed text'.[9] It was a Hasidic assumption that 'God's actual speech, the idiom of immediacy known to Adam and common to men until Babel, can still be decoded, partially at least, in the inner layers of Hebrew and, perhaps, in other languages of the original scattering'.[10] This helps to explain why the idea of Babel was so important to both Kafka and Borges. At the beginning of 1917 Brod wrote to Martin Buber that Kafka was drifting 'unawares into Judaism';[11] in the summer of 1917 he started to study modern Hebrew, using a text-book by Moses Rath.[12] By 10 September he had worked his way through forty-five lessons. One of his 1917 notes runs: 'If the Tower of Babel could have been built without climbing it, this would have been allowed.'[13] And in 'Beim Bau der chinesischen Mauer' ('The Great Wall of China'), a story he wrote during the spring of 1917 in a style that sometimes parodies Talmudic commentary, he associates the tower with the wall, mentioning a book by a scholar who maintained that the real reason the tower collapsed was that its foundations were not built securely enough and that the Great Wall could now provide a firm foundation for it.[14] But, through his Chinese persona, Kafka professes himself puzzled by the argument: the wall is not circular but shaped more like a half-circle or a quarter-circle.

Though it never becomes a mere symbol for the Law, Kafka is now addressing himself to the question of how the Law was evolved, and at the same time writing a miniature allegorical history of the Jews during the Diaspora.[15] The tower then represents an attempt to use the Law as a base for reaching from the material to the spiritual. Committed by their superiors to a system of piecemeal construction, the builders had a secret maxim: 'Strive with all your might to understand the orders you're given, but only up to a certain point: then stop racking your brain.'[16] The wall was to serve as a protection against the people of the north, but the writer comes from the south-east of China, where the people were in no danger, so why had they streamed northwards to help? Who gave the orders for them to be drummed out of their beds? Probably it was not a gathering of mandarins. 'Probably the authority (*Führerschaft*) has always existed, and so has the commandment about building the wall.'[17]

The story roots back to the stultifying sense of provincial remoteness from the unapproachable centre at which all the key decisions are taken – a knot of resentment which is taking on an increasing metaphysical load.

The Emperor of China stands in simultaneously for the ineffectual political and administrative centre of the disintegrating Austro-Hungarian
Empire, and for God. Nietzsche's image of a dead God is replaced by an
image of a remote and dying emperor. Perhaps he is lying on a couch,
which is perhaps quite large, perhaps narrow and short. Sometimes he
yawns. But how can people thousands of miles to the south know anything about that? Even if he were being executed, they would not know.
What if the emperor on his death-bed directed a message to one of his
ordinary subjects? The messenger, trying to push his way through the
throng, wears out his strength while still in the innermost palace. It would
take thousands of years for him to reach the outermost gate. All the
subject can do is sit at his window, dreaming about the message that will
never arrive. [18] The personal message is reminiscent of the door intended
for one individual, while the messenger parable anticipates a diary entry
about a shabby king who knows all his subjects by name. He stops in the
doorway of the tailor's shop where Franz is working in a dark corner. The
king asks for Franz, and when he pushes his way out of the dark corner
through the journeymen towards the doorway, the king says: 'Come
along.' As they leave he tells the tailor: 'He's moving into the castle.' [19]
Ionesco's play *Les Chaises* (*The Chairs*) forms a kind of corollary to Kafka's
fragment: an invisible emperor arrives at the house of an old man who
thinks he has a message for the world, but the orator he employs to
expound it is dumb.

In German *Schloss* means both 'castle' and 'lock'; Kafka's despair was at
ever finding the key. Clues to its whereabouts were to be found both in
the scriptural laws and in the laws that lawyers studied, but most of the
clues were either useless or misleading.

In the story about the Chinese wall the people in the province are
equally untouched by political revolutions or contemporary wars. Once a
leaflet published by rebels in another province was brought along by a
beggar, but the dialect is different, and the written language looks
archaic, so it provoked only laughter. 'People are so willing here to
obliterate the present.' [20] The fault is partly that of the empire, which fails
to extend its workings over the whole of its territory, and partly that of the
people, who are guilty of 'weakness in imagination or faith', being unable
'to draw the empire out of its demoralized preoccupations in Pekin into a
vivid, vital embrace with its subjects'. [21] Kafka wrote the story in the
Schönborn Palace, itself a palpable reminder of the imperial past.

Among the more frequently recurrent images in his work are the wall,
with its associations of impenetrability, and the door or gate, which is less
often a point of admission than a reminder of exclusion. In the dream-like
story 'Der Schlag am Hoftor' ('The Knock at the Manor Gate') the

punishment will be out of all proportion to the misdeed, which was committed – if it was committed at all – by someone else. The narrator can no longer remember whether his sister mischievously knocked at the gate as they passed or merely raised her fist, but the terrified villagers make warning signs, and soon horsemen are riding through the gateway. After telling her to go home and change into better clothes so as to make a good impression, he is left alone to face the judge and the two other men who ride up. They take him to a cell-like room in the village inn. 'Big stone flags, completely bare wall, an iron ring embedded somewhere in the middle, the plank bed like an operating table.'[22]

The series of events and images is like a nightmare, caused mainly by Kafka's equation of marriage with imprisonment. Felice came to Prague in July, and, for the second time, they were engaged. It was conventional for engaged couples to pay formal visits on friends and relations. They took this seriously, even calling on the Brods. 'The sight of the slightly embarrassed couple, above all Franz in a strange high stiff collar, was rather moving, and at the same time horrifying.'[23] Two days later they went to see Felice's sister in Hungary, stopping on the way to Arad at Budapest, where Jizchak Löwy had been living since the beginning of the war. Once again Kafka tried to help him, suggesting he should write an article on the situation of the Yiddish actor. Löwy liked the idea and Kafka recommended it for *Der Jude*. [24]

The quarrel with Felice was sudden. It happened either in Hungary or on the journey. He left her in Budapest, travelling alone to Vienna, where he met Rudolf Fuchs, a poet and translator, who afterwards said he had given the impression that the relationship with Felice had no future. [25] He wrote at least two letters to her from Prague during the four weeks after his return, but they are no longer extant; she may have destroyed them. He called them monstrous and unanswerable, [26] but probably they were not intended to create a final breach. His letter of 27 July to Kurt Wolff expresses the intention of marrying after the war and moving away from Prague, 'possibly to Berlin'. [27]

18 Haemorrhage

It was early in August 1917 that he first spat blood, without paying much attention to it.

> It was hot, beautiful, everything outside my head was in order – in the swimming bath I spat out something red. That was strange and interesting, wasn't it? I looked at it a little while, and then forgot it. After that it happened quite often, and usually when I wanted to spit, I produced something red, whenever I felt like it. It was no longer interesting, just boring, and I forgot it again.[1]

He neither told anyone about it nor worried about it until about four o'clock in the morning of 10 August:

> I wake up, surprised at the quantity of saliva in my mouth, spit it out, switch the light on, strange, it's a blob of blood. And now it begins. Haemoptysis, I don't know whether I've spelt it right, but that's a good name for this wellspring in the throat. I thought it was never going to stop. How could I block it up when I hadn't opened it? I got up, walked around the room, to the window, looked out, went back – continuous blood, finally it stopped, and I slept, better than I had for ages.[2]

In the morning, when the hunchbacked flower-girl came in and saw the blood, she said: 'Herr Doktor, it's soon going to be all over with you.'[3] But he went to the office as usual, and did not see a doctor until the afternoon.[4] Dr Mühlstein thought he had bronchial catarrh, and gave him three bottles of medicine, telling him to come back in a month's time, if there was no more bleeding, or, if there was, straight away.[5] There was more bleeding that night, but not so much. When he went back, the doctor said it might be a chronic chill. Another possibility, which could be discounted, he said, was tuberculosis; another was congestion of the lung.[6] Kafka confided in Brod, who advised him to see a specialist, but it was not until 4 September that he consented. The entry in Brod's diary for 24 August is: 'Action à propos Kafka's illness. He describes it as psychical, at the same time as rescuing him from the marriage. He calls it his ultimate defeat. But he's been sleeping well since.'[7]

Certainly Kafka felt relieved at not having to go on either with the internal battle or with the engagement. The last entry in his diary before the haemorrhage was: '"No, leave me alone! No, leave me alone" I shouted without stopping all the way along the streets, and again and again she grabbed at me, again and again the siren's clawed hands struck sideways or across my shoulders at my breast.'[8] Felice was kept in ignorance of the haemorrhage for over four weeks, nor did he confide in his parents or in anyone else except his cousin Irma, and Ottla, revealing to her his relief at being defeated:

A victory (such as might be won in marriage, for example, Felice is perhaps only a representative of what's probably the good principle in this conflict) I mean a victory with half-way tolerable bloodshed would, in my private history, have been almost Napoleonic. Now it looks as though this is the way I'm going to lose the battle. And indeed, as if something had been blown away, I've been sleeping better since that incident at 4.00 a.m., though not much better, but the main thing is that the headache, which was driving me mad, has stopped completely. I think they were all partners in the haemorrhage – the persistent sleeplessness, headaches, feverish conditions, tensions weakened me so much that I was receptive to something tubercular.[9]

He is viewing himself as passive or plural – a battleground, or a loose confederation of principalities. And this is how he went on thinking about it. Three years later he wrote:

What happened was that the brain could no longer stand the troubles and pains being loaded on to it. It said: 'I'm giving up. But if there's anyone else interested in continuing the whole thing, he can take over some of my burden, and things can go on for a while.' The lung volunteered, probably not having much to lose anyway. I wasn't informed about these negotiations between brain and lung, and they may have been ghastly.[10]

The image is a development of the one he had used to Felice in October 1914 about a wrestling match between two selves. But the onset of the tuberculosis made it still harder for him to believe in himself as a single entity: how could all that aggression come from inside the self? Even if the presence of the bacilli was due to self-critical ovulation, they could have been fertilized only by the Other, the Judge. Throughout his adolescent and adult life, he had constantly been asking himself whether he was not unworthy to stay alive. Tuberculosis must have seemed like an answer from outside, a judgment written on his body, a harsh reminder of the Law which he had never found, never been able to obey.

After the haemorrhage he was short of breath and coughed a lot. Sometimes he ran a temperature, and sometimes sweated, especially at night.[11] On 29 August he went back to Dr Mühlstein, who auscultated his lungs and pronounced them to be better, insisting there was no danger of tuberculosis. He did not suggest an X-ray, but it did not become normal until the thirties for X-rays to be used in diagnosis. When Kafka finally went with Brod to a specialist, Professor Friedl Pick, he was told that both lungs were congested and liable to become tubercular. Brod wrote: 'He regards the illness as a punishment, because he has often wished for a violent solution. But this is too crude for him. Against God he quotes from *Die Meistersinger:* "I'd thought he was more refined."'[12] Pick ordered him to rest for three months.

Just before the haemorrhage he had been working on 'In der Straf-kolonie'. For three days he had been writing fragments of the story in his diary. Once again, as at the end of *Der Prozess,* death is associated with dogs, but the traveller, though he runs about on all fours, refuses to take the easy way out. 'I'll be a dirty dog (*Hundsfott*) if I give in to that.'[13] On 8 August Kafka wrote: 'And even if everything remained the same, the spike was still there, sticking crookedly out of his shattered forehead as if bearing witness to some truth.' But the last phrase is crossed out. In the entry for the next day, the day before the haemorrhage, a pre-Hitlerian phrase occurs when the traveller has to resist the feeling that with the torture and the death a perfect solution has been achieved (*vollkommene Ordnung geschaffen*).[14] Presumably the condemned man was not going to be reprieved in the story as Kafka was now intending to write it. But after his execution the traveller would see him again, or believe he was seeing him again, apparently quite unharmed, while the officer, though still talking and walking about, would have a spike in his forehead and would complain that he had been executed in accordance with the traveller's commands.[15] The narrative idea is in line with the strand in *Der Prozess* which leads to Franz's punishment in consequence of Josef K.'s complaints, though K. had no desire for him to be punished. 'In der Straf-kolonie' points forward with an uncanny accuracy to the concentration camps, but the underlying preoccupation seems to be personal and existential, while the image of the penal colony appears to derive at least partly from the racking headaches. The solution is death. If God resorted to tuberculosis as a delaying tactic, this was crude but logical.

After paying a second visit to Professor Pick, again accompanied by Brod,[16] Kafka was given three months' leave of absence. Though previously he had opted for holidays in a sanatorium, he would not hear of going to one now.[17] He decided to stay with Ottla in Zürau, though Professor Pick would have preferred him to be in Switzerland: in Zürau, he said, there would be no doctor to look after him.[18] After giving up the flat he moved back with his parents on 1 September, living in Ottla's room till the 12th, when he joined her in Zürau. He was to stay there for eight months, longer than he had ever been away from Prague.

19 Zürau

In Zürau he immediately felt at ease. He had to put up with farmyard noises and banging – someone was hammering against metal, someone else, from six in the morning, against wood – and with piano-playing from 'the only piano in north-west Bohemia'.[1] But his room was well-furnished,[2] 'excellent, airy, warm, and all this with almost complete silence in the house'.[3] His window looked out on a single cottage and, beyond it, the open fields.[4] Living with Ottla he could feel that she was 'literally carrying me on her wings through this difficult world'.[5] His room faced north-east but he found a spot nearby that was ideal for sunbathing, a space in the centre of a broad valley, surrounded by low hills. Confident of being unobserved, he lay in an easy chair with two hassocks in front of it, wearing nothing but his trousers and resting on average eight hours a day.[6] The villagers spoke dialect, and his relationship with them was 'so loose it's quite unearthly'.[7]

He felt a certain affinity with a tramp who was twice fed by Ottla. A man of sixty-two, he had never married because his mother, who had been dead for only ten years, had always advised him against it, and recently he had been feeling unable to take pleasure in anything. He had been drinking heavily and tramping the roads without any plan, often travelling in a circle, which did not matter, because the people who fed him hardly ever recognized him.[8]

The disease in Kafka's lungs seemed less like an enemy than like the skirts of a mother. He was the child who could cling to them. It was his writing that was killing him, and Brod's was no less suicidal. 'It's the same knife. Our throats, our poor pigeon's throats, one here, one there, are pressing themselves against its edge. But so slowly, so provocatively, so bloodlessly, so heartbreakingly, leaving the hearts so broken.'[9]

He enjoyed being in the country. 'You leave the house, turn the corner and on the garden path come face to face with the goddess of Fortune.'[10] 'The village square surrendered to the night. The sagacity of children, supremacy of animals. – Cows, crossing the square with the utmost casualness. My sofa across the country.'[11] Surely he had as much opportunity as anyone ever had 'to make a new start. Don't throw it away. You won't be able to avoid the muck that wells up out of you if you want to go deep inside. But don't wallow in it.'[12]

Ottla said he could stay in Zürau till the end of the war and then buy a cottage there with a garden and a field for planting potatoes. 'I myself believe that God sent him this illness: without it he'd never have escaped from Prague.'[13] Meanwhile he worked happily in her vegetable garden, cut wood, drove a plough and a cart.[14]

On arriving in Zürau he weighed 61.5 kilos;[15] within a week he had put on a kilo.[16] He was delighted: it was only if he started losing weight that Dr Pick might force him to move. But by early October his weight had gone up to 65 kilos.[17] He felt so at ease in Ottla's company he called the relationship 'a small, good marriage; not the usual high-voltage marriage but one based on the mild current of the low voltages'.[18] Felice who knew from his one letter or from his protracted silence that she was losing him, made a thirty-hour journey to see him, arriving on the 20th.

I should have forestalled it. As I see it, she's extremely unhappy, and it's my fault. Over details she's unjust, unjust in defending her imaginary – or real – rights, but all in all she's an innocent woman condemned to vicious torture; I've done the wrong for which she's being tortured, and, what's more, I'm wielding the instruments of torture.[19]

All their conversations in Zürau could be summed up, he realized, in four lines:

I: So this is what I've come to.
F: This is what *I've* come to.
I: This is what I've brought you to.
F: That's true.[20]

When she left with Ottla for the station, the carriage circled round the pond and he cut across to be close to her one last time. The day ended with a headache, which seemed like the residue of a performance he had been putting on.[21]

When a letter arrived from her, he did not at first open it; when he did, he found it had been written before her visit and delayed because she had addressed it to Flohau in Moravia. When two more letters came on 1 October, he did not open them until the evening, and then wrote to her. 'There's nothing to which I'd give myself with more complete confidence than death'[22] – but if a death sentence had now been passed on Kafka, it did not mean that the trial was over, and his willingness to die did not mean that he was indifferent to the proceedings. He wrote to her as if two courts were considering his case, one human, the other not. He had tried, with her, not to tell lies, but

if I cross-examine myself about my ultimate objective, it emerges that I don't really go all out to be a good man and meet the requirements of a supreme court, but, quite on the contrary, I try to survey the whole human and animal community, to recognize its basic preferences, desires, conventional ideals, to reduce them to simple principles, and to orient myself to them as quickly as possible, so as to be thoroughly acceptable to everyone, and indeed (this is the trick) so acceptable that I can expose all my vicious secrets without forfeiting everyone's love, so that I can be the only sinner who isn't roasted. In other words, what matters to me is the human law court, which I wish to deceive without practising any deception. [23]

Sometimes he identified the human law court entirely with Felice,[24] sometimes thought of her as a partisan in the battle that constituted his existence,[25] and sometimes as the prize for which the war was being fought, a territory he had hoped to annex. 'Privately, in fact, I don't consider this illness to be tuberculosis, or at least not primarily. I think it's my general bankruptcy. I thought the war would go on, and it didn't. The blood is coming not from the lung, but from a crucial stab inflicted by one of the two combatants.'[26]

An unanswerable question: could he have sidestepped the disease if he had chosen a different woman or a different woman had chosen him? Was there a tension inside his body which could never be released inside hers and which found its only possible outlet in an illness he could not survive? If he had had a hunch when he met her that this might happen, the irreversible judgment he imposed on himself was nothing less than a death sentence and 'Das Urteil' was, as he had said, her story. But he was still free to move around, like Josef K. after the two warders came to arrest him. There was no chance that the court would acquit him, but the haemorrhage was less an end than a beginning. For the last seven years of his life Kafka would breathe with more difficulty, but with less anxiety.

It was not easy, though, for him to relinquish his claim on Felice. One word from her, he said, and he would be at her feet again.[27] But then the tuberculosis would force him away from her again. 'In comparison with such a weapon the almost innumerable ones used earlier, from "physical incapacity" to "work" and even to "meanness", all look makeshift and primitive.'[28] He knew he would never be well again. He resisted the idea, but

I ought to be convinced by the remote darkness that falls all round me at each attempt to work or think. Just because it's not a tuberculosis that can be put in a reclining chair and nursed back to health but a weapon that remains indispensable so long as I stay alive. And both of us can't stay alive.[29]

When Felix Weltsch said that what he most needed was the will to recover, his reply was:

I have that, but – if this can be said unaffectedly – I also have the opposite desire. It's a special illness, which has been, if you like, conferred preferentially, quite unlike any I've previously had. In the same way a happy lover might say: 'Everything else was just infatuation. I'm in love for the first time.'[30]

This complacency provoked Brod into concluding. 'You're happy in your unhappiness,'[31] a simplification which was understandable but irritating. With this phrase, Kafka retorted, the mark was probably printed on Cain.

If someone is 'happy in unhappiness', it means not only that he's fallen out of step with the world, but that everything's fallen apart for him, or is falling apart, that no voice can reach him clearly, and that he therefore can't respond to anything without loss of integrity. Things aren't quite that bad with me or at least haven't been so far; I've had complete experience of happiness and unhappiness.[32]

Four days later, in his last letter to Felice (or the last which has been preserved), answering her complaints about his behaviour in Zürau,[33] he accused her of taking the same view as Brod, and accused himself not of being happy that their long relationship had finally petered out, but of not having been unhappy, as she had. 'I didn't so much feel the whole calamity as see it, recognize it, assess it in all its overwhelming monstrosity, which exceeds my strength (at least my strength as one of the living) and in this recognition I remained relatively calm, my lips shut tight, very tight.'[34] The implication of the parenthesis is that dying was, for him, the only possible response. Not concealing her own unhappiness 'over the purposeless journey, over my incomprehensible behaviour, over everything',[35] Felice was obviously angered by his refusal or inability to seem more perturbed. He conceded: 'I was probably putting on a bit of an act,'[36] – which tallied with the feeling he had had about the headache. But he did not blame himself. 'The prospect in front of me (admittedly, not for the first time) was so hellish one naturally tried coming to the spectators' aid with a distracting bit of music.'[37] And again Kafka complained that Brod had been using terms applicable to Cain: 'The man who bears the mark has destroyed the world and, incapable of bringing it back to life, he will be hunted through the ruins.'[38]

To Kafka it seemed that he had failed the test, failed to make good, 'in relation to city life and to family, as well as professionally, socially and in love'.[39] He believed that his failure was worse than anyone else's.[40] Though the idea of unlived life, of wasted opportunity, caused him less suffering, he said, than the underlying circumstances, the suffering was too meaningless for him to continue with it indefinitely.[41] Since childhood the idea of suicide had been on the horizon, but how could he be so ambitious? 'You, who can't do anything, think you can bring off something like that? How can you even dare to think about it? If you were capable of it, you certainly wouldn't be in need of it.'[42]

Dying of tuberculosis was an easier alternative, 'which I wouldn't have found with my own resources (except in so far as tuberculosis belongs to "my resources")'.[43] He thought he had not yet opted for this way out – merely become aware of it; to take it, all he must do was carry on exactly as he was. What was new was the feeling of working his passage. 'Our ever-increasing closeness', he wrote to Brod, 'will consist in this: that we are both "in motion"; in the past I've all too often felt I was a burden on your back.'[44] To Kafka his friend was the man who could pass all the tests, rebut each point in the case for the prosecution: 'You can hold all the conflicting elements together; I can't, or at least not yet.'[45] That his writing would come to rank above Brod's was a possibility that never occurred to Kafka, partly because he was so uninterested in getting his work into print. *Der Prozess*, like *Der Verschollene*, had remained unfinished and unpublished: Kafka had contented himself with publishing his favourite sequences – the chapter about the stoker and the legend about the door-keeper. And in November 1917, when Brod wanted him to send something for an evening of readings at Frankfurt, his answer was: 'If I send it, I'm prompted only by vanity, if I don't send it, it's also vanity, but not mere vanity, so it's something better. The pieces I could send really mean nothing at all to me, I respect only the moments at which I wrote them.'[46] The same attitude was behind his final instructions to Brod: that all his unpublished writings should be destroyed. Later, when Elsa Brod wanted to read some of his work in public, he did not send either *Der Verschollene* or *Der Prozess*.

Why resuscitate old labours? Only because I haven't burnt them yet? . . . I hope it will have happened before my next visit to you. What's the point of preserving such miscarried works, even if the miscarriage was artistic? Because one hopes these fragments will coalesce into my entirety? Some kind of appeal court I can turn to when I'm in need?[47]

If he had not taken this idea seriously he would not have needed to deride it, but he never took it seriously enough to explore the novels' full potential, to work them into completion.

Seven years before his death the possibility of dying made him feel 'no longer ashamed of wanting to die'.[48] 'This feeling "No anchoring here" and straight away you feel supported by the tide of the flood.'[49] 'One can now ask to be moved from the old cell, which one hates, to another, which one will only slowly come to hate. A residue of faith is also taking effect: during the move perhaps the master will come along the corridor to look at the prisoners and say: "This man's not to be locked up any longer. He's coming with me".'[50] The fantasy is almost the same as in the fragmentary story about the shabby king, while another story still alive in Kafka's mind was the one about the dying emperor's message.

> They were given the chance of becoming kings or royal messengers. Like children, they all wanted to be messengers. That's why there are so many messengers all racing about the world and giving each other messages which, because there are no kings, have become meaningless. They'd gladly put an end to their miserable lives, but daren't break their oath of loyalty.[51]

Aware that his fictional methods derived partly from dreams, partly from Hasidic stories that had a clear moral, Kafka saw himself as one of these useless messengers: it was possible to tell the truth about personal experience but not to bridge the gap between experience and Law. 'Our art consists of being dazzled by the truth: the light on the vanishing grimace is true, but nothing else is.'[52] In *Das Schloss* Kafka will develop the image of the messenger who does his ineffectual best to carry meaningful messages between the two areas.

At the same time as giving him more self-confidence and freedom, the tuberculosis was making his thinking more transcendental. It was a matter of having to believe – not in a God who had struck at him but in an absolute and in a higher reality without any law of gravity or any mockery for things that to us seem ridiculous.[53] Pulling against gravity is a 'heavenly collar and chain' which chokes us if we try to stay on earth, while the gravitational collar and chain chokes us if we try to reach heaven.[54] But only the spiritual is real.

Possibly Kafka was trying to console himself by teaching himself to love the world less. He was perhaps identifying with Jesus when he questioned the motivation behind the incarnation. In pulling himself away from absolute goodness, had Jesus been fighting to preserve his identity, 'because he could save himself from loving the world only by destroying it'?[55] 'Martyrs don't undervalue the body, they let it be elevated on the cross. In this they're at one with their opponents.'[56] In these notes Kafka was undeniably taking pleasure in paradox for its own sake, and this is itself symptomatic of both dwindling faith in the relevance of the word to the world, and of a desire to explore the no-man's land between the meaningful and the meaningless. Abstracting himself as far as he could from his diseased body, Kafka wanted to feel passive in the caress of his own phrases. At the same time, both in thought and expression, he was repeating rhythms and symmetries found in the Bible and in Kabbalistic writings, and he was influenced by Hasidic ideas about the value intrinsic to language. The Zohar, a mystical exegesis of the Torah,[57] rests on the tradition that the divine word has no specific meaning but is imbued by

God with meaning that must always remain largely obscure to the human intelligence. Not that Kafka believed himself to be divinely inspired, but he was aware of a divergence between his words and his convictions, and of the effect that formulation could have on faith. 'Formulation doesn't fundamentally signify a weakening in belief – this would be nothing to regret – but a weakness of conviction.'[58]

His struggle for faith was a struggle to salvage his existence even if his body was beyond repair. 'Believing means: releasing what's indestructible in the self, or better: releasing the self, or better: being indestructible, or better: being.'[59] He was reading *Der Jude* and taking pleasure in its anti-materialism. One writer[60] called the Bible sacramental and the world excremental.[61] We are separated from God, wrote Kafka, on two sides: by the Fall and by the Tree of Life.[62] Paradise remains intact and immune to the curse laid on mankind.[63] This was why 'human judgment of human actions is true and futile – first true and then futile'.[64] For Aristotle 'the end for which we live is a certain kind of activity, not a quality'.[65] Kafka was setting even less value than before on any kind of activity, and more on a certain kind of quality. People who immersed themselves in activity now struck him as misunderstanding the two ideological questions posed by the human condition: about the credibility of this life and of their objectives.[66] Their assumption that there was no alternative to living secreted 'the crazy strength of faith: in this negation it takes form'.[67] The aphorisms in these notebooks deal mainly with guilt, Original Sin and the Fall. From preoccupation with private guilt Kafka was moving out towards solidarity with other sinners.

Kafka was not in pain, and, physically at least, he was hardly aware of being ill.[68] Sitting or lying down he did not feel short of breath; walking or working 'I just breathe twice as fast as I used to';[69] it was hard to talk while walking.[70] He was not writing much, and when he tried to work in the vegetable garden, soon felt exhausted.[71] But, thanks to the illness, he had liberated himself from the office routine and from Prague. On 27 October, when Brod came to address a Zionist meeting, Kafka went to hear the speech and went on with him and Ottla the next day to Prague, where he stayed to see his doctor and his dentist, and to settle a few matters for the institute. But three days before the journey he had felt 'Sad, nervous, physically ill – fear of Prague – in bed.'[72] The three days in Prague would be 'a departure from liberty into serfdom and wretchedness'.[73]

No one else could have made him feel as relaxed as Ottla did. 'Nowhere else would I have so few distractions ... nowhere would I tolerate the domestic and culinary arrangements with less resistance, irritation or impatience.'[74] He enjoyed the proximity of so many animals. Once, while he was sun-bathing, he noticed that the tastiest leaves were too high for the goats, so he bent the branches down for them.

These goats, incidentally, look very much like Jewish types, mostly doctors, though there are also approximations to lawyers, Polish Jews and a few young girls. Dr W., the doctor who treats me, is strongly represented among them. The committee of three Jewish doctors I fed today was so pleased with me that in the evening it was reluctant to be driven home for milking.[75]

One night in the middle of November he heard a nibbling noise. When he got out of bed it stopped at once, but he was woken up again by a rustling around the bed. Mice were running up and down the coal box and across the room. 'Nothing to hold on to anywhere in my being, didn't dare get up or put the light on, the only possibility was a bit of shouting, trying to scare them.... In the morning I was too disgusted and depressed to get up till one.'[76] He took the cat, which secretly he had hated, into his room, but it was not house-trained and each time it dirtied the floor he had to fetch the maid from downstairs.[77] He kept the cat in the room every night after that, but did not like undressing in front of it, and hated it to jump into his lap when he was writing or onto his bed when he was in it. He connected his fear of mice 'with the impression they give of having an unexpected, unwanted, inescapable, largely silent, dogged secret intention, together with the feeling that the walls all round are riddled with their tunneling, and that they're lurking there, and that because of the night-time, which belongs to them, and because of their tininess, they're alien from us and therefore all the harder to attack'.[78] When he tried to persuade the cat that some places were better than others for urinating and excreting, it chose one of his slippers.[79] He told himself that if the excrement repelled the mice, it was not altogether despicable.[80] The problem was eventually solved by leaving a box of sand in the room.[81]

For Christmas Kafka went to Prague, leaving Zürau on 22 December – earlier than he wanted to, because Felice was coming to meet him.[82] They did not give each other an easy time, except on the first day together, when they avoided all discussion of the main issue.[83] But he had made his mind up to break with her. They spent the evening of Christmas Day with the Brods. 'Both unhappy, don't talk,' Brod recorded.[84] In the morning Kafka came back at 7.30. 'Wants me to give my morning to him. Café Paris. But he doesn't want my advice, his mind is admirably made up. Just to pass the time. Yesterday he made everything very clear to Felice. We spoke about everything except that.'[85] Discussing Tolstoy's *Resurrection* Kafka said: 'You can't write salvation, only live it.' Possibly he was identifying with Odysseus in 'Das Schweigen der Sirenen' ('The Silence of the Sirens') the story he had written in October. To protect himself from being tempted, Odysseus stuffed wax into his ears and had himself chained to the mast. But their silence was an even stronger weapon than their singing, and they were silent when they saw him, either knowing him to be wily, or distracted by the reflected radiance in his eyes, which were fixed on the distance. Perhaps he thought they were singing or perhaps he knew and 'was putting on this act for them and the gods merely to shield himself'.[86]

In the afternoon Kafka and Felice went on an outing with the Brods, the Baums and the Weltsches. According to Brod's diary Kafka told him: 'What I have to do I can only do alone. Become clear about the ultimate things. The Western Jew is not clear about them, and therefore has no right to marry. Here there are no marriages. Or only for people who aren't interested in these things. Businessmen, for instance.'[87] Probably he felt more hopeful of achieving clarity about the ultimate things than he had ever been of marrying successfully.

In the morning Kafka took Felice, who was in tears,[88] to the railway station, and then went to see Brod at his office. 'His face was pale, hard and firm,' Brod wrote. 'But suddenly he burst into tears. It was the only time I saw him weep.'[89] The official who shared the room with Brod was at his desk, and Kafka was sitting on a small chair positioned near Brod's desk for debtors, pensioners and petitioners. With tears pouring down his cheeks he gulped: 'Isn't it frightful that something like this has to happen?'[90] Later he told Ottla: 'On the last morning I wept more than at any time since childhood.'[91] In his notebook he wrote: 'Everything hard, unjust and yet right.'[92] And, three days later: 'Not essentially disappointed.'[93] Later still: 'Voluntarily, like a fist, he twisted away from the world.'[94]

After Felice had left, Kafka wanted to see Pick, who was away till 31 December or 2 January, so he went to Dr Mühlstein, who approved both the decision to apply for a pension, and the decision against marrying.[95]

In November Ottla had let her parents into the secret about his lungs, so it was not difficult to explain why he had broken off the engagement, and, far from blaming them for creating conditions that had induced tuberculosis, he felt sorry for them: they could not understand why both their unmarried children needed to live so far away from home. Still under trial, Kafka acquitted himself from the paternal charges of madness and ingratitude, but writing to Ottla about their father he irrationally conceded that they

have things too easy (regardless of whether it's his fault or thanks to his efforts); he acknowledges no other way of being put to the test than hunger, poverty and perhaps illness, and since we haven't had to withstand the pressures –

indubitably taxing – of the first two, he assumes the right to deny us freedom of speech. There's some truth, and therefore some good in what he says.[96]

The disease had not cured him of overrating his father's powers of judgment; nor did it occur to him that undernourishment, which had possibly weakened his resistance to the tuberculosis bacillus, may have done more damage to him than it ever had to his father.

At the end of January, after correcting the proofs of the fifteen short stories Kurt Wolff was publishing under the title *Ein Landarzt* (*A Country Doctor*), Kafka asked for a dedication page to be inserted, inscribed 'To my Father'.[97] But he did think of his disease in relation to childhood intimidation. After two successive nights of coughing blood in quantity, he was not expecting to live long. Not unlike Georg Bendemann, he was carrying out the sentence implicit in his father's threats. He was tearing himself to pieces. 'In fact he never laid a finger on me but now the threat is being realized independently of him. The world – F. is its representative – and my ego, relentlessly in conflict, are tearing my body apart.'[98] He also remembered his father's ruthlessness toward a tubercular shop assistant: 'He ought to die, the sick dog.'[99] But the lack of bitterness is remarkable.

Staying on in Prague to see Pick and to make arrangements about a pension, Kafka felt impatient to be back in the country; he was at ease with no one now except Ottla and Brod.[100] But during his last evening with the Brods, a marital squabble broke out. Elsa told Max, who was pacing about the room, that he was not fit for marriage, and Kafka felt inclined to agree.[101] 'Of course you married wholeheartedly, but staring into the distance (*mit dem Fernblick*) in a way characteristic of that split in you.'[102] This is like the phrase he used in the story for Odysseus ('. . . seinen in die Fernegerichteten Blicken').

After being refused a pension, he went back to Zürau about 6 January 1918 with his blind friend Oskar Baum, who was to stay with him there till 13 January. Kafka was left feeling 'gloomy, weak, impatient'.[103] Before the end of the month he had arrived at a variation on the Bendemann story: 'The suicide is the prisoner who sees a gallows erected in the prison yard, mistakenly believes it is for him, breaks out of his cell during the night, goes down and hangs himself.'[104]

By the end of January it was six to eight degrees below freezing point in Zürau, but Kafka was sleeping with the window open and standing naked for his early morning wash. He would break the layer of ice in the pitcher, only to find that ice formed again in the wash-bowl. But, though he had become accustomed to having the stove going day and night, he did not catch cold.[105] The market square was covered in snow, and when a funeral service was held at the church for a poor man from a neighbouring village, the hearse, because of a trench cutting half-way across the square, had to detour around the frozen goose-pond. He watched from his reclining chair at the window.[106]

His stamina was low, and he was enervated by a wound on his thumb which refused to heal: he had cut it while digging in the garden.[107] But he was coming to believe that exhaustion, self-contempt, dissatisfaction and his sense of constriction would all disappear if he could stop wanting to discriminate between internal and external. Surely, what had always seemed to be offering stimulation, refreshment, satisfaction, freedom, had not been extraneous but integral to the self.[108] Similarly, the part of himself that issued commands to him was not separate, even if he felt he could interrogate it and write down the dialogue:

– It's impossible that only a commandment is implanted in such a way that you just hear it and nothing else happens. Is it a continuous commandment or only occasional?
– I can't be sure but I think it's continuous though I'm only occasionally aware of it.[109]

But he was taking a more positive view of what he saw as his failure in living and literature. It was not due to inertia or perversity or incompetence, but he had had no ground under his feet, no breathing space, no super-ego.

It's my task to create these, not in order to catch up on what I've missed: I'll have missed nothing, for this task's as good as any other. In fact it's the most basic task or at least a reflection of it. . . . Nor is this exceptional, the task is sure to have been set before. Whether on the same scale I don't know. I've no qualifications for life, so far as I know, except the usual human weakness. With this – in this respect it's an enormous strength – I've vigorously incorporated what's negative in my period, which is very close to me, and I've no right ever to go against it, only in some measure to represent it. I had no inherited share of either the faintly positive or the violently negative that overturns into the negative. I wasn't, like Kierkegaard, led into life by the frail and failing hand of Christianity nor, like the Zionists, did I catch hold of the retreating hem of the Jewish prayer shawl. I am end or beginning.[110]

In the middle of February Kafka went back to Prague to make sure he was exempt from military service. On his return he felt 'completely inebriated, as if I were in Zürau for the sake of sobering up and as soon as I was on the way to sobriety, would immediately set out for Prague again, to get drunk'.[111] Re-acclimatizing himself to rustic calm and boundless leisure, he felt not only disinclined to make any statement but incompetent. It was as if symbols were being physically actualized in his breathlessness.

It happens of its own accord, my world is progressively impoverished by the silence; I've always thought it was my particular misfortune ... not to have enough lung power to breathe into the world all the diversity which our eyes tell us it has. I no longer even try. [112]

From the end of March he worked in the garden Ottla had laid out during the summer, and, reading Kierkegaard, he agreed with Brod that the philosopher's preoccupation had been with how to arrive at a true marriage. [113] But Kafka no longer felt he had any affinity with Kierkegaard: 'the man in the next-door room has somehow turned into a star'. [114] 'So much light emanates from Kierkegaard that some of it penetrates into all corners.' [115] Kerkegaard's fiancée, Regine Olsen, was lucky to have escaped 'that instrument of torture which was no longer touching her'. [116] Similarly Kafka thought Felice was lucky to have escaped him. He may have been thinking of himself when he measured an aphorism of Kierkegaard's against Freud's remark that Jesus was always healthy: 'To lead a true spiritual life while physically and psychically in a state of perfect health – that no man can do.' [177]

Much as he would have liked to stay on in Zürau, Kafka knew that unless his sick leave was extended, he could not hold out much longer against the insidious pressure the institute was putting on him by continuing, uncomplainingly, to pay his salary. [118] Then, on 18 April, Ottla returned from Prague with the news that he had had all the leave he was going to be given. Though he had always complained of office work as wasting energy he needed for writing, the wish to stay in Zürau had nothing to do with any wish to write fiction, write letters or even to talk. [119] If he thought of himself as a writer, it was mainly in a negative way: to write was not so much to produce something that might be analysable ('to cough up the moon' as he put it, implicating his illness in the metaphor) [120] as to withdraw from reality: 'we've moved, with everything we possess, to the moon ... we've lost ourselves for the sake of having a home on the moon.' [121]

20 Julie

He left Zürau on 30 April 1918, and on 2 May resumed his work in the institute. Once again he was living in his parents' home, and, writing to Ottla, said he had settled into her room but not into living in the city.[1] At first he had felt only half awake. He was sleeping badly, breathing with difficulty, and missing her. 'I tried to make Elli into a confidante, but she isn't the right one.'[2] By the middle of the month he was better adjusted: 'it's harder to live here than in Zürau, but that's certainly no reason for not trying.'[3] In the afternoons he would go to do gardening work at the pomological institute in Troja. According to a note Brod made on 1 July, 'He feels better in Prague because in Zürau he was idling the time away. Here he regards Hebrew and gardening as the positives in his life. Wants to keep these entirely unadulterated, they are "rural" things. Wants to withdraw from everything else.'[4] When Johannes Urzidil approached him for a contribution to his Expressionist magazine *Der Mensch*, Kafka said he had nothing he wanted to publish.[5]

During the summer he made a number of journeys to the clinic he had helped to found in Frankenstein. In October the Royal Bohemian State Office for the Welfare of Returning Ex-Servicemen would apply for him to be awarded a first-class decoration in recognition of his work.

Sometimes Brod would meet him at Troja to go for a walk, sometimes they would go swimming together, but they were seeing less of each other.[6] 'Sleepless night because of Kafka,' Brod noted on 3 July.

> I feel abandoned but respect his determination. There's been no quarrel. I've often felt comforted – and been given fundamental principles – by his admirable way of looking at what's positive in everything (even in those who are against him) of seeing how far they're in the right and how far they can't help what they're doing ... I've been encouraged by his confidence that a pure intention, an objective piece of work is never futile, that nothing good can ever be wholly lost.[7]

Not that their relationship was sufficiently moribund to need the 'obituary' Brod felt this to be.[8]

Kafka was fairly consistent, throughout the summer, in minimizing intellectually strenuous activity, but his health went on deteriorating. In the autumn he was 'beginning to be really ill',[9] but he still refused to go into a sanatorium.[10] Katherine Mansfield and D. H. Lawrence, contemporary victims of the disease, were equally stubborn in refusing the discipline of institutionalized therapy.[11]

Like Gregor in 'Die Verwandlung' who lovingly intended to subsidize his sister's training as a violinist, Kafka encouraged Ottla to study agricultural economy. In Zürau she had tried to learn from individual farmers, but made serious mistakes and lost money: in August he wrote around on her behalf to a number of possible colleges. Perhaps it did not matter much which one she chose. 'If you really want to learn, you can learn all you need anywhere, if necessary with help from books.'[12] She must not discuss the cost of the course with their father. 'I'll very gladly pay for it. Money has less and less value anyway, and if I invest in you it will be the first mortgage on your future economy.'[13] He would go with her, if she liked, to look at some of the colleges.[14]

During the second half of September he was convalescing at a hotel in Turnau. 'I learn nothing at all, just try to keep hold of what I have, and that's the way I wanted it, I'm in the garden all day long.'[15] He liked the hotel, which was clean and efficiently managed, while the cooking was good. Meat and eggs were plentiful; vegetables, bread, milk and butter in short supply. The loaves distributed by the municipality were inferior, but the fruit was good.[16] The surrounding woods were 'very beautiful, quite on a par with the woods of Marienbad, beautiful heart-warming views on every side.'[17]

He went back to Prague at the end of September, and in October Ottla arrived from Zürau. There was an epidemic of Spanish 'flu all over Europe, and in the middle of the month Kafka succumbed to it. His temperature was abnormally high (105.8 degrees) and when his life appeared to be in danger, he was moved into his parents' bedroom. 'Mother wept the whole day,' wrote Ottla. 'I comforted her as best I could.'[18] His father came quietly to poke his head round the door of the room, and raised his hand gently in greeting. 'At times like that one lay back and wept for joy, as I weep again now describing it.'[19] He had enormous trouble with his breathing, and seemed to be sweating endlessly. It was nearly four weeks before he could get up, and by then, the Austro-Hungarian Empire had finally disintegrated. On 14 September it had made a peace offer which the allies had rejected. On 4 October a German–Austrian note was sent via Switzerland to the US, proposing an armistice, and on the 12th, Germany and Austria agreed to Woodrow Wilson's terms – that they should both retreat to their own territory before the armistice was signed. On 9 November, two days after Kafka got up, Kaiser Wilhelm abdicated. On 11 November the armistice between the Germans and the allies was signed; on 14 November the Czechoslovak national assembly had its first session in Prague. Karel Kramář declared the House of Habsburg to be deposed, proclaiming the Czech state as a republic, and Tomáš Masaryk was elected as its first President.

Kafka resumed work on 19 November, but in less than a week he was ill again, with a high temperature, difficulty in breathing and outbreaks of sweating. He had to 'spend the whole week half lying, half sitting',[20] but he went on teaching himself Hebrew.[21] It was his mother's idea that he should convalesce in Schelesen near Liboch, and she travelled with him on 30 November to install him in the Pension Stüdl. He intended to stay for less than four weeks; in fact he stayed four months. 'It's not as good here as it was in Zürau, but not at all bad, of course, and, like everywhere, instructive. Besides, it's amazingly cheap: 6 francs a day.'[22] Before leaving Prague he had promised to send Brod a list of questions on Hebrew grammar, mostly written in Hebrew. They could all be answered briefly, and Brod could reply in Hebrew.[23] He sent the questionnaire with his first letter from Schelesen, but he was not trying to do much work. 'The day is short, there's not much paraffin and I lie out in the open air for hours. I'm not even reading my books, just those in the hotel library.'[24]

Ottla was in Friedland at the Agricultural Economy Winter School. Either she could come to Schelesen for Christmas or he could go back to Prague. He was worrying about her. She was homesick, without enough to eat and without a room of her own – in almost every way worse off than she had been in Zürau. 'If either your studies or your health suffers, you must of course come back.'[25] Reporting on his own condition, he tried to be reassuring: 'I'm really quite well, even if the breathing has become rather weaker and the heartbeats louder.'[26]

It looked as though illness was going to make the remainder of his life more solitary, but it seemed to him that there were only two types of people who were not 'social through and through': 'those who lead a vagabond life right on the edge, and soon fall off, and then those who have a superhuman ability to contain the whole of society within their own narrow breast'.[27] This is the category to which he would have liked to belong.

He went back to Prague for Christmas, and on 12 January 1919 applied for another three months' sick leave. He was granted only three weeks, but on 22 January he went back to Schelesen, where the local doctor, Ernst Fröhlich, wrote medical reports which he posted to the institute.[28] On 7 February his sick leave was extended for four weeks.[29]

Though condemned to see little of Brod, in the flying dreams Kafka often had, Brod sometimes featured as an onlooker who was either slightly wronged or kept waiting for a long time, but was always tolerant and understanding.[30] He also needed to reconstitute Ottla's presence in his dreams. 'I woke at about five and heard you at the bedroom door calling "Franz" – quite softly but I heard it distinctly. I answered straight away but heard nothing else. What did you want?'[31] His mother was occasionally present in his dreams – for instance in one about driving around Lapland in a troika.[32]

Early in the year Kafka became involved with a young woman who reminded him of Grete Bloch. Julie Wohryzek, the twenty-seven-year-old daughter of a Prague shoemaker and synagogue official, was staying at the same pension, convalescing.

Not a Jewess and not a non-Jewess, not German, not non-German, mad about films, operettas and comedies, in face-powder and veil, with an inexhaustible and irrepressible supply of pungent slang, generally fairly ignorant, more cheerful than depressed – that's roughly what she's like. If you wanted to describe her genetic origin, you'd have to say that she belonged to the race of shopgirls. But at heart she's brave, honest, unselfconscious – such great qualities in a creature who's certainly not without physical beauty, but is as skimpy as the mosquitoes that fly up against my lamp.[33]

At first their only way of communicating was laughter. 'For several days we laughed continuously whenever we met – at meal-times, out walking, sitting opposite each other. This laughter wasn't really agreeable, there was no obvious reason for it, it was painful, embarrassing.'[34] It made them, after the first few days, want to avoid each other, even at meal-times, and he stopped wanting to read to her.

He was too weak not to notice how much energy an emotional relationship consumes. 'To open oneself to new human beings, and especially to their sufferings and above all to their struggle – you come to think you know more about it than they do – all this is the counterpart to giving birth.'[35] Julie had been engaged, but her fiancé had been killed in the war.[36] The conversation gave Kafka one of his first sleepless nights for nearly a year: all the old wounds seemed about to reopen.[37] He reverted to spending most of his time alone, lying on his balcony, looking out over the wooded hills,[38] watching peasants working in the turnip fields and overhearing snatches of conversation.[39] He was disinclined to read. There was less to be learnt from books, he now felt, 'than from suffering, provided one has the strength to resist it where necessary.'[40]

But Julie and he were thrown back together by the wintry weather. They were virtually alone together in the pension, and 'each of us is a necessity to the other, quite regardless of pleasure or pain'.[41] They did not become intimate sexually and went on addressing each other in the formal plural – but the strain on his heart made him feel like consulting a doctor every day.[42] She did not want to marry, she said, and no longer wanted to have children. He intended not to see her again in Prague, and though they had exchanged notes in the pension, they did not correspond after she left early in March, [43] and when, on the 6th, his sick leave was extended, he had no doubt that he wanted to stay on in Schelesen, alone, until the end of the month.

Ottla's friend Josef David had been serving in the army and then gone back to his job at the municipal savings bank. In November he'd paid her parents a formal visit. They were outraged at the idea of her wanting to marry a Christian, and a penurious one at that, but her emancipation was already under way, and Kafka encouraged it. To marry Josef, he told her, would be better than marrying ten Jews. [44] In February she went to Turnau, ostensibly about a job, actually to meet Josef; Kafka said she had done the right thing but given the wrong pretext. [45] Half aware that he was countering the intolerance of their father by playing a tolerantly paternal role towards the sister nine years his junior, he dreamed about pushing a pram and asking the child in it what her name was. 'Ottla,' she said. [46]

As soon as he returned to Prague he contacted Julie. 'We flew together as if we were being chased. . . . For neither of us was there any alternative. . . . And now came a relatively happy and peaceful time.' [47] They went together into the woods, they went swimming in Černosič, they went for walks in the city, but still without any intention of marrying. [48] It was the thirty-six-year-old Kafka who, compulsively, changed the basis of their relationship. Marriage was what he craved, and, after five years of literary self-indulgence and physical frustration with Felice, he felt incredulously glad to be in such a close relationship. Though he was uneasy with some of Julie's friends, [49] the prospects of being happily married were better than ever before.

And in the summer, when Kafka told his father that Julie had accepted his proposal of marriage, his reaction was something like: 'I suppose she put on one of those blouses. Prague Jewesses are good at that sort of thing. And of course you made your mind up straight away to marry her. And as soon as you possibly can, what's more, in a week's time, tomorrow, today. I just don't understand you. You're supposed to be a grown man, and you live in the city and yet you can do no better than marry a girl who'd give herself to anybody. Aren't there any alternatives? If you're afraid, I'll go along with you myself.' [50] He spoke more coarsely than this, though his wife was in the room, and his son, who was not accustomed to humiliation, had never suffered more. 'Perhaps things became a little misty in front of my eyes.' [51] His mother, apparently in complete agreement with her husband, picked up something from the table and walked out of the room. [52]

In Julie's company Kafka was liable to feel simultaneously sincere and insincere, 'play-acting when I sighed, truthful in my commitment, confidence and feeling of safety. Uneasiness in my heart.' [53] He was making the second entry in a new diary he had started three days earlier, but he made only one other brief entry before December: 'Constantly the same thought, desire, anxiety. But certainly milder than before, as if a major development was taking its course, while I feel its distant tremors. Too much said.'[54] He had lost faith not only in the possibility of analysing and controlling events, but in the wisdom of trying to.

The violence of his father's reaction ruled out any possibility of a helpful discussion: no one could have been less capable of providing the sympathy his son so desperately needed. Kafka's main handicap, as always, was self-doubt. When it was so hard to cope with his own existence, how could he assume responsibility for a wife and children? Could he hope to make Julie happy when the additional strain on his nerves and his lungs might precipitate a breakdown? 'The whole affair was a race between external circumstances and inner debility.'[55] It was a race he only just lost. They found a cheap one-room flat in Prague-Wrschowitz. The banns were published. But two days before the wedding they lost the flat and Kafka decided against marrying with nowhere to live. The loss of the flat seemed not so much a stroke of bad luck as a condemnation from some higher authority, a rebuke for his presumptuousness in thinking himself qualified to graduate into married life. As with the haemorrhage, it seemed like a sign – apparently from outside, secretly to be welcomed.

21 Milena

In der Strafkolonie was published in October 1919. When Kafka gave a copy to his father, the only response was: 'Put it on the bedside table.'[1] The rebuff hurt Kafka deeply, but at this time the main practical problem was whether he should move to Munich, and whether Julie would live with him there. Meanwhile he should not have stayed in Prague. 'If ever you've had good advice from me,' pleaded Brod, who was on holiday in Heringsdorf, 'listen to me and come here.'[2]

At about the end of October he received a letter which had been sent to his publisher by a young writer, Milena Jesenská Polaková, who wanted to translate some of his work into Czech. He had met her briefly in a Prague café during 1919, but she was married to an Austrian, Ernst Polak, and living in Vienna. Kafka could not remember her face. 'Only how you walked away between the café tables, your figure, your dress, I can still picture those.'[3] He wrote to her, and he showed her letter to Julie.[4] Early in November he and Brod left Prague together to spend a week at the Pension Stüdl in Schelesen. It was here that Kafka wrote most of the long letter to his father, which reveals his conviction that he was mentally unfit for marriage. 'The proof is that from the moment I make my mind up to marry, I can't sleep, my head burns day and night, I don't feel alive, I totter about in despair.'[5]

He had sometimes thought about the way, very early in life, irrevocable mistakes can be made. As if a runner in a race headed off course at the first hurdle. 'To the judge it's quite clear that this man won't win, at least not on this plane, and it must be very instructive to analyse how, right from the beginning, he puts all his efforts into breaking away – and all in utter seriousness.'[6] Kafka's letter to his father was an attempt at analysing what had made him put so much effort into running in the wrong direction.

It was also an attempt to answer the question his father had posed in Prague: why was he afraid of him?[7] But, more important, it was an attempt – skilful in execution but clumsy in misconception of its own *raison d'être* – to manufacture a surrogate for the sympathetic understanding his father would never be able to provide. Could Kafka at least prove theoretically that he was entitled to more love? For his father the only serious worries were material. From childhood onwards Kafka could remember unsympathetic reactions to his preoccupations: 'an ironic sigh, a shake of the head, tapping your finger on the table, "Is that all?" or "I wish I had your worries", or "If only I had time to worry about that sort of thing" or "Buy yourself something with that."'[8] His business success had absolved his son from any need to worry, so imaginary worries were not only superfluous but insultingly symptomatic of ingratitude. Even now Hermann Kafka was a relentless grumbler, and the letter makes a good case for the defence, but Kafka could never stop self-accusation from breaking in. Had he not failed – as perhaps Valli had succeeded – in giving back the warmth their father needed from his children?[9] The letter is like a course of psycho-analysis conducted without therapeutic intention. Kafka could see that 'for me as a child, everything you shouted was a divine commandment, I never forgot it, it remained my chief means of judging the world, and above all of judging you'.[10] He had been snared into the evaluative syndrome and armed with sharp criteria which could not fail to cut against each other, and, eventually, against him, while the damage was exacerbated by the love for his father that still welled up so overpoweringly. This love was immune to all awareness of his father's deficiencies. Kafka's fiction 'was about you, I was only complaining about what I couldn't complain about on your breast. It was a deliberately protracted farewell to you.'[11] Success as a writer could never redeem failure as a man because he was conditioned to believe – 'and I had conclusive proof in your disapproving expression – that the more success I had, the worse it would finally be for me.'[12] So how could he want children? The phrase 'accepting all the children that come' occurs in both the letter to his father and the letter he wrote later in the month to Julie's sister. Nothing seemed more desirable or further out of reach.

Often I picture a map of the world spread out and you lying across it. And then it seems as if the only areas open to my life are those that are either not covered by you or are out of your reach. . . . What necessarily belongs to supporting a family and to being its head is what I've recognised in you.[13]

At the end of the letter Kafka makes an effort to identify with his father's viewpoint: how might Hermann Kafka have rebutted the charges against him? The father makes an imaginary speech accusing his son of parasitism. Franz has always fought against him – not chivalrously but like an insect that sucks its lifeblood from another body.

You're not capable of living, but to give yourself a clear and easy conscience, you set out to prove that I've taken all your capacity for living and stuffed it into my pocket. . . . I should have told you you were dishonest, equivocal, parasitical. Unless I'm much mistaken, this letter is just another piece of parasitical sucking.[14]

While the phrase 'not capable of living' is reminiscent of the death sentence passed in 'Das Urteil', written seven and a half years earlier, in 1912, the image of the parasitical insect is in line with 'Die Verwandlung', written later in 1912. Both ideas had developed out of paternal invective, but the fictional outlet had not done enough towards relieving the emotional pressure.

Sharing a room in Schelesen with Brod he had less freedom than previously. He could not lie on the bed, half asleep, until eleven, went out walking more than he wanted to, and, because Brod worked in the bedroom, felt guilty about disturbing him.[15] Two other young men were staying at the pension, and a nineteen-year-old girl from Teplitz, Minze Eisner, who was convalescing, after a long illness. At first Kafka disliked her,[16] but he talked to her a good deal, encouraging her to believe in work as a means of self-improvement.[17] Like Ottla, who came to spend a couple of days in Schelesen, Minze was intending to study agriculture.

He went back to Prague just after the middle of the month, only to fall ill again almost immediately, and he did not return to work until the 21st. When Minze sent him some photographs, he told her she had potential as an actress or dancer, 'and the divine impertinence (in the best sense) of standing up to being looked at and enjoying it. I hadn't expected that.'[18] He asked her to go on writing to him: 'After all perhaps it's not such a bad thing to have a good friend.'[19]

With Julie he was less in command of what he did. 'Thursday. Cold. Silently with J. In Rieger Park. Seduction on the Graben. It's all too difficult. I'm not sufficiently prepared. In one way it's the same as it was twenty-six years ago when my teacher Beck, without knowing what a prophetic joke he was making, said "Leave him in the 5th class, he's too weak, over-exertion will take its toll later."'[20]

At the institute Kafka was again listed as sick from 22–9 December but on 1 January 1920 he was promoted to the status of institute secretary, and a salary rise followed on 18 February.

Secretly he was working against the institute. Together with a colleague, Janouch, he advised workmen on how to claim what was due to them, and paid for a lawyer to represent an old labourer whose leg had been smashed on a building site by a crane. Otherwise he would have lost his case against the institute.

In the spring of 1920 Janouch introduced his seventeen-year-old son Gustav, who was writing verse. Kafka took a friendly interest in the boy, who made notes on their conversations. He describes Kafka's 'brown face' as being unusually animated. 'He uses his facial muscles instead of words whenever he can – smiling or contracting or pursing his lips.' He would also use physical gestures instead of laughter, throwing back his head, parting his lips and closing his eyes to slits as if lying in the sun. Or he would lay his hand on the desk, raise his shoulders, draw in his bottom lip and shut his eyes, as if someone were going to shower him with water.

He struck Janouch as 'apologizing for being so slender and tall. His whole figure seemed to be saying: "I am, pardon me, quite unimportant. You'll be doing me a great service if you overlook me."' He had big, strong hands, with broad palms, prominent knuckles and thin fingers.[21]

Between the middle of January and the end of February Kafka again took to writing about himself in the third person. 'He lives in the Diaspora. His elements, a loose-living horde, are scattered through the world. Sometimes he sees them in the distance, but only because his room is integral to the world. How is he to take responsibility for them? Is it still called responsibility?'[22] The identification with the Jewish people is ironical, but the irony is possible only because he felt so much less disconnected from it than he had before he became interested in Yiddish theatre.

One note in this notebook suggests that somewhere there is someone unknown to him who spends the whole time worrying about him, and only him. This is the source of his headaches.[23] Another note says he has a host of judges, like birds perching in a tree with their voices mingling inextricably. There is one judge who maintains that you can be saved simply by opting decisively for goodness, but this judge has never yet recognized a single case as coming within his competence.[24]

Kafka went on corresponding with Minze, who wanted his photograph, but he replied: 'If in your memory my eyes are really clear, young and calm, let them stay there like that, for they're in better care than they are with me.'[25]

He would obviously need another holiday before the spring,[26] but the doctor advised him against Munich, recommending Meran in South Tirol, which Kafka thought would be too expensive.[27] Weakening in his determination not to go to a sanatorium, he wrote to the one in Kainzenbad, in Bavaria, but there were no vacancies until the end of March.[28] He thought of going to the Bavarian Alps. 'My head, I believe, prefers the north, my lungs the south.'[29] When the sanatorium cabled him about an unexpected vacancy at the beginning of March, he intended to go there,[30] but at the end of February he took to his bed again, with a temperature.[31] 'It's not really illness but certainly it isn't health.... Certainly it's the lungs but then again it's not the lungs. Perhaps I'll go to Meran after all, or then perhaps to the moon, where there's no air at all, so it's the best place for the lungs to rest.'[32] At the end of February the medical reports from Dr J. Kodym secured him sick leave for six to eight weeks.[33]

'We are nihilistic thoughts that come into God's head,' he told Brod on 28 February. Brod mentioned the Gnostic idea that the creation was the misdeed of an evil god. 'No,' said Kafka. 'I don't think we're such a serious lapse as that on God's part – just one of his bad moods, a bad day.'

'So outside our world there'd still be hope?' 'Plenty of hope – for God – unlimited hope. Only not for us.'[34]

Before a visa could be issued for him to stay in Kainzenbad, Kafka was told, he needed an entry permit from the municipality. He wrote to the sanatorium, but instead of obtaining the permit for him, the director replied that since all foreign visitors were banned, he should apply to the district authorities. So Kafka settled on Merano.[35]

After leaving at the beginning of April, he stayed for a few days at the Hotel Emma, but went out on Easter Monday, 5 April, to look for somewhere cheaper, and found the Pension Ottoburg in Untermais, to the south of the town. Three days later he moved. In comparison with the big hotel, the pension had 'something of the family vault about it, no that's wrong, something of the mass grave'.[36] The landlady was a cheerful, plump, red-cheeked lady who immediately recognised Kafka's Prague German and expressed interest in his vegetarian diet, but showed no understanding of it.[37]

Self-conscious about it and about his determination to masticate thoroughly – the American nutritionist Horace Fletcher recommended up to thirty chews per bite – he asked for a separate table in the dining-room, but on his first day a colonel invited him to the large table with such cordiality that he could not refuse. Used napkins in rings showed which places were reserved for residents.[38] A general sat down opposite him, and in the conversation it soon emerged that he was from Prague. Was he Czech? No. Someone suggested 'German-Bohemian', someone else 'West Bank'. At the end of the meal, the general drew him aside to discuss his accent. Kafka mentioned his Jewishness as if that explained it. It may have been coincidental that the others all got up to leave the table. 'The general too is very restless, but out of politeness he brings the little chat to some kind of conclusion before striding hurriedly out.'[39] Acutely embarrassed, Kafka was also relieved that he would be able to sit at a separate table from now on.[40] In 1912, after two weeks in the sanatorium at Jungborn, Kafka had complained to Brod how Prague frustrated his need to be in other people's company; during the subsequent seven years, the dietary laws and eating habits he had imposed on himself – no less austere than those of orthodox Judaism – had helped to cut him off from society.

Otherwise the place was pleasant enough. 'Merano is incomparably more free, more spacious, more complex, more splendid than Schelesen, while the air is cleaner and the sun stronger.'[41] He could sit on his balcony, which dipped into a garden overgrown with flowering shrubs.[42] 'The sun shines strongly on me till six in the evening, the greenness all round is beautiful, birds and lizards approach me closely.'[43] But the sun did not go on shining strongly. 'Cordial greetings from the warm south,' he wrote to Minze, '(warm, that is, when the stove's on and I'm almost leaning on it).'[44] And some days were rainy. 'What else could one expect so close to Prague? It's only the vegetation that's deceptive, in weather that would almost make the puddles freeze in Prague the blossoms are slowly opening here in front of my balcony.'[45] There was no sugar to be had in Merano, but, though he hated saccharin, Kafka was nervous of writing for sugar to be sent from home. He could imagine his father's reaction: 'Just like our son. See what sort of a hole he's crept into. They don't even have sugar there.'[46]

It was in Merano that he started writing to Milena Jesenská Polak, who had written twice before he left Prague but not replied to his letter.[47] He hoped he had not offended her in it.[48] Why didn't she consider a trip to Merano? He would take continued silence to mean 'I'm all right'; otherwise she should send him a few lines.[49] She did. She too had a lung disease. 'Half of Western Europe has more or less defective lungs,' he reassured her,[50] adding that in three years the disease had brought him more good than harm. He soon had a strong enough sense of affinity with her to write a detailed account of the haemorrhage that had woken him in the middle of the night. She, he was sure, could not be seriously ill. Struggling with his memory of her, he could recall 'the almost peasant-like freshness alongside the sensitivity'. She had sent him a manuscript, 'which touches me and shames me, makes me sad and pleased'.[51] But she must not sacrifice any sleep to translating his work, he insisted, no less solicitous than when he had been desperate to hear from Felice but nervous that she was starving herself of sleep in order to write. The early letters to Milena follow the pattern of the letters to Felice: on the basis of a brief meeting he was writing with great frequency, at great length, and with a progressive intimacy. He developed a fantasy in which the Milena figure did not have much to do with the actual woman. He pictured a deck-chair ready for her in the garden, half in the shade, and ten glasses of milk within easy reach.[52]

He liked her translation of 'Der Heizer': 'I wouldn't have believed such fidelity was possible in the Czech language, and you show such beautiful natural authority in it.'[53] She had been writing to him in German; now he asked her to write in Czech: it was only in Czech he could get to know the whole Milena. Later, when she complied, he told her: 'I see you more clearly, the movements of the body, the hands, so quick, so decisive, it's almost a meeting, but actually when I then try to look up at your face, what breaks into the flow of the letter – a fine story, this – is fire and I see nothing but fire.'[54] He used the same image when he wrote to Brod about her relationship with her husband:

She's a living fire, such as I've never seen before, a fire, incidentally, that in spite of everything burns only for him. But extremely tender, brave, clever and she puts everything into the sacrifice, or, if you like, gets everything she has out of the sacrifice. What sort of man must he be to inspire it?[55]

Ernst Polak was a German-speaking Jew, and their affair had caused a scandal. Her father, a professor and a Czech nationalist, had put up with a lot of provocation – she had stolen gold from him to give her lovers – but he had reacted like an eighteenth-century nobleman: he had had her interned in a mental clinic outside Prague.[56] Released after eight months, she married Polak and went to live with him in Vienna, where he became a member of the neo-positivist Vienna Circle. He attempted neither to conceal his infidelities nor to include her in his social and intellectual life. She felt unloved, isolated and disliked; sometimes she resorted to cocaine.[57] Kept short of money, she took to journalism as a means of earning independently. Grasping the lifeline of sympathy Kafka was holding out, she confided in him about the 'real horror' of her life.[58] As they began to exchange letters almost daily, the sense of being needed by her intensified his need for her. 'It's true I have only a small room, but the real Milena, who apparently ran away from you on Sunday, is here, and, believe me, it's wonderful to be with her.'[59] 'I'd be lying if I said I missed you, it's the most perfect, most painful magic, you're here, exactly as I am, and stronger ... sometimes I think to myself that you, who are really here, are missing *me* and asking "Where is he then? Didn't he write that he's in Merano?" '[60] He told her there was no prospect of marriage to Julie. The relationship 'isn't actually alive or rather is living an independent life at the expense of people'.[61] That life was eclipsed by a correspondence that became quite different from the one with Felice: Milena's sensitivity was more nearly on a par with his own, and she could project it into her prose. 'One leans right back and drinks the letters, oblivious of everything except that one doesn't want to stop drinking.'[62] Soon he was offering to lend her money so that she could leave Vienna for a while.[63] More acceptable was his reassurance that she must not feel guilty: 'One would have, Milena, to take your face in one's hands and look steadily into your eyes to make you recognize yourself in the other eyes so that from then on you'd no longer be in a position even to think the things that you've written in your letter.'[64] With Felice he had achieved epistolary intimacy by imposing it; Milena was desperate enough for no literary rape to be necessary. The need for intimacy was mutual.

But her letters did not save him from fantasies of seducing the chambermaid.[65] He was putting on weight but suffering once again from sleeplessness.[66] Living almost *en famille* with the hotel residents, Kafka was often embarrassed by remarks about Jews. The colonel, talking to him confidentially, accused the general of 'stupid anti-Semitism',[67] but the general, a tall, thin, well-preserved man of sixty-three, turned out to be friendlier than the colonel. Taking Kafka to be much younger than thirty-six, he described the sort of girl he expected him to marry.[68] Undeterred by Kafka's presence, the hotel guests chatted about

Jewish roguery, brashness, cowardice (stories about the war provide many opportunities, also frightful things, e.g. a sick Eastern European Jew who the evening before marching to the front sprayed V.D. germs into the eyes of twelve Jews, is that possible?) they laugh with a certain admiration, and also apologize afterwards to me.[69]

In this letter to Brod, Kafka, denying that the Jews were ruining Germany's future, concedes that 'it's possible to imagine they're spoiling Germany's present. They've long been imposing on Germany things it could perhaps have achieved slowly in its own way, but has opposed, as coming from outsiders.'[70] And when Milena asked whether he was Jewish, Kafka answered: 'perhaps this is only a joke, perhaps you're only asking whether I'm one of those Angst-ridden Jews'.[71]

At first he seemed to be making headway against the tuberculosis. On 6 April his weight was 57.40 kg; on the 28th it was 59.55, and when he saw Dr Josef Kohn at the end of April, 'he finds my lung excellent, i.e. he can find almost nothing to worry about'.[72] But before the end of May Kafka was told he had no hope of recovering.[73] Writing in June to Brod, he implied that the news confirmed the verdict he had passed thirteen years ago: in the story 'Die Insel Carina', when he described Carus as a mere aesthete. Brod's dismissive criticism of him had been in line with God's; without tougher qualities he did not deserve to live. Kafka was now more convinced than ever of his inferiority to Brod, who had stood in April, albeit unsuccessfully, as candidate of the Jewish Party at the elections for the national assembly of the new state, Czechoslovakia.

You have a mighty fortress, unhappiness may have climbed over one of the outer ramparts but you are in the innermost stronghold or wherever you want to be, and you work, disturbed as you work, restless, but you carry on working, while I'm burning myself up, suddenly I've got nothing at all, a few beams, and if I didn't prop them up with my head, they'd collapse and the whole hovel would catch fire.[74]

Vis-à-vis Milena he felt more disqualified by unworthiness than by disease:

I know how enormously and for me perhaps unattainably remote from my present position is the point at which I'd begin to deserve an occasional glance (even from myself – let alone others!) . . . Someone is lying in the filth and stench of his death-bed, and the angel of death, the most blessed of all angels, arrives and looks at him, Can this man presume to die? He turns over, buries himself deeper than ever in bed, it's impossible for him to die.[75]

His sick leave ran to the end of May, but, entitled to five weeks' holiday, he asked permission to stay in Merano till the end of June.[76] He could sleep but could not stay asleep, and the valerian tea Dr Kohn prescribed was ineffectual, as were both beer and bromine.[77] Lying in a deck-chair, naked, half in the sun, half in the shade, he wrote to tell Milena: 'Too light for sleep I kept circling round you.'[78] And, using her phrase 'what's fallen into my lap', he said he was scared at what had fallen into his.[79] 'I can't cry out, and nothing cries out within me, and I don't say a thousand foolish things, they aren't in me ... and that I'm on my knees perhaps doesn't become obvious until, quite close to my eyes, I see your feet, and caress them.'[80] She had unexpectedly fulfilled the fantasy he had entertained ever since writing his earliest stories. One day a beautiful woman, listening intently to what they said, would understand him completely. With her there was no need of such tortuous self-explanation as had distended the letters to Felice; Milena could read his fiction and give it back to him in the language of his native land. He felt

as if I were leading you by the hand behind me through the subterranean, dark, low, ugly corridors of the story, almost endlessly (that's why the sentences are endless, didn't you realize?) almost endlessly ... so that then, arriving at the way out in broad daylight, I hope I have the sense to disappear.'[81]

He was the self who could stay in bed while the fiction went out into the world.

She wanted him to stop at Vienna on his way back to Prague. As with Felice, when she had asked him to spend Christmas in Berlin, he baulked. How could he stand the mental strain?[82] Julie, who had opened a ladies' hat shop, had sent him a telegram, suggesting a meeting in Karlsbad. Perhaps he would go there.[83] Milena was so young; he was so old, he said, nearly thirty-eight.[84] (He wasn't yet thirty-seven.) 'I'm quite definitely not coming, but if I do – it won't happen – shock myself by arriving in Vienna, I'll need neither breakfast nor supper but a stretcher.'[85] She could write to him in Karlsbad, no, not till he got to Prague.[86] She threatened to break off the correspondence if he did not go to Vienna.[87] She became ill; he worried about her, but 'now no longer, now I think only of my illness and my health, and both of these, the first as well as the second, are you'.[88] He began to dream about going to Vienna and being rebuffed. 'To be honest,' she told him in one dream, 'I thought you'd be smarter.'[89] In another she was warding off his advances.[90] Awake, he had equally disturbing fantasies about the meeting:

Then a tall, lean man will be standing there with a friendly smile (this will last, he had it from an old aunt, who also smiled constantly, but they both do it unintentionally, out of embarrassment) and he'll then sit down where he's told to. This will really be the end of the ceremony, for he'll scarcely talk, lacking the necessary vitality.[91]

Writing of himself in the second person he told her: 'you're not tired but restless, but afraid to take a step on this earth, which is littered with traps, and therefore have both feet simultaneously in the air'.[92] Perhaps the best time in his life had been the eight months in the village, 'when you believed you'd finished with everything'.[93] But the letter ended: 'if towards the end of the fortnight you still want me to come as much as you did on Friday, then I'll come'.[94]

Three days later, insisting '*you belong to me*, even if I were never to see you again', he controlled himself by means of deliberate contradictions. 'My world's collapsing, my world's building itself up, watch out how you (this you am I) survive it … what I'm complaining about is the building itself up, and my own weakness, and being reborn, and the sunlight.'[95] What could they do? If her response to his letters was positive, she could not stay in Vienna, but 'I don't think I'll dare to hold out my hand to you, girl, this dirty, quivering, clawed, unsteady, uncertain, hot-cold hand.'[96]

He was no stranger to ambivalence, but it had never been so painful. 'I lay in bed as on the rack, answering you all night long, complaining to you, trying to scare you away from me, cursing myself.'[97] The next day, together with an engineer acquaintance, he travelled into the Dolomites, but the mountain air failed to clear his head. 'I don't earn much', he wrote, after returning to Merano alone, 'but it would be enough for both of us, I believe, provided of course there's no illness.'[98] He was still unsure whether he would go to Vienna. 'I saw a map of Vienna today, momentarily it was incomprehensible to me that such a large city had been built when you need only one room.'[99]

He left Merano on 27 June and after two sleepless nights wrote a letter-card to her at 10 o'clock on the morning of Tuesday the 29th from a café near the Südbahnhof: '(what sort of cocoa is this, and pastry, is this what you live on?) but I'm not entirely here'. The letter-card would take two hours to reach her, so they shouldn't meet until tomorrow morning. At ten o'clock in front of his hotel, the Hotel Riva. 'Please, Milena, don't surprise me by approaching from the side or back, I won't either.'[100]

Later he would write to Brod: 'The only happiness was fragments of four days torn from the night, already they were literally unattainable, locked in a box, happiness was the straining towards this attainment.'[101] But this fragmentary happiness was intense, despite bedbugs which covered him in bites, [102] and despite the noises from the nearby garage. The best moments were in the woods, where she said she had not imagined it differently from the way it was. This was on their second day together. [103] But the best day was the fourth. Afterwards it seemed he had been too unsure of everything on the first, too sure on the second, too remorseful on the third. [104] He was in love as never before:

> I love the whole world, which includes your left shoulder, no, the right one was the first, so I kiss it if I want to (and you're good enough to pull your blouse out of the way) and that includes your left shoulder and your face above me in the woods and resting on your almost naked breast. So you're right when you say we were already one, and I'm not at all afraid of it. [105]

She understood what it was that nearly always made him afraid:

> I knew his anxiety before I knew him. Understanding it, I could armour myself against it. In the four days Frank was with me he lost it. We laughed at it. . . . When he felt this anxiety he looked into my eyes, we waited a while as if we couldn't catch our breath or as if our feet hurt, and after a while it went away. Not the slightest effort was needed, everything was simple and clear, I dragged him over the hills behind Vienna, I ran ahead because he walked slowly, he tramped behind me, and if I close my eyes I can still see his white shirt and his sun-tanned neck and how he was exerting himself. He walked the whole day, up, down, walked in the sun, didn't once cough, ate an awful lot and slept like a log, he was simply healthy, and to us in those days his illness was rather like a slight cold. [106]

The moment of saying goodbye on the platform of the railway station was 'a natural phenomenon ... such as I've never seen: sunlight being obscured not by clouds but by itself'. [107]

His Austrian visa had expired, but in Merano he had been told it would not be needed for the journey. He had no trouble at the Austrian border, but in Gmünd a frontier official said he must go back to get a re-entry visa from a police-station in Vienna. It meant two extra journeys of four and a half hours to Vienna and back, besides the journey to Prague that would still be ahead of him. But the inspector relented at the last minute, giving him time to collect his luggage, rush to the passport office and the customs and, with the help of a porter, board the train just before it moved off. [108]

Immediately he arrived in Prague he told Julie about Milena. 'She didn't say even one remotely angry word about you or me,' [109] but, nervous she would fall seriously ill, he promised to see her again the next day, Monday 5 July. [110] She was calmer when they met. 'But when the main question came up again – for minutes at a stretch the girl, next to me on the Karlsplatz, was trembling all over her body – all I could say was that with you there everything else, even if it hadn't changed in itself, disappeared, became nothing.'[111] Finally Julie said: 'I can't leave you, but if you send me away, I'll go. Are you sending me away?' But when he said 'Yes', her answer was 'I still can't go.' Then she began to argue. She was sure Milena loved her husband, she said. She abused Milena, demanded to see her letters. He refused. Then she said she wanted to write to her. When he agreed to this, she quietened down.[112] 'And isn't it deeply degrading to you, my fear that in her desperation she may write something insidious that could turn you against me?'[113] 'And despite everything, I often feel that if a man can die from happiness it will happen to me. And if happiness can keep a man alive who's marked down for death, then I'll stay alive.'[114]

Kafka's Uncle Alfred had not been to Prague for eight years, but now a telegram arrived to say that he was coming.[115] To make room for him in the flat Kafka moved out to Elli's flat – she was in Marienbad.[116] In the evening he went to the station twice, first to meet his uncle, and then his parents, who were coming back from Franzensbad.

Fear of what Julie would write gave way to fear that Milena still loved her husband. Kafka was coughing a lot – at night sometimes for fifteen minutes at a stretch.[117] And on 13 July, the doctor said he was no better than when he had left for Merano in April. The disease was firmly ensconced in the apex of his left lung, and the only gain in weight was a negligible three kilograms.[118] Considering how Milena was squandering her health, he thought 'that instead of ever living together, all we'll be able to do together is lie down and die'.[119]   On 15 July Ottla was married to Josef David. Kafka had been consistent in his encouragement. 'We shouldn't both get married, that would be dreadful, and since you're certainly more suited to it than I am, you're doing it for both of us. . . . So I'll stay single for both of us.'[120] But, appalled at the prospect of losing her, he had such a bad headache it was hard to get through the wedding meal, sitting between his two new sisters-in-law.[121]

In the office it was hard to keep his mind off Milena. 'When I don't happen to be writing to you, I lie back in my armchair and look out of the window.'[122] But, for fear of missing a telegram or a special delivery letter from her, he had taken to spending the whole afternoon there.[123] Often he would plead with Brod to come and help him pass the time.[124]

Could she make up her mind to leave Ernst and come to Prague?

I, I, Milena, know absolutely that you will be doing the right thing, whatever you do, whether you stay in Vienna or come here or stay hovering between Vienna and here, or now do one and now the other. *After all, what would I be having to do with you if I didn't know that?* . . . I used to think I couldn't bear life. . . . But you're now proving to me it wasn't life I found intolerable.[125]

As he had written in the diary during 1915, to have just one person who fully understood him, a woman for instance, 'would be to have a foothold on every side, to have God'. The sensation of having his existence confirmed by that understanding, of basking in that sunshine, was more important to him than to make love. But it was hard to hold the anxiety at bay, as it had been even when they were together. 'You're right to accuse me of anxiety *à propos* my behaviour in Vienna. . . . I don't know its inner laws, I know only its hand at my throat, and that's truly *the most terrible thing I've ever experienced or could experience.'* [126] Was it just unreasonable defeatism which was telling him that her letters, indispensable though they had become, were contradicted and possibly invalidated by her absence: if she felt committed to him, as he did to her, why wasn't she in Prague? [127] 'What I'd prefer', she wrote, 'is a third way out which leads neither to you nor back to him but to no matter what kind of solitude.' [128] Meanwhile she was still with Polak, which made Kafka feel like a mouse, allowed to run across the noble household's carpet once a year. [129] She wanted him to come to Vienna; he wrote that he probably would not. [130] Perhaps she would come to Prague next month. 'I'd almost like to ask you "Don't come".' [131] She wanted reassurances that he loved her, and when he started to demur, she began to feel a desperate need to be with him: would he not come to spend a day with her in Vienna? [132] He cabled that he could not come. [133] She cabled, imploring him to come, telephoned him, wrote letters, always making an impact but never overcoming his resistance. [134] He did not want to ask for time off from the office, he said. Nor could he lie to his director, unless it were either out of fear or out of necessity. [135] 'To me the office is a living creature – and so were school, university, family, everything – which gazes at me out of innocent eyes, wherever I am. A person with whom I have somehow become involved, although he's stranger to me than the people I can now hear driving cars over the Ring.' [136] Milena was furious.

Frank can't live. Frank has no capacity for living. Frank will never be healthy. Frank will die soon. . . . He's absolutely incapable of lying, as he is of getting drunk. There's nowhere he can take refuge. He's exposed to everything the rest of us protect ourselves from. He's like a naked man where everyone else wears clothes. Nor is it even truth all he says, all he does, all he is. It's a predetermined Being, in and for itself, stripped of all the accessories that could help him to distort life into beauty or suffering – either. [137]

In Vienna she had not known how ill he was. When she had found out from Brod, she had written to him confidentially, promising to do everything she could – if necessary even come to Prague – to coax him into a sanatorium. [138] And on his next visit, the doctor said there was no alternative, recommending the sanatoria in Grimmenstein and in the Wiener Wald. Kafka hesitated. 'These are exclusively lung clinics, feverish houses which cough all over, day and night. You have to eat meat there, and ex-hangmen twist your arm if you resist injections, and Jewish doctors, stroking their beards, are as strict with Jews as with Christians.'[139] At the same time, he was trying to encourage Milena, who had been spitting blood too, to see a doctor.[140] She must not go on living her 'heroically joyful life, living as if you were telling the blood "Come on then. For goodness sake, come on."'[141] He had been writing to her, as he once had to Felice, trying to plan a weekend meeting at Gmünd, on the border, where they could spend the Saturday night together,[142] but they seemed to be drifting apart. Did they have nothing in common but a death wish?[143] Suddenly she was urgently demanding a meeting in Gmünd. 'I ought to be very happy about it, but I can't be, because your letter contains some kind of secret fear, whether for me or against me I don't know.'[144] But he still believed her to be incapable of making anyone suffer.[145] And when she cancelled the arrangement to meet, 'Now look, Milena, it doesn't matter, for my part I wouldn't even have had the temerity ... to ask to see you again after "only" four weeks.'[146]

When, during the first week in August, she wrote explicitly that she could not leave her husband, that she loved him too much, that he needed her too much, Kafka's answer was that he had known all along. 'It was behind nearly all your letters, it was in your eyes ... it was in the lines on your forehead, I knew it like someone who's spent the whole day sunk in some sleep-dream-anxiety behind closed shutters.'[147] Two days later he sent her an account of his first sexual experience with a girl.

And as it was then, so it has always remained. My body, often silent for years, would again be shaken beyond endurance by this longing for a slight, for a quite specific vileness, for something slightly repulsive, painful, filthy; even in the best things there were for me here, there was something of that, some kind of slightly bad smell; some sulphur, some hell. This drive had in it something of the eternal Jew, senselessly attracted, senselessly wandering through a senselessly filthy world.[148]

The idea is close to one formulated by de Sade: 'horror, nastiness and the frightful are what give pleasure during fornication', and, echoing him, Baudelaire wrote: 'the unique and supreme pleasure of love lies in the certainty of doing evil'. It was Milena who seemed to have liberated him, after all this time, from taking pleasure in what seemed nasty: 'I simply don't see anything dirty, anything of that kind, which provokes from outside, only everything that produces life from within.'[149]

The disease had made no inroads yet on his face. It was still possible to mistake him for a boy. This happened when an instructor at the 'Civilian Swimming School' on the Sophieninsel, an island on the Moldau, asked him whether he would like to go for a row. A building speculator wanted to be rowed to the Judeninsel, another island. When the owner of the swimming bath asked whether the boy could swim, Kafka said nothing, but the instructor said he could. In the boat the speculator praised him for rowing so fast, but, disappointingly, failed to give him a tip.[150]

Finally, in the middle of August, he did have a weekend meeting with Milena in Gmünd but, inevitably, the reality sank under the weight of his expectations. He arrived 'like a house-owner; odd, that with all the restlessness which never leaves me, this complacency of ownership is still possible'.[151] For much of the time they were like strangers;[152] the familiarity which had grown up in their almost daily exchange of letters was so extreme that their behaviour could not match it. She asked him whether he had been unfaithful to her in Prague.[153] (How could she ask this when she had read his letters?[154] How could she ask this when she knew he knew she had been sleeping with her husband?) With a mixture of flippancy, seriousness and indifference he answered: Yes, he had been faithful to her.[155] And in the evening, when they were in a meadow together and she was lying back and he was talking about one of his friends, he had the impression she was hardly listening.[156] Something had been ruined, and, as always, he blamed himself.[157] His main fear was that he had alienated her. 'Don't let yourself be scared off from me, even if I disappoint you once or a thousand times or right now or perhaps always right now.'[158] She had told him a great many things he would have preferred not to know: one was about polishing her husband's boots and how she enjoyed doing it well.[159] This time he had not been able to make love without feeling unclean. 'I'm dirty, Milena, infinitely dirty, that's why I make so much fuss about cleanliness. No song is purer than the one sung in the deepest hell; that's what sounds angelic.'[160]

Why can't one make up one's mind that it's right to live in this extraordinary, suspended, suicidal tension (once you suggested something similar, I tried then to laugh you out of it) instead of deliberately loosening it, wriggling out of it like an irrational animal (loving this irrationality, like an animal). Letting so much electricity that's become uncontrollable, disturbed, into the body, one's almost burnt up.[161]

But he was still addicted to the fantasy Milena who was always with him. 'What do I need a letter for when yesterday for example I spent the whole day and evening and half the night conversing with you – a conversation in which I was as sincere and serious as a child with its mother.'[162]

But while she had given up almost nothing – peace of mind was a luxury she had not had since early childhood – he had given up Julie and, compulsively, he was gambling high emotional stakes on an unreliable allegiance. 'There's no limit to the dependency. The Either-Or is too great. Either you're mine, and then it's good, or you're lost to me, then it's not so much bad as annihilating – nothing at all would remain, no jealousy, no suffering, no worrying.'[163] Nevertheless, he held on to his longing for her: it was the only truthful emotion available to him, since hopelessness was no deterrent. 'Perhaps it isn't really love when I say you're what I love most; love is that to me you're the knife I turn inside myself.'[164] His desires were subject to a force he did not understand: 'what it wants in the long run I don't know'; what it wanted at the moment was 'quiet, darkness, creeping inside myself'.[165] In any case he was helpless in his dependence on it: 'if it ceases, I cease too, it's the condition of my participation in life . . . I'll always be frightened, of myself most of all'.[166] Having admitted defeat, he could use her almost like a diary. 'To you as to no one else one can tell the truth both for one's own sake and for yours, yes one can actually find out from you the truth about oneself.'[167]

At first he felt no compulsion to write anything except letters to her, but as the letters became more diary-like, he wanted to resume the literary work he had abandoned over three years earlier. Apart from the long letter to his father, he had written virtually nothing except brief letters since the haemorrhage. But at the end of August 1920 he went back to his routine of sleeping in the afternoon instead of staying in the office. After waking up, he would take a two-hour walk and then sit at his writing-table as long as he could.[168] At first the routine was fairly unproductive, but the first sketches for *Das Schloss* belong to this period. In one of these, determined to penetrate into the lord of the manor's family, K. tries to bypass waiting for an introduction through a common acquaintance. Not that the lord of the manor is anything more than a decent, hard-working man, or that K. is either in need of a job from him or in love with his daughter.[169] Another sketch is in the form of a dialogue in which two speakers discuss what is dimly visible in the distance, a town or big village with a castle in it on the top of a hill.[170]

Sometimes Kafka wrote aphoristically on the same theme. 'There's only an objective, no way. What we call a way is hesitation.'[171] Sometimes he wrote about the disease as if it were the active cause of his ambivalence towards it: 'Under each intention the disease is lying curled up as if under a leaf. Bend down to look at it, and, knowing itself to be discovered, it jumps away, the lean silent malignity, and wants to be not crushed but fertilized by you.'[172] Something of the same willing connivance with destructive forces is present in the story 'Der Geier' ('The Vulture'). The man, too feeble to fight the vulture off, lets it peck at his feet. When a passer-by offers to fetch his gun, the bird drives its beak through its victim's mouth, only to drown in the rush of blood.[173] Sometimes, Kafka wrote about provinciality, as in 'Die Abweisung' ('The Rejection') and 'Zur Frage der Gesetze' ('The Problem of Our Laws') which ends with the sentence, 'The one visible indubitable law imposed on us is the nobility, and could we want to deprive ourselves of this one law?'[174]

His behaviour too, was based on acquiescence in the disease: it was a damp autumn, and the winter, which came early, was unusually hard,[175] but he was determined to stay in Prague till October.[176] His situation was like that of 'In der Strafkolonie' with himself as both executioner and victim. Without mentioning the story, he sent Milena a drawing of a simple torture machine with the hands and feet of the delinquent fastened to rods which pull outwards until he is torn apart in the middle. Another man lounges against a pillar, watching.[177]

In September he had a very bad week, with a high temperature, a lot of coughing, and so much difficulty in breathing he was sometimes nervous of standing up.[178] He had received brochures from the sanatoria at Grimmenstein and in the Wiener Wald. Both were expensive, and he felt more inclined, anyway, to go into the country and learn a craft.[179] In October Ottla effectively overruled him by going to the institute, where she spoke to the director about his illness. The consequence was a medical examination.[180] The apexes of both lungs were now infected, according to Dr Kodym, who recommended three months in a sanatorium.[181] Trying to reserve a room at Grimmenstein, Kafka found that he needed first to apply for a residence permit,[182] while his reluctance to leave Prague was being eroded by new outbreaks of anti-Semitic rioting.

I've spent the whole afternoon in the streets luxuriating in the anti-Jewishness. I've now heard them called a 'mangy race'.... To stay on here regardless would be no more heroic than cockroaches are when they can't be driven out from the bathroom. Just now I looked out of the window: mounted police, *gendarmerie* ready for a bayonet charge, screaming crowds running in all directions.[183]

Anti-German feelings and anti-Jewish feelings were confused in what the Prague Bürgermeister permissively called an 'assertion of national consciousness'.[184] During the second half of November crowds vandalized the printing presses of German newspapers, the German Landestheater was occupied, documents in the archive of the Jewish Town Hall were destroyed and parchment scrolls of the Hebrew Pentateuch were burned in front of the Altneu synagogue.

But Kafka had procrastinated so much over the journey to the sanatorium that he was not only too dispirited to travel but almost too ill.

One night he coughed nearly continuously from 9.45 till 11.00 and then, after an hour's sleep, had another hour of coughing.[185] In his depressed state he was only half ironic in his willingness to agree with the *Venkov*, the journal of the reactionary agrarian party, that the Jews corrupted everything and caused it to decompose.[186] He now called himself 'the most Western-Jewish' of all Western Jews, meaning that 'not a single peaceful second is given to me, nothing is given, everything has to be earned, not only the present and the future, but also the past'.[187] The premisses of psycho-analysis were nonsensical. All the so-called neuroses or illnesses were 'matters of faith, desperate attempts to find anchorage in no matter what maternal soil'.[188] According to psycho-analysis, religion had its sources in the same needs as neurosis. But the anchors that really gripped were integral to the personality; they could not be given to a patient by a therapist.[189]

Milena's guilt-feelings were now rising to the surface: 'It's against me', she wrote, 'that he dashed himself to pieces.' No, he answered, paraphrasing a proverb, the pitcher was broken long before it went to the well.[190] Eventually he found there was no need to wait in Prague for permission to stay in Austria; he could get the permit in Vienna. Still ambivalent about going to Grimmenstein, he was sure he did not want to meet Milena: 'I already find the idea of standing in front of you intolerable, I can't bear the pressure on the brain.'[191] It was only one more step to the realization that they should not go on writing to each other. He felt an *'irresistibly strong voice, actually your voice*, that's demanding silence from me'.[192] 'These letters are nothing but torture, *produced by torture, irremediable, cause only torture, irremediable'*.[193]

22 Matliary

On 13 December 1920 he was formally released from his duties for three months.[1] Although he had received a residence permit, he had decided against Grimmenstein in favour of a chest clinic in Matliary 900 metres up in the High Tatra mountains in Slovakia, about 200 kilometres north of Budapest. He made the journey on 18 December. Ottla had been planning to accompany him and stay for a few days, but he travelled alone. A sledge awaited him at the station, and he had a beautiful moonlit journey through the snow-covered mountains.[2] His first impressions of the clinic were so unfavourable that he thought of leaving the next day. In the room that had been reserved in the annexe, there was no central heating, nothing but an iron bed with a bolster and a blanket, a cupboard with a broken door, and a balcony with a door that did not properly fit. The proprietress, Frau Forberger, was unhelpful. After Christmas, she said, he could move into the main building, which was centrally heated; here he would at least have a doctor living in the same corridor. When she had gone, the maid suggested he should sleep in the next-door room, which had been prepared for Ottla; it had no balcony but during the day he could lie on the balcony of this room. He agreed, and in the morning everything seemed different, even Frau Forberger.[3]

There were about thirty residents. 'I took most of them for non-Jews, they're so entirely Hungarian, but most of them are Jewish, starting with the head waiter.'[4] The balcony was sunny,[5] and he decided to stay on in the annexe, which was quieter than the main building. The doctor wanted to start Kafka on a course of arsenic treatment, but, after agreeing to a flat rate of 6 kronen for daily visits, he prescribed milk five times a day and cream twice.[6] All Kafka's previous troubles with his stomach and his nerves had been due, he said, to the lung infection, which had not yet revealed itself.[7]

During his first week at the clinic Kafka gained 1.6 kilos in weight.[8] 'Budapesters used to spend their summer holidays here, so it's clean, and the cooking is good.'[9] Of the other patients there the one he liked best was a twenty-five-year-old Hungarian boy who had only just learned to speak German. He could scarcely see anything out of one eye and mostly kept it closed.[10] 'Charming, in the Eastern Jewish way. Ironic, restless, moody, confident but in great need. To him everything is "interesting, interesting", only that means not what it usually means but something like

"Fire, fire!" '[11] He was as solicitous towards Kafka 'as a mother to her child'.[12]

Kafka instructed Milena: 'Don't write, and avoid meeting me, just fulfil this request for me in silence, it's the only way I can somehow go on living, anything else would do more damage.'[13] She obeyed, but wrote to Brod:

Am I guilty or not?... I'm on the brink of madness. I've tried hard to act conscientiously in behaviour, life, thinking, feeling, but there *is* guilt some-where. . . . I want to know whether I'm someone who made Frank suffer as he did with every other woman so that his illness got worse, so that, in his anxiety he had to run away from me too and so that I must also disappear, whether I'm at fault or whether it's consequential on his own nature.[14]

Her next letter, which was calmer, acknowledged that if she had gone to Prague with him after their four days together in Vienna, she could have given him what he needed. 'With me he'd have been able to find peace.'[15] But, apart from loving her husband too much, 'perhaps I was too much of a woman to have the strength to subject myself to this life, which, I knew, would permanently involve the strictest asceticism.'[16] She still hoped to have a child and live a simpler life, close to the soil.

What looks like Frank's abnormality is actually his chief quality. The women who've been with him were ordinary women who didn't know how to live in any other way than as women. I prefer to believe that we're all of us – the whole world, everybody – sick and that he's the only healthy man who perceives and feels rightly, the only pure human being. . . . He knows ten thousand times more about the world than anyone else. His anxiety was well-founded. . . . He always believes himself to be the one who's guilty and weak. But there's no other man in the whole world who has his enormous strength, this absolute, undeviating drive for perfection, purity and truth.[17]

If she had understood that earlier, she might have found the strength to dedicate herself to him. But 'at that time I was just an ordinary woman like all the women in the world, a little, conative woman. That's why he was anxious.'[18] Kafka's *post mortem* on the relationship arrived at a different conclusion. He diagnosed in himself 'a disease of the instinct, an efflores-cence of the period' and he lacked the vitality to find ways of dealing with it.[19] Since adolescence

I'd be tempted by the body of one girl out of two, but not at all by that of the girl in whom I (therefore?) placed my hopes. So long as she refused me (F) or so long as we were one (M) it was only a distant threat, and not even so distant, but the slightest triviality could make everything collapse. Obviously on account of my dignity, my arrogance (even when he looks so humble, the crafty Western Jew) I can love only what I can place so high above me that it's out of reach.[20]

In Matliary he went on gaining in weight – 4.2 kilos altogether in his first five weeks[21] – but in spite of everything he had written about torture (or perhaps because he was so allergic to the idea) he was susceptible to the sufferings of fellow-patients. One bed-ridden old man showed him a drawing of his abscesses and demonstrated how he had to insert a small mirror deep into his throat to reflect sunlight on to them, while looking in a large mirror to adjust the small one. Kafka staggered to the balcony, and sitting in the cold air, recovered sufficiently to leave the room, but it was only by holding on to the walls and the bench on the landing that he got back to his own room. Treatment for terminal diseases seemed worse than torture. 'Here the torturing goes on for years, with pauses for effect, so that it isn't over too quickly and – the speciality – the victim is himself forced, of his own free will, out of his poor inner self, to prolong the agony.'[22]

Kafka spent much of the time resting on the balcony, well wrapped up, reading and looking up to watch skiers in the mountains. He was coughing less convulsively, if not less frequently, but there was no improvement in his breathing. The second friendship to grow in the clinic was with another Jewish boy, who arrived at the beginning of February, a twenty-one-year-old medical student from Budapest, Robert Klopstock, who had served as an officer on the Eastern front and in Italy. He resembled Werfel – tall, broad, red-cheeked, blond, and strong-looking,[23] with no sign of the tuberculosis he had contracted in the army.[24] Kafka asked Ottla to post some of his books (Kierkegaard, Plato, a biography of Dostoevsky, and Brod) so that he could lend them to Klopstock.[25] Kafka himself was now less interested in reading such books than in reading the Bible.[26]

He was planning to go home when his three months of sick leave ended on 20 March, but he was coughing more than ever, finding it more difficult to breathe, and feeling generally enfeebled.[27] He had no appetite, but forced himself to eat, even to eat meat, though he had haemorrhoids, and it seemed to make them worse.[28] 'How vile it is, for example, to sit opposite a larynx patient (blood-relation of the consumptive, the sadder brother) who faces you amiably, harmlessly, with the transfigured eyes of the consumptive, coughing into your face through his spread fingers droplets of pus from his tubercular abscess.'[29] During the second week in March the doctor warned Kafka that if he went back to Prague he might collapse. He should stay on till the autumn.[30]

The time slipped unnoticeably past. A letter, begun in a burst of energy, would remain unfinished for days, and, not having dated it, he wouldn't even know how many. 'I must often have been lying in a twilight state, as my grandparents did when I was a child, and it always surprised me.'[31] There was still snow in the woods, but he would lie on his balcony or in the outdoor pavilion, wishing vaguely he could be working somewhere in a garden.[32] His letters to Brod were full of envying admiration for the way he was keeping his marriage intact while carrying on both an increasingly active literary career and a relationship with a woman, Emmy Salveter – a chambermaid, when Brod met her, later an actress. 'It seems to me that I'm wandering around like a child in the forests of maturity.'[33] But this feeling did not make it easier for Brod to influence him. He had shown one of Kafka's letters to a doctor, Heinrich Kral, who said Matliary was the wrong sanatorium. 'Only systematic treatment with tuberculin could help you.'[34] Kral knew cases from his own practice where injections had led to complete recovery. 'Why should you think that what helps others can't help you?'[35] Why wasn't his sputum even being examined in Matliary? Why couldn't his parents pay for a more expensive sanatorium, such as Plesch?[36]

But scepticism about Matliary stood less chance of making Kafka move than the threatened arrival of Milena, whose lungs had deteriorated badly. In the middle of April she wrote, saying that her father had suggested the Tatra Mountains. Kafka asked Brod to keep him informed of her movements, so that if she came to the mountains he could leave.[37] When the Austrian expressionist Albert Ehrenstein came on a visit, he tried to persuade Kafka that in Milena life was reaching out its hand, that he had the choice between life and death. 'The only stupidity was in seeming to believe I had a choice. If there were still a Delphic Oracle, I'd have consulted it, and the answer would have been: "Choice between life and death? How can you hesitate?"'[38]

April brought milder weather. Still spending most of his time lying down, he was coughing less, expectorating less, and breathing more easily except on chilly evenings.[39] Altogether he had gained 6.5 kilograms since arriving.[40] But Brod was instructed not to go on writing about recovery: 'Just look at this body, surviving unwillingly, which the brain, frightened at what it has arranged, is now trying to push back towards life. Surviving unwillingly, it can't eat, and an ulcerous wound – the bandage was removed yesterday – needs a whole month to heal inconclusively.'[41] On 5 May, fifteen days before his leave was due to run out, he obtained a new medical certificate which he forwarded to the institute. His leave was then extended to 20 August.

Noise had never ceased to worry him, and at the end of May a man installing stoves in the adjoining rooms regularly started work at five in the morning and went on, hammering, singing and whistling till ten in the evening.

But it isn't a matter of the noise here, it's the noise of the world, or rather my own noiselessness.... If the world shouts sacrilegiously into this gravelike unworldliness, I go berserk, really batter my head against the door of madness, which is never shut except by someone leaning on the other side.[42]

And he hated to be surrounded by illness. 'It's all dirty – constantly being ill and the contradiction between the appearance of the face and of the lung. It's only with revulsion that I can watch other people expectorate, and I have no sputum jar, as I should have.'[43]

Seen in this context, 'writing was only an expedient, as for someone writing his will shortly before hanging himself – an expedient that can well last a lifetime'.[44] In 'this small world of German–Jewish literature'[45] it was apparent that 'in German only the dialects and the most individual High German are really alive, while the rest, the linguistic middle ground, is nothing but embers, which can be brought to a semblance of life only when inordinately lively Jewish hands rake through them'.[46] Most of the young Jews who took to writing in German wanted to leave Jewishness behind them.

But their hind legs were still stuck in parental Judaism while their forelegs found no purchase on new ground. Despair about that was their inspiration ... They lived between three impossibilities ... the impossibility of not writing, the impossibility of writing German, the impossibility of writing differently. You could add a fourth impossibility, the impossibility of writing (since the despair, which couldn't be appeased by writing, was hostile to both life *and* writing ...). So the literature was impossible in every way, a gypsy literature which had stolen the German child from its cradle and somehow hastily trained it, because someone has to dance on the tightrope.[47]

Samuel Beckett, in his Dialogues with Georges Duthuit, uses strikingly similar terms to condemn the art that never stirs 'from the field of the possible'. Art should prefer 'The expression that there is nothing to express, nothing with which to express, nothing from which to express, no power to express, no desire to express, together with the obligation to express.'[48]

For six months now – longer than ever before – Kafka had been cut off from the family. His parents had not troubled to visit him, and Ottla now had a baby daughter, Věra, who had been born in March. He went on sleeping until the end of April in the room that had originally been got ready for Ottla. When he was finally moved into the room with the balcony, taking most of the furniture with him, he soon realized it was the better room, airier and lighter.[49] As the weather improved he spent more time in the woods, happy to escape from the sanatorium sounds into silence broken only by birdsong, running water and wind in the trees.[50] 'The degree of quiet I need doesn't exist in the world, which means one shouldn't need that much quiet.'[51] For hours at a stretch he would rest with only a bottle of milk beside him, either in the woods or in a three-walled wind-shelter. 'If every afternoon were like this and the world would leave me here, I'd stay until I had to be carried away on the reclining chair.'[52]

He had been intending to resume work at the institute on 20 August, but he was too ill to make the journey till the 26th.[53] The train was too full for him to find a seat until it had passed Vruthy, when the conductor let himself be persuaded to make a first-class compartment into a second-class one by pasting a big 2 on the glass door.[54] Kafka started work again on the 29th and, after a couple of most exhausting days, realized that he would have to go to bed every afternoon as soon as he got home.[55] His temperature did not go above 99 degrees, but did go above 98.6 every day.[56] It was obvious that he could not stay in Prague, but he did not want to go back to Matliary. 'Besides the doctors are demanding a proper sanatorium with massage, compresses, quartz lamps and a better diet.'[57] A cold that developed into a bad cough kept him away from the office for at least one day during the last week in September,[58] and when he heard that Milena was coming to Prague, he found it even harder to stay asleep at night.[59] They met several times and, early in October, still wanting her as a witness to the experience of being Kafka, he gave her his diaries to read,[60] about fifteen large exercise books. He would never have shown them to Felice, and never to Milena while he still hoped for a shared future. But he was free now of the compulsion that had necessitated them: 'I no longer need to drive the detail of such things into my consciousness, I'm not so forgetful as I was, I'm a memory that's come to life, hence the insomnia.'[61]

Depression was verging on desperation. After going to a party and then on to a café with some friends, he came home trembling:

I can't even bear to be looked at (not out of misanthropy, but just people's eyes, their presence, sitting there and looking at me, it's all too much for me). I coughed for hours, sank into a morning slumber and would have liked most of all to have swum out of life, which seemed easy, because the distance was so small.[62]

Walking in the park and looking at girls, he felt excluded from the possibility of such happiness.[63] Every married couple seemed enviable; was there anyone else whose inner plight resembled his?[64] 'The systematic destruction of myself in the course of the years is astonishing, it was like a slow, self-widening breach in a dam, a deliberate action. The spirit which achieved that must be celebrating its triumph; why won't he let me join in?'[65]

But he could not even join in when his father, at the eternal card-game with his mother, invited him to take a hand, or at least watch. He made an excuse, but why had he always rejected such invitations? Perhaps it was just weakness of will. [66] A few evenings later, he did make himself join in to the extent of keeping score for his mother, but he was bored and resented the waste of time. 'That's how it's always been. This frontier territory between solitude and sociality I have crossed extremely seldom.'[67] He felt helpless. Why was he fascinated by human bodies with their blinking eyes and talking mouths? 'Because you belong to the same species? But you don't belong to the same species, that's why you raised this question.'[68]

In the story 'Erstes Leid' ('First Sorrow'), which must have been written during October, the trapeze artist arranges to spend all his time, day and night, on the high wire. Specially made containers are hauled up and down to take care of his needs. He speaks to no one but fellow-acrobats, and occasionally a workman or a fireman who has to come up to his level. For train journeys a whole compartment is reserved, and he travels on the luggage rack.

On 17 October Kafka had been examined by the doctor his parents wanted to see him, Dr O. Herrmann, [69] who diagnosed catarrh of the lungs on both sides and prescribed a course of treatment lasting several months. Dr Herrmann struck him as 'at the same time impressive and childishly ridiculous, as they mostly are', [70] but the institute approved the course of treatment and gave him three months' leave starting from 5 November, although Dr Kodym sent in a report on 22 October, recommending that he should be pensioned off since there was 'little probability' of complete cure. [71]

Milena came to see him four times before she left Prague on 2 December. Though her behaviour was 'sweet and dignified as always', [72] she gave him the impression she was making a dutiful effort, 'as if visiting the sick'. [73] Returning to Prague, she came to see him again on 22 or 23 January. Except for the four days in Vienna and the brief meeting in Gmünd, the relationship had been no less literary than the relationship with Felice, and even in giving her his diaries, Kafka had been using the written word in a compulsive bid for her sympathy. But he was coming to distrust the comfort writing could give. Literature was both too dependent on metaphor and too dependent on the world – on the maid looking after the fire, on the cat warming itself. 'All such activity as this is self-sufficient, with its own laws; it's only writing that's helpless, incapable of self-contained life. It's a joke and it's despair.'[74]

In January 1922 he came closer to complete breakdown. 'It all seemed to be over ... it was impossible to sleep, to stay awake, to tolerate life, or rather its sequentiality. The clocks disagree: the inner one races at a diabolical or demonic or in any case inhuman speed, while the outer one stumbles along at its usual pace. What else can happen unless the two different worlds split or tear themselves fearfully apart?'[75]

He was exhausted and exasperated by introspection. For years he had been worrying at the same problems, and however accurate his insights were, the cerebration had not ameliorated his condition but exacerbated it by heightening his nervous anxiety. By analysing what it was that isolated him he was fortifying his isolation, and now the process was carrying him to the brink of madness. Rejecting psycho-analysis, he had no tool but metaphor, and the metaphorical suggestion that he was launching an attack on the ultimate worldly frontier felt no more useful than the idea that he was being attacked from above.[76] Words were only helping him to feel that he was disintegrating.

Defensively, he advised himself to relax into the present moment, to rest on it. 'It's not terrible, it's just fear of the future that makes it terrible. And retrospection, too, admittedly.'[77] Relentlessly tormented still by sexual appetite, he could not forget that he had wasted the gift of sexuality. To achieve satisfaction he would have to overcome fear, sadness and shame as soon as the first opportunity presented itself, but it was wrong, he believed, even to play with the idea of overcoming them. The compromise he had always made was to tempt opportunities to him, but this was wrong too – shameful.[78]

Imprisoned in his self-consciousness, he went on looking enviously at married couples, and at parents with their children. He was nervous that when reading his diaries Milena might have found 'something decisive' against him.[79] And he was almost regretful to find himself calming down, 'as though I got the true feeling of myself only when I'm unbearably unhappy'.[80] But it took little effort to cultivate his unhappiness: he had only to think of past enthusiasms and of how abortive they had all been. Inside brackets he gave a list of examples: 'piano, violin, languages, German language, anti-Zionism, Zionism, Hebrew, gardening, carpentry, literature, attempts at marriage, a flat of my own'.[81] What he would most like now would be to exist alongside himself, to look at the locus of his life as if it were someone else's.[82]

For three weeks he had almost no sleep.[83] His sick leave was due to expire on 4 February, but using Dr Kodym's report of 22 October, he applied on 24 January for an extra three months, and, after seeing Dr Herrmann on the 26th, he was given another report to submit.[84] On Friday 27 January the extension was granted, and he left the same day for Spindlermühle, a resort in the mountains at the foot of the Schneekoppe – the mountain on the Polish border. He went tobogganing and mountain climbing without at first feeling any the worse for it, but after a few nights of sleeping comparatively well, he reverted to sleeplessness.[85] He was feeling like a citizen of another world 'which bears the same relationship to the ordinary world as the desert to cultivated land (it's forty years since I wandered away from Canaan)'.[86]

The next evening, he was taken ill while walking through the snow.[87] He was not well enough to be staying at a hotel with no one to look after him. He would have liked it if Brod could have joined him,[88] but felt incapable of making or even tolerating a new relationship.[89] His friends liked him (so he now believed) 'because they feel that on a different plane I enjoy the freedom of movement that's completely denied to me here'.[90] Even if Milena had joined him at the hotel, he would have been plunged 'into a world in which I can't live'.[91]

The next day, expecting pneumonia to declare itself, he felt less afraid of the illness than of other people's reactions to it.[92] Perhaps it was only for his mother's sake that he wanted to stay alive: his attitude to her had been changing, as hers had to him. 'With what, at her age, is infinite strength, she's trying to compensate for my being so cut off from life.'[93]

But he never felt too disconnected to comment on normality. He was as liable to romanticize it as he had been to romanticize his father or Milena. He never came to understand how much he had deceived himself about his father but he did come to see the correspondence with her as 'communication with ghosts'.[94] One's own ghost

emerges under one's hand in the letter one's writing. . . . How could we ever have believed it was possible to communicate through letters? You can think about someone who's not there and you can touch someone who is there, everything else lies beyond our capacity. . . . Written kisses never arrive at their destination: they're drunk en route by the ghosts.[95]

It did not occur to him that they would intercept the kisses he sent to the imaginary Kafka who lived an ordinary life. Feeling tired in the evening of the first day in February, he thought enviously and idealizingly of the waggoner 'who experiences all his evenings as I do this one, and even better. . . . It's just before falling exhaustedly asleep that one's really cleansed of ghosts, they've all been driven out.'[96] Kafka thought on these lines often enough for the idea of learning a trade to keep recurring, but so did the imagery of spirits. Both had Jewish roots. Zionism was partly a reaction against the shopkeeper mentality of the generation that worshipped financial security as the guarantee of freedom from the ghetto; the pioneers in Palestine worked on the soil, using their hands and their physical strength. What Kafka still had in common with the Zionists of his generation was a quasi-religious faith in manual labour, though the desire to work with his hands also had some of its roots in the wish to live 'dans le vrai', and something in common with Wittgenstein's decision to work as an elementary school teacher and as a gardener, though Kafka never apparently questioned the motivation behind his carpentry and his gardening. There were also areas of his mental activity that remained unanalysed. He does not seem to have been aware of how much sediment the Yiddish plays had left in his imagination, and while the Hasidic tales and the Kabbalah were invaluable to his fiction, they had also dragged him back into pre-modern premisses.

Writing about his illness, Kafka often used transcendental language, suggesting – at least half-seriously – that scientific concepts made the malaise harder to cure than the idea of possession did. Wasn't it still an open question whether weakness caused evil spirits to invade the body or whether 'weakness and illness are already a stage in possession, the preparation of the human body as a bed for unclean spirits to copulate in'?[97]

At the same time he was thinking of himself as being personally assaulted by God. In his diaries God is never mentioned by name, but on 10 or 11 February he wrote 'New attack by G.' A few sentences later, reversing the image, he equates God not with the enemy but with the general who is leading the despairing multitudes through mountain passes no one else can find in the snow.[98] The idea leads straight to a fragment of fiction. Standing at the window of the dilapidated hut, the general watches the troops' moonlight march through the snow. Occasionally a soldier detaches himself from the marching column to peer through the window. One of these men is hauled through the window and questioned. Why did he look inside? 'To see whether you're still here.'[99]

One attraction of manual work was that it would use up energy that kept short-circuiting into self-analysis: he would be too tired to go on chewing the cud of his central failing. 'It's a mixture of anxiety, shyness, verbosity and half-heartedness'.[100] 'I haven't the slightest contact with people except when they create it.'[101] 'Obviously there's no other way you can know me', he told Robert Klopstock, 'than through the hatred my behaviour must ultimately induce.'[102] (He was wrong, of course. What Klopstock came to feel was nothing less than love.) Kafka attributed 'the origin of my downfall' to 'crazy egocentricity', not concern for 'a higher self', but 'anxiety for my vulgar well-being'.[103] Addiction to physical comfort had led him to 'begging, weeping, sacrificing things that matter more'.[104]

He went back to Prague about 20 February, and with over two months of sick leave still in hand he began to write, 'in order to save myself from what they call nerves'.[105] He wanted to concentrate on fiction, but

Writing withholds itself from me. Hence project for autobiographical investigations. Not biography, but investigation and discovery if possible of the small components, which I'll use to reconstruct myself, like a man whose house is unsafe and who wants to build a safe one next door, preferably using the same materials.[106]

The idea is strikingly close to one formulated by Nietzsche, who also wanted to cancel the unhealthy present in favour of the permanence that work could offer: the writer 'experiences an almost malicious joy as he watches the erosion of his body and spirit by time. It's as if he were in a corner watching a thief at the safe, knowing it to be empty, his treasure being elsewhere.' The artefact is being made at the expense of the organism; Kafka even refers explicitly to the danger of being caught with the original house half demolished and the new one not yet ready: 'What follows is madness, or something like a Cossack dance between the two houses, with the heels of the Cossack's boots scraping and burrowing into the earth until his grave is dug.'[107]

Of all Kafka's short-story-length allegorizations of his existential predicament, 'Erstes Leid' and 'Ein Hungerkünstler' ('A Hunger Artist') are the ones which most clearly reveal the frailty of the barrier between fiction and self-analysis, or between 'writing' and 'autobiographical investigations'. 'Erstes Leid' was written in the same exercise-book as his diary, but he tore it out before lending the diary to Milena.[108] The self-analysis in the diaries and fragments deploys many metaphors and similes; in 'Ein Hungerkünstler', as in 'Erstes Leid', 'Die Verwandlung' or 'In der Strafkolonie', the narrative develops a single image dramatically. In all four stories Kafka is writing about himself as his father's victim. Arguably he never wrote about anything else. His genius was in making what he wrote so resonant, so relevant to the problems and failings of people apparently unlike him but actually, beneath the surface, not altogether dissimilar. The achievement depends partly on the stubborn logicality in his thinking. Life had not offered the food he needed; he had not adapted to what it offered. The only way of snatching back the initiative was self-destructive: like suicide, the option of starving himself was always available and never wholly unattractive. But his ontological curiosity was so strong that he preferred to go on investigating the human condition by postulating a consciousness even more abstemious than his own, even more critical of the only diet available.

The hunger-artist fasts inside a barred cage. People buy tickets to watch as he sits among straw, wearing black tights. His ribs stick out and sometimes he reaches through the bars, so that people can feel how thin he is. He is watched, day and night, by representatives of the public, usually butchers. But he is the only one who knows he never cheats.

Nevertheless, he is dissatisfied with himself: no one else knows how easy it is to fast. He has sustained it for forty days but he is as reluctant, even at the end, to leave the cage as Kafka's trapeze artist is to leave his high wire.[109] The hunger-artist feels there are no limits to his capacity for starving. The impresario who makes a speech praising the artist's self-denial is paralleling Brod's mistake in thinking Kafka saint-like.

But fashion changes. The crowds no longer come. Leaving the impresario, the artist joins a circus. But he is no longer famous enough to be presented as part of the show; his cage is left outside the main tent, and, in the interval the audience, on its way to the menagerie, takes little interest. His reaction is not to fast less but more. No one counts or announces the number of days he goes without food, and, finally, at the point of death, he insists that there is nothing admirable in all the fasting he has done, 'Because I couldn't find any food I liked. If I had, believe me, I wouldn't have made any fuss about it, I'd have stuffed myself full like everybody else.'[110]

It would be as simplistic to equate food with writing as to suggest that Kafka was merely cheering himself up about the waste of his sexuality, but obviously the story is developed out of self-criticism, while images of caging, chains and imprisonment were recurrent in his conversation. 'The "I" is nothing', he told Janouch, 'but a cage from the past, its bars intertwined with incessant dreams about the future.'[111] The story also reflects his hyper-fastidiousness about food. This affected Ottla, a plump Jewish girl with a healthy appetite – she turned vegetarian.[112]

Another story that belongs, as the beginning of *Das Schloss* does, to the same period of activity and the same zone of emotional low pressure, is the dreamlike 'Fürsprecher' ('Advocates'), a two-page story which bridges between *Der Prozess* and *Das Schloss*. The narrator is uncertain whether he has any defending counsel and whether he is in a law court. The corridors are like those of a museum or library; there is a distant droning noise. He needs a barrister, for judgment is passed according to the law, and life made possible by the assumption that this is not being done irresponsibly. But all the faces he sees are unfriendly, and he may be in the wrong place. Why did he run headlong into a house without reading the sign over the door? But there is no question of turning back. 'The time measured out to you is so short that if you lose one second, you've lost your whole life, it's never any longer than the time you're losing.'[113]

In the first paragraph of *Das Schloss* K. stands for some time on a wooden bridge between the country road and the village, staring into the 'apparent emptiness' where the hill and castle are.[114] The village is covered in deep snow. He is surrounded by fog and darkness. There is no light to betray the castle's presence. We assume he is unaware of it, and when he is roused from sleep at the village inn to be told that the village belongs to the castle, he asks: 'Which village is it I've mistakenly come to? Is there a castle here?' His interlocutor, Schwarzer, who introduces himself as the castellan's son, says that he cannot stay the night without a permit from the count, and cannot obtain a permit in the middle of the night. K. then contradicts the implications of his previous questions by claiming that he is a land-surveyor, that the count is expecting him, that his assistants will be arriving tomorrow. (The amateur evangelist at Jungborn had been a land-surveyor.) When Schwarzer telephones the castle to check, we expect K.'s bluff to be called, as it immediately is, but the telephone rings again, and after listening to the voice at the other end, Schwarzer accepts K. as a land-surveyor. The castle seems to have taken up the challenge K. has casually thrown down: both Schwarzer and the innkeeper treat him more respectfully. It is like a reversal of the situation in Gogol's *Inspector General* – which Kafka had recently both seen and read [115] – but, more disturbingly, Schwarzer's father is described as one of the lowest castellans, though even he is powerful. This is reminiscent of the hierarchy among the doorkeepers. K. tells the innkeeper he has no power himself, 'And consequently have probably no less respect than you have for those who are powerful, only, not being so open as you are, I don't always show it.' [116] Kafka is trying to build a house next-door to his own with the same materials. He may even be thinking of this image when he writes that K. is reminded of his home town by the castle, which is only a cluster of small buildings with plaster flaking off and the stone underneath crumbling away. 'If it was just a matter of sightseeing, it was a pity K. had come so far, it would have been better to revisit his old home, which he hadn't seen for such a long time.' [117]

Gradually the ambiguities surrounding K.'s uncertain position in the village make it analogous to the situation of the Jew in an anti-Semitic environment and, more resonantly, to the human condition. As in the story of the humanized ape, Kafka is not specifying the Jew's awareness of anti-Semitism but generalizing it into an image of alienation. Without any apparent freedom of choice he has arrived in the place, and it is impossible for him to make contact with those in authority. No one is willing to explain what is required of him, but he does not feel free simply to leave, though no visible pressure is put on him to stay. Having claimed to be a land-surveyor he is saddled with an identity, and it is bolstered disconcertingly by the two assistants who materialize. From his conversation with the Superintendent, who receives him in bed (like the lawyer Josef K. consults in *Der Prozess*), it is clear that he had never seen the two men before they presented themselves to him in the village, and the superintendent says they were assigned to him.[118]

It was characteristic of Kafka that looking at his situation in life he should question the need for his presence. Feeling useless, he asked what his function could be, unable to look at the question from the viewpoint of other people, but, thanks to his genius, able to look at it from a viewpoint not identical with that of his everyday self. Told there is no work for a land-surveyor, K. reacts in the way a new-born baby might if magically endowed with adult articulacy and awareness of future redundancy: 'I certainly haven't made this endless journey just to be sent back again!'[119] It is already clear that K. won't be sent back again, and later he is told explicitly: 'Nobody's keeping you here but that doesn't mean you're being thrown out.[120] In the meantime his status is uncertain. The superintendent, though inferior in rank to the official who has written confirming his appointment as land-surveyor, casts doubt on the validity of the letter, and himself maintains that K. should not be taken on as land-surveyor, though he promises friendly help on other matters.[121] The unpredictability of the officials combines with the mixture of hostility, coldness, indifference and helpfulness that K. encounters among the peasants and villagers to undermine his security.

Insofar as Kafka thought of the law as a code defining demands on the individual or at least defining his social function, it was natural for him to associate the administrative inefficiency of the Austro-Hungarian Empire with the incomprehensible vagaries in God's administration of the universe or at least to devise a fiction in which echoes of one would mingle suggestively with echoes of the other. Amusingly, the confusion over the appointment of the land-surveyor is shown to derive from inter-departmental failures of communication; as an insurance official Kafka had had plentiful experience of bureaucratic inefficiency, and the description of the way that clerks and telephonists behave in the castle implies a much bigger administrative unit than would actually be involved if it were only the castle's hegemony over the village that were in question. Once again provincialism is one of the underlying themes: Kafka's painful confusion as a child about what his father wanted from him made it harder for him to live as an adult in a capital city that was not the imperial capital: the empty castle was a prominent reminder of the emperor's absence.

Once the novel had begun to take shape, Kafka was excitedly aware he had been leaving great areas of his talent unexplored. His one-word diary entry for 19 February is 'Hopes?'[122] And a week later, 'I admit . . . there are possibilities in me, quite close at hand, which I'm not yet familiar with . . . this means a villain can become an honest man and happy to be honest.'[123]

But the flicker of happiness was feeble. His physique was so enfeebled that one afternoon of bad sleep could make him feel defeated,[124] and at the beginning of March he had to stay in bed again.[125] The night of 6 March seemed like the worst he had ever had,[126] but on the 9th he felt worse still, as if 'oppressive introspection could either reduce the opening through which one flows out into the world or close it altogether.... A stream flowing backwards.'[127] The only possibility was to take sides against himself: 'Make the enemy's horse into your own mount.... But what strength and skill are called for.'[128]

On 15 March he read the beginning of *Das Schloss* to Brod,[129] and afterwards went on trying to write his way into it, 'but it's nothing, a dug-out scratched up with fingernails in the world war, and next month it stops and the office starts'.[130] With his life nearly over, he felt as though it had not yet begun: 'Not born yet and to be forced already to walk in the streets and talk to people.'[131] However much he had yearned for death, its proximity gave him accesses of terror. 'How it lies in wait for one. On the way to the doctor, for instance, often there.'[132] Talking to his mother and trying to make jokes about the future, he was suddenly terrified.[133]

While writing *Das Schloss* he clung to the book in a spirit of resentful dependence. He told Klopstock: 'desperate rats like us, hearing the master's footsteps, run in different directions, for example to women, you towards no matter which, I towards literature, but it's useless'. Since leaving Matliary, he had 'been whipped through periods of madness', while in a way that was 'frightful for everyone around me' the writing had become 'the most important thing on earth to me, like delusion to a madman – without it he'd go "mad", or like pregnancy to an expectant mother.... Therefore, in fearful trembling, I keep the writing protected from any disturbance.' Solitude seems more desirable than the friendship proffered in Klopstock's letters. 'What's the use of such unwieldy things to tramps?... If one feels some sense of moving in the same direction, there's enough of a bond in that. Let's leave the rest to the stars.'[134]

On 26 April Kafka had obtained another report from Dr Kodym and, submitting it the next day, asked for permission to take his normal five-week holiday from 5 May. On 3 May permission was granted.[135]

Having overcome his resistance to Buber's versions of Hasidic stories, he was reading a new anthology featuring Rabbi Dow Baer of Mezritch, a disciple of the Baal Shem.[136] One of the stories is about a rabbi who fasts for a week. On the last day, he feels proud of his success in mastering the temptation to drink from a well. Aware that pride is more dangerous than failure, he goes back to drink from the well, but no longer feels thirsty. 'Patchwork', is his teacher's contemptuous dismissal of his achievement.[137] In 'Der Hungerkünstler' Kafka had already exposed impurities among motives for ascetism – as in all these semi-allegorical stories, an argument is spinal – but the fundamental criticism was of himself. 'I have a great talent for patchwork', he wrote,[138] and, shelving the novel, he ironically developed the self-criticism in the story that was subsequently titled 'Forschungen eines Hundes' ('Investigations of a Dog'), once again taking pleasure in identification with an animal. As in the ape story, Kafka was capitalizing on his uncertainty about whether he was a full member of either the human race or the Jewish people: this dog is no longer living as a dog among dogs or sharing their preoccupations. Kafka uses him in the way Pascal used triangles when he said that if they had a god it would be three-sided. The story is an attack on human presumptuousness in expecting to arrive at a full understanding of reality. The deficiencies of human vision are satirized by presenting a dog-philosopher who assumes dogs to be the most intelligent species in existence. The central joke in this much misunderstood story is that the dog is therefore blind to the existence of human beings. It seems to him that food appears from above as a direct result of canine activities – passing water on the earth to nourish it, scratching it, barking incantations. Whether wilfully or voluntarily blind to humanity, he cannot see the laps underneath lap-dogs – to him they appear to be hovering in the air – and he is mystified by the dogs who have been trained to perform in a circus. The satire may be directed partly against the philosophy and science that claim to explain the natural while denying the supernatural.

At the same time Kafka was caricaturing the ontological probing he was himself conducting in *Das Schloss*: hence, probably, the need to write the story before finishing the novel. The animal identification was partly an antidote to the guilt he felt at taking himself so seriously. He complained (as Nietzsche had) that his task was the heaviest ever assigned to a human being. 'It could be said that it's not a task at all, not even an impossible one, it's not even impossibility itself, it's nothing.'[139] Or, 'When others came to this frontier – and just to have come here is pitiful – they turned aside. But I can't. It seems to me as though I didn't come here at all but was brought here as a tiny child and chained here.'[140] K.'s confusion about coming to the village is not dissimilar, but the diaries make statements which the fiction has to repudiate, undermine, satirize. Intent on sniffing out the truth, the dog cannot tell whether other dogs remain silent because they know it or because they don't. Or would the marrow inside be poisonous? Again the underlying question is Nietzschean: aren't we perhaps wrong to assume that knowledge of the truth is desirable?

The dog takes to ascetism, sits with his head buried between his paws.[141] Becoming more fastidious, he fasts, lies down in a solitary spot, experiences his own reality more intensively, through his hunger, and begins to moralize – here the narrative parodies the rabbinic style of argument and Talmudic accounts of disagreements between rabbis – about whether fasting is prohibited. Towards the end he is feeling uncertain – as Kafka was – whether he is dying from hunger or neglect. 'It was clear enough that nobody was bothering about me, nobody below the earth, nobody on it, nobody above it, it was their indifference that was destroying me, their indifference said "he's dying", and that's what would happen.'[142]

In his diaries Kafka would never have opened the throttle like this on his sense of being a victim. He would more likely revert to writing about himself in the third person, to make some such point as 'In someone else's company he feels more abandoned than when alone.'[143] It was beyond Kafka's power to remedy the isolation or to staunch the resentment, but by dragging both into his fiction he could enjoy the illusion of having both under control.

On 27 May, while taking a walk in the evening, he felt 'momentary disorientation, helplessness, hopelessness, immeasurable void, nothing else'.[144] He traced the malaise back to four fairly trivial vexations he had had during the day, but his lungs seemed to have deteriorated more during the spring than during the winter.[145]

On 7 June, four days before the end of his holiday, he applied to the institute for temporary retirement. Recovery, said Dr Kodym, was not to be expected for several years, and Kafka was retired with effect from 1 July. It was almost fourteen years since he had joined the institute as an assistant. Frau Svátková, who cleaned his office, told Janouch: 'Kafka came and went as quietly as a mouse. . . . In his wardrobe there was only his grey threadbare second-best coat he kept there for a rainy day. I've never seen him with an umbrella.' Treml ordered her to take away the 'rubbish' on his desk – a slender glass vase holding two pencils and a penholder, the blue and gold teacup and saucer he used for drinking milk and sometimes tea.[146]

23 The Problem of Space

On 23 June he left Prague to stay with Ottla at Planá in south-eastern Bohemia. It was a two-hour journey by express train. At first he felt 'afraid of the country. . . . But on the second day here it's fine; it's strange to have a relationship with the earth.'[1] He was glad to have Ottla looking after him again, for the first time since the birth of her baby and, when he sat at the table in the large, warm living-room, she tried to leave him in peace, taking Věra and the maid into a smaller, colder room.[2] One of the things Ottla and her husband enjoyed was waking up to such a splendid view from the bed, with woods in the distance. But within a few days they made Kafka sleep in their bed, while they and Věra slept in a much smaller room that looked out only on a neighbour's courtyard and the chimney of the saw-mill.[3] Unfortunately for Kafka, the grassy road and the fenced-in meadow outside the house made it popular among local children as a play-space, and the considerate Ottla was constantly trying to persuade them to go somewhere else, but she often failed, and Kafka got little relief from the wax and cotton-wool earplugs he was using.[4]

In Georgenthal Oskar Baum and his wife had taken trouble to find a room for him that was comfortable and quiet, but the invitation filled him with fear – fear of the journey, 'fear of change, fear of attracting the attention of the gods through what, for me, is a major act'.[5] Nevertheless he wrote a letter of acceptance; the fear must be overcome. But when, on his way to post the letter, he met Ottla and told her he had not given an exact date for going, she said he should. The letter remained unposted and after a sleepless night – with the decision to go he was putting too much pressure on himself – he wrote saying he would not go.[6]

Another reason for refusing was that it would keep him away from *Das Schloss* for several days.[7] Writing, as he said, sustained the kind of life he was living 'on unsteady or non-existent ground, above a darkness from which the dark powers emerge whenever they want to, ravaging my life without paying any attention to my stuttering'.[8] His only means of keeping madness at bay,[9] writing was 'a sweet, a wonderful reward, but for what?'[10] No doubt he was being rewarded 'for serving the devil. This descent to the dark powers, this unchaining of spirits bound by nature, these questionable embraces and whatever else may happen down there – you're ignorant of all this if you write stories in the sunlight.'[11] As in his fiction, he was now using language in a way that merged metaphor into objective presentation of fact and surmise, constantly drawing on the imagery of possession. The dog story had fortified his transcendentalism. The diabolical element in his writing 'seems to me very clear. It is the vanity and lust for pleasure that buzzes about one's own form or someone else's and sucks pleasure from it; the movement then proliferates, becoming a solar system of vanity.'[12] In 'Das Urteil' the father passed the death sentence on the son who had become devilish; soon Kafka will condemn his own 'devilish' writing to destruction.

Summarizing anxieties of a sleepless night when he 'let everything go unremittingly backwards and forwards between aching temples',[13] Kafka abrasively compares writing with the idle desire so many people entertain to know how friends would react to news of their death: a writer 'dies (or fails to live) and never stops mourning for himself'.[14] He has an enormous fear of death because he has not begun to live, though he believes himself capable of living, but also believes he has hastened the onset of death by enacting it in his work.[15] 'The writer in me will of course die immediately, because such a figure has no base, no substance, isn't even made of dust, is only a construct of indulgence, just about possible in the most abandoned, earthly living.'[16] The little life the writer had enjoyed had been at the expense of the self: 'I've remained clay, haven't used the sparks for making fire, only for illuminating my corpse.... The soul has obviously abandoned the real self, but only to become a writer, nothing more.'[17]

The compulsion to leave so much work unfinished was partly superstitious: he wanted to stop short of potentializing it. 'We can't escape the ghosts we release into the world,' he told Janouch. 'Again and again evil returns to its point of departure.' He wanted none of his unfinished work to survive him, and felt no great desire for even the finished work to be preserved. When Janouch had 'Die Verwandlung', 'Das Urteil' and 'Der Heizer' bound in dark brown leather, Kafka was not pleased. 'My scribbling ... is nothing more than my own materialization of horror. It shouldn't be printed at all. It should be burnt.' And when Janouch reminded him of his own comment on Picasso – that art was like a clock running fast to foretell the future – his answer was: 'Probably that's why I can't complete anything. I'm afraid of the truth. ... If one can give no help one should remain silent. No one should let his own hopelessness cause the patient's condition to deteriorate.'[18]

The noise of the saw-mill was bearable for short intervals, but not when the circular saw was in use, and Kafka found himself lusting for silence and moving desperately between one room and the other. It was probably this that gave him the idea for the conditions of K.'s employment in *Das Schloss* as janitor in the school. (We know that the first nine chapters of the novel were completed by 20 July.)[19] K. is to have the right of living in either of the two classrooms, but when only one is in use for teaching, he will have to move into the other.[20] When the beautiful young school-teacher and the children arrive in the morning, K., Frieda and the assistants are not yet dressed, and the room is untidy. After making a fuss, the teacher takes her charges into the other room. The disruption of the teaching may reflect Kafka's guilt-feelings about disrupting the life in Ottla's house. There must also have been a neurotic residue from living so long in his parents' various flats, where he had complete freedom of movement only inside his bedroom. In his fiction the *alter ego* often feels he can gain freedom only by invading territory that is not his, as when K. is left in the courtyard where he would not normally be allowed. But he can never relax in these spaces, or expect to be left undisturbed. When the head teacher finds K. and Frieda sitting peacefully at the table in the schoolroom, he says: 'Pardon my intrusion, but tell me when the clearing up in here will finally be done. It's like a cattle-truck there, it's so crowded, and the teaching's suffering, but you're spreading yourselves out here in the big gymnasium like lords and you've even sent the assistants away so as to have still more room.'[21] If Kafka had spent more of his life in possession of a space that was indubitably his, he would have been a happier man but would have been without one of the tensions that needed to find release in his work.

On the afternoon of 14 July he heard that his father had been taken ill in Franzensbad, and was being brought back to Prague. There was an obstruction because of a navel hernia, and an operation would be necessary. Alarmed – his father was now seventy, and weakened by heart disease – Kafka left immediately for Prague. Within two days of the operation the old man was out of danger. At first he seemed pleased to have his son there but this did not last: 'yesterday he couldn't get me out of the room fast enough, while he pressed Mother to stay'.[22] He considered his tubercular son was entirely to blame for his own illness: he should never have moved out of the parental home into such an unhealthy room at the Schönborn Palace.[23]

After about five days in Prague, Kafka went back to Planá. Illness had given him freedom not to work, freedom to live wherever he chose. His situation was like that of K. after he has failed to trap Klamm into a conversation by waiting in the courtyard by his coach:

It seemed to K. as if everyone had broken off all relations with him and as if he now in fact had more freedom than ever before, and could wait as long as he wanted here in the place that was normally forbidden to him, and that he'd battled for this freedom, as almost nobody else could have, and no one must touch him or drive him away or even speak to him, but – this conviction was at least as strong –

as if, at the same time, there was nothing more senseless, or more hopeless than this freedom, this waiting, this invulnerability.[24]

When he was proposed as a possible successor to Martin Buber as editor of *Der Jude*, his reaction was: 'With my unbounded ignorance of things, total disconnection with humanity, and with no firm Jewish ground under my feet, how could I consider anything of the kind? No, no.'[25]

He had four 'breakdowns', as he called them, in Planá.[26] One was on a day the children were intolerably noisy; the second was when he had to decide about Baum's invitation. The third came when Ottla said she was going back to Prague early in September: he could stay on in the house, but he would have to eat at the inn. This interrupted his work on the novel.[27]

At the end of the month he spent four days in Prague, where, knowing he had not long to live, he found it painful to look at girls in their summer dresses. He reminded himself that female contours were not very durable. 'It's soft flesh, very retentive of water, gently bloated, stays fresh only a few days; in reality it's long-lasting, but that only proves how short human life is, if flesh like that . . . survives for a large part of it.'[28] Back in the country he felt deflated,[29] but not too self-involved to fret about other people. He was concerned about both his father, who had to put up with 'pain, discomfort, restlessness, fear',[30] and his mother, who was being ruthless towards herself in nursing him so devotedly. He was also worrying – and again dreaming – about Brod, who had been looking exhausted and ill – impatient for letters from Emmy Salveter, the ex-chambermaid, who was in Leipzig, but still more dispirited when they arrived. Kafka called her 'the letter-writer who's working for your destruction *while denying that this is what she wants*'.[31] Later, when she wrote to him, he replied politely, but to Brod he wrote: 'As for E., she does hate me and I'm almost frightened to meet her.'[32]

Back in Planá, although the chapters of *Das Schloss* he had written there struck him as better than the early ones, he could not regain his momentum. 'I've had to abandon the castle story – evidently for ever.'[33] The fourth 'breakdown' occurred after he had successfully dropped hints which made the landlady offer to cook for him if he stayed on after Ottla left. Scared of returning to Prague, he was even more scared of solitude in Planá. Fortunately Ottla intervened. It would be too cold and foggy for him, she said, informing the landlady he would be leaving when she did: 'I stand there like Gulliver while the gigantic women talk to each other.'[34] Afterwards, mainly for his sake, Ottla decided to stay on herself for most of September.[35]

Looking back on his life he could see a pattern in the vacillation: 'Insofar as I can be said to have "organized" my life, it was always to accommodate solitude.'[36] But total isolation scared him.[37] (If it had not, he would not have anchored himself for so much of the time to his parents and to Ottla.)

Incidentally it's revealing that I feel so at ease in empty flats, not totally empty, but full of human memories and prepared for further living, flats containing matrimonial bedrooms, children's rooms, kitchens, flats where mail for other people arrives in the early morning, and other people's newspapers are stuffed through the letter-box.[38]

It was this vicarious relationship with life *dans le vrai* that made him write as he did. With Felice and again with Julie he had come close to translating a fantasy about married life into a reality that would soon have developed into something very different from what he had imagined. The Frieda episodes in *Das Schloss* were written more or less as memoirs of the marriage he had never had, indoor reconstructions of a walk he had never taken into the fresh air. Frieda is the same name he had used for the Felice figure in *Der Prozess*, and in *Das Schloss* Frieda tells K.: 'I'm not good enough to live with you. If you were rid of me you might be able to achieve everything you want. Out of concern for me you knuckle under to the tyrannical teacher, you take over this wretched job.'[39] Which corresponds to Kafka's former fears about having less time for writing if he married, and became more dependent on his job, while, within the novel, there is no differentiation between Frieda's view of the sacrifices K. is making for her and his view: 'everything worried him only in relation to her. He must therefore try to keep this job, which gave Frieda some security, and he mustn't complain if he had to put up with more from the teacher than he'd otherwise have had to take.'[40] When Frieda suspects that K. wants to use her as a means of securing his foothold in the village and making contact with Klamm, Kafka seems to be empathizing retrospectively with Felice's less articulate suspicions that he wanted a marriage certificate as a visa for his passage across the frontier into *le vrai*. The implacable landlady, Frieda's confidante, friend and adviser, sometimes acts as an intermediary, as Grete Bloch had, while the dialogue distils – if it does not actually reproduce – the conversation at the Askanische Hof. But K. is more adept than Kafka at living. Where Josef K., like his creator, had usually submitted over-eagerly to the pressure, real or imaginary, to consider himself on trial, K. refuses to give Momus the answers he needs for his protocol.[41]

Kafka's memory was an echo chamber in which paternal threats, reprimands and criticisms went on reverberating. One remark about seductive blouses was enough to make him go on associating white blouses with irresistible attraction. The ruin of the Barnabas family derives from a white blouse 'swelling high in front, one row of lace on top of another'.[42] The father says: 'Today, you can take my word for it, Amalia's going to find a husband.'[43] But it is a castle official, Sortini, who is captivated, and her rejection of him is revenged mercilessly. Generally the castle officials' shameless sexuality is reminiscent of the courtroom episodes in *Der Prozess*, while in the treatment of the two clownish assistants, who introduce a counterpoint like that of the comedy in a Shakespearian tragedy, there are covertly autobiographical elements. With their adult faces and their childish behaviour, they are divided, as Kafka felt himself to be, between boyhood that cannot be outgrown and maturity that must be short-lived. Their pathetic desire to be constantly in K.'s company not only parodies Kafka's fixation on his father, but reflects his fear of the children he never had and the demands they would have made on his time. His mother was obviously the model for Hans's mother: 'Above all she never did anything against his father's wishes, she gave in to him about everything, even when their unreasonableness was clearly apparent to him, Hans.'[44] Kafka may also have been thinking of his mother when he made Frieda intervene on behalf of the two assistants. Realizing that paternity would have made him in some ways more like his father, he gives K. stern moments of grumbling about Frieda's 'willingness to forgive their bad behaviour and stroking their hair and constant sympathizing with them. "Poor things, poor things," you say over and over again, and finally this last thing happened – you don't mind sacrificing me to save the assistants from a beating.'[45]

If Kafka, throughout most of his life, had been starved not only of food and sex but also of space – space he could call his own – *Das Schloss* is the novel which deals with this, exploring the way in which literature can represent an alternative space. Because he had felt free and relaxed while writing, it had come to seem like an area in which he could stretch his limbs, feeling himself to be the unchallenged and unchallengeable possessor of all the land that he could survey. Writing to Felice, he had felt as if he was escaping from Prague to Berlin;[46] writing to Milena from Meran, he had felt he was conjuring up her presence next to him. Paper as magic carpet; pen as wand. One of the reasons doors and windows are so important in his work is that they offer ways of imaginative escape, access to territory he can imaginatively appropriate, just as a landscape-painter may feel proprietorial towards a terrain he has captured on canvas, having occupied every fold and hollow with his vision, having studied every contour. In writing the story about the doorkeeper, Kafka had been able to feel that, unlike the man from the country, he was defying the vetoes; at least he was making a statement, however Kabbalistic, about one of the ways in which the Law functions – the way in which it conceals its own nature from those who are incapable of 'non-folly'. Kafka had been fairly unsuccessful in his own efforts to cultivate non-folly, but K. is more determined and single-minded. As he says in one version – finally rejected – of the novel's opening,

> I've a difficult task in front of me, and I've dedicated my whole life to it. I do this gladly, without asking for pity from anyone. But because it's all I have – the task I mean – I ruthlessly reject anything that may distract me. I tell you, I can be mad in my ruthlessness.

This may be too explicit, but it is possible that a more decisive reason for rejecting it was that it points too revealingly at the correspondence between K.'s task and Kafka's. K.'s obsession about penetrating to the castle reflects Kafka's relentless determination to go wherever his writing led him, to colonize as much as he could of the world inside his head, even if it meant defying the God who did not want him to write. His task involved him in besieging the forbidden castle, making contact with the Absolute, confronting the unconfrontable, looking God in the face and then doing his best to break the Second Commandment by constructing a graven image. He must defy all the doorkeepers.

Max Brod was not entirely wrong to associate K.'s isolation in the village with the alienated Jew's isolation in Czechoslovakia, but, as always, Kafka was not only allegorizing his own life: he was also writing about his own experience of writing. It is not K.'s prime objective to graft himself on to the village community: he is less interested in Frieda as a passport to living *dans le vrai* than as a means of making contact with Klamm. In another suppressed passage Kafka wrote: 'The conquest of Frieda meant changing his plans: here he gained a means to power that might obviate the necessity for the whole period of working in the village.' K. is interested in Frieda for the same reason that he is interested in Hans's mother and in Barnabas: they are all footholds to be used ruthlessly in clambering towards the castle. But non-folly does not help K. Like Karl Rossmann and Josef K. he is a gauche tactician who alienates people who could have helped him, while squandering his energies on the wrong allies. He despises and bullies his two assistants, treating them rather in the way Kafka's father had treated the 'paid enemies' in his shop, but the assistants have been sent to K. by Klamm, and possibly they could have been more valuable as allies than any of the women. Frieda tells him that to keep her he would have to take her to live somewhere else. He has no wish to live somewhere else. Why would he have come here, he argues in a masterly piece of question-begging, if he did not want to be here? But despite his determination to be ruthless and not to let himself be distracted, he is always liable to be led astray by the women who find him attractive. Like Josef K., he overrates their potential usefulness.

On 18 September Kafka returned to Prague, and within eight days he was in a state of collapse,[47] but he still had not seen a doctor by the end of the month.[48] At the beginning of October he received a letter from Michal Mareš, enclosing one from Milena. He replied to her, saying little about his lung, 'it can't be so very bad, though, when for example I could chop wood outside – holy vanity! – for an hour and more, without getting tired, and I was happy, momentarily'.[49]

Most of *Das Schloss* was probably written before he came back to Prague, but, although it was nearing completion, the novel is excluded from the will he wrote in pencil, probably after the publication of 'Ein Hungerkünstler' in the October issue of the monthly *Neue Rundschau*:

> Dear Max, perhaps this time I won't get up again, after the month of pulmonary fever the onset of pneumonia is likely enough, and writing this down, though it has some power, won't keep it away.
>
> In case, then, my last will for everything I've written.
>
> Of all my writings the only valid ones are the books *Urteil, Heizer, Verwandlung, Strafkolonie, Landarzt*, and the story *Hungerkünstler*. (The few copies of *Betrachtung* can remain, I don't want to give anyone the trouble of pulping them, but nothing from it is to be reprinted.) When I say that those five books and the story are valid, I don't mean that I want them to be reprinted and passed on to the future, on the contrary, if they should disappear completely this corresponds to my real wish. But since they're there, I'm not preventing anyone from keeping them if he wants to.
>
> But everything else I've written (in periodicals, papers, manuscripts or letters) is without exception, insofar as it can be obtained or recovered from the addressees ... all this is without exception to be burnt, preferably unread (I won't stop you from looking at it, I'd like it best of all if you didn't, but in any case nobody else must see it) – I ask you to burn it all as soon as possible –
>
> Franz[50]

He did not succumb to pneumonia, but was far from feeling well enough to write, even in his diary. The next entry is for 14 November: 'Evening always 99.6, 99.9. Sit at the desk and get nothing done, hardly ever go out. But Tartufferie to complain about the illness.'[51]

In December he received a visit from Otto Pick and Franz Werfel, who invited him to Venice in the spring. After Pick had left, Kafka, who had read Werfel's new play *Schweiger*, which was to be staged in January, began to criticize it. 'I couldn't help it, and I vented some of my disgust in chat. But I suffered from the consequences the whole evening and the whole night.'[52] He still admired Werfel – though 'in this instance only for having the strength to wade through all this three-act slime'[53] and afterwards he felt contrite enough to write at least two drafts of a long letter apologizing for

> my weakness, which not only affects my thinking and speaking but brings on a kind of swooning without loss of consciousness. For instance I try to criticize the play, and before I've completed two sentences the swoon interrupts me with questions like 'What are you talking about? What's the matter? Literature, what is that? Where does it come from? What use is it?'[54]

Though he stayed in bed for much of the time, he was not too ill at the end of the year to take regular Hebrew lessons from a nineteen-year-old Palestinian girl, Puah Bentovim, who came to the flat several times each week, and talked to him about Palestine. He also gave Valli's ten-year-old daughter Marianne her first Hebrew lessons, working with her from a Hebrew newspaper. He was doing some writing, but both the stories 'Ein Kommentar' and 'Das Ehepaar' ('The Married Couple') are defeatist. 'Ein Kommentar', which is extremely short, may draw on his memory of losing his way in Reichenberg, thirteen years earlier, and getting no help from the police. But the memory is only a whisper inside the echo chamber where a death sentence has been pronounced.

> It was very early in the morning, the streets clean and empty, I went to the station. Comparing a tower clock with my watch I saw it was already much later than I'd believed, I must hurry, the shock of this discovery made me feel unsure of my direction, I didn't yet know my way around this town, fortunately a policeman was nearby, I ran to him and breathlessly asked him the way. He smiled and said: 'You want me to tell you the way?' 'Yes', I said, 'since I can't find it myself.' 'Give it up, give it up,' he said, and turned away very abruptly, like a man who wants to be alone with his laughter.[55]

In 'Das Ehepaar' an apparent death is made into the subject of a mirthless comedy. Kafka now uses 'K.' as a name for a character more like his father than himself – a tall, cantankerous businessman with a short, devoted wife and a grown-up son who is sick. The narrator, eager to do business with K., pursues him into his home, and the fusillade of sales-talk appears to kill the old man:

> K. sat with his eyes open, glassy, bulging, only momentarily usable, tremblingly craning forward, as if someone were holding or hitting him in the neck, the lower lip, in fact the whole lower jaw was hanging down with gums fully exposed, the whole face was unhinged; he was still breathing, if with difficulty, but then, as if released, he fell back against the armchair, shut his eyes, the expression of some kind of enormous strain passed over his face and then it was all over.[56]

Kafka could not have written this without thinking of his own death, but the old man has merely gone to sleep. Afterwards, when he settles down to sleep on his son's bed with two cushions hastily fetched by his solicitous wife, we are reminded of the sequence in 'Das Urteil' where the son picks the father up and carries him to his own bed.

In April Kafka's old school-friend Hugo Bergmann came back to Prague. After the war he had settled in Jerusalem, where he had been appointed as librarian at the Hebrew National Library and as professor at the university. 'It's exciting and delightful to be together with him.'[57] Kafka, who was going out now very little, attended his lecture for the Zionist organization *Keren Hayessod* about the cultural situation in Palestine. 'You gave that lecture for me,' he told Bergmann afterwards. Bergmann invited him to Palestine, and for months he went on playing with the idea.

At the beginning of May he went to convalesce in Dobrichovitz, 'But it's not so much a journey as a flapping of wings that are quite useless.'[58] He neither slept well in the hotel nor felt settled, though the place was 'immeasurably beautiful'.[59] 'But I'm frightened of the expense, first of all – it's so dear here that one should stay only for the last few days before dying, so that nothing is left over – and, secondly, of heaven and hell. Apart from that the world lies open to me.'[60]

He went back to Prague before the middle of May, and in June he worked at both Hebrew and Italian, translating passages into a blue exercise-book.[61] This was the month in which he made the last entries in his diary:

Ghastly times, recently, innumerable, almost uninterrupted. Walks, nights, days, unfit for anything except pain. . . .

Increasingly terrifying as I write it down. It's understandable. Each word twisted in the ghosts' hands – this twisting of the hands is their characteristic movement – becomes a spike forced back into the speaker. Especially a remark like this one. And so on ad infinitum. The only consolation would be: it happens whether you like it or not. And what you want doesn't help noticeably. What's more than consolation: you too have weapons.[62]

He was hoist on the petard of his imagery. If the ghosts had once been metaphorical, they were now quite real for him.

At the beginning of July he left Prague to go with Elli and her two children, Felix and Gerti, to Müritz, a seaside resort to the north-east of Rostock. He broke the journey in Berlin to meet Emmy Salveter, who made a favourable impression, though he was tired and feverish.[63] 'She's charming. And so entirely oriented to you. Nothing came up that failed to cue a remark about you.'[64] She kept making comments such as, 'It's remarkable how one takes over the opinions of someone one loves, even when they're opposed to what one previously believed.'[65] Kafka's verdict was: 'A really sturdy originality, directness, seriousness, childishly endearing seriousness.'[66] He wanted to take her to Eberswalde, a town to the north-east of Berlin, where Puah Bentovim was helping to teach at a Jewish children's camp. But he had not realized that it was a twenty-nine-mile journey,[67] and they went only half-way, stopping at Bernau. 'There she took enormous pleasure in a stork's nest, which she spotted incredibly quickly. She was very nice to me.'[68]

24 Dora

At Müritz, as always at a new place, Kafka felt better for the first few days. It was the first time for ten years that he had seen the sea, and he insisted that it had changed – become more beautiful – 'more varied, livelier, younger'.[1] He was very happy to see the children in the holiday camp affiliated to the Jewish People's Home where Felice had been working.[2] The camp was only fifty yards from his balcony. 'Through the trees I can see the children playing. Happy, healthy, spirited children. . . . Half the days and nights the house, the woods and the beach are filled with singing. When I'm with them, I'm not happy but on the threshold of happiness.'[3] And on Friday evening 13 July he took part with the children (for what, so far as he could remember, was the first time in his life) in the Jewish service for the eve of Shabbos.[4]

It was during a performance staged by the children that Kafka made friends with a sixteen-year-old girl from Berlin, Tile Rössler. Afterwards she often came to chat with him when he was sitting on the beach in his wicker chair, and she invited him to the camp. Minze Eisner had been eighteen when he made friends with her: he could communicate uninhibitedly with girls of this age, taking, as he did, a generous and genuine interest in what was going on in their lives, while, unlike most men of his generation, he was able to converse with them unpatronizingly, honestly and imaginatively. He also enjoyed playing games, as he had with his sisters when they were younger. At the camp he met Dora Dymant (or Diamant), the girl who became the last love of his life while still in her early twenties. One of the games he later played with her was making shadows on the wall with his hands. 'He was extremely clever at it. . . . He loved to play; he was the born playmate, always ready for some mischief.'[5] Having achieved more intimacy with Ottla than he ever had – except in letters – with Felice or Milena, he could talk to Minze, to Tile and to Dora like an older brother, and, now that his favourite sister was a mother, he needed a substitute for her.

Dora was a pretty, dark-haired girl, who was working as a volunteer in the kitchen. But she had already noticed him on the beach, playing with Elli and the two children. She took him to be their father. 'I was particularly struck by the man. I couldn't shake off the impression he made on me. I even followed them into the town.'[6] When he saw her in the kitchen, scaling fish, his vegetarian instincts were outraged. 'Such gentle hands and such bloody work!'[7]

In the evening we were all sitting on benches at long tables. A little boy got up and, as he went away, was so embarrassed that he fell down. Kafka said to him, his eyes shining with admiration: 'What a clever way to fall, and what a clever way to get up again.'... He was tall and dark-skinned and had a loping walk that at first made me believe he must be a half-breed Indian and not a European. He swayed a little, but held himself straight. Only he carried his head a little on one side.... Kafka had the bearing of a lonely man who's always in relation to something outside himself.... The essential characteristics of his face were very open, sometimes even wide-open eyes, whether he was talking or listening.... His eyes were brown and shy. When he spoke they lit up, there was humour in them but it wasn't so much irony as mischievousness.... But he was entirely without solemnity. Generally he had a very lively way of talking and he liked talking.... Sometimes one got the impression of a craftsmanlike satisfaction, when he succeeded in expressing well what he wanted to say. He had long, ethereal fingers, speaking fingers which took on shapes while he was telling a story and accompanied what he said much more than his hands did.[8]

She was a good Hebrew student and his enthusiasm for the language gave them a bond; one of their earliest conversations culminated in her reading from Isaiah in Hebrew.[9] Like Jizchak Löwy she rebelled against parental orthodoxy: her father was an orthodox Polish Jew, a follower of the Hasidic rabbi from Gera. After leaving Poland, she had found herself jobs in Breslau and Berlin (where she was a seamstress at a Jewish orphanage),[10] before coming to Müritz to work at the camp. Kafka met her on 13 July. For the next three weeks he went to the camp every evening.[11] That the idea of going to live with her in Berlin was already forming in his mind in the second week can be inferred from a postcard he wrote to Robert Klopstock trying to dissuade him from settling in Prague: 'Life ought to be different from the life we lead there. You must organize yours differently next year, leave Prague perhaps, e.g. for the dirty Jewish streets in Berlin.'[12]

Tile had left the camp by the end of July, but not without exchanging presents – she gave Kafka a vase, he gave her a bowl, which, he said, was intended as a question: 'Hey, Tile, how long before you smash me?'[13] Early in August Puah Bentovim came to Müritz, staying in the camp, though barely for a day.[14] Kafka was spending less time there now, and instead of being lulled by the proximity of the children's dormitory,[15] he felt it was depriving him of sleep. 'But perhaps it will give some back later, it's a living relationship.'[16]

He could have stayed on alone in Müritz after Elli and the children left, but he went to Berlin, where, together with three girls, he saw a performance of Schiller's *Die Räuber* (*The Robbers*) without paying much attention, he said, to anything but his own fatigue.[17] Though due to meet Brod in a few days, he wrote to him from the garden of a restaurant, wanting 'to have a physical connection with you . . . from hour to hour the evil effect of being alone for the first day is affecting me strongly.'[18] But he was not intending to see Emmy. 'I'm too weak, and what's more I don't quite know what Emmy thinks of me, and I always fear the worst.'[19]

The next day he left for Prague, and met Brod on 16 August. 'His anxiety – ghosts, nothing specific.'[20] He read out the curses from Leviticus, and told Brod that he wanted Tefillim – the philacteries used by orthodox Jews for morning prayers every day except Saturday.[21] We also know that during 1923 he borrowed his parents' Hebrew prayerbook.[22] He stayed only a few days and later went on to Schelesen where he stayed with Ottla and her children till 21 September. When he arrived, his weight was only 54.5 kilos.[23] He had been hoping that Ottla's cooking and the country environment would help him to regain something of what he had lost, but it did not[24] and his temperature was moving upwards.[25] 'I must be a valuable prize for those anti-forces, they fight like – or are – the devil.'[26] He had intended to go home for his father's birthday on 14 September – his mother was in Paris, where her brother had died – but decided against the journey.[27] Having always looked younger than he was, he now looked so old and ill that one day an elderly gardener stopped him to say: 'You've seen better days.'[28] Kafka chatted for a while with the old man. 'Then, with his basket on his back, he went into the woods to refill it with a gigantic quantity of dry wood, and I began to take my pulse – well above 110.'[29]

Returning to Prague, he stayed only a day and a half before leaving for Berlin,[30] in spite of his parents' resistance to the idea of his settling there.[31] With Dora he moved into Miquelstrasse in Berlin-Steglitz. According to Dora he regarded his success in tearing himself away from Prague as the greatest achievement in his life.[32] She looked after him even more devotedly and lovingly than Ottla had, and, as an 'Eastern Jewess', she symbolized for him immunity to the materialistic corruption of the West. Living with her he was happily rejecting everything his parents worked so hard for.

This whole Berlin thing is so delicate, it's been landed with the last of my strength, which has probably made it more vulnerable. You know the tone of voice which, thanks to Father's influence, is often used to discuss my affairs. There's nothing evil about it . . . but it's Prague, as I not only love it but fear it.[33]

At first Berlin was intended to be only a stepping-stone on the way to Palestine,[34] and it was not easy to settle in Berlin when inflation was so steep. They had two rooms with a verandah, which used to cost 28 kronen, but the rent was 70 for September and going up to 180 for October.[35] Nor was he indifferent to other people's sufferings. 'Whatever might happen around him,' wrote Dora, 'he had no right to shut himself off from it. . . . He could stand in queues for hours, not with the intention of buying something, but simply with the feeling: blood was flowing, so his must flow too.'[36] But he could not have lived in the centre of Berlin: 'My road is the last one that's more or less urban, then everything dissolves peacefully into gardens and villas, each street is a peaceful garden walk, or can be.'[37]

He would get up at around nine and spend a lot of the day lying down, especially in the afternoon.[38] During his first month in Berlin, he and Dora ate only twice in restaurants,[39] while inflation had made theatre tickets too expensive for him. He was seeing Emmy, who came to his room in Steglitz, bringing flowers,[40] and he reported on her to Brod: 'She seems a little restless, nervous, almost overworked, but brave and terribly full of yearning.'[41] One day they went together to the botanical gardens.[42] He had wanted to see Ibsen's *Enemy of the People* with her but had to give up the idea.[43] When he had left Prague he had brought little money with him, partly because he did not know how long he would be staying, but the pension would go on being sent to his parents and although his mother, who had not been able to give him the October cash in advance, had promised to send money in each letter from the first of the month, and although he had reminded her several times, by 16 October he had received only 70 kronen. 'Yesterday it made me dizzy and I find the city centre frightful. . . . But out here, at present, everything's peaceful and lovely. These warm evenings, when I step outside the house, I walk into odour from the lush gardens, stronger and more delicate than I've ever encountered in Schelesen or Meran or Marienbad.[44] Writing about his sleeplessness and his physical deterioration, he used the imagery of possession by evil spirits. 'Recently the phantoms of the night have tracked me down.'[45] And, complaining he had had no intimate conversations with Brod since their holiday together ten years ago, he described their innocence then, when 'the evil powers, on good or bad missions, were only lightly touching the entrances through which they were already planning, with intolerable pleasure, to break in'.[46]

He was thinking of taking a course at the State Gardening Institute in Dahlem, which was only fifteen minutes away, but after listening to the descriptions of a Palestinian student there, he knew that the practical work would have been too strenuous, while even the theoretical work would have been beyond his current powers of concentration.[47] Nor did he want to go out of doors when the weather was bad.[48] He was ambivalent about emigrating to Palestine, but it was partly in order to prepare himself that, together with Dora, he was studying the Old Testament, with the commentary in Hebrew by Rashi.[49]

The landlady was consistently antagonistic, and so aggressive about the electricity consumed when he worked through the night that Dora bought him a paraffin lamp, which he loved. He enjoyed filling it and trimming the wick himself.[50] It was the strain in their relationship with the landlady that precipitated the story 'Eine kleine Frau' ('A Little Woman'), which uses the first person to explore the groundless animosity of a woman who has no connection with the narrator and no grounds for disliking him. Why she sees him so often is not explained in the narrative: the landlady–tenant relationship is hinted at only in the key passage:

I shall go on leaving the house in the elation that comes in the early morning and seeing this face, saddened by me, the lips twisted with anger, the critical and prematurely condemning gaze which travels over me without missing anything, however quickly it moves, the bitter smile cutting deeply into the girlish cheeks, the complaining glance upwards to heaven, the placing of the hands on the hips, to fortify herself, and then, as rage erupts, the pallor and trembling.[51]

After braving her hostility, Kafka and Dora were given notice to leave at the end of their sixth week in the house.[52] They moved in the middle of November to two rooms in the house of a lady doctor, Dr Rethburg, at 13 Grunewaldstrasse. Dora moved their possessions while Kafka went to the Academy for Hebrew Studies (Lehranstalt für die Wissenschaft des Judentums, an institute for training rabbis and scholars), using almost the last of his strength – the last chances of going out – to attend two lectures on the Talmud. Though it was in the centre of Berlin, he was going twice a week. He kept in touch with Emmy, and tried to mediate between her and Brod, arguing that it was not unreasonable of her to demand that he should spend two days a month with her in Berlin. He should also be more tolerant towards her jealousy: it was not enough to retort 'that only duty keeps me in this marriage'.[53] Kafka also tried to dissuade them from bombarding each other with letters and telephone calls.[54]

One day in the street he saw a small girl, crying because she had lost her doll. He explained that the doll, whom he had only just met, had to go away but had promised to write to her. For weeks afterwards he sent her letters in which the doll described her travel adventures.[55]

He could not write much, but according to Dora he completed the longish story 'Der Bau' ('The Burrow') in one night, working from evening till early morning.[56] Having maintained after writing 'Das Urteil', eleven years earlier, in one session, that this was the only way to work, he produced in 'Der Bau' a work that corresponded as truthfully and as intimately with his innermost self as 'Das Urteil' did. If the 1912 story was about his relationship to his father, the 1923 story is about a relationship that had become no less important to him, his relationship with his work.

His desire to escape himself was so strong, his imagination so volatile, that he could never observe anything or describe anything without a degree of empathy. The fictional identifications with animals go back at least as far as the 1904 incident when his dog persecuted a mole, and he was amused at the little creature's distress as it 'looked in vain for a hole in the hard road'.[57] The letter to Brod (see above, p. 43) makes no mention of intervening, but soon he found that his head began to droop, and the simile based on identification with the mole precedes the account of the incident. We 'tunnel through ourselves like a mole and emerge quite blackened and velvet-haired from our sandy underground vaults, our poor little red feet sticking out pitifully in hope of sympathy'.[58] For nearly twenty years Kafka had gone on tunnelling into himself and finding himself no less in need of a way out, a hole, than if he were still on the hard road. In one fragment he identifies with a doomed animal too badly mauled by hounds to be capable of burrowing into the earth.[59] The resonance of the story 'Der Bau' – the title means both 'building' and 'burrow' – depends partly on the autobiographical fact that creativity and disease have simultaneously tunnelled into him. The burrow also takes on associations with a grave. When the relationship with Milena was ending, he called himself a forest animal that felt secure only in darkness.[60] When they met, he said, he had been

lying somewhere in a dirty ditch (dirty only as result of my presence, of course) then I saw you outside in the open, the most wonderful thing I'd ever seen. . . . You had, even if you stroked me with the kindest of hands, to recognize peculiarities indicative of the forest . . . it grew increasingly clear to me what an unclean pest I was, what a nuisance I was for you everywhere . . . I had to go back into the darkness, I couldn't bear the sun, I was desperate, really like an animal gone mad.[61]

The animal narrator of 'Der Bau' progresses from confidence through desperation to recognition of defeat. He is the proud possessor of exactly what was needed by the mole in 1904, a hole which leads to safety, a burrow, its entrance camouflaged by moss. Nearby is another hole which leads nowhere – the result of an unsuccessful excavation, but left in sight to mislead enemies.[62] But Kafka keeps the animal mask tightly against his narrative face, submerging the equation between disease and the animal's death-bringing enemy: 'I live peacefully in the innermost recess of my house and meanwhile, slowly and silently, the enemy is burrowing towards me from somewhere or other.'[63] The animal – its species remains unnamed – can stay for days in his burrow, feeding on smaller under-ground creatures it encounters, and repairing the earthworks wherever the pattering of soil makes it sound necessary. Kafka does not use the word *Schloss* but the word *Burgplatz* for the central area in the burrow (the Muirs' translation 'Castle Keep' is misleading), but the narrative is full of private jokes and veiled references to his literary activity. Comparing life in the 'open woods'[84] with life in the burrow, the animal recognizes that he is not really free in either place. The food is better in the woods, if harder to find, and he can use muscles which became cramped while underground. Looking at the burrow from outside, he feels at first as though he is watching protectively over his own sleep, but really it is more like identifying with the enemy: 'it's I who am asleep while the predator watches'.[65] And there are dangers in re-entering the burrow. What if an enemy is watching?[66]

Once back inside the burrow he feels as though he has awakened from deep sleep,[67] and time makes itself felt differently: 'inside the burrow I always have infinite time – since everything I do there is good and important and gives me some satisfaction'.[68] As in *Das Schloss*, the attitude to space is that of a man who has never had a house or flat of his own.

The terror begins when, inside the inner sanctum, the animal wakes up to hear an almost inaudible whistling noise. At first he thinks the sound is being produced by air caught in an old tunnel which has been intersected by a new tunnel made in his absence by the smaller creatures. Or perhaps it is being made by tinier creatures than he has ever encountered.[69] Or some larger beast that is pursuing him.[70] Once, when he was young, he had thought that perhaps he was building his burrow inside the burrow of a larger animal which was now boring its way towards him.[71] There was still time then to choose another site, but now he can only retreat to spaces where the whistling is inaudible.

The story was completed, but the final pages are missing. They may have been destroyed by Kafka or by Dora, who, at his instructions and in his presence, had to burn many of his manuscripts, including a play and the story about an Odessa trial for ritual murder. 'Time and again he said to me "I wonder if I've escaped the ghosts".... He wanted to burn everything he'd written in order to free his soul from these "ghosts". What he really wanted to write was to come afterwards, only after he had gained his "liberty".'[72] He told her she was the innermost recess in the burrow, and she concluded that the fiction was motivated by fear of losing his freedom, of being forced back to imprisonment in his parents' flat. Writing, constantly associated with the world of the father and the fan-tasy of escape, produced the symptoms of depression. 'Kafka used to walk around heavily and uneasily before he began to write. Then he spoke little, ate without appetite, took no interest in things and was very sad. He wanted to be alone.'[73]

No visits were to be expected from his parents, who looked down on Eastern Jewesses and on unmarried love,[74] but they were helping him financially. He was reluctant to accept money from them but could not have lived on his pension, though inflation had been checked by the stabilization of the currency in November. At the turn of the year he was suffering from high temperature, chills, feverishness and digestive troubles. (His parents felt sure that Dora was giving him the wrong food.)[75] She was cooking for him on two methylated spirit stoves and an oven improvised out of a tin.[76] On New Year's Day 1924, because they had no spirit, she used candles to heat their food.[77] He tried to consult a doctor only once, a well-known professor, who had been recommended to him, but, instead of coming himself, he sent his assistant, a young man who could find nothing wrong, except the temperature, and gave no advice, except that Kafka should stay in bed. His fee for this was 20 marks or 160 kronen, but Dora persuaded him to halve it.[78] In the Jewish hospital a second-class bed would have cost 64, but this did not include consultations or treatment.[79] The room was not adequately heated and when his temperature went above 100, as it often did, especially in the evenings, he was afraid to get out of bed.[80] Even the rent had become too much for him and they had to start looking for a cheaper room. All the ones they liked were too dear.[81] But he did not want to go back to Prague or to Schelesen. He would have preferred a Bohemian or Moravian country town or Vienna,[82] but he was in no state to make decisions, and Dora was too young to put much pressure on him.

Finally they found a room in Zehlendorf, not far from the Grunewald. His condition had begun to deteriorate more rapidly. He went on reading in Hebrew – a little every day – but he had given up going to the Academy,[83] and it was hard to make him react realistically. When Brod went to see him, he would joke about going to Palestine where he would be a waiter and Dora a cook.[84] Eventually Brod alerted Kafka's Uncle Siegfried, the country doctor from Triesch, who went to visit him in Berlin, and confirmed that he could not possibly be left there.[85] His temperature was averaging 100.4, but he was still unwilling to go into a sanatorium.[86] 'It's very unpleasant to think one should lose one's freedom especially in those few warm months which are earmarked for freedom.'[87] But whenever he tried to walk, he faltered. He had prolonged fits of coughing regularly every morning and every evening, while the bottle for sputum was nearly full at the end of each day.[88]

On 14 March Brod was in Berlin for the première of Janáček's opera

Jenufa at the Staatsoper and three days later Kafka travelled back to Prague with him. Robert Klopstock, who had come to Berlin despite Kafka's efforts to dissuade him from the journey,[89] took him to the railway station, but Dora did not travel to Prague until later in the month: he did not want a confrontation between her and his parents in 'the house where all his disasters had come from'.[90]

He wrote to her every day,[91] and he asked Brod to visit him every day. 'Previously he'd never spoken so peremptorily, had always been most considerate about the pressure of my work. Now he spoke as though he knew we wouldn't have each other much longer. "Come again tomorrow at the same time." '[92]

Home in his parents' flat again, he wrote his last story 'Josefine die Sängerin oder Das Völk der Mäuse' ('Josefine the Singer or the Mouse People'). Having said that writing was connected with the naïve wish to know how other people would react to the news of one's death, he produced a humorously sophisticated epitaph for himself, implicitly equating his art with the singing of a female mouse who may not even be singing at all, but only squeaking, like the other mice.[93] If anything, her voice seems to differ from theirs by being weaker.[94] 'We admire in her what we don't admire at all in ourselves. . . . Is it her singing that charms us or isn't it rather the solemn stillness that surrounds the feeble little voice?'[95] She pleads for exemption from work on the grounds that the strain of working (though less than the strain of singing) is bad for her voice.[96] Rebuffed, she cuts back on her coloratura and finally disappears.

The main focus in the story is social. The narrator's primary concern is with the relationship between the prima donna and the people; one of Kafka's underlying concerns is with his own relationship with the Jewish people and Jewish culture. The mouse people is described as 'nearly always on the move, scuttling to and fro for reasons that often aren't clear',[97] and also as 'not only childish but in some respects prematurely old, childhood and old age don't come to us as to others'.[98] Many of his Jewish contemporaries had also been deprived of a normal childhood and a normal maturity. But his links with the Jewish people were more negative than he would have liked; given respite from harassment, the mice dream 'as if they could stretch and relax in the great warm bed of the community'.[99] Writing earlier about his fear of mice, he had called them 'alien from us'; this feeling may have led him to associate them with the perpetually persecuted Jews.

And how will the people manage without Josefine? Even if she was not their saviour, the mice had listened to her more intently during periods of crisis. But the mouse people 'has always, somehow or other, saved itself, though not without sacrifices which fill historical researchers with horror'.[100] (Who but Kafka could have compared Jews and mice so tell-ingly that the parable looks prophetic?) But the memory the mice will retain of Josefine will not be so very different from the impression they had of her when she was present. Was her actual squeaking noticeably louder and livelier than the memory of it will be? Was it anything more than mere memory while she was alive? Hasn't the people, in its wisdom, put such a high value on Josefine's singing precisely because it would be, in this way, impossible to lose?[101]

On first encountering Buber's renderings of Hasidic legends, Kafka had been embarrassed, partly perhaps because they implied a folkish solidarity; what embarrassed him now was awareness of his indebted-ness to them. The only oblique acknowledgement occurs in this story: Josefine denies any connection between her art and folk-squeaking, smiling with brazen arrogance when anyone points out the similarity.[102] But the story raises the question of whether Kafka may sometimes have wished his fiction to serve the same function as folk art (or as Yiddish theatre): when the mass mouse audience listens attentively to Josefine, the squeaking 'comes almost like a message from the people to the individual'.[103] This would be the ideal message for a royal messenger to carry if the king is dead. 'Our life is very disturbed, every day brings surprises, anxieties, hopes and fears; without support from his fellows, all this would be unbearable for the individual.' Josefine believes that she protects the people. If her art does not drive away the evil, at least it gives others the strength to bear it.[104] Kafka could not seriously believe that his fiction would have this effect, but he could seriously play with the idea.

Contradicting it, though, was the fear that his work was corrosive. Another story which may have been somewhere in his mind when he wrote 'Josefine' was one he had read in a history of devil-worship and repeated in a letter to Felice.[105] A clergyman had such a sweet voice that everyone who heard it was enraptured, until a priest, denouncing it as diabolical, exorcized the demon, leaving nothing of the clergyman except a stinking and disintegrating corpse. The determination of the dis-integrating Kafka to have his work destroyed was based on a serious fear that evil spirits had been speaking through it.

Just after finishing the story he told Klopstock: 'I think I started investi-gating animal squeaking at the right moment.'[106] The same evening he complained of a strange burning sensation in his throat when he was drinking, and especially when drinking fruit juice. He was nervous that his larynx might be affected.[107] When his old classmate from the Altstädter Gymnasium, Emil Utitz, came to visit him, he could not speak out loud, but his smile struck Utitz as being identical with the smile of his boyhood.[108]

25 Hunger Artist

At the beginning of April Kafka was moved into the Wiener Wald sanatorium, about forty-five miles to the south-west of Vienna. Dora accompanied him on the journey, and stayed with him. He was fairly sure he had tuberculosis of the larynx, though the doctors equivocated. 'Everyone withdraws into a reticent, evasive, glassy-eyed manner of speaking. But "swelling at the back", "infiltration", "not malignant", and "we can't say anything definite yet" in combination with very malignant pains are probably enough.'[1] They gave him Demropon, which was ineffective against the coughing, and Anastesin lozenges. His weight was down to 49 kilos, fully clothed, and he could now talk only in a whisper, though he had not had much trouble with his voice until his third day in Prague.[2] The treatment was obviously going to be very expensive; he instructed Brod to give the Josefine story to Otto Pick, a friend of the editor-in-chief of the *Prager Presse*.[3] There would also be some money coming in from Die Schmiede, a new publishing company to which Brod had introduced him in Berlin. It had accepted 'Ein Hungerkünstler', 'Eine kleine Frau' and 'Erstes Leid' to be published as a collection: Brod was also to offer the Josefine story, either now, if the *Prager Presse* rejected it, or later, if it accepted. It did. The story was published in its literary supplement.[4]

Within a few days Kafka's larynx was so swollen that he could not eat. 'What do you suppose it looks like inside?' he asked the sister. 'Like a witches' kitchen,' she answered.[5]

'All terrors eclipsed on 10 April', wrote Brod in his diary, 'by the news that Kafka was to be sent back from the "Wiener Wald" San. Vienna Clinic. Tuberculosis of the larynx confirmed. Catastrophic day.'[6] Kafka, who now weighed only 43 kilos, was told that he needed alcohol injections into the nerve, and possibly an operation.[7] The car provided for the forty-five-mile journey to Vienna was an open one, and it was raining. Dora stood up all the way, trying to shield him with her body.[8] 'The mad Dr Klopstock', as Brod jealously called him,[9] was on the point of giving up his studies to be with Kafka, who did his best to dissuade him:

Robert, dear Robert, no acts of violence, no sudden journeys to Vienna. . . . I'm better, the treatment in the hospital has done me good (except for details), it doesn't hurt so much to swallow, and there's less burning. No injections so far, they've only sprayed the larynx with menthol oil.[10]

Although Brod asked Werfel to intervene on Kafka's behalf, the doctor in charge, Professor Hayek, refused to give him a private room: 'A certain Werfel has written to say I should do something for a certain Kafka. Who Kafka is I know. He's the patient in No. 13. But who's Werfel?'[11] The patient in the next bed was dying. He had pneumonia and the doctors had been allowing him to walk around with a temperature of 106.[12] According to Dora,

> Someone died every night. He 'told' me about it by pointing once to a bed that was empty. Another time he showed me a patient, a jolly man who walked about a lot, enjoyed eating and had a tube in his throat. He had a moustache and shining eyes. Kafka was very pleased that he had such a good appetite. The next day he pointed to his empty bed. Kafka wasn't shaken but positively angry, as if he couldn't grasp that the man who'd been so gay had had to die. I will never forget his malicious, ironic smile.[13]

Hayek said Kafka should not be moved from the hospital, where they had all the right equipment and medicine,[14] but Klopstock and Dora arranged for him to be transferred at the end of April to the sanatorium Kierling, in Klosterneuburg, where he had a room to himself. Advised to use his voice as little as possible, he communicated with them by writing on slips of paper: 'How long will I be able to bear it that you're bearing it?'[15]

The owner of the sanatorium, Dr Hofmann, was 'a sick old gentleman', and his 'very unpleasant' assistant had more of a social than a professional relationship with Kafka.[16] Coughing caused such acute pains in his larynx that Dora called in two of the doctors from the hospital, first Professor Neumann, and on 2 May Dr Beck. The tuberculosis was affecting his epiglottis, and swallowing had become so painful he was effectively starving himself to death, like his hunger artist. The idea had overtaken him. All they could do was give alcohol injections in the upper laryngeal nerve. They agreed that his expectation of life was about three months, and Beck advised Dora to take him back to Prague, but she did not want to make him aware that he was dying.[17] To save her from spending money on calling in specialists, Beck made it clear that nothing could be done for Kafka except by administering pain-killers.[18]

His mind turned a good deal on swimming and demonstrations of physical prowess. Both in the letter to his parents and in the conversation slips he referred to the swimming lessons his father had given him, followed by beer and sausages. His cousin Robert had come to swim at the Sophieninsel, 'a splendid man' who 'jumped into the water and threshed around there with the strength of a beautiful wild animal, gleaming from the water, with shining eyes, and then he was off towards the weir'.[19]

In the first half of May one specialist, Professor Tschiassny, told Kafka that his throat was looking a little better. Kafka wept for joy, embraced Dora again and again, saying he had never had so much desire to live. He wanted to marry her, and he had written to her father asking for permission. Admitting that he had never been an orthodox Jew, he described himself as 'a penitent', 'one who is returning'.[20] Her father took Kafka's letter to the rabbi who, without any explanation, said 'No'. Kafka received her father's rejection on 11 May, the day Brod paid his last visit to his friend. 'Dora took me to one side and whispered to me that an owl had appeared that night at Franz's window. The bird of death.'[21]

He wrote afterwards to apologize for not having been more cheerful during a visit to which he had so much looked forward.[22] 'But it wasn't a specially bad day, you mustn't think that, it was just worse than the previous day, but that's the way that time and the fever move on.'[23] 'To think that at one time I could simply dare to take a large gulp of water,' he wrote ruefully on one of the conversation slips.[24] He was now in the same self-torturing situation as the old man at Matliary who had shown Kafka the abscesses in his throat. 'The victim is himself forced, of his own free will, out of his poor inner self, to prolong the agony.'

Kafka was achieving the 'frightful union' he had described in 1922:

From the primitive viewpoint the real, incontestable truth, disturbed by nothing (except martyrdom, sacrifice for someone else's sake) is physical pain. Remarkable that the god of physical pain didn't become the principal god of the early religions (as perhaps he did of the later ones). To each invalid his own household god, to the tubercular the god of suffocation. How can his approach be tolerable unless you've already taken part in the terrible union?[25]

The loving care that Dora and Klopstock were lavishing on him was never taken for granted. 'What a pest I am, it's quite mad.'[26] 'Of course it hurts me more because you're so good to me.'[27] When the galley proofs of 'Ein Hungerkünstler' came from Die Schmiede, he corrected them. As Klopstock wrote:

Kafka's physical condition at this time and the whole situation – that he was literally starving to death – was really lurid. As he finished the correcting, which must have been not only a monstrous psychological effort but also a kind of disturbing spiritual confrontation with himself, tears went on rolling down his cheeks. It was the first time that I'd seen an emotional outburst of this kind. He's always had a superhuman power of self-control.[28]

In fact only the first galley is corrected in his handwriting.

After one of the doctor's visits he wrote: 'So the help goes away again without helping.'[29] He knew that his larynx was not going to get any better,[30] and that it was 'probable that my present intake of food isn't sufficient for any recovery to get under way'.[31] But he could still make jokes: 'Infinite amount of sputum, easily and still pain in the morning, in the confusion it went through my head that for this quantity and this effortlessness somehow the Nobel Prize.'[32] Not that he could always be good-humoured. 'You praise so haphazardly when I've eaten enough, today I've eaten a lot and you're complaining, and sometimes you praise me just as unfairly.'[33] And there were moments when he just needed comfort. 'Let me have your hand on my forehead for a minute to give me courage.'[34] But still he went on identifying with other forms of life. He was surrounded by flowers. 'How wonderful that is, isn't it? the lilac – still drinks while it's dying, still swigs away.'[35]

In his last few days he took intense pleasure in the fragrance of flowers and fruit. He talked a great deal about fruit and drinks, asking other people to take long drinks of water and beer in front of him: he could share in their pleasure.

Now at last his parents were prepared to pay him a visit. It would be pleasant, he wrote on 2 June, to spend a few days quietly with them in a beautiful place. He could not remember when that had last happened. There had been a few hours in Franzensbad. But he raised difficulties. His father might have trouble in getting a passport. His mother would concentrate on him too much. And since he could speak only in whispers, perhaps they should postpone the visit.[36]

At four in the morning of 3 June he was breathing so badly that Dora called Klopstock, who woke the doctor. Kafka was given a camphor injection, and an ice-pack was put on his throat. He demanded morphine, telling Klopstock: 'You've been promising it to me for four years. You're torturing me, always have been. I'm not speaking to you any more. That's how I'm going to die.' After being given two injections he said: 'Don't cheat me. You're giving me an antidote. Kill me, or you're a murderer.' When he was given Pantopon he was pleased: 'That's good, but more, more, it's not helping.' Then he slowly lost consciousness. When he came to, Klopstock was holding his head, and he thought it was Elli: 'Go away, Elli, not so close, not so close.' He was nervous of infecting her. Klopstock moved away slightly. 'Yes, that's better.' Then he summoned all his strength to tear off the icepack and throw it across the room. 'No more torture. Why prolong it?' As Klopstock moved away from the bed to clean something on the syringe, 'Don't go away.'

'I'm not going away.'

'But I'm going away.'[37]

When Brod tried to ring up about midday he was too late.[38]

After the body had been taken down to the mortuary Dora could not stop whimpering, but Klopstock could make out only the words 'My love, my love, my dearest.' He promised her that if she would lie down, they could go and see the body again in the afternoon. She obeyed, still talking about him 'who is so alone, yes, so quite alone, there's nothing for us to do and we sit here and we leave him there, alone in the darkness, all uncovered, oh my dear, my sweet. . . .'

'What's happening to us', wrote Klopstock, 'can't be described and shouldn't be. . . . Now we're going down again, to Franz. His face is so stiff, firm, unapproachable, as pure and firm as his spirit was. Firm – a king's face from the noblest, oldest stock. The gentleness of his human existence has gone, only his incomparable spirit is shaping his stiff, dear face. It's as beautiful as an old marble bust.'[39]

Kafka's body was taken back to Prague and buried on 11 June 1924 in the Jewish cemetery in Straschnitz. At the funeral Max Brod made a speech, and Dora Dymant threw herself on the new grave, weeping. 'She fainted,' reports an eye-witness, Hans Demetz, 'but no one moved. On the contrary, Kafka's father turned his back, which stirred the mourners into motion. I don't remember who took care of the girl who'd broken down. I still feel ashamed that I did nothing to help the poor girl.'[40]

In the newspaper announcement of the funeral his parents indicated that they did not want to receive visits of condolence. In 1931 his father and in 1934 his mother were buried in the same grave.

Notes

Note Page references to Kafka's books are to the Fischer paperback editions. Details of other books are given here only when they are not listed in the Bibliography. Roman numerals refer to the numbers of volumes. 'Brod' refers to *Brod über Kafka*.

1 The Turning Point: 1912

1 *Tagebücher*, 23.9.12, p. 183.
2 Ibid.
3 P. 184.
4 25.9.12, p. 184.
5 Ibid.
6 Ibid.
7 Brod, p. 112.
8 *Tagebücher*, 11.2.13, p. 186.
9 23.9.12, p. 183.
10 *Brief an den Vater*, p. 40.
11 Pp. 58–9.
12 *Tagebücher*, 11.2.13, p. 186.
13 Cf. Freud, *Gesammelte Werke XIII*, p. 287 for a discussion of ego and superego.
14 *Sämtliche Erzählungen*, p. 83.
15 Letter to Hedwig Weiler, probably beginning of 1908, *Briefe*, p. 55.
16 Letter to Brod, spring 1910 (Brod dates it spring 1919), p. 254.
17 *Sämtliche Erzählungen*, p. 189.
18 Letter to Brod 3.4.13, pp. 114–15.
19 Letter to Felice 30.8.13, p. 458.
20 *Tagebücher*, 21 or 22.7.13, p. 196.
21 Janouch.
22 Footnote by Brod to diary entry for 23.12.22.
23 *Sämtliche Erzählungen*, p. 108.
24 P. 121.

2 After the Ghetto

1 F. Stamm, *Verhältnisse der Land- und Forstwirtschaft des Königreiches Böhmen* (Prague 1856), p. 57. Cited by Stölzl.
2 Alfred Meissner, *Geschichte meines Lebens* (Wien-Teschen 1884) II, p. 47. Kafka read it in 1918. Letter to Brod

beginning of December 1918, p. 247.
3 Brod, p. 14.
4 *Brief an den Vater*, p. 29.
5 Unpublished autobiographical sketch by Julie Kafka.
6 *Brief an den Vater*, p. 29.
7 Brod, *Der Prager Kreis*, p. 111.
8 Stölzl, p. 38.
9 Julie Kafka.
10 *Tagebücher*, 24.10.11, p. 74.
11 Hugo Bergmann, 1966.
12 Letter to Felice, 19–20.12.12, p. 193.
13 Věra Saudková.
14 Marianna Steiner.
15 Janouch.
16 Binder (1979) I, p. 117.
17 Unpublished letter from Ottla to Josef David, 2. and 5.12.16.
18 *Brief an den Vater*, p. 17.
19 Ibid.
20 Pp. 17–18.
21 P. 20.
22 Ibid.
23 Letter to Ottla, 13.11.19, p. 76.
24 *Brief an den Vater*, pp. 11–12.
25 Ibid., passim.
26 *Tagebücher*, 24.10.11, p. 74.
27 Marianna Steiner.
28 *Brief an den Vater*, p. 28.
29 Pp. 32–3.
30 P. 34.
31 P. 11.
32 *Briefe an Milena*, p. 49.
33 Bergmann (1966).
34 Autobiographical epilogue to Oskar Baum's novel *Die Memoiren der Frau Marianne Rollberg* (Berlin 1910).
35 *Tribüne*, 15.12.1882. Cited by Stölzl.

36 *Tribüne,* 11.12.82.
37 H. Rauchberg, *Der nationale Besitzstand in Böhmen* (Leipzig 1905) pp. 152 and 389.
38 Documentation of German Bohemian Anti-Semitism in the Státní ústřední archiv (Central State Archive) Prague.
39 Letter to Brod, 13.1.21, p. 289.
40 Janouch.
41 Ibid.
42 *Tagebücher,* 24.10.11, p. 74.
43 *Brief an den Vater,* p. 46.
44 Letter to Felice, 16.9.16, p. 700.
45 P. 14.
46 *Tagebücher,* 1911.
47 P. 141.
48 P. 142.
49 Ibid.
50 *Brief an den Vater,* p. 13.
51 Conversation slip quoted by Brod, p. 180.
52 Letter to Felice, 10–11.1.13, p. 245.
53 Cited by Wagenbach (1958), p. 196.
54 Wagenbach (1958), p. 30.
55 *Brief an den Vater,* p. 52.
56 Ibid.
57 Letter to his sister Elli, autumn 1921, p. 345.
58 Ibid.
59 *Tagebücher,* p. 540.

3 Gymnasium

1 Emil Utitz (cited by Wagenbach, 1958).
2 *Brief an den Vater,* pp. 52–3.
3 *Tagebücher,* 18.1.22, p. 346.
4 3.2.22, p. 356.
5 Hecht, p. 3.
6 W. Weizsäcker, 'Auf Altprager Schulbanken' in *Prager Nachrichten V* (1954) 2–3.
7 Hecht, p. 6.
8 Bergmann (1966).
9 26. *Jahresbericht über das Staats-Gymnasium mit deutscher Unterrichtssprache in Prag-Altstadt für das Schuljahr 1897–8* (Prague 1898).
10 Emil Gschwind, 'Anschauungsunterricht auf dem Gymnasium und Verteilung der

Realerklärung aus der römischen Alterthumswissenschaft auf die einzelnen Klassen des Obergymnasiums', in 28. *Jahresbericht über das Staatsgymnasium mit deutscher Unterrichtssprache in Prag-Altstadt für das Schuljahr 1899–1900* (Prague 1900).
11 Ibid.
12 *Zeitschrift für die osterreichischen Gymnasien.*
13 F. Deml, 'Betrachtung der Mittel zur Erreichung klarer und gewandter Ausdrucksweise in der deutschen Sprache', in 24. *Jahresbericht über das Staats-Gymnasium mit deutscher Unterrichtssprache in Prag-Altstadt für das Schuljahr 1895–96* (Prague 1896).
14 22. *Jahresbericht 1893–4.*
15 Binder (1966).
16 Ibid.
17 Weizsäcker.
18 Fritz Mauthner, *Erinnerungen* (Munich 1918).
19 Binder (1966).
20 Brod, p. 16.
21 *Brief an den Vater,* p. 46.
22 Ibid.
23 Fragmente in *Hochzeitsvorbereitungen auf dem Lande* (1953) p. 228.
24 Utitz.
25 Zylberberg, Helene, 'Das tragische Ende der drei Schwester Kafkas' in *Wort und Tat I* (1946–7) 2.
26 25. *Jahresbericht 1896–7.*
27 Bergmann, cited by Wagenbach (1958).
28 Hecht, p. 7.
29 Ibid.
30 Wagenbach (1958) p. 60.
31 *Tagebücher,* p. 12.
32 P. 430.
33 Ibid.
34 Letter to Oskar Baum, 21.9.22, p. 419.
35 Robert S. Wistrich, 'Georg von Schoenerer and the Genesis of Modern Austrian Antisemitism' in *The Wiener Library Bulletin XXIV* (1976) 39–40.
36 Státní ústřední archiv (Central State Archive in Prague).
37 Riff.
38 R. Kestenburg-Gladstein, *The Jews of*

Czechoslovakia I (Philadelphia/New York 1968).

39 Felix Weltsch, cited by Wagenbach (1958) p. 40.
40 Wagenbach (1958) p. 59.
41 *Tagebücher*, December 1911, p. 139.
42 Wagenbach (1958) p. 19.
43 *Sämtliche Erzählungen*, p. 14.
44 *Briefe an Milena*, pp. 111–12.
45 K. F. Kummer and K. Steyksal, *Deutsches Lesebuch für osterreichische Gymnasien* (Vienna 1898).
46 H. Frank and K. Šmejkal, 'Ze vzpomínek vychovatelky v rodině Franze Kafky' in *Plamen* VI (1964). Cited by Binder (1979).
47 *Tagebücher*, 10.4.22, p. 361.
48 *Brief an den Vater*, pp. 60–2.
49 Bergmann (1969).
50 Utitz (Wagenbach 1958).
51 Letter to Felice, 28.10.16, p. 736 and Stölzl, p. 71.
52 See above, p. 15.
53 Utitz (Wagenbach 1958).
54 Letter to Max Brod, mid-September 1917, p. 164.
55 Letter to Max Brod, mid-August 1907, p. 37.
56 Letter from Selma Kohn Robitschek to Max Brod quoted in his (German) edition of the letters.
57 Entry in Selma Kohn's album. *Briefe*, p. 9.
58 Bergmann cited by Wagenbach (1958).
59 Ibid.
60 Postcard to his sister Elli, 24.8.01.

4 University

1 *Brief an den Vater*, p. 53.
2 P. 56.
3 Pp. 55–6.
4 P. 56.
5 P. 54.
6 Bergmann (1966).
7 *Brief an den Vater*, p. 56.
8 Letter to Oskar Pollak, 4.2.02, p. 9.
9 Pp. 10–11.
10 Bauer.
11 Letter to Felix Weltsch, mid-October 1917, p. 184.
12 Letter to Oskar Pollak, 24.8.02, Brod deleted from this letter a denunciation of Sauer.
13 Emil Utitz, 'Erinnerungen an Franz Brentano' in *Wissenschaftliche Zeitschrift der Martin Luther Universität*, Halle–Wittenberg IV (1954) 4.
14 Ibid.
15 Bergmann (1972).
16 Brod, p. 175
17 Letter to Oskar Pollak, postmarked on arrival 12.8.02 p. 11.
18 Letter to Oskar Pollak, 24.8.02, p. 13.
19 Letter to Oskar Pollak, autumn 1902, p. 14.
20 Ibid.
21 Brod, p. 43.
22 Letter to Oskar Pollak, postmarked 20.12.02, p. 14.
23 P. 16.
24 Brod, p. 198.
25 Anna Pouzarová in Frank and Šmejkal.
26 Ibid.
27 Brod, p. 43.
28 According to Brod, whose memory was unreliable, the lecture was on Schopenhauer and Nietzsche; titles of lectures were published in the monthly bibliographies.
29 Gustav Meyrink, 'Violetten Tod'.
30 Brod, pp. 46–7.
31 Letter to Oskar Pollak, 6.9.?03, p. 17.
32 *Brief an den Vater*, p. 56.
33 *Briefe an Milena*, p. 138.
34 Pp. 138–9.
35 Ibid.
36 Letter to Oskar Pollak, 6.9.?03, pp. 17–18.
37 P. 18.
38 Ibid.
39 Ibid.
40 P. 19.
41 Letter to Oskar Pollak, 9.11.03, p. 21.
42 P. 20.
43 Ibid.
44 P. 19.
45 Letter to Oskar Pollak, 10.1.04, p. 24.
46 Friedrich Hebbel, *Tagebücher 1825–63*.

The four volumes were in Kafka's library.

47 Letter to Oskar Pollak, 27.1.04, pp. 27–8.
48 Letter to Oskar Pollak, 9.11.03, p. 20.
49 Letter to Max Brod, 1903 or 1904, p. 24.
50 Postscript, p. 25.
51 Brod, pp. 53–4.
52 Brod. Unpublished note.
53 Brod, p. 54.
54 Ibid.
55 Ibid.
56 Brod, p. 295.
57 Letter to Max Brod postmarked 21.10.05. English ed., p. 20. Missing from German edition.
58 Wagenbach (1958), pp. 52 and 135.
59 Letter to Max Brod, 28.8.14, p. 28.
60 Pp. 28–9.
61 P. 29.
62 Ibid.
63 *Sämtliche Erzählungen*, p. 202.
64 Letter to Max Brod, 28.8.04, p. 29.
65 Ibid.
66 P. 30.
67 *Sämtliche Erzählungen*, pp. 230–1.
68 P. 232.
69 P. 197.
70 P. 198.
71 Pp. 199–200.
72 Pp. 200–1.
73 P. 201.
74 Ibid.
75 P. 207.
76 P. 202.
77 P. 203.
78 P. 204.
79 Pp. 217–18.
80 P. 218.
81 P. 193.
82 Oskar Baum, cited by Brod, p. 96.
83 Ibid.
84 Brod, *Die Insel Carina*.
85 Brod, *Zauberreich*.
86 Brod, p. 64.
87 Pp. 64–5.
88 Letter to Max Brod postmarked 25.10.08, p. 80.
89 Bruno Kafka, 'Horaz Krasnopolski–ein Nachruf' in *60. Bericht der Lese- und Redehalle der deutschen Studenten in Prag* (Prague 1909).
90 Hans Gross, *Criminalpsychologie* (Graz, 1898) and *Handbuch für Untersuchungsrichter, Polizeibeamten und Gendarmen* (Graz 1899).
91 Letter to Max Brod, postmarked on arrival 24.7.05, p. 32.
92 Letter to Max Brod, mid-July 1916, p. 139.
93 *Sämtliche Erzählungen*, p. 247.
94 P. 248.
95 Postcard to Max Brod, 19.2.06, English ed., p. 20, omitted from German ed.
96 Letter to Max Brod, 21.10.05.
97 Brod, *Streitbares Leben*, p. 169.
98 Letter to Max Brod, 21.10.05.
99 Postcard to Max Brod, 19.2.06.
100 Janouch (1971).
101 Letter to Max Brod postmarked 29.5.06, p. 33.
102 Letter to Max Brod postmarked 7.6.06, English ed., p. 21, omitted from German ed.
103 Letter to Max Brod postmarked 13.8.06, p. 34.
104 *Sämtliche Erzählungen*, p. 234.
105 Ibid.
106 Ibid.
107 P. 241.
108 Ibid.
109 Pp. 235–6.
110 P. 236.

5 Good Conduct

1 Letter to Max Brod, mid-August 1907, p. 36.
2 Brod, p. 72.
3 Letter to Max Brod, mid-August 1907.
4 Bauer, pp. 99–106.
5 Letter to Max Brod, mid-August 1907.
6 'Die Abweisung', probably written in late 1920. *Sämtliche Erzählungen*, p. 312.
7 P. 313.
8 Ibid.
9 Brod, p. 59.
10 Letter to Max Brod, 12.2.07, p. 35.

11 Letter to Max Brod, probably May 1907, p. 36.
12 Postcard to Max Brod, May 1907, English ed., p. 24.
13 Postcard quoted in letter to Max Brod, May 1907, English ed., p. 24.
14 Letter to Max Brod, May 1907, English ed., p. 24.
15 Probably May 1907, p. 36.
16 Mid-August 1907, pp. 36–7.
17 Ibid.
18 Letter to Felice, 21.11.12, p. 111.
19 Letter to Max Brod, mid-August 1908, pp. 36–7.
20 Ibid.
21 Pp. 37–8.
22 Letter to Hedwig Weiler, 29.8.07, p. 39.
23 P. 40.
24 Letter to Hedwig Weiler early September 1907, p. 40.
25 Pp. 40–1.
26 Jens Peter Jacobsen, *Niels Lyhne* (New York undated).
27 Letter to Hedwig Weiler early September 1907, p. 41.
28 P. 42.
29 Ibid.
30 Letter to Hedwig Weiler early September 1907, p. 44.
31 P. 43.
32 Ibid.
33 Ibid.
34 Letters to Hedwig Weiler early September and early October 1907, pp. 43 and 48–9.
35 Letter of 2.10.07 from the Prague Office of the Assicurazioni Generali.
36 Letter to Hedwig Weiler 19.9.07, p. 45. Almost the same sentences occur in a letter to Max Brod, 22.9.07, p. 46.
37 Letter to Hedwig Weiler, 15.9.07, p. 44.
38 Ibid.
39 Letter to Hedwig Weiler early September 1907, p. 43.
40 24.9.07, p. 47.
41 19.9.07, p. 45.
42 Ibid.
43 Ibid.
44 Ibid.
45 Ibid.
46 Letter to Hedwig Weiler, 24.9.07, pp. 46–7.
47 P. 47.
48 Medical report by Dr Wilhelm Pollak, 1.10.07.
49 Ibid.
50 Letter to Hedwig Weiler, probably November 1907, p. 50.
51 Letter to Max Brod postmarked 4.10.07, English ed., p. 34.
52 Letter to Hedwig Weiler early October 1907, pp. 48–9.
53 Letter to Max Brod postmarked 21.10.07, English ed., p. 36.
54 Letter to Hedwig Weiler early October 1907, p. 49.
55 Ibid.
56 Letter to Hedwig Weiler probably November 1907, p. 49.
57 Pp. 49–50.
58 P. 50.
59 Ibid.
60 Letter to Hedwig Weiler, November 1907, p. 51.
61 Continuation of the letter 22.11.07, p. 51.
62 Brod, pp. 73–4.
63 Letter to Max Brod, end of November 1907, p. 52.
64 Pp. 51–2.
65 Postcard to Max Brod postmarked 21.12.07, English ed., p. 39.
66 *Sämtliche Erzählungen*, p. 18.
67 Letter to Max Brod postmarked 11.1.08, p. 54.
68 Letter to Hedwig Weiler probably early 1908, p. 54.
69 *Sämtliche Erzählungen*, p. 16.
70 P. 15.
71 Letter to Hedwig Weiler probably early 1908, p. 55.
72 Ibid.
73 Ibid.
74 Willy Haas, 'Um 1910 in Prag' in *Forum IV* (1957) 42.
75 *Sämtliche Erzählungen*, p. 13.
76 Ibid.
77 P. 14.
78 Ibid.

79 Letter to Max Brod, May 1908,
   pp. 56–7.
80 2.9.08, p. 58.
81 August 1908, p. 59.
82 Ibid.
83 Letter to Max Brod postmarked 29.3.08,
   p. 56.
84 *Brief an den Vater*, p. 32.
85 *Tagebücher*, 19.1.15, p. 284.

6 The New Job

1 Postcard to Max Brod, 13.11.17, p. 194.
2 Louzil, p. 62, cited by Binder (1979).
3 *Hochzeitsvorbereitungen*, p. 428.
4 Report reproduced in Wagenbach
   (1958).
5 Janouch (1971).
6 Postcard to Max Brod postmarked
   2.9.08, p. 58.
7 Letter to Max Brod, September 1908,
   p. 59.
8 Postcard to Max Brod, September 1908,
   p. 59.
9 Brod, *Zauberreich*.
10 Benjamin (1970), p. 142.
11 Benjamin and Scholem (1980), p. 293.
12 Brod, p. 61.
13 Ibid.
14 Letter to Max Brod, 12.11.08, English
   ed., p. 46.
15 Postcard to Max Brod, 21.11.08, p. 60.
16 Another postcard, same date, English
   ed., p. 47.
17 Ibid.
18 Letter to Max Brod, 10.12.08, p. 61.
19 15.12.08, p. 61.
20 31.12.08, p. 63.
21 Letter to Hedwig Weiler, 7.1.09, p. 65.
22 Ibid.
23 Letter to Hedwig Weiler mid-April
   1909, p. 67.
24 Ibid.
25 *Tagebücher*, p. 41.
26 Qualificationsliste 16.4.09, cited by
   Wagenbach (1958).
27 Letter to Max Brod postmarked 13.3.09,
   p. 66.
28 Postmarked 23.3.09, English ed., p. 52.
29 Mid-April 1909, p. 67.
30 Postmarked 21.4.09, English ed.,
   p. 54.
31 Postcard to Max Brod postmarked
   8.5.09, p. 69.
32 Letter to Max Brod, early July 1909,
   p. 70.
33 Ibid.
34 Letter to Max Brod postmarked 15.7.09,
   p. 72.
35 Brod (1969), pp. 19–22.
36 Letter to Max Brod, summer 1909,
   p. 73.
37 Early July 1909, p. 70.
38 Postcard to Max Brod postmarked
   11.10.09. p. 74.
39 Letter to Max Brod, early July 1909,
   p. 70.
40 Brod, p. 92.
41 'Die Aeroplane in Brescia.'
42 Ibid.
43 Ibid.
44 Brod, pp. 92–3.
45 'Die Aeroplane in Brescia.'
46 Ibid.
47 Ibid.
48 Ibid.
49 Ibid.
50 Brod, p. 93.
51 P. 94.
52 Ibid.
53 Ibid.
54 Postcard to Max Brod, ?1909, pp. 76–7.
55 Letter to Ernst Eisner, probably 1909,
   p. 76.
56 Ibid.
57 A. Gütling, 'Erinnerungen an Franz
   Kafka', *Prager Nachrichten* II, pp. 3–5
58 Qualificationstliste 11.9.09.
59 Loužil, p. 354.
60 Letter to Felice, 30.11.12, p. 142.
61 Letter to Max Brod postmarked
   13.10.09, p. 74.
62 Michal Mareš. Memoir in Wagenbach
   (1958).
63 Ibid.
64 Postcard to Max Brod probably
   31.10.09, p. 80.
65 Brod (1979), p. 23.
66 Letter to Max Brod postmarked 12.3.10,
   English ed., p. 63.

67 Brod, 'Zirkus auf dem Lande' in *Die Schaubühne*, 1.7.09.
68 Postcard to Max Brod postmarked 21.12.09, English ed., p. 60.
69 Postmarked 29.1.10, p. 79.
70 Brod (1966).
71 Postcard to Max Brod postmarked 10.3.10, p. 79.
72 Brod, p. 60.
73 Postcard to Max Brod postmarked 18.3.10, p. 80.
74 Ibid.
75 Ibid.
76 Letter to Max Brod, spring 1909, dated by Brod spring 1919, p. 254.
77 Natalie Bauer Lechner, *Erinnerungen an Gustav Mahler* (Leipzig 1923), p. 60.
78 Nietzsche, *Genealogie der Moral*, second essay: '"Schuld", Schlechtes Gewissen und Verwandtes'.

7 The Ladder in Mid-Air

1 *Tagebücher*, 1910, p. 11.
2 Pp. 430–1.
3 Pp. 11–12.
4 Letter to Felice, 8–9.1.13, pp. 237–8.
5 Pp. 239–40.
6 *Tagebücher*, 1910, p. 12.
7 Postcard to Max Brod postmarked 9.12.10, p. 84.
8 *Tagebücher*, 1910, p. 9.
9 Ibid.
10 P. 10.
11 Brod, p. 98.
12 *Tagebücher*, 8.10.11, p. 57.
13 *Tagebücher*, 1910, p. 10.
14 Ibid.
15 *Tagebücher*, 1910, pp. 13–14.
16 *Sämtliche Erzählungen*, p. 22.
17 *Tagebücher*, 1910, p. 14.
18 Loužil, p. 63.
19 Postcards to Max and Otto Brod postmarked 20.10.10, p. 82.
20 Ibid.
21 *Tagebücher*, 21.2.11, p. 30.
22 Postcard to Max Brod postmarked 4.12.10, p. 83.
23 Ibid.
24 Letter to Max Brod, 15.12.10, pp. 84–5.

25 *Tagebücher*, 16.12.10, p. 20.
26 Ibid.
27 P. 85.
28 Ibid.
29 *Tagebücher*, 15.12.10, p. 20.
30 Postcard to Max and Otto Brod postmarked 20.10.10, p. 82.
31 Postcard to Max Brod postmarked 4.12.10, p. 83.
32 Ibid.
33 *Tagebücher*, 17.12.10, p. 21.
34 Ibid.
35 Letter to Felice, 29–30.12.12, p. 219.
36 See below, p. 213.
37 *Tagebücher*, 12.1.11, p. 27.
38 18.12.10, p. 22.
39 R. Haubrichs. Cited by Binder (1979) vol I, p. 448.
40 18.12.10, p. 22.
41 *Tagebücher*, 20.12.10, p. 22.
42 Letter to Max Brod, 15 or 17.12.10, p. 85
43 22.12.10, p. 23.
44 26.12.10, p. 24.
45 24.12.10, p. 23.
46 25.12.10, p. 24.
47 Ibid.
48 12.1.11, p. 27.
49 12.1.11, p. 27.
50 7.1.11, p. 26.
51 19.1.11, p. 28.
52 Ibid.
53 Ibid.
54 Brod, p. 343.
55 *Tagebücher*, 19.1.11, p. 28.
56 The travel diaries (*Reisetagebücher*) are printed at the end of the diaries in both German and English editions.
57 Postcard to Max Brod, 1.2.11, p. 87.
58 *Reisetagebücher*, January–February 1911, pp. 370–1.
59 P. 371.
60 P. 372.
61 Ibid.
62 Ibid.
63 Ibid.
64 Ibid.
65 P. 373.
66 *Reisetagebücher*, p. 373.
67 Ibid.
68 Ibid.

69 *Tagebücher*, 19.2.11, p. 29
70 Ibid.
71 *Tagebücher*, p. 39.
72 'Die städtische Welt, *Tagebücher*, p. 31.
73 Ibid.
74 P. 32.
75 P. 33.
76 P. 32.
77 *Tagebücher*, 19.2.11, p. 29
78 Ibid.
79 21.2.11, p. 30.
80 Binder (1976), p. 50.
81 Binder (1967), p. 135.
82 Binder (1979), vol. I, p. 373.
83 P. 376.
84 *Tagebücher*, 28.3.11, pp. 37–8.
85 Ibid.
86 Wagenbach (1958) p. 175.
87 *Tagebücher*, 26 or 27.3.11, p. 36.
88 Pp. 38–9.
89 Postcard to Max Brod postmarked
   23.4.11, p. 89.
90 Brod, pp. 97–8.
91 P. 97.
92 Loužil, p. 64.
93 Brod diary, 25.5.11.
94 *Tagebücher*, 27.5.11, p. 39 and letter to
   Max Brod, 27.5.11, p. 89.
95 Brod diary, 15.6.11.
96 *Tagebücher*, 15.8.11, p. 40.
97 20.8.11, p. 40.
98 Ibid.
99 Ibid.
100 Ibid.
101 Ibid.
102 *Tagebücher*, entry dated 26.8.11, but
   the same date is given for his
   departure.
103 Ibid.
104 Ibid.
105 Ibid.

8 Holiday and Malaise

1 *Reisetagebücher*, p. 374.
2 P. 376.
3 Ibid.
4 P. 378.
5 Ibid.
6 Ibid.
7 P. 380.
8 Brod, p. 106.
9 *Reisetagebücher*, 5.9.11, p. 385.
10 Brod, p. 106
11 P. 97.
12 *Tagebücher*, 26.9.11, p. 44.
13 21 or 22.11.11, p. 108.
14 P. 107.
15 Ibid.
16 Ibid.
17 Ibid.
18 Ibid.
19 Ibid.
20 Ibid.
21 Ibid.
22 *Reisetagebücher*, p. 375.
23 28.8.11, p. 379.
24 Brod diary, 2.9.11.
25 *Reisetagebücher*, 4.9.11, p. 382.
26 P. 383.
27 P. 384.
28 Pp. 384–5.
29 P. 385.
30 Ibid.
31 P. 386.
32 Letter to Max Brod, 17.9.11, p. 90.
33 *Reisetagebücher*, p. 384.
34 Brod, p. 341.
35 *Reisetagebücher*, pp. 394–5.
36 *Tagebücher*, 11.11.11, pp. 97–8.
37 *Reisetagebücher*, pp. 394–5.
38 P. 397.
39 P. 398.
40 P. 400.
41 Ibid.
42 Pp. 400–1.
43 P. 401.
44 Ibid.
45 P. 395.
46 P. 399.
47 *Tagebücher*, p. 42.
48 *Reisetagebücher*, p. 389.
49 P. 390.
50 Letter to Max Brod, 17.9.11, p. 90.
51 *Reisetagebücher*, p. 391.
52 Ibid.
53 Letter to Oskar Baum, 19.9.11, p. 92.
54 Pines, *Histoire de la littérature
   judéo-allemande*.
55 *Tagebücher*, 26.9.11, p. 44.

56 30.9.11, p. 46.
57 P. 47.
58 27.9.11, p. 45.
59 29.9.11, p. 45.
60 1.10.11, p. 47.
61 P. 48.
62 Levin, Meyer (ed. and tr.), *Classic
   Hassidic Tales* (New York 1932, 1975,
   p. xii).
63 30.9.11, p. 46.
64 P. 47.
65 Ibid.
66 Ibid.
67 2.10.11, p. 48.
68 3.10.11, p. 50.
69 Ibid.
70 Pp. 48–9.
71 P. 49.
72 P. 50.
73 Letter to Felice, 10–11.13, p. 333
   (misdated 1912).
74 *Tagebücher*, 2.10.11, p. 49.
75 Pp. 49–50.
76 P. 51.
77 P. 50.
78 4.10.11, p. 51.
79 5.10.11, p. 73.

9 The Yiddish Actors

1 Löwy, Yizchak, 'Tsvey Prager Dichter'
   in *Literarishe Bleter XXXIV* (1934).
   Article on Kafka and Brod. Tr. in Beck.
2 *Tagebücher*, 7.1.12, p. 148.
3 5.10.11, pp. 52–3.
4 Janouch (1971).
5 *Tagebücher*, 8.10.11, p. 58.
6 5.10.11, p. 53.
7 Letter to Felice, 11. 3. 12.
8 *Tagebücher*, 8.10.11, p. 47.
9 5.10.11, p. 53.
10 Ibid.
11 Ibid.
12 Ibid.
13 8.10.11, p. 56.
14 9.10.11, p. 58.
15 Ibid.
16 Pp. 59–60.
17 11.10.11, pp. 60–1.
18 10.10.11, p. 60.
19 Bauer, p. 108.
20 *Tagebücher*, 13.10.11, pp. 62–3.
21 14.10.11, p. 63.
22 P. 64.
23 Ibid.
24 Löwy's article on 'Tsvey Prager
   Dichter'. See Beck.
25 *Tagebücher*, 16.10.11, p. 66.
26 P. 65.
27 Ibid.
28 P. 66.
29 Ibid.
30 17.10.11, p. 67.
31 20.10.11 p. 69.
32 Pp. 69–70.
33 17.10.11, p. 66.
34 Ibid.
35 20.10.11, p. 70.
36 Ibid.
37 P. 67.
38 Ibid.
39 P. 68.
40 Ibid.
41 P. 69.
42 21.10.11, p. 71.
43 22.10.11, p. 71.
44 P. 72.
45 Ibid.
46 28.10.11, p. 78.
47 Ibid.
48 23.10.11, p. 73.
49 Ibid.
50 27.10.11, p. 75.
51 Ibid.
52 26.10.11, p. 75.
53 Ibid.
54 29.10.11, p. 80.
55 1.11.11, p. 86.
56 16.11.11, p. 102.
57 26.10.11, p. 76.
58 P. 77.
59 30.10.11, p. 82.
60 P. 83.
61 22.10.11, p. 72.
62 30.10.11, p. 83.
63 31.10.11, p. 84.
64 Ibid.
65 See for instance 29.10.11, p. 81.
66 1.11.11, p. 84.
67 Ibid.

68 24 and 29.11.11, pp. 109–13.
69 5.11.11, p. 90.
70 Ibid.
71 24.12.11, p. 127.
72 5.11.11, pp. 90–1.
73 7.11.11, p. 93.
74 Ibid.
75 5.11.11, pp. 90–1.
76 7.11.11, pp. 93–4.
77 P. 95.
78 P. 96.
79 8.12.11, p. 114.

10 Bachelor Life

1 8.11.11, p. 95.
2 14.11.11, p. 101.
3 *Sämtliche Erzählungen*, p. 264.
4 *Tagebücher*, 11.11.11, p. 98.
5 15.11.11, p. 102.
6 31.11.11, p. 107.
7 P. 108.
8 Ibid.
9 13.12.11, p. 119 and 19.12.11, p. 124.
10 8.12.11, p. 114.
11 P. 116.
12 Ibid.
13 P. 117.
14 Ibid.
15 13.12.11, p. 20.
16 24.12.11, p. 129.
17 5.1.12, p. 146.
18 18.12.11, p. 126.
19 23.12.11, p. 126.
20 19.12.11, p. 124.
21 19 and 23.12.11, p. 125.
22 24.12.11, p. 129.
23 Pp. 128–9.
24 P. 129.
25 3.1.12, p. 144.
26 4.1.12, p. 145.
27 Ibid.
28 5.1.12, p. 146.
29 Ibid.
30 6.1.12, p. 147.
31 7.1.12, p. 148.
32 Ibid.
33 Pp. 150–1.
34 3.1.12 and 31.12.11, pp. 143 and 138.
35 3.1.12, p. 143.
36 Janouch, 1912, p. 151.

37 Ibid.
38 Ibid.
39 24.1.12, p. 142.
40 M. Pines, *Histoire de la littérature judéo-allemande* and Jakob Fromer, *Der Organismus des Judentums*.
41 *Tagebücher*, 24.1.12, p. 152.
42 *Tagebücher*, 4.2.12, p. 154.
43 P. 153.
44 Ibid.
45 Ibid.
46 Ibid.
47 Ibid.
48 5.2.12, p. 230 of English ed. (missing from German) reproduced – without mentioning names – in *Betrachtung*, *Sämtliche Erzählungen*, p. 12.
49 Ibid.
50 Northey in Flores (1977).
51 *Tagebücher*, 5.12.11, p. 155.
52 8.2.12, p. 156.
53 25.2.12, p. 158.
54 P. 157.
55 *Hochzeitsvorbereitungen*, p. 426.
56 *Tagebücher*, pp. 157–8.
57 P. 158.
58 *Selbstwehr* 23.2.12, cited and trans. by Beck.
59 *Tagebücher*, 26.2.12, p. 159.
60 Ibid.
61 Brod (1966), p. 150.
62 *Tagebücher*, 25.2.12, p. 158.
63 27.3.12, p. 171.
64 Letter to Felice, 19.1.13, p. 258.
65 *Tagebücher*, 8.3.12, p. 166.
66 P. 167.
67 10.3.12, p. 167.
68 Ibid.
69 Pp. 167–8.
70 11.8.12, p. 177.
71 16.3.12, p. 168
72 Ibid.
73 Binder (1979) vol I, pp. 120 and 260.
74 2.6.12, p. 175.
75 *Amerika*, ch. 7.
76 *Tagebücher*, 6.5.12, pp. 172–3.
77 Loužil, p. 64.
78 Letter to Felice, 18.9.16, p. 702.
79 *Reisetagebücher*, 28.6.12, p. 407.
80 Ibid.

81 29.6.12, p. 407.
82 P. 408.
83 Ibid.
84 30.6.12, p. 408.
85 P. 409.
86 Ibid.
87 2.7.12, p. 410.
88 Ibid.
89 Brod's diary (unpublished).
90 *Reisetagebücher*, 5.7.12, p. 412.
91 P. 413.
92 6.7.12, p. 414.
93 Ibid.
94 7.7.12, p. 416.
95 8.7.12, p. 416.
96 9.7.12, p. 417.
97 8.7.12, p. 416.
98 9.7.12, p. 417.
99 Ibid.
100 Ibid.
101 Letter to Max Brod, 17.7.12, p. 99.
102 Ibid.
103 *Reisetagebücher*, 11.7.12, p. 99.
104 Ibid.
105 Ibid.
106 Ibid.
107 Ibid.
108 19.7.12, p. 423.
109 20.7.12, p. 423.
110 10.7.12,, p. 418
111 15.7.12, p. 420.
112 Letter to Max Brod, 17.7.12, p. 98.
113 10.7.12, p 96.
114 9.7.12, p. 95.
115 10.7.12, p. 96.
116 22.7.12, p. 100.
117 Ibid.
118 14.7.12, p. 420.
119 Ibid.
120 12.7.12, p. 419.
121 15.7.12, p. 420.
122 20.7.12, p. 424.
123 Letter to Max Brod, 22.7.12, p. 101.
124 Ibid.

11 Felice

1 Letter to Max Brod, probably 7.8.12 but dated by Brod July, p. 99.
2 *Tagebücher*, 11.8.12, p. 176.
3 Letter to Felice, 27.10.12, p. 55.
4 *Tagebücher*, 20.8.12, p. 178.
5 Letter to Felice, 27.10.12, p. 58.
6 20.9.12, p. 43.
7 A line from Ludwig Fulda's *Der Talisman*, slightly altered.
8 Letter to Felice, 27.10.12, p. 59.
9 15.8.16, p. 681.
10 27.10.12, pp. 60–1
11 *Tagebücher*, 15.8.12, p. 177.
12 Ibid.
13 Ibid.
14 16.8.12, p. 178.
15 30.8.12, p. 179.
16 21.8.12, p. 179.
17 Ibid.
18 30.8.12, p. 179.
19 Ibid.
20 4.9.12, p. 180.
21 5.9.12, pp. 179–80.
22 15.8.12, p. 177.
23 30.8.12, p. 179.
24 *Reisetagebücher*, 16.7.12, p. 421.
25 *Tagebücher*, 8.9.12, p. 180.
26 11.9.12, p. 180.
27 15.9.12, p. 181.
28 Letter to Felice, 17–18.1.12, p. 255.
29 20.9.12, p. 44.
30 Pp. 43–4.
31 Letter to Max Brod and Felix Weltsch, 20.9.12, p. 104; letter to Felice, 20.9.12, p. 43.
32 *Tagebücher*, 23.9.12, p. 184.
33 Letter to Felice, 2.6.13, p. 394.
34 Ibid.
35 Ibid.
36 Letter to Max Brod, 7 or 8.10.12, p. 108.
37 *Sämtliche Erzählungen*, p. 27.
38 P. 28.
39 Janouch (1971).
40 *Sämtliche Erzählungen*, p. 30.
41 *Brief an den Vater*, p. 63.
42 *Sämtliche Erzählungen*, p. 30.
43 Ibid.
44 Beck, p. 73.
45 *Tagebücher*, 24.11.11, p. 109.
46 Binder in Flores, *The Problem of 'the Judgment'*.
47 *Tagebücher*, 9.8.12, p. 176.
48 J. P. Stern in Flores.

49 Brod, p. 101.
50 Letter to Felice, 27–8.12.12, p. 213.
51 15–16.12.12, p. 185.
52 5.8.13, p. 435.
53 28.9.12, p. 45.
54 P. 46.
55 *Tagebücher*, 23.9.12, p. 183.
56 Brod, p. 113.
57 Ibid.
58 *Tagebücher* 10.8.12, p. 176.
59 Letter to Felice, 27.10.12, p. 60.
60 *Amerika p.* 6.
61 P. 7.
62 Pp. 8–9.
63 Janouch (1971).
64 *Amerika*, p. 28.
65 P. 24.
66 Letter to Felice, 28.11.12, p. 136.
67 Letter to Max Brod, 8.10.12, p. 107.
68 P. 108.
69 Ibid.
70 P. 109.
71 Postscript to letter to Max Brod, 7–8.10.12, p. 109.
72 Brod, pp. 86–7.
73 P. 87.
74 Undated letter later enclosed with letter to Felice, 20–1.12.12, p. 198.
75 13.10.12, p. 47.
76 23.10.12, p. 50.
77 24.10.12, p. 51.
78 P. 53.
79 27.10.12, pp. 55–62.
80 29.10.12, p. 62.
81 31.10.12, p. 63.
82 1.11.12, p. 65.
83 P. 66.
84 P. 67.
85 P. 68.
86 2.11.12, pp. 68–9.
87 P. 69.
88 3 and 6.11.12, pp. 72 and 77.
89 Postscript to letter to Felice, 3.11.12, p. 73.
90. 5.11.12, p. 76.
91 P. 74.
92 7.11.12, p. 78.
93 Ibid.
94 Brod, p. 367.
95 Letter to Felice, 7.11.12, p. 79.

96 Ibid.
97 P. 80.
98 8.11.12, p. 81.
99 P. 82.
100 Draft of letter to Felice, 9.11.12, pp. 83–4.
101 Second letter to Felice dated 11.11.12, p. 87.
102 Ibid.
103 pp. 85–6.
104 P. 86.
105 Third letter to Felice dated 11.11.12, p. 88.
106 Ibid.
107 P. 89.
108 Note to Felice, 13.11.12, p. 88.
109 Letter from Max Brod to Felice, 15.11.12, p. 96.
110 Ibid.
111 Ibid.
112 Letter to Felice, 9–10.3.13, p. 332.
113 *Tagebücher*, 8.10.17, p. 334.
114 Letter to Max Brod, 13.11.12, p. 111.
115 Second letter to Felice, 11.11.12, p. 86.
116 14.11.12, p. 89.
117 P. 90.
118 Third letter to Felice, 11.11.12, p. 89.
119 P. 90.
120 Pp. 91–2.
121 Pp. 92–3.
122 P. 93.
123 Letter to Felice (undated), p. 99.
124 Ibid.
125 15.11.12, pp. 93–4.
126 17.11.12, p. 101.
127 Letter from his mother to Felice, 16.11.12, p. 100.
128 Ibid.

12 Captive Insect

1 Letter to Felice, 17.11.12, p. 101.
2 *Sämtliche Erzählungen*, p. 56.
3 Letter to Felice, 18.11.12, p. 105.
4 Benjamin (1970), p. 122.
5 Letter to Felice, 20.11.12, p. 106.
6 Second letter to Felice dated 20.11.12, p. 107.

Notes

7 Letter to Felice, 18.11.12, p. 104.

8 Unfinished letter to Felice, 18.11.12, posted 28.12, p. 138.

9 4.12.12, p. 154.

10 5.12.12, p. 159.

11 Ibid.

12 21.11.12, p. 109.

13 22.11.12, p. 114.

14 Ibid.

15 Second letter of 21.11.12, pp. 111–12.

16 6–7.12.12, p. 163.

17 23–4.11.12, p. 117.

18 P. 116.

19 23–4.11.12, p. 117.

20 25.11.12, p. 125.

21 26.11.12, p. 130.

22 27.11.12, p. 135.

23 7.12.12 (dated 8.12), p. 168.

24 30.11.12 (night of 29–30), p. 142.

25 17–18.12.12, p. 187.

26 11–12.12.12, p. 176.

27 11.12.12, p. 175.

28 22.12.12, pp, 200–1.

29 Robert Musil, *Der Mann ohne Eigenschaften,* Book II, part 1, ch. 32.

30 Wittgenstein, *Tractatus,* 6.421.

31 Letter to Felice, 22–3.12.12, p. 222.

32 Pp. 201–2.

33 23–4.12.12, p. 204.

34 30–31.12.12, p. 222.

35 1–2.2.13, p. 280.

36 23–4.12.12, p. 204.

37 25–6.12.12, p. 208.

38 30–31.12.12, p. 222.

39 31.12.12–1.1.12, p. 222.

40 P. 224.

41 Ibid.

42 3–4.1.13, pp. 228–9.

43 5–6.1.13, p. 233.

44 10–11.1.13, p. 243.

45 P. 244.

46 11–12.1.13, p. 246.

47 p. 247.

48 13–14.1.13, p. 249.

49 14–15.1.13, p. 250.

50 A translation of the lecture appears in Buber, *On Judaism* (New York 1967).

51 Letter to Felice, 16.1.13, p. 252.

52 19.1.13, p. 257.

53 17–18.1.13, p. 254.

54 19.1.13, p. 257.

55 23–4.1.13, p. 267.

56 Ibid.

57 26.1.13, p. 271.

58 26–7.1.13, p. 272.

59 1–2.2.13, p. 257.

60 19.1.13, p. 257.

61 1–2.2.13, p. 282.

62 2.2.13, p. 282.

63 Ibid.

64 5–6.2.13, p. 286.

65 P. 287.

66 Letter dated 9–10.2.13, but presumably written 7–8, p. 290.

67 P. 289.

68 Ibid.

69 Note apparently enclosed in letter to Felice, 21–22.2.13, p. 310.

70 9–10.2.13, p. 291.

71 10–11.2.13, p. 293.

72 11–12.2.13, p. 294.

73 17–18.2.13, p. 304.

74 Born *et al., Symposium,* p. 130.

75 Letter to Felice, 14–15.2.13, p. 300.

76 18–19.2.13, p. 306.

77 21–2.2.13, pp. 309–10.

78 23.2.13, p. 311.

79 Ibid.

80 9.3.13, p. 330.

81 *Tagebücher,* 28.2.13, pp. 187–90.

82 Letter to Felice, 1.3.13, p. 320.

83 2.3.13, p. 321.

84 2–3.13, p. 323.

85 16–17.3.13, p. 340.

86 17–18.3.13, p. 341.

87 22.3.13, p. 345.

88 23.3.13, p. 345.

89 8.4.13, p. 360.

90 28.3.13, p. 347.

91 Ibid.

92 1.4.13, pp. 351–2.

93 Canetti, p. 43.

94 *Tagebücher,* 14.8,13, p. 198.

95 Postscript to letter to Felice, 1.4.13, p. 352.

96 *Tagebücher,* 24.5.13, p. 192.

97 21.8.13, p. 200.

98 21 or 22.7.13, p. 195.

99 Letter to Felice, 7.4.13, p. 358.

100 10.4.13, p. 362.

101 14.4.13, p. 365.
102 17.4.13, p. 366.
103 20.4 13, p. 368.
104 Ibid.
105 28.4.13, p. 371.
106 29–30.4.13, p. 373.
107 *Tagebücher*, 2.5.13, p. 191.
108 Letter to Felice, 2.5.13, p. 375.
109 4.5.13, p. 377.
110 *Tagebücher*, 4.5.13, p. 191.
111 Letter to Felice, 15.5.13, p. 383.
112 Letter dated 1.7.13 (?written 1.8), p. 418.
113 12–3.5.13, pp. 380–1.
114 P. 382.
115 23.5.13, pp. 388–9.
116 P. 389.
117 27.5.13, p. 390.
118 1.6.13, p. 393.
119 *Prager Tagblatt*, 1.6.13.
120 Letter to Felice, 10.6.13, p. 396.
121 Ibid.
122 16.6.13, p. 400.
123 P. 401.
124 19.6.13, p. 405.
125 *Tagebücher*, 21.6.13, p. 192.
126 Letter to Felice, 21. (22 and 23) 6.13, p. 407.
127 Pp. 407–8.
128 P. 408.
129 23.6.13, p. 410.
130 Ibid.
131 Ibid.
132 Letter dated 7.6.13 and written 7.7, p. 422.
133 29.10.13, p. 467.
134 *Tagebücher*, 21 or 22.7.13, p. 195.
135 Ibid.
136 Ibid.
137 Ibid.
138 Letter to Felice, 28.6.13, pp. 414–15.
139 p. 415.
140 3.7.13, p. 419.
141 p. 420.
142 7.7.13, p. 424.
143 Letter dated 6.7.15 but written 5.7.15, p. 421.
144 13.7.13, p. 427.
145 Ibid.
146 Ibid.

147 2.8.13, p. 432.
148 4.8.13, p. 434.
149 Ibid.
150 6.8.13, p. 436.
151 Ibid.
152 Ibid.
153 7.8.13, p. 438.
154 *Tagebücher*, 13.8.13, p. 197.
155 14.8.13, p. 197.
156 p. 198.
157 Letter to Felice, 14.8.13, p. 444.
158 *Das literarische Echo* XV 22, 15.8.13.
159 Letter to Felice, 22.8.13, p. 450.
160 p. 451.
161 Ibid.
162 *Tagebücher*, 15.8.13, p. 198.
163 Ibid.
164 p. 199.
165 Kierkegaard, *Journals*.
166 Letters to Felice, 24.8.13 and 24–5.8.13, pp. 452–4.
167 30.8.13, p. 459.
168 2.9.13, p. 460.
169 Ibid.

13 Grete Bloch

1 Binder (1979) vol I, p. 451.
2 Letter to Felice, 27–8.2.13, p. 318.
3 Postcard to Felice, 9.9.13, p. 462.
4 *Tagebücher*, 12.12.13, p. 214.
5 23.1.14, p. 221.
6 Binder (1967).
7 Letter to Felice, 9.9.13, p. 462.
8 Note dated 10.9.13 printed with the letters to Felice, p. 433.
9 Ibid.
10 Postcard to Felice, 15.9.13, p. 465.
11 Letter to Felice, 16.9.13, p. 466.
12 Letter to Max Brod, 16.9.13, p. 120.
13 Letter to Grete Bloch printed with the letters to Felice, p. 472.
14 Note enclosed in letter to Felice, 6.11.13, p. 472.
15 Letter to Max Brod, 28.9.13, p. 121.
16 Ibid.
17 Ibid.
18 Ibid.
19 *Tagebücher*, 20.10.13, p. 203.
20 Ibid.

21 Ibid.
22 Ibid.
23 Letter to Felice, 29.12.13, pp. 484–5.
24 29.10.13, p. 468.
25 Ibid.
26 Letter to Grete Bloch, 21.5.14, p. 582.
27 10.11.13, p. 473.
28 6.11.13, p. 476.
29 10.11.13, p. 476.
30 Pp. 474–5.
31 18.11.13, p. 479.
32 Marianna Steiner.
33 Ibid.
34 Postscript to letter to Grete Bloch, 18.11.13, pp. 479–80.
35 *Tagebücher*, 4.12.13, p. 211.
36 Letter to Grete Bloch, 19.2.14, p. 504.
37 *Tagebücher*, 4.12.13, p. 211.
38 Ibid.
39 William Blake, 'Proverbs of Hell'.
40 *Tagebücher*, 5.12.13, p. 212.
41 8.12.13, p. 212.
42 Ibid.
43 12.12.13, p. 214.
44 Letter to Grete Bloch, 15–16.12.13, pp. 480–1.
45 28.1.14, p. 492.
46 Letter to Felice, 29.12.12, p. 482,
47 Quoted by Kafka, p. 483.
48 p. 483.
49 p. 485.
50 p. 488.
51 Ibid.
52 Letter to Grete Bloch, 28.1.14, p. 491.
53 5.2.14, p. 496.
54 7.2.14, p. 496.
55 P. 497.
56 11.2.14, p. 500.
57 Letter started 21 or 22.2.14, finished 25.2, p. 505.
58 Ibid.
59 2.3.14, pp. 507–8.
60 *Tagebücher*, ca 9.3.14, p. 229.
61 Letter to Grete Bloch, 3.3.14, p. 510.
62 Ibid.
63 Letter to Felice, 2.3.14. No longer extant.
64 Letter to Grete Bloch, 4.3.14, p. 511.
65 6.3.14, p. 512.
66 p. 514.
67 9.3.14, p. 516.
68 Letter dated 12.3.14 but probably written 11.3.14, p. 517.
69 Letter to Felice, 13.3.14, p. 518.
70 *Tagebücher, ca* 9.3.14, p. 229.
71 P. 230.
72 Ibid.
73 Ibid.
74 Letter to Grete Bloch, 13.3.14, p. 521.
75 16.3.14, p. 522.
76 18.3.14, p. 523.
77 Telegram quoted in letter written to Felice later the same day, 18.3.14, p. 525.
78 Letter from Julie Kafka to Felice, 18.3.14, p. 525.
79 Letter to Grete Bloch, 19.3.14, p. 525.
80 Letter to Felice's parents, 19.3.14, p. 526.
81 Letter to Felice, 21.3.14, pp. 527–8.
82 Letter to Grete Bloch, dated 20.3.14 but written 21.3, p. 531.
83 Ibid.
84 Letter to Felice, 25.3.14, p. 534.
85 Ibid.
86 3.4.14, pp. 538–40.
87 Letter to Grete Bloch, 5.4.14, p. 541.
88 7.4.14, p. 544.
89 14.4.14, p. 549.
90 p. 550.
91 15.4.14, p. 556.
92 Ibid.
93 16.4.14, p. 552.
94 16.3.14, p. 522.
95 Letter to Felice, 14.4.14, p. 548.
96 p. 549.
97 Letter to Felice's mother, 19.4.14, p. 556.
98 Letter to Felice, 17.4.14, p. 553.
99 20.4.14, p. 559.
100 Ibid.
101 24.4.14, p. 563.
102 Letter dated 25.4.14, possibly written 26.4, p. 564.
103 Letters to Grete Bloch, 26 and 29.4.14, pp. 565 and 567.
104 Letter to Grete Bloch, end of April 1914, p. 569.
105 *Ca* 3.5.14, p. 570.

106 7.5.14, p. 571.
107 Letter to Felice, end of October/beginning of November 1914, p. 620.
108 Letter from Sigmund Freud to Martha Bernays, 18.8.82.
109 Letter to Grete Bloch, 8.5.14, p. 572.
110 Ibid.
111 Ibid.
112 24.5.14, p. 588.
113 16.5.14, p. 576.
114 Letter to Felice, 22.5.14, p. 584.
115 Ibid.
116 Letter to Grete Bloch, 29.5.14, pp. 592–3.
117 *Ca* 2–3.6.14, p. 593.
118 *Tagebücher*, May 1914, p. 234.
119 Letter to Grete Bloch, 29.5.14, pp. 592–3.
120 *Ca* 2–3.6.14, p. 593.
121 Cited in Brod, p. 210.
122 *Briefe an Felice*, p. 470.
123 *Tagebücher*, May 1914, pp. 236–7.
124 Pp. 237–9.
125 Letter to Grete Bloch, 4.6.14, p. 593.
126 *Tagebücher*, 6.6.14, p. 240.
127 Letter to Grete Bloch, 6.6.14, p. 595.
128 *Tagebücher*, pp. 243–9.
129 Ibid.
130 Letter to Grete Bloch, 8.6.14, p. 597.
131 *Tagebücher*, p. 242.
132 Ibid.
133 Quoted in letter to Grete Bloch, 11.6.14, p. 598.
134 Ibid.
135 16 or 17.6.14, p. 601.
136 Postscripts to this letter, p. 602.
137 Letter dated 20.6.14, but probably written 24.6, p. 603.
138 Letter to Felice, 17–18.1.13, p. 255.
139 *Tagebücher*, 30.6.14, p. 254.
140 Ibid.
141 Letters to Grete Bloch, 30.6.14, 2.7, and 3.7, pp. 606–8.
142 Draft or copy of letter for Grete Bloch, 3.7.14, p. 608.
143 3.7.14, p. 609.
144 Letter from Julie Kafka to Felice's parents 4.7.14, p. 611.
145 *Tagebücher*, 23.7.14, p. 254.
146 Letter to Felice, late October to early November 1914, p. 617.
147 *Tagebücher*, 23.7.14, p. 254.
148 Ibid.
149 Ibid.
150 Ibid.
151 P. 255.
152 Letter to Felice's parents, 13.7.14, p. 611.
153 *Tagebücher*, 27.7.14, p. 255.
154 Ibid.
155 Pp. 255–6.
156 Letter to Max Brod and Felix Weltsch, late July 1914, p. 131.
157 Ibid.
158 Ibid.
159 Letter to his parents in *Briefe an Ottla*, p. 23.
160 Pp. 23–4.
161 *Tagebücher*, 28.7.14, pp. 256–7.
162 Letter to Felice, late October to early November 1914, p. 616.
163 *Tagebücher*, 28.7.14, p. 257.
164 Ibid.
165 P. 256.
166 Unpublished draft of letter to Musil c. July 1914.
167 *Tagebücher*, 2.8.14, p. 261.
168 Letter from Kafka's mother to Felice's mother, 7.8.14, p. 613.

14 Trial

1 *Tagebücher*, 29.7.14, p. 258.
2 Pp. 258–9.
3 6.8.14, p. 261.
4 4.8.14, p. 261.
5 6.8.14, p. 261.
6 Ibid.
7 Ibid.
8 15.8.14, p. 263.
9 29.8.14, p. 271.
10 Ibid.
11 *Tagebücher*, 30.8.14, p. 271.
12 Letter to Grete Bloch, 15.10.14, p. 615 and *Tagebücher*, p. 273.
13 *Brief an den Vater*, p. 40.
14 Pp. 40–1.
15 Letter to Grete Bloch, p. 615.
16 *Der Prozess*, pp. 10–11.
17 P. 22.
18 P. 45.

19 Telegram to Felice, 27.10.14, p. 615.
20 Letter to Felice, end of October to beginning of November 1914, p. 617.
21 Ibid.
22 Ibid.
23 *Tagebücher*, 1.9.14, p. 272.
24 Ibid.
25 13.9.14, p. 272.
26 Ibid.
27 7.10.14, p. 272.
28 Letter to Felice, end of October to beginning of November 1914, p. 618.
29 *Tagebücher*, 15.10.14, p. 273.
30 Ibid.
31 *Amerika*, p. 200.
32 P. 204.
33 Ibid.
34 Ibid.
35 P. 274.
36 Pp. 273–4.
37 *Tagebücher*, between 15 and 30 October 1914, p. 274.
38 Ibid.
39 3.11.14, p. 275.
40 25.10.14, p. 274.
41 Ibid.
42 4.11.14, p. 275.
43 Ibid.
44 2.12.14, p. 277.
45 Ibid.
46 *Der Prozess*, p. 44.
47 P. 37.
48 Pp. 53–4.
49 Letter to Felice, 27.10.12, p. 59.
50 *Der Prozess*, p. 14.
51 Canetti, p. 67.
52 Letter to Felice, 27.10.12, p. 59.
53 *Der Prozess*, p. 78.
54 *Tagebücher*, 20.11.14, p. 276.
55 *Der Prozess*, p. 133.
56 P. 183.
57 P. 182.
58 *Tagebücher*, November 1911.
59 M. Friedlander, *Die religiösen Bewegungen innerhalb des Judentums im Zeitalter Jesu* (Berlin 1905).
60 Oppenheim.
61 *Der Prozess*, p. 11.
62 *The Trial*, p. 13.
63 G. Scholem, *On the Kabbalah and its Symbolism* (London 1965), p. 76.
64 P. 297.
65 *Tagebücher*, 30.11.14, p. 276.
66 5.12.14, p. 277.
67 13.12.14, p. 279.
68 The usual English title is 'The Giant Mole'.
69 *Sämtliche Erzählungen*, p. 252.
70 *Tagebücher*, 19.12.14, p. 280.
71 Ibid.
72 24.1.15, p. 287.
73 26.12.14, p. 281.
74 27.12.14, p. 281.

15 Exodus

1 *Tagebücher*, 4.1.15, p. 283.
2 31.12.14, p. 282.
3 19.12.14, p. 280.
4 4.1.15, p. 283.
5 Ibid.
6 6.1.15, p. 283.
7 18.1.15, p. 284.
8 Ibid.
9 19.1.15, p. 284.
10 17.1.15, p. 283.
11 24.1.15, p. 287.
12 P. 286.
13 Ibid.
14 Ibid.
15 P. 287.
16 Ibid.
17 Ibid.
18 Letter to Felice, 25.1.15, pp. 624–5.
19 P. 625.
20 11.2.15, p. 626.
21 *Tagebücher*, 29.1.15, p. 287.
22 9.2.15, p. 288.
23 Letter to Felice, 11.2.15, p. 626.
24 P. 627.
25 Ibid.
26 3.3.15, p. 628.
27 11.2.15, p. 627.
28 *Tagebücher*, 1.3.15, p. 289.
29 Letter to Felice, 21.3.15, p. 630.
30 P. 631.
31 End of December 1916 or beginning of January 1917, p. 749.
32 *Tagebücher*, 13.3.15, p. 290.

33 17.3.15, p. 291.
34 Letter to Felice, 21.3.15, p. 631.
35 5.4.15, p. 632.
36 P. 633.
37 Pp. 632–3.
38 P. 633.
39 Ibid.
40 *Tagebücher*, 27.4.15, p. 292.
41 P. 295.
42 Ibid.
43 3.5.15, p. 296.
44 4.5.15, p. 296.
45 Ibid.
46 Letter to Felice postmarked on arrival 6.5.15, p. 637.
47 Ibid.
48 Brod, p. 89.
49 Letter to Felice postmarked on arrival 4.6.15, p. 638.
50 P. 637.
51 Postcard to Felice postmarked 26.5.15, p. 639.
52 Postcard postmarked 27.5.15, p. 640.
53 Ibid.
54 *Tagebücher*, 27.5.15, p. 297.
55 Letter to Felice, 20.7.15, p. 641.
56 20.7.15, p. 641.
57 End of July 1915, pp. 641–2.
58 9.8.15, p. 643.
59 Ibid.
60 P. 642.
61 Ibid.
62 P. 643.
63 Pp. 643–4.
64 P. 644.
65 *Tagebücher*, 14.5.15, p. 296.
66 Ibid.
67 27.5.15, p. 297.
68 13.9.15, p. 297.
69 Ibid.
70 Ibid.
71 16.9.15, English ed., Vol. II, p. 129. Omitted from German ed.
72 16.9.15, p. 298.
73 Ibid.
74 Ibid.
75 28.9.15, p. 298.
76 30.9.15, p. 299.
77 3rd Octavo Notebook 13.12.17, *Hochzeitsvorbereitungen*, p. 94.

78 J. J. White, 'Endings and Non-endings in Kafka's Fiction' in Kuna.
79 *Der Prozess*, p. 191.
80 P. 222.
81 Ibid.
82 *Tagebücher*, 20.7.16, p. 316.
83 *Der Prozess*, pp. 193–4.
84 P. 194.
85 Ibid.
86 Ibid.
87 P. 222.
88 Letter to Verlag Kurt Wolff, 25.10.15, p. 136.
89 Ibid.
90 *Tagebücher*, 5.11.15, p. 303.
91 6.11.15, p. 303.
92 19.11.15, p. 303.
93 21.11.15, p. 304.
94 Ibid.
95 Letter to Felice, 5.15.15, p. 645.
96 Ibid.
97 Postcard to Felice postmarked on arrival 24.12.15, p. 645.
98 Ibid.
99 Postcard to Felice, 26.12.15, p. 646.

16 Hopeful Interlude

1 Letter to Felice, 18.1.16, p. 647.
2 P. 648.
3 Postcard to Felice, 24.1.16, p. 648.
4 Letter to Felice, March 1916, p. 650.
5 P. 649.
6 Ibid.
7 Ibid.
8 14.4.16, p. 652.
9 Postcard to Felice, 25.4.16.
10 19.4.16, p. 653.
11 Ibid.
12 *Tagebücher*, April or May 1916, p. 307.
13 April or May (probably Easter) 1916, p. 307.
14 P. 309.
15 P. 310.
16 Letter to Felice, probably 14.5.16, p. 656.
17 *Tagebücher*, 11.5.16, p. 311.
18 Letter to Felice, probably 14.5.16, pp. 656–7.

19 Postcard to Felice, mid-May 1916, p. 657.
20 Ibid.
21 26.5.16, p. 657.
22 Another postcard dated 26.5.16 and a letter, presumably 28.5.16, p. 658.
23 Letter to Felice, presumably 28.5.16, p. 659.
24 Postcard to Felice, 31.5.16, p. 660.
25 Ibid.
26 *Tagebücher*, 2.6.16, pp. 311–12.
27 19.6.16, p. 312.
28 P. 313.
29 Postcard to Max Brod, 9.7.16, p. 138.
30 *Tagebücher*, between 6 and 13.7.16, p. 314.
31 Ibid.
32 3.7.16, p. 313.
33 Postcard to Max Brod, 5.7.16, p. 137.
34 Ibid.
35 *Tagebücher*, 4.7.16, p. 313.
36 5.7.16, p. 314.
37 6.7.16, p. 314.
38 Between 6 and 12.7.16, p. 318.
39 Letter to Felice's mother, 10.7.16, p. 663.
40 Letter to Ottla, 12.7.16, p. 30.
41 *Tagebücher*, 13.7.16, p. 315.
42 P. 315.
43 Letter to Max Brod, 12–14.7.16, p. 139.
44 Ibid.
45 P. 140.
46 Letter to Max Brod, mid-July 1916, p. 144.
47 Letter to Dr Siegfried Löwy, 1916, pp. 151–2.
48 Ibid.
49 Postcard to Felice, 14.7.16, p. 664.
50 Ibid.
51 Letter to Kurt Wolff Verlag, 22.4.14, p. 127.
52 Letter to Max Brod, mid-July 1916, p. 144.
53 P. 145.
54 P. 146.
55 Postcard to Felice, 18.7.16, p. 666.
56 27.7.16, p. 672.
57 19.7.16, p. 667.
58 *Tagebücher*, 20.7.16, p. 316.
59 Ibid.
60 Postcard to Felice, 24.7.16, p. 670.
61 25.7.16, p. 671.
62 Ibid.
63 26.7.16, p. 671.
64 28.7.16, p. 672.
65 26.7.16, p. 671.
66 29.7.16, p. 673.
67 30.7.16, p. 673.
68 1.8.16, p. 674.
69 Ibid.
70 9.8.16, p. 677.
71 1.9.16, p. 690.
72 Letter to Felice, 11.9.16, p. 695.
73 Fragment dated 20.8.16, *Hochzeitsvorbereitungen*, p. 238.
74 *Tagebücher*, 27.8.16, pp. 318–19.
75 Two postcards to Felice, 31.8.16, p. 689.
76 Postcard to Felice, 1.9.16, p. 690.
77 7.9.16, p. 691.
78 8.9.16, p. 693.
79 10.9.16, p. 693.
80 Letter to Felice, 23.10.16, p. 732.
81 End of December 1916 or beginning of January 1917, p. 750.
82 12.9.16, p. 616.
83 3.10.16, p. 716.
84 12.10.16, p. 724.
85 5.10.16, p. 718.
86 6.10.16, pp. 718–19.
87 *Tagebücher*, October 1916, p. 319.
88 Letter from Julie Kafka to Felice, 8.10.16, pp. 720–1.
89 Letter to Felice, 11.10.16, p. 723.
90 Quoted in his letter to Felice, 19.10.16, p. 729.
91 Letter to Felice, 19.10.16, p. 729.
92 Pp. 730–1.
93 Pp. 729–30.
94 P. 730.
95 Ibid.
96 Pp. 730–1.
97 P. 731.
98 30.10.16, p. 737.
99 Postcard to Felice, 7.12.16, p. 744.
100 Ibid.
101 Letter to Gottfried Kolwel, 3.1.17, p. 153.
102 Ibid.
103 Ibid.
104 Eugen Mondt, *München-Dachau, Ein*

Literarisches Erinnerungsbüchlein.
Typescript in Stadtbibliothek, Munich.
105 Letter from R. M. Rilke to Kurt Wolff,
17.2.22. Wolff, *Briefwechsel*, p. 152.
106 Postcard to Felice, 23.11.16, p. 741.
107 21.11.16, p. 741.
108 Letter to Felice, end of December 1916
or beginning of January 1917, p. 750.
109 Pp. 750–1.
110 Postcard to Felice, 23.11.16, p. 742.
111 4.12.16, p. 743.
112 7.12.16, p. 743.
113 8.12.16, p. 745.
114 Oppenheimer.
115 Martin Buber, *Die Legende des
Baalschem* (Frankfurt 1908).
116 *Sämtliche Erzählungen*, p. 145.

17 The Modern Kabbalist

1 Typed letter dated 8.3.17 (unpublished)
in State Archive, Vienna.
2 Letter to Felice, end of December 1916
to beginning of January 1917, p. 752.
3 Letter to Ottla, 19.4.17, p. 32.
4 P. 33.
5 *Sämtliche Erzählungen*, p. 154.
6 P. 155.
7 Letter to Martin Buber, 12.5.17, English
ed., p. 132. Omitted from the German
ed.
8 George Steiner, *The Tower of Babel*
(Oxford 1975), p. 67.
9 P. 66.
10 P. 61.
11 Pazi, p. 136.
12 Binder (1979) I, p. 488.
13 3rd Octavo Notebook 9.11.17,
Hochzeitsvorbereitungen, p. 82.
14 *Sämtliche Erzählungen*, pp. 291–2.
15 Clement Greenberg, 'At the Building of
the Great Wall of China' in Flores
(1958).
16 *Sämtliche Erzählungen*, p. 293.
17 P. 294.
18 P. 296.
19 *Tagebücher*, 29.7.17, p. 323.
20 *Sämtliche Erzählungen*, p. 298.
21 Pp. 298–9.

22 P. 300.
23 Brod, p. 140.
24 Letter to Martin Buber 20.7.17, English
ed., p. 133. Omitted from German ed.
25 Rudolf Fuchs, 'Reminiscences of Franz
Kafka' in 1960 New York ed. of Brod's
biography.
26 Letter to Felice, 9.9.17, p. 753.
27 Letter to Kurt Wolff, 27.7.17, p. 158.

18 Haemorrhage

1 Letter to Milena, p. 123.
2 Letter to Ottla, 29.8.17, p. 39.
3 Letter to Milena, p. 8.
4 Ibid.
5 Letter to Ottla, 29.8.17, p. 39.
6 Ibid.
7 Brod, p. 144.
8 *Tagebücher*, 9.8.17, p. 329.
9 Letter to Ottla, 29.8.17, p. 40.
10 Letter to Milena, p. 8.
11 Postcript to letter to Felice, 29.9.17,
p. 754.
12 Brod, p. 144.
13 *Tagebücher*, 6, 7 or 8.8.17, p. 327.
14 *Tagebücher*, 9.8.17, p. 328.
15 Pp. 328–9.
16 Brod, p. 144.
17 P. 145.
18 Letter to Ottla, 8.9.17, p. 45.

19 Zürau

1 Letter to Oskar Baum, mid-September
1917, p. 166.
2 Letter to Felix Weltsch, 22.9.17, p. 169.
3 Letter to Max Brod, mid-September
1917, pp. 160–1.
4 Letter to Felix Weltsch, after 17.10.17,
p. 186.
5 Ibid.
6 Letter to Felix Weltsch, 22.9.17, p. 169,
and letter to Max Brod, end of
September 1917, p. 171.
7 Letter to Felix Weltsch, after 17.10.17,
p. 186.
8 Letter to Oskar Baum, mid-September
1917, pp. 162–3.

9 Letter to Max Brod, mid-September 1917, p. 161.
10 *Tagebücher*, p. 330.
11 Ibid.
12 *Tagebücher*, 15.9.17, p. 329.
13 Binder (1968), p. 443.
14 Ibid.
15 Letter to Max Brod, mid-September 1917, p. 165.
16 Letter to Oskar Baum, mid-September 1917, p. 165.
17 Letter to Felix Weltsch, beginning of October 1917, p. 180.
18 Letter to Max Brod, mid-September 1917, p. 165.
19 *Tagebücher*, 21.9.17, p. 331.
20 28.9.17, p. 333.
21 21.9.17, p. 331.
22 Letter to Max Brod, end of September 1917, p. 171.
23 Letter to Felice, 1.10.17, pp. 755–6.
24 P. 756.
25 Ibid.
26 Ibid.
27 P. 757.
28 Ibid.
29 Ibid.
30 Letter to Felix Weltsch, beginning of October 1917, p. 180.
31 Quoted in letter to Felice, 16.10.17, p. 757.
32 Letter to Max Brod, 12.10.17, p. 181.
33 *Tagebücher*, 8.10.17, p. 333.
34 Letter to Felice, 16.10.17, p. 758.
35 Pp. 757–8.
36 P. 758.
37 Ibid.
38 Ibid.
39 Letter to Max Brod, mid-November 1917, pp. 194–5.
40 P. 195.
41 Ibid.
42 Ibid.
43 Ibid.
44 P. 196.
45 Ibid.
46 Beginning of November 1917, p. 191.
47 End of December 1917, pp. 216–17.
48 *Betrachtungen* No 13. *Hochzeitsvorbereitungen*, p. 40.
49 No 76, p. 47.
50 No 13, p. 40.
51 No 47, p. 44.
52 No 63, p. 46.
53 3rd Octavo Notebook, *Hochzeitsvorbereitungen*, pp. 71–2.
54 *Betrachtungen* No 54, p. 44.
55 *Hochzeitsvorbereitungen*, p. 85.
56 *Betrachtungen* No 33, p. 42.
57 Written by Simeon ben Yochai in the second century and by Moses de Leon in the thirteenth.
58 *Hochzeitsvorbereitungen*, p. 76.
59 P. 89.
60 Stein, 11.12.17.
61 *Hochzeitsvorbereitungen*, p. 80.
62 P. 101.
63 Ibid.
64 24.11.17, p. 86.
65 Aristotle, *On the Art of Poetry*, tr. Ingram Bywater, Section 6.
66 4th Octavo Notebook, p. 123.
67 *Betrachtungen* No 109, p. 54.
68 Letter to Max Brod, beginning of October 1917, p. 177.
69 Ibid.
70 10.12.17, p. 208.
71 24.11.17, p. 200.
72 Note of 25.10.17 in 3rd Octavo Notebook, p. 80.
73 Postcard to Max Brod, 22.10.17, p. 189.
74 Letter to Max Brod, beginning of November 1917, p. 191.
75 Letter to Max and Elsa Brod, beginning of October 1917, p. 176.
76 Letter to Felix Weltsch, mid-November 1917, p. 198.
77 Ibid.
78 Letter to Max Brod, beginning of December 1917, p. 205.
79 Ibid.
80 P. 206.
81 10.12.17, p. 207.
82 Letter to Felix Weltsch, 20.12.17, English ed., p. 184. Omitted from German ed.
83 Letter to Ottla, 28.12.17, p. 47.
84 Brod, p. 147.
85 Ibid.
86 *Sämtliche Erzählungen*, p. 305.

87 Ibid.
88 *Hochzeitsvorbereitungen*, p. 97.
89 Ibid.
90 P. 148.
91 Letter to Ottla, 28.12.17, p. 47.
92 *Hochzeitsvorbereitungen*, p. 97.
93 Ibid. Note of 30.12.17.
94 16.1.18, p. 98.
95 Letter to Ottla, 28.12.17, p. 47.
96 P. 48.
97 Letter to Kurt Wolff Verlag, 27.1.18, p. 228.
98 *Hochzeitsvorbereitungen*, pp. 131–2.
99 *Brief an den Vater*, p. 33.
100 Ibid.
101 Letter to Brod, probably 13.1.18, p. 219.
102 P. 220.
103 14.1.18, *Hochzeitsvorbereitungen*, p. 98.
104 25.1.18, *Hochzeitsvorbereitungen*, p. 104.
105 Postcard to Felix Weltsch end of January 1918, English ed., p. 193. Omitted from German ed.
106 Letter to Felix Weltsch, beginning of February 1918, p. 231.
107 16.1.18, *Hochzeitsvorbereitungen*, p. 99.
108 7.2.18, p. 110.
109 Pp. 110–11.
110 25.2.18, pp. 120–1.
111 Letter to Max Brod, beginning of March 1918, pp. 234–5.
112 P. 235.
113 Ibid.
114 Ibid.
115 End of March 1918, p. 238.
116 Ibid.
117 P. 240.
118 Letter to Max Brod, beginning of April 1918, p. 246.
119 Letter to Felix Weltsch, end of April 1918 (misdated by Brod May–June), p. 242.
120 Letter to Max Brod, beginning of April 1918, p. 240.
121 P. 241.

20 Julie

1 Letter to Ottla, 5.5.18, p. 53.
2 Ibid.
3 *Ca* 14–15.5.18, p. 54.
4 Brod, p. 149.
5 Letter to Johannes Urzidil, spring 1918, p. 241.
6 Brod, p. 149.
7 Ibid.
8 Ibid.
9 Letter to Felix Weltsch, probably autumn 1918, p. 243.
10 Ibid.
11 Jeffrey Meyers, *Katherine Mansfield: A Biography* (London 1978).
12 Letter to Ottla, 8.9.18, p. 55.
13 P. 56.
14 P. 57.
15 Postcard to Max Brod, 27.9.18, p. 243.
16 Letter to Felix Weltsch, September 1918, p. 244.
17 Ibid.
18 Letter to Ottla, p. 183.
19 *Brief an den Vater*, p. 26.
20 Letter to Max Brod, September 1918, p. 246.
21 Binder (1979) I.
22 Letter to Max Brod, beginning of December 1918, p. 247.
23 September 1918, p. 246.
24 Beginning of December 1918, p. 247.
25 Letter to Ottla, 11.11.18, p. 59.
26 11.12.18, p. 61.
27 Postcard to Max Brod, 16.12.18, p. 248.
28 2.3.19, p. 253.
29 Loužil, p. 72.
30 Letter to Max Brod, January 1919, p. 251.
31 Postcard to Ottla, 1.2.19, p. 63.
32 Letter to Max Brod, 6.2.19, p. 251.
33 P. 252.
34 Letter to Julie Wohryzek's sister. Born et al., *Symposium*, pp. 45ff.
35 Ibid.
36 Letter to Max Brod, 2.3.19, p. 253.
37 Letter to Julie Wohryzek's sister.
38 Ibid.
39 Letter to Ottla, 20.2.19, pp. 67–8.
40 P. 68.
41 Letter to Julie Wohryzek's sister.
42 Ibid.
43 Ibid.

44 Letter to Ottla, p. 69.
45 24.2.19, p. 69.
46 P. 70.
47 *Symposium,* p. 48.
48 *Symposium.*
49 Ibid.
50 *Brief an den Vater*, p. 63.
51 Ibid.
52 Ibid.
53 *Tagebücher*, 30.6.19, p. 336.
54 3.7.19, p. 336.
55 *Symposium.*

21 Milena

1 *Brief an den Vater*, p. 51.
2 Letter from Max Brod, 1.8.19 (unpublished).
3 Letter to Milena, p. 5.
4 P. 47.
5 *Brief an den Vater*, p. 66.
6 Letter to Max Brod, 2.3.19, p. 253.
7 *Brief an den Vater*, p. 5.
8 P. 14.
9 P. 9.
10 P. 16.
11 P. 51.
12 P. 55.
13 Pp. 67–70.
14 Pp. 72–3.
15 Letter to Ottla, beginning of November 1919, p. 74.
16 *Ca* 10.11.19, p. 75.
17 Olga Stüdl (pseud. Dora Gerrit), Memoir in *Bohemia*, 27.2.31.
18 Letter to Minze Eisner, winter 1919, p. 256.
19 P. 257.
20 *Tagebücher*, 11.12.19, p. 336.
21 Janouch (1971).
22 'Paralipomena', *Hochzeitsvorbereitungen*, p. 418.
23 Ibid.
24 P. 419.
25 Letter to Minze Eisner, February 1920, p. 259.
26 Letter to Kurt Wolff, February 1920, p. 261.
27 Letter to Minze Eisner, February 1920, p. 262.
28 Letter to Kurt Wolff, February 1920, p. 261.
29 Letter to Minze Eisner, February 1920, p. 262.
30 Letter to Kurt Wolff, February 1920, pp. 262–3.
31 Letter to Minze Eisner, end of February 1920 (misdated March by Brod), p. 265.
32 Ibid.
33 Loužil, p. 73.
34 Brod, p. 71.
35 Letter to Kurt Wolff, end of March 1920, p. 268.
36 Letter to Ottla, 6.4.20, p. 77.
37 P. 78.
38 Ibid.
39 Letter to Max Brod and Felix Weltsch, 8.4.20 (misdated 10.4. by Brod), p. 271.
40 Ibid.
41 Letter to Ottla, 6.4.20, p. 77.
42 Letter to Milena, p. 7.
43 Letter to Max Brod and Felix Wolff, p. 269.
44 Postcard to Minze Eisner, April 1920, p. 271.
45 Ibid.
46 Letter to Ottla, 17.4.20, p. 79
47 The letter printed second in *Briefe an Milena* was written from Prague before the one printed first, which was written from Meran.
48 Letter to Milena, p. 5.
49 Ibid.
50 Postscript to letter to Milena, p. 7.
51 Ibid.
52 P. 9.
53 Ibid.
54 Pp. 15–16.
55 Letter to Max Brod, beginning of May 1920, p. 275.
56 Buber–Neumann, p. 64.
57 Pp. 66–72.
58 Letter to Milena, p. 16.
59 P. 17.
60 P. 18.
61 P. 10.
62 P. 21.
63 P. 24.

64 P. 26.
65 P. 140.
66 P. 11, and letter to Max Brod, end of
    April 1920, p. 272.
67 Letter to Max Brod, beginning of May
    1920, p. 275.
68 Letter to Ottla, end of May 1920, p. 91.
69 Letter to Max Brod, beginning of May
    1920, p. 275.
70 p. 274.
71 Letter to Milena, p. 33.
72 Letter to Ottla, *ca* 1.5.20, p. 83.
73 Letter to Max Brod, June 1920, p. 276.
74 Ibid.
75 Letter to Milena, p. 22.
76 Letter to Ottla, 4 May 1920, p. 84.
77 Mid-May, p. 87.
78 Letter to Milena, p. 29.
79 Ibid.
80 Letter to Milena, p. 31.
81 P. 35.
82 P. 37.
83 P. 38.
84 P. 37.
85 P. 39.
86 Ibid.
87 P. 40.
88 P. 43.
89 P. 45.
90 P. 50.
91 P. 52.
92 Pp. 50–1.
93 P. 51.
94 P. 53.
95 Ibid.
96 P. 54.
97 Ibid.
98 P. 55.
99 P. 56.
100 P. 58.
101 Letter to Max Brod, mid-April 1921,
    pp. 317–18.
102 Letter to Milena, p. 63.
103 P. 106.
104 Ibid.
105 P. 114.
106 Letter from Milena to Max Brod. Brod,
    p. 203.
107 P. 59.
108 Pp. 62–4.
109 p. 60.
110 Ibid.
111 P. 65.
112 Pp. 65–6.
113 P. 66.
114 P. 65.
115 Pp. 66–7.
116 P. 69.
117 P. 74.
118 P. 78.
119 Ibid.
120 Letter to Ottla, mid-May 1920, p. 87.
121 Letter to Milena, p. 81.
122 P. 82.
123 Brod, pp. 194–5.
124 Ibid.
125 Letter to Milena, p. 84.
126 P. 86.
127 Ibid.
128 Quoted in his letter to Milena, p. 88.
129 P. 89.
130 P. 88.
131 P. 92.
132 Letter from Milena to Max Brod. Brod,
    p. 199.
133 Letter to Milena, p. 105.
134 Letter from Milena to Max Brod. Brod,
    p. 199.
135 Letter to Milena, p. 105.
136 P. 106.
137 Letter from Milena to Max Brod. Brod,
    p. 200.
138 Letter from Milena to Max Brod,
    29.7.20, pp. 197–8.
139 Letter to Milena, pp. 120–1.
140 Pp. 122–3.
141 Pp. 110–11.
142 P. 110.
143 P. 111.
144 P. 116.
145 Ibid.
146 P. 126.
147 P. 136.
148 Pp. 138–9.
149 P. 140.
150 Pp. 144–5.
151 P. 163.
152 P. 157.
153 Ibid.
154 Ibid.

155 Ibid.
156 P. 161.
157 P. 178–9.
158 P. 155.
159 P. 156.
160 P. 159.
161 P. 160.
162 Pp. 162–3.
163 P. 167.
164 P. 172.
165 Ibid.
166 P. 173.
167 Ibid.
168 P. 159.
169 *Hochzeitsvorbereitungen,* p. 298.
170 P. 33.
171 17.9.10, p. 303.
172 P. 302.
173 *Sämtliche Erzählungen,* pp. 318–19.
174 P. 315.
175 Janouch (1971), p. 176.
176 *Sämtliche Erzählungen,* p. 130.
177 Letter to Milena, p. 175.
178 P. 181.
179 P. 182.
180 P. 183.
181 Louzil, p. 73.
182 Letter to Milena, p. 184.
183 Ibid.
184 Krolop, p. 61.
185 Letter to Milena, p. 186.
186 Pp. 187–8.
187 P. 189.
188 P. 188.
189 Ibid.
190 P. 191.
191 P. 192.
192 P. 193.
193 P. 194.

22 Matliary

1 Loužil, p. 73.
2 Letter to Ottla, *ca* 21.12.20, p. 95.
3 Pp. 96–7.
4 Letter to Max Brod, 31.12.20, p. 286.
5 Letter to Ottla, 21.12.20, pp. 97–8.
6 P. 98.
7 Letter to Max Brod, 31.12.20, p. 285.
8 Ibid.
9 13.1.21, p. 291.
10 P. 286.
11 Ibid.
12 Letter to Max Brod, p. 289.
13 Quoted in letter from Milena to Max Brod. Brod, p. 202.
14 Brod, p. 202.
15 P. 204.
16 P. 203.
17 P. 204.
18 Ibid.
19 Letter to Max Brod, mid-April 1921, p. 317.
20 Ibid.
21 End of January 1921, p. 296.
22 P. 294.
23 Beginning of February 1921, p. 302.
24 Mid-April 1921, p. 319.
25 Letter to Ottla, *ca* 10.2.21, p. 108
26 Letter to Max Brod, mid-April 1921, p. 315.
27 Beginning of March 1921, p. 304.
28 Mid-March 1921, p. 306.
29 Beginning of March 1921, p. 305.
30 Ibid.
31 Letter to Minze Eisner, end of March 1921, p. 311.
32 P. 312.
33 Letter to Max Brod, mid-April 1921, p. 313.
34 Letter from Max Brod, 9.3.21 (unpublished).
35 Ibid.
36 Ibid.
37 Letter to Milena, p. 316.
38 Letter to Max Brod, beginning of May 1921, p. 322.
39 P. 319.
40 Answer to questionnaire sent by Max Brod and returned with letter in June 1921, p. 338.
41 Letter to Max Brod, beginning of May 1921, p. 322.
42 End of May/beginning of June 1921, pp. 328–30.
43 June, p. 335.
44 P. 338.
45 P. 336.
46 P. 337.
47 Pp. 337–8.

48 Beckett, *Three Dialogues*. Reprinted in *Proust* (London 1965, p. 103).

49 Letter to Ottla, June 1921, p. 123.

50 Letter to Ottla, beginning to middle of June 1921, p. 125.

51 P. 126.

52 Ibid.

53 Letter to Max Brod postmarked 23.8.21, p. 339 and letter to Robert Klopstock, 2.9.21, p. 348.

54 P. 348.

55 Letter to Robert Klopstock, beginning of September 1921, p. 350.

56 Mid-September 1921, p. 352.

57 End of September 1921, p. 354.

58 Postcard to Robert Klopstock, 23.9.21, p. 353.

59 Letter to Robert Klopstock, end of September 1921, p. 353.

60 *Tagebücher*, 15.10.21, p. 338.

61 Ibid.

62 Loose sheet enclosed with letter to Robert Klopstock, 9.10.21, p. 357.

63 *Tagebücher*, 16.10.21, p. 338.

64 17.10.21, p. 339.

65 Ibid.

66 25.10.21, p. 341.

67 29.10.21, pp. 341–2.

68 30.10.21, p. 342.

69 Loužil, p. 77.

70 Letter to Robert Klopstock, November 1921, p. 364.

71 Loužil, pp. 77ff.

72 *Tagebücher*, 19.11.22, p. 347.

73 Ibid.

74 6.12.21, p. 343.

75 16.1.22, p. 345.

76 Ibid.

77 18.1.22, p. 346.

78 Ibid.

79 19.1.22, p. 347.

80 20.1.22, p. 347.

81 23.1.22, p. 350.

82 24.1.22, p. 350.

83 Letter to Robert Klopstock, end of January 1921, p. 369.

84 Loužil, p. 78.

85 Letter to Robert Klopstock, end of January 1921, p. 370.

86 *Tagebücher*, 28.1.22, p. 352.

87 29.1.22, p. 353.

88 Postcard to Max Brod postmarked on arrival 8.2.22, p. 370.

89 *Tagebücher*, 29.1.22, p. 353.

90 Ibid.

91 P. 354.

92 30.1.22, p. 354.

93 Ibid.

94 Letter to Milena, *ca*. March 1922, p. 199.

95 Ibid.

96 *Tagebücher*, 1.2.22, p. 355.

97 Postcard to Robert Klopstock postmarked 1.3.21, p. 372.

98 10 or 11.2.22, p. 357.

99 Ibid.

100 *Tagebücher*, 3.2.22, p. 356.

101 10.2.22, p. 357.

102 Letter to Robert Klopstock dated by Brod 22.11.22, but more likely written in December 1921, p. 422.

103 *Tagebücher*, 12.2.22, p. 358.

104 14.2.22, p. 358.

105 Letter to Robert Klopstock dated by Brod spring 1922, probably end of March. See Binder (1976) p. 346.

106 'Fragmente', *Hochzeitsvorbereitungen*, p. 388.

107 Ibid.

108 Born *et al.*, *Symposium*, p. 71.

109 *Sämtliche Erzählungen*, p. 165.

110 P. 171.

111 Janouch (1971), p. 57.

112 Věra Saudková.

113 *Sämtliche Erzählungen*, p. 323.

114 *Das Schloss*, p. 7. See p. 267 for variant beginnings.

115 Postcard to Max Brod postmarked on arrival 26.6.22, pp. 375–6.

116 *Das Schloss*, p. 11.

117 P. 12.

118 P. 54.

119 P. 52.

120 P. 64.

121 P. 61.

122 *Tagebücher*, 19.2.22, p. 358.

123 26.2.22, p. 359.

124 27.2.22, p. 359.

125 5.3.22, p. 359.

126 7.3.22, p. 359.

127 9.3.22, p. 359.

128 Ibid.
129 Brod, p. 163.
130 Letter to Robert Klopstock, spring 1922, p. 374.
131 *Tagebücher*, 17 or 18.3.22, p. 360.
132 24.3.22, p. 360.
133 6.4.22, pp. 360–1.
134 Letter to Robert Klopstock dated end of March 1923 by Brod but probably end of April 1922, p. 430.
135 Loužil, p. 78.
136 *Tagebücher*, 12.5.22, p. 362.
137 M. Buber, *Tales of the Hasidim* (New York 1947) p. 316.
138 Cited by Politzer.
139 *Tagebücher*, 21.1.23, p. 348.
140 Between 24 and 27.1.22, p. 351.
141 P. 334.
142 P. 335.
143 19.5.22, p. 363.
144 26.5.22, English ed., p. 230. Omitted from German ed.
145 Letter to Robert Klopstock, June 1922, p. 374.
146 Janouch (1971) p. 190.

23 The Problem of Space

1 Postcard to Max Brod postmarked on arrival 26.6.22, p. 375.
2 Postcard to Robert Klopstock postmarked 26.6.22, p. 376.
3 Letter to Max Brod, 16.8.22, p. 408.
4 Letter postmarked on arrival 30.6.22, p. 379.
5 5.7.22, p. 384.
6 Letter to Oskar Baum, 5.7.22, pp. 387–8.
7 P. 386.
8 P. 384.
9 Ibid.
10 Ibid.
11 Ibid.
12 P. 385.
13 P. 384.
14 P. 385.
15 Ibid.
16 Ibid.
17 Pp. 385–6.
18 Janouch (1971) p. 150.

19 Letter to Max Brod postmarked 20.7.22, p. 396.
20 End of July 1922, p. 401.
21 *Das Schloss*, p. 91.
22 Letter to Max Brod postmarked 20.7.22, p. 396.
23 End of July 1922, p. 401.
24 *Das Schloss*, p. 91.
25 Letter to Max Brod postmarked on arrival 31.7.22, pp. 403–4.
26 Draft of letter to Emmy Salveter, August 1922, p. 411.
27 Ibid.
28 Letter to Max Brod, beginning of August 1922, p. 405.
29 P. 407.
30 Ibid.
31 Ibid.
32 Draft of letter to Emmy Salveter, August 1922, p. 411.
33 Letter to Max Brod postmarked on arrival 11.9.22, p. 416.
34 Ibid.
35 P. 416.
36 P. 415.
37 Ibid.
38 Pp. 415–16.
39 *Das Schloss*, p. 118.
40 P. 126.
41 P. 100.
42 P. 159.
43 P. 160.
44 P. 126.
45 P. 118.
46 E.g. letter to Felice, 19.1.13, p. 258.
47 *Tagebücher*, 26.9.22, p. 364.
48 Letter to Milena, p. 198.
49 Ibid.
50 *Der Prozess*, p. 224.
51 *Tagebücher*, 14.11.22, p. 364.
52 Letter to Max Brod, December 1922, p. 424.
53 Ibid.
54 *Hochzeitsvorbereitungen*, pp. 276–7.
55 'Ein Kommentar' was Kafka's title. Brod called it 'Gib's Auf' when he published it in 1936.
56 *Sämtliche Erzählungen*, p. 357 (in this edition the initial K. is replaced by N.).

57 Letter to Robert Klopstock, mid-April
   1923, p. 433.
58 Postcard to Milena postmarked 9.5.23
   but written a few days earlier.
59 Postmarked 9.5.22, p. 204.
60 Ibid.
61 Hartmut Binder, 'Kafkas
   Hebräischstudien' in *Jahrbuch des
   Deutschen Schillergesellschaft* XI (1967),
   p. 541.
62 *Tagebücher*, 12.6.23, p. 365.
63 Postcard to Robert Klopstock
   postmarked 13.7.23, p. 435.
64 Postcard to Max Brod postmarked
   10.7.23, p. 435.
65 Ibid.
66 Ibid.
67 Postcard to Robert Klopstock
   postmarked 13.7.23, p. 435.
68 Postcard to Max Brod postmarked
   10.7.23, p. 435.

24 Dora

1 Letter to Elsa Brod, 13.7.23, p. 437.
2 Postcard to Max Brod postmarked
   10.7.23 and postcard to Robert
   Klopstock postmarked 13.7.23,
   p. 435.
3 Letter to Hugo Bergmann, July 1923,
   p. 436.
4 Letter or postcard to Else Bergmann,
   13.7.23, p. 437.
5 Hodin, p. 37.
6 P. 35.
7 Brod, p. 171.
8 Hodin, pp. 36-7.
9 Brod, p. 172.
10 Letter to Max Brod, mid-January 1924,
   p. 438.
11 Letter to Tile Rössler, 3.8.23, p. 439.
12 Postcard to Robert Klopstock
   postmarked 24.7.23, p. 438.
13 Letter to Tile Rössler postmarked
   3.8.23, p. 440.
14 Ibid.
15 Postcard to Robert Klopstock
   postmarked 24.7.23, p. 438.
16 Letter to Robert Klopstock, beginning
   of August 1923, p. 441.

17 Letter to Max Brod postmarked 8.8.23,
   p. 442.
18 Ibid.
19 Ibid.
20 Brod diary 17.8.23 (unpublished).
21 Ibid.
22 Unpublished memoir of Julie Kafka's.
   See also Binder (1979) I, p. 499.
23 Postcard to Max Brod, 29.8.23, p. 443.
24 Postmarked 14.9.23, p. 446.
25 Postcard to Robert Klopstock, 13.9.23,
   p. 445.
26 Ibid.
27 Postcard to Max Brod postmarked
   13.9.23, p. 445.
28 14.9.23, p. 446.
29 Ibid.
30 Postcard to Oskar Baum, 26.9.23,
   p. 447.
31 Postcard to Ottla, 26.9.23, p. 133.
32 Hodin, p. 43.
33 Letter to Ottla, 8.10.23, p. 137.
34 Letter to Ottla last week in October
   1923, p. 146.
35 Postcard to Max Brod, 2.10.23, p. 448.
36 Hodin, p. 37.
37 Postcard to Robert Klopstock
   postmarked 16.10.23, p. 452.
38 Letter to Max Brod, 25.10.23, p. 453.
39 Postcard to Max Brod postmarked on
   arrival 27.10.23, pp. 457-8.
40 Postcard to Max Brod postmarked
   28.9.23, p. 448.
41 Ibid.
42 8.10.23, p. 449.
43 Letter to Max Brod postmarked on
   arrival 2.11.23, p. 461.
44 Postcard to Ottla postmarked 2.10.23,
   pp. 134-5.
45 Postcard to Max Brod postmarked on
   arrival 16.10.23, p. 451.
46 Letter to Max Brod postmarked on
   arrival 25.10.23, p. 452.
47 P. 455.
48 Ibid.
49 Weltsch (1957), p. 38.
50 Hodin, p. 40.
51 *Sämtliche Erzählungen*, p. 161.
52 Letter to Valli, November 1923,
   p. 462.

53 Letter to Max Brod postmarked on arrival 5.11.23, p. 464.
54 Ibid.
55 Brod, p. 339.
56 Hodin, p. 38.
57 Letter to Max Brod, 28.8.04, p. 29.
58 Ibid.
59 8th Octavo Notebook, *Hochzeitsvorbereitungen*, p. 160.
60 Letter to Milena, p. 171.
61 Pp. 171–2.
62 *Sämtliche Erzählungen*, p. 359.
63 P. 360.
64 P. 366.
65 P. 368.
66 P. 369.
67 P. 373.
68 P. 374.
69 P. 379.
70 P. 383.
71 P. 385.
72 Hodin, pp. 38–9.
73 P. 38.
74 Věra Saudková.
75 Ibid.
76 Brod, p. 176.
77 Letter to Ottla, first week in January 1924, pp. 153–4.
78 Brod, pp. 176–7.
79 Ibid.
80 Ibid.
81 Postcard to Robert Klopstock postmarked 26.1.24, p. 474.
82 Pp. 472–3.
83 Letter to Robert Klopstock postmarked 29.2.24, p. 477.
84 Brod, p. 176.
85 Ibid.
86 Letter to Robert Klopstock, beginning of March 1924, pp. 477–8.
87 P. 478.
88 Ibid.
89 Ibid.
90 Hodin, p. 43.
91 Ibid.
92 Brod, p. 178.
92 *Sämtliche Erzählungen*, p. 172.
94 P. 173.
95 Pp. 173–4.
96 P. 181.
97 P. 175.
98 P. 179.
99 P. 180.
100 P. 183.
101 P. 185.
102 P. 173.
103 P. 178.
104 P. 177.
105 Letter to Felice, 30.11.12, p. 144.
106 Note by Robert Klopstock printed in *Briefe*, p. 521.
107 Ibid.
108 Memoir by Utitz. Wagenbach (1958) p. 268.

25 Hunger Artist

1 Postcard to Robert Klopstock postmarked 7.4.24, p. 480.
2 Ibid.
3 Postcard to Max Brod postmarked 9.4.24, p. 48.
4 Ibid.
5 Postcard to Robert Klopstock postmarked 13.4.24, p. 480.
6 Brod, p. 178.
7 Postcard to Robert Klopstock postmarked 13.4.24, p. 480.
8 Ibid.
9 Brod diary 17.3.24 (unpublished).
10 Postmarked 18.4.24, p. 481.
11 Brod, p. 178.
12 Conversation slips, *Briefe*, p. 487.
13 Hodin, p. 46.
14 Letter from Franz Werfel to Max Brod. Brod, p. 178.
15 Conversation slips, p. 487.
16 Letter to his parents, *ca* 19.5.24, *Briefe an Ottla*, p. 156.
17 Letter from Dr Oskar Beck to Felix Weltsch, 3.5.24, Brod, p. 179.
18 Ibid.
19 Brod, p. 180.
20 P. 181.
21 P. 182.
22 Postcard to Max Brod postmarked 20.5.24, p. 483.
23 Ibid.
24 Conversation slips, p. 485.

25 *Tagebücher*, 1.2.22, p. 355.
26 Conversation slips, p. 486.
27 P. 487.
28 *Briefe*, pp. 520–1.
29 Conversation slips, p. 491.
30 P. 489.
31 P. 488.
32 P. 490.
33 Ibid.
34 P. 491.

35 Ibid.
36 Letter to his parents, *Briefe an Ottla*, pp. 155–6.
37 Testimony of Robert Klopstock, Brod, pp. 183–5.
38 Postcard from Max Brod to Oskar Baum, 4.6.24 (unpublished).
39 Letter from Robert Klopstock to Max Brod, 4.6.24.
40 Janouch (1965), p. 164.

Select Bibliography

Kafka's Works

Betrachtung (Leipzig 1913)
Die Verwandlung (Leipzig undated 1915)
Der Heizer (Leipzig 1916)
Das Urteil (Leipzig 1916)
In der Strafkolonie (Leipzig 1919)
Ein Landarzt (stories) (Munich and Leipzig undated 1919)
Ein Hungerkünstler (four stories) (Berlin 1924)

POSTHUMOUS
Der Prozess (Berlin 1925)
Das Schloss (Munich 1926)
Amerika (Munich 1927)
Beim Bau der chinesischen Mauer (stories) (Berlin 1931)

STANDARD EDITIONS
Der Prozess (New York 1946; Frankfurt 1950)
Das Schloss (New York 1946; Frankfurt 1951)
Tagebücher 1910–23 (New York and Frankfurt 1951)
Amerika (New York 1946; Frankfurt 1953)
Hochzeitsvorbereitungen auf dem Lande (New York and Frankfurt 1953)
Beschreibung eines Kampfes (New York 1946; Frankfurt 1953)
Briefe an Milena, ed. Willy Haas (New York and Frankfurt 1952)
Briefe 1902–24 (New York and Frankfurt 1958)
Briefe an Felice, ed. Erich Heller and Jürgen Born (New York and Frankfurt 1967)
Sämtliche Erzählungen, ed. Paul Raabe (Frankfurt 1970)
Briefe an Ottla und die Familie, ed. Klaus Wagenbach and Hartmut Binder (Frankfurt 1975)

ENGLISH TRANSLATIONS
The Trial, tr. Willa and Edwin Muir (London and New York 1937). New edition with additional material tr. E. M. Butler (London 1945). With additional material tr. Tania and James Stern (London 1956)
The Castle, tr. Willa and Edwin Muir (London and New York 1930). New edition with additional material tr. Eithne Wilkins and Ernst Kaiser (London 1953)
America, tr. Willa and Edwin Muir (London 1949)
Diaries 1910–13, ed. Max Brod, tr. Joseph Kresh (London 1948)
Diaries 1914–23, ed. Max Brod, tr. Martin Greenberg with Hannah Arendt (London 1949)
Letters to Milena, tr. Tania and James Stern (London and New York 1953)
Letters to Felice, tr. James Stern and Elizabeth Duckworth (New York 1973; London 1974)
Wedding Preparations in the Country and other Stories, tr. Ernst Kaiser and Eithne Wilkins (New York 1953; London 1954)
Metamorphosis and other Stories, tr. Willa and Edwin Muir (London 1961)

Select Bibliography

Description of a Struggle and other Stories, tr. Willa and Edwin Muir, Malcolm Pasley, Tania and
James Stern (London 1979)
Dearest Father: stories and other writings, tr. Ernst Kaiser and Eithne Wilkins (New York 1954)

Political and Social Background

Demetz, Peter, 'Kafka, Freud, Husserl: Probleme einer Generation' in *Zeitschrift für
Religion und Kunstgeschichte* VIII (1955)
Gay, Peter, *Freud, Jews and Other Germans: Masters and Victims in Modernist Culture* (New
York 1978; Oxford 1979)
Grunfeld, Frederic V., *Prophets without Honour: a Background to Freud, Kafka, Einstein and
Their World* (London and New York 1979)
Haas, Willy, *Die Literarische Welt. Erinnerungen* (Munich 1957)
Herz, Julius M., 'Franz Kafka and Austria: National Background and Ethnic Identity' in
Modern Austrian Literature XI 3–4.
Janik, Allan and Toulmin, Stephen, *Wittgenstein's Vienna* (New York 1973)
Kann, Robert A., *The Multinational Empire: Nationalism and Reform in the Habsburg Monarchy
1848–1918* (New York 1950)
Pick, Otto, 'Prager Dichter' in *Das jüdische Prag.* (Prague 1917)
Pulver, Max, *Erinnerungen an eine europäische Zeit.* (Zürich 1953)
Riff, Michael A., 'Czech Antisemitism and the Jewish Response before 1914' in the *Wiener
Library Bulletin* XXIX (1976) 39–40
Ripellino, A. *Praga Magica* (Turin 1973)
Robert, Marthe, *From Oedipus to Moses: Freud's Jewish Identity*, tr. Ralph Manheim (New
York 1976)
Schorske, Carl E., *Fin-de-Siècle Vienna: Politics and Culture* (New York 1979; London 1980)
Stölzl, Christoph, *Kafkas böses Böhmen: zur Sozialgeschichte eines Prager Juden* (Munich 1975)
Tramer, Hans, 'Prague – City of Three Peoples,' *Leo Baeck Institute Yearbook* IX (1964)
Williams, C. E., *The Broken Eagle: the Politics of Austrian Literature from Empire to Anschluss*
(London 1974)

Biographical, Critical and Interpretative

Adorno, Theodor W., 'Aufzeichnungen zu Kafka' in *Prismen* (Frankfurt 1955)
Anders, Günther, *Franz Kafka*, tr. A. Steer and A. K. Thorlby (London and New York 1960)
Arendt, Hannah, 'Franz Kafka: a Revaluation' in *Partisan Review XI* (1944) 3
Auden, W. H., 'Kafka's Quest' in *Flores* (1946)
Barthes, Roland, 'La Réponse de Kafka' in *Essais critiques* (Paris 1964)
Bataille, Georges, *La Littérature et le mal* (Paris 1957)
Bauer, Johann, *Kafka and Prague*, tr. P. S. Falla (London and New York 1971)
Baumer, Franz, *Franz Kafka*, tr. Abraham Farbstein (New York 1971)
Beck, Evelyn T., *Kafka and the Yiddish Theatre: Its Impact on his Work* (Wisconsin 1971)
Beissner, Friedrich, *Der Erzähler Franz Kafka* (Stuttgart 1952)
Benjamin, Walter, 'Franz Kafka: On the 10th Anniversary of his Death' and 'Max Brod's
Book on Kafka' in *Illuminations*, tr. Harry Zohn (New York 1968; London 1970)
Benjamin, Walter and Scholem, Gershom, *Briefwechsel* (Frankfurt 1980)
Bergmann, Hugo, 'Schulerinnerungen an Franz Kafka' in *Mitteilungsblatt* (Tel Aviv) 9.9.66;
'Erinnerungen an Franz Kafka' in *Universitas* XXVII (1972)
Bezzel, Christoph, *Natur bei Kafka* (Nuremberg 1964); *Kafka-Chronik. Daten zu Leben und Werk*
(Munich 1975)

Select Bibliography

Binder, Hartmut, 'Franz Kafka and the Weekly Paper *Selbstwehr*' in *Publications of the Leo Baeck Institute, Yearbook XII* (1967); 'Kafka und seine Schwester Ottla' in *Jahrbuch des deutschen Schillergesellschaft XII* (1968); *Kafka Kommentar zu sämtlichen Erzählungen* (Munich 1975); *Kafka in neuer Sicht* (Stuttgart 1976); *Kafka-Handbuch* (2 vols) (Stuttgart 1979) *Kafka: ein Leben in Prag* (Munich 1982)

Bloom, Harold (ed.), *Franz Kafka* (New York 1994)

Borges, Jorge Luis, 'Kafka and his Precursors' (1952), reprinted in *Labyrinths* (New York 1962)

Born, Jürgen, Dietz, Ludwig, Pasley, Malcolm, Raabe, Paul and Wagenbach, Klaus, *Kafka-Symposium* (Berlin 1965)

Brod, Max, *Über Franz Kafka* (contains: *Franz Kafka: eine Biographie* (1954). *Franz Kafkas Glauben und Lehre* (1948) and *Verzweiflung und Erlösung im Werk Franz Kafkas* (1959) (Frankfurt 1974); *Der Prager Kreis* (Stuttgart 1966); *Streitbares Leben* (Munich 1969)

Buber, Martin, 'Kafka and Judaism' in Gray (1962)

Buber-Neumann, Margarete, *Mistress to Kafka: the Life and Death of Milena*, tr. anon. (London 1966)

Camus, Albert, 'L'espoir et l'absurde dans l'oeuvre de Kafka' in *Le Mythe de Sisyphe* (Paris 1948)

Canetti, Elias, *Kafka's Other Trial: the Letters to Felice*, tr. Christopher Middleton (London and New York 1974)

Carrouges, Michel, *Franz Kafka* (Paris 1948); *Kafka contre Kafka* (Paris 1962)

Citati, Pietro, *Kafka* (London 1990)

Cohn, Dorrit, 'Kafka's Eternal Present: Narrative Tense in "Ein Landarzt" and Other First Person Stories' in *Publications of the Modern Languages Association LXXXIII*

Currie, Robert, *Genius: an Ideology of Literature* (New York 1974)

Deleuze, Gilles and Guattari, Felix, *Kafka. Pour une littérature mineure* (Paris 1975)

Dietz, Ludwig, *Franz Kafka* (Stuttgart 1975)

Dodd, W. J., *Kafka and Dostoevski* (London 1992)

Dymant, Dora, 'Ich habe Franz Kafka geliebt' in *Die neue Zeitung* (18.8.48) and in J. P. Hodin (1948 and 1949)

Eisner, Pavel, *Franz Kafka and Prague*, tr. Lowry Nelson and René Wellek (New York 1950)

Emrich, Wilhelm, *Franz Kafka. A Critical Study*, tr. Sheema Zeben Buehne (New York 1968)

Fickert, Kurt, *Kafka's Doubles* (Berne 1979); *End of a Mission: Kafka's Search for Truth in His Last Stories* (Columbia, South Carolina 1993)

Flores, Angel (ed.), *The Kafka Problem* (New York 1946); (with Swander Homer, ed.) *Franz Kafka Today* (Wisconsin 1958); *The Kafka Debate* (New York 1976); *The Problem of 'The Judgment'* (New York 1976); *A Kafka Bibliography 1908–76* (New York 1976)

Fowles, John, 'My Recollections of Kafka' in *Mosaic* III (1970) 4

Fraiberg, Selma, 'Kafka and the Dream' in *Art and Psychoanalysis*, ed. William Phillips (New York 1957)

(Franz-Kafka-Gesellschaft) *Kunst und Prophetie*, reprint of lectures by Hans Mayer, Claude David, Jost Schillemeit, Peter Dettmering, Jürgen Born, Peter Kampits and Roman Karst delivered at a Symposium held in Klosterneuburg, June 1979

Friedmann, Maurice, *Problematic Rebel: Melville, Dostoevsky, Kafka, Camus* (New York 1963)

Frynta, Emmanuel and Lukas, Jan, *Kafka and Prague*, tr. John Layton (London 1960)

Goldstücker, Eduard (ed.), *Franz Kafka aus Prager Sicht 1963* (Prague 1965); *Weltfreunde. Konferenz über die Prager deutsche Literatur* (Prague 1967)

Goodman, Paul, *Kafka's Prayer* (New York 1947)

Grandin, John M., *Kafka's Prussian Advocate: A Study of the Influence of Heinrich von Kleist on Franz Kafka* (Columbia, South Carolina 1987)

Select Bibliography

Gray, Richard T., *Constructive Destruction – Kafka's Aphorisms: Literary Tradition and Literary Transformation* (Tübingen 1987)

Gray, Ronald, *Kafka's Castle* (Cambridge 1956); (ed.) *Kafka: A Collection of Critical Essays* (New Jersey 1962); *Franz Kafka* (Cambridge 1973)

Greenberg, Clement, 'The Jewishness of Franz Kafka' in *Art and Culture* (Boston 1961)

Greenberg, Martin, *The Terror of Art: Kafka and Modern Literature* (New York 1968; London 1971)

Grözinger, Karl Erich, *Kafka and Kabbalah*, tr. Susan Hecker Ray (New York 1994)

Hall, Calvin S. and Lind, Richard E., *Dreams, Life and Literature. A Study of Franz Kafka* (Chapel Hill, North Carolina 1970)

Hamalian, Leo (ed.), *Franz Kafka. A Collection of Criticism* (New York 1974)

Hecht, Hugo, 'Zwölf Jahre in der Schule mit Franz Kafka' in *Prager Nachrichten* XVII (1966) 8

Heller, Erich, 'The World of Franz Kafka' in *The Disinherited Mind* (Cambridge 1952); *Franz Kafka* (London and New York 1975)

Heller, Peter, *Dialectics and Nihilism: Essays on Lessing, Nietzsche, Mann and Kafka* (Amherst, Mass., 1966); 'On not Understanding Kafka', *German Quarterly* XLVII (1974) 3

Henel, Ingeborg, 'The Legend of the Doorkeeper and Its Significance' in Rolleston (1976)

Hermsdorf, Klaus, *Kafka: Weltbild und Roman* (Berlin 1961)

Hodin, J.P., 'Memories of Franz Kafka' in *Horizon* No 97 (1948); 'Erinnerungen an Franz Kafka' in *Der Monat* I (1949) No 8–9

Hughes, Kenneth (ed.), *Franz Kafka: An Anthology of Marxist Criticism* (London 1981)

Jaffe, Adrian H., *The Process of Kafka's 'Trial'* (Michigan 1967)

Janouch, Gustav, *Conversations with Kafka, Notes and Reminiscences*, tr. Goronwy Rees. Enlarged ed. (London and New York 1971); *Franz Kafka und seine Welt. Eine Bildbiographie* (Vienna 1965)

Karl, Frederick R., *Franz Kafka: Representative Man* (New York 1991)

Kautmann, František, 'Franz Kafka und die tschechische Literatur' in Goldstücker (1965)

Kraft, Werner, *Franz Kafka: Durchdringung und Geheimnis* (Frankfurt 1968)

Krolop, Kurt, 'Zu den Erinnerungen Anna Lichtensterns an Franz Kafka' in *Germanistica Pragensia* V (1968)

Kuna, Franz, *Franz Kafka: Literature as Corrective Punishment* (Indiana 1974); (ed.) *On Kafka: Semi-Centenary Perspectives* (London 1976)

Loužil, Jaromír, 'Dopisy Franze Kafky Dělnické úrazové pojištövné pro Čechy v Praze' in Sbnorník Národníko muzea v Praze (Prague 1963)

Lukács, Georg, 'Franz Kafka or Thomas Mann?' in *The Meaning of Contemporary Realism*, tr. J. and N. Mander (London 1962); retitled *Realism in Our Time* (New York 1964)

Mailloux, Peter, *A Hesitation before Birth: A Life of Franz Kafka* (Newark and London 1989)

Mann, Thomas, Foreword to *The Castle* (New York 1941), repr. in *Gesammelte Werke* (Frankfurt 1960) vol. X

Muschg, Walter, 'Der unbekannte Kafka' in *Von Trakl bis Brecht* (Munich 1961)

von Natzmer Cooper, Gabriele, *Kafka and Language in the Stream of Thoughts and Life* (Riverside, California 1991)

Neumeyer, Peter F. (ed.), *Twentieth-Century Interpretations of 'The Castle': A Collection of Critical Essays* (New Jersey 1969)

Northey, Anthony D. '*Amerika*' in Flores (1976); *Kafka's Relatives: Their Lives and His Writing* (New Haven and London 1991)

Parry, Idris, 'Kafka, Gogol and Nathaniel West' in Gray (1962)

Pasley, Malcolm, 'Franz Kafka Mss: Description and Select Inedita' in *Modern Language*

Review LVII (1962); 'Zur Entstehungsgeschichte von Franz Kafkas Schloss-Bild' in Gold-stücker (1967)

Pawel, Ernst, *The Nightmare of Reason: A Life of Franz Kafka* (London 1984)

Pazi, Margarita, *Max Brod. Werk und Persönlichkeit* (Bonn 1970)

Politzer, Heinz, *Franz Kafka: Parable and Paradox* (Ithaca 1962); (ed.) *Franz Kafka: Wege der Forschung* (Darmstadt 1973)

Rahv, Philip, 'An Introduction to Kafka' and 'The Death of Ivan Ilyich and Joseph K' in *Literature and the Sixth Sense* (Boston 1969; London 1970)

Robert, Marthe, *Kafka* (Paris 1968) (new ed.); *L'Ancien et le nouveau: De Don Quichotte à Kafka* (Paris 1963); *Seul comme Franz Kafka* (Paris 1979)

Robertson, Ritchie, *Kafka, Judaism, Politics and Literature* (Oxford 1985)

Rolleston, James, *Kafka's Narrative Theatre* (Pennsylvania 1974); (ed.) *Twentieth-Century Interpretations of 'The Trial'* (New Jersey 1976)

Sheppard, Richard, *On Kafka's Castle: A Study* (New York 1973; London 1974)

Slochower, Harry (ed.), *A Franz Kafka Miscellany* (New York 1946)

Sokel, Walter, *Franz Kafka. Tragik und Ironie. Zur Struktur seiner Kunst* (Munich/Vienna 1964); *Franz Kafka* (New York 1966)

Spann, Meno, *Franz Kafka* (Boston 1976)

Spilka, Mark, *Dickens and Kafka: A Mutual Interpretation* (London 1963)

Starobinski, Jean, 'Kafka et Dostoevski' in *Obliques* (1973) no 3

Steiner, George, 'Kafka' in *Language and Silence* (London 1967)

Stern, J. P., 'The Law of *The Trial*' in Kuna (1976); 'The Judgment' in Flores (1976)

Stern, J. P., and White, J. J. (eds.) *Paths and Labyrinths: Nine Papers from a Kafka Symposium* (London 1985)

Tauber, Herbert, *Franz Kafka: An Interpretation of His Works* (London 1948; New York 1968)

Thorlby, Anthony, *Kafka: A Study* (London and Totowa, New Jersey, 1972)

Udolff, Alan (ed.), *Kafka and Contemporary Critical Performance: Centenary Readings* (Bloomington 1987)

Urzidil, Johannes, *There Goes Kafka*, tr. Harold A. Basiliny (Detroit 1968)

Vivas, Eliseo, 'Kafka's Distorted Mask' in Gray (1962)

Wagenbach, Klaus, *Franz Kafka. Eine Biographie seiner Jugend 1883–1912* (Bern 1958); *Franz Kafka in Selbstzeugnissen und Bilddokumenten* (Hamburg 1964)

Walser, Martin, *Beschreibung einer Form. Versuch über Franz Kafka* (Munich 1971)

Weltsch, Felix, *Kafkas Glauben und Lehre* (Munich 1948); 'The Rise and Fall of the Jewish-German Symbiosis: The Case of F. K.' in the *Leo Baeck Institute Yearbook* 1956; *Religion und Humor im Werk Franz Kafkas* (Berlin 1957)

Wilson, Edmund, 'A Dissenting Opinion on Franz Kafka' in *Classics and Commercials* (New York 1950)

Winkler, R. O. C., 'Significance of Kafka' in *Scrutiny VII* (1938) 3

Glossary of German and Czech Names

Note In the text I have given the German names of buildings, streets, rivers and islands because it is by these that they were known during Kafka's lifetime. Their Czech names are listed below.

Alchimistengässchen	Zlatá ulička
Altneu Synagoge	Staronová synagoga
Altstadt	Staré město
Altstädter Ring	Staroměstské náměstí
Aussig	Ústí nad Labem
Belvedere Park	Letenské sady
Bilekgasse	Bílkova ulice
Bodenbach	Podmokly
Brünn	Brno
Budweis	České Budějovice
Castle Ober Studenec	Zámek Horní Studenec
Cech (bridge)	Čechův most
Cernosic	Černošice
Dobrichowitz	Dobřichovice
Eisengasse	Železná ulice
Elbe	Labe
Ferdinandstrasse	Ferdinandova třída, *now* Národní třída
Fleischmarkt	Masný trh
Flöhau	Blšany
Franzensbad	Františkovy Lázně
Franz Josef Station	nádraží dráhy císaře Frantiske Josefa, *now* Hlavní nádraží
Friedland	Frýdlant
Gablonz	Jablonec
Geistgasse	Dušní ulice
Georgenthal	Jiřetín
Graben	Na Příkopě
Grosser Ring	Staroměstské náměstí
Heinrichsynagoge	Jerusalémská synagoga
Hybernergasse	Hybernská ulice
Iser Mountain	Jizerské hory
Jacobskirche	kostel sv. Jakuba
Josefstadt	Josefov
Josephsplatz	Náměstí Republiky
Judeninsel	Židovský ostrov
Jungmannstrasse	Jungmannova ulice
Karlsbad	Karlovy Vary
Karlsbrücke	Karlův most
Karlsplatz	Karlovo náměstí

Glossary of German and Czech Names

Karolinenthal	Karlín
Kleiner Ring	Malé náměstí
Kleinseite	Malá strana
Königssaal	Zbraslav
Komotau	Chomutov
Kratzau	Chrastava
Kuchelbad	Chuchle
Kuttenberg	Kutná hora
Langengasse	Dlouhá třída
Länderbank	Zemská banka
Laurenziberg	Petřín
Leitmeritz	Litoměřice
Liboch	Liboc (probably)
Maiselgasse	Maislova ulice
Marienbad	Mariánské Lázně
Marktgasse	Tržiště
Matliary	Matljary
Mattersdorf	Vratislavice
Moldau	Vltava
Moravian Silesia	Moravské Slezsko
Müritz	*now* Graal-Müritz
Niklasstrasse	Mikulášská ulice, *now* Pařížská třída
Obstmarkt	Ovocný trh
Pilsen	Plzeň
Pinkassynagoge	Pinkasova synagoga
Plesch	Pleš
Podiebrad	Poděbrady
Porschitschenstrasse	Na Poříčí
Pulverturm	Prašná brána
Reichenberg	Liberec
Riegerpark	Riegrovy sady
Roztok	Roztoky
Rumburg	Rumburk
Schelesen	Želízy
Schneekoppe	Sněžka
Schützen (Island)	Střelecký ostrov
Sophieninsel	Žofín
Spindlermühle	Špindlerův Mlýn
Spitzberg	Špičák
Stechowitz	Štěchovice
Strakonitz	Strakonice
Straschnitz	Strašnice
Teplitz	Teplice-Šanov, *now* Teplice
Tetschau	Děčín
Teyn church	Týnský kostel
Triesch	Třešť
Turnau	Turnov
Vrutky	Vrútky
Warnsdorf	Varnsdorf
Wenzelsplatz	Václavské náměstí

Glossary of German and Czech Names

Wossek	Osek
Wotawa	Otava
Wrschowitz	Vršovice
Zalezly	Zálezly
Zeltnergasse	Celetná ulice
Ziegengasse	Kozí ulice
Zigeunersynagoge	Velkodvorská synagoga (*probably*)
Zuckmantel	Cukmantl
Zürau	Siřem

Index

343

Index

Index